The *New* Book of

BESTS

EXPLORING THE WORLD OF QUALITY

The *New* Book of

BESTS

EXPLORING THE WORLD OF QUALITY

A Guide to the Best Things Life Has to Offer

**By the Editors of *The Best Report*
with a foreword by Stanley Marcus**

Andrews, McMeel & Parker
A Universal Press Syndicate Affiliate
Kansas City • New York

Library of Congress Cataloging-in-Publication Data

The New book of bests.

    Rev. ed. of: The Book of bests. 1983.
    Includes index.
    1. Consumer education.   2. Shopping—Directories.
I. Book of bests.   II. Best report.
TX335.B63   1986   380.1'45   86-22280
ISBN 0-8362-7933-6

FOREWORD

THERE is nothing as rewarding to an author as a letter from a reader attesting to the fact that his book has been a decisive influence in shaping the reader's decision in a critical matter. Serious as you may be as a writer, it is a little awesome to realize that your words were taken that seriously. Equally, there's nothing as flattering as learning that your book has stimulated the founding of a new publication and, in turn, another book.

I refer to my book, *Quest for the Best,* published in 1978 by Viking Press, which I believe struck a responsive chord in Michael Bartlett and Norman Aronson. Perhaps they had been thinking about the subject of "Best" for months or even years before my book came out; perhaps my book simply stimulated them to action, realizing that I had merely skimmed the surface of this broad subject. At any rate, they started publishing *The Best Report* in September, 1981; and with the success of that venture have now come forth with this book, *The New Book of Bests.*

I was more concerned with the philosophical and psychological implications of the subject that with an encyclopedic exposition which is the course the authors of *The New Book of Bests* have taken. I tried to elucidate the concept of "Best" and to explain the motivations of people of different ages and occupations to achieve it. Then, through a dozen or more case examples, I attempted to describe the differences between "better and best" and the effect that our contemporary economic culture and technology have had on the attainment of the "best."

I attributed a decline in the quality of goods and services to the bigness of our business institutions, to public ownership, which erased the pride of authorship, and to the decreased discrimination of customers who seemed to me to have too willingly accepted standards of mediocrity. These were my observations as a social observer, not those of a moralist. I did suggest that the remedies existed in the power of management to devote more time in observing both customers and product, and the willingness of customers to become more vigorous in complaints about product and service deterioration.

Finally, in a very presumptive way, I ended the book with a list of things I considered "The Best" and another with my pet peeves which I labeled "less than the best."

Now comes *The New Book of Bests,* which attempts to systematically and unequivocally qualify the best in a wide range of categories from art museums to wine events, from fellowships to hot dogs, and from classic wallpapers to jigsaw puzzles. That's one whale of a lot of expertise. That demanded the talents of a modern Diderot.

Stanley Marcus

CONTENTS

Four   FINE TASTING   95

Five   PERSONAL GOODS   173

CONTRIBUTORS

DURING the almost five years since we conceived the idea for a systematic exposition of the world's best things, our records show over 1,400 people—creators, critics, expert practitioners from a variety of fields—have contributed encouragement, counsel, insight, and information toward the creation of our database which we call BEST-BANK™. Unfortunately, only a representative few can be listed here. The following deserve special thanks:

First, those who sustain and direct the work at Best Publishing, Inc.: Norman L. Aronson, Jerry Jontry, James C. Mote, Barbara N. Lo Re, Eugene P. Gorman.

Second, the *Best* editorial staff and regular contributors: Jaala Weingarten, Peter Filichia, Elizabeth J. Field, Dan Richards, Michael Hofferber, Amy Kurtz, Richard Sullivan, Mary Ziegler, Beatrice Naiman, Gina Algarotti.

Third, some of our experts: Peter Andrews (Contributing Editor, *American Heritage, Saturday Review*); Caskie Stinett (Contributing Editor, *Signature*); Xavier Hermès (Hermès); Eloise Ricciardelli (Registrar, Museum of Modern Art); Alistair Cooke (Author); Joan Hartmann-Goldsmith (Director, Institute for Asian Studies); Angela Cummings (Designer, Tiffany & Co); Annalynn Swan (Music Critic, *Newsweek*); Joanne Fishman (Boating Editor, *New York Times*); Judson Mead (Associate Editor, *Americana*); Roger Stewart (De Casi Custom Clothing); Morten Lund (Contributing Editor, *Ski Magazine*); A. Jerry Ross (Director of Choreography, University of Miami); Dave Bell (Dave Bell Communications); John Fink (Editor, *Chicago* Magazine); William Bendig (Editor, *Artgallery* Magazine); Tony Assenza (Automotive Editor, *Popular Mechanics*); André Soltner (Owner, Lutèce); Bill Pence (Director, Telluride Film Festival); Nicola Bulgari (Bulgari); Jan Hansum (Vice-President, Kent of London); Bill Mckeown (Editor, *Outdoor Life*); Cathleen Stratos (Perfumer's Workshop, Bloomingdale's); Bonnie Burnham (Executive Director, International Foundation for Art Research); Jack Whitaker (ABC-TV Sports); Donal Henehan (Music Critic, *New York Times*);

Sacha Lichine (Wine Expert); Cecil Behringer (Metallurgist and Custom Bike Builder); Albert Sack (Israel Sack Antiques); Louise Deutschman and Jerry Gorovoy (Sydney Janis Gallery); Francis G. Mandrano (The Maserati Information Exchange); Jacques Pepin (Chef, Author); Steven Zeitlin (Smithsonian Institute); Christopher Blackwall (Director, U.S. Rowing Association); Jacques Francais (Jacques Francais Rare Violins); Peter Solmssen (Director, Arts International Agency); Neil Shapiro (Electronics Editor, *Popular Mechanics*); Bob Gillen (Editor, *Ski Business*); Wendy Amos (Alvin Ailey School); Ernest Burns (Owner, Cinemabilia); Tamiko Hanafusa (Co-Director, Bizen Gallery); Thomas Neal (Administrative Director, Howard Business School Executive Education Program); Dominique Mazeaud (Modern Master Tapestries); Nika Hazelton (Food Writer); Susan Colgan (Editor, *Art and Antiques* Magazine); Roger Yaseen (Publisher, *Gastronome*);

Neil Leifer (Photographer, *Sports Illustrated*); Don Gold (Managing Editor, *Playboy*); Robert Persky (Publisher, *The Photograph Collector*); William Barry Furlong (Writer); Park Beeler (Publisher, *Jacksonville Monthly*); Deborah Evetts (Morgan Library); David Wexler (Publisher, *Restaurant Institutions*); Norman Block (Dunhill Tailors); Alex McNab (Managing Editor, *Tennis* Magazine); Peter Landau (Editor, *Insitutional Investor*); Clifton Fadiman (Author); Alan Flusser (Designer, Men's Fashion); Donald Wintergill (London Correspondent, *Art & Auction*); Douglas Pleasanton (Ballantyne); Larry Cici (Pringle); Montague Moss (Moss Bros., Inc., London); Melissa Marek (Cartier); Otto Perl (Custom Tailor); Charles Case (Cartographer, National Geographic Society); Nancy Bongiovani (Dunhill, Tobacconist); Larry Rabin (President, New York Dart League); B. Warren Brown (President, Arthur Brown Bros.); Robert Wiener (Manager, Crouch & Fitzgerald Luggage); Vincent Thurston (Manager, T. Anthony Luggage); Tom Bryant (Associate Editor, *Road & Track*); William Shannon (Poulson & Skone, London); Donald Kayner (Iwan Ries, Tobacconist); Robert Clerk

(Aston Martin); Robert Wexler (President, Tourneau, Inc.); George Holmes and Helene Huffer (Editors, Jewelers Circular-Keystone); Maurice de la Valette (Revillon Furs);

John H. Steinway (Chairman, Steinway & Sons); Bonnie Selfe (Pearl Buyer, Cartier); Benjamin Gingiss (Gingiss Formalwear); Margaret Pisant (Fashion Editor, *Vogue*); Victor Borge (Performer); Jack McDonald (President, Oxxford Clothes, Inc.); Bob Persons (Mark Cross); Michael Worthington-Williams (Director, Motorcycle Sales, Sotheby's, London). Robert Brooks (Director, Vintage Vehicle Sales, Christie's, London); Robert Bright (Wells of Mayfair, Savile Row); John Mandeville (Director, American Kennel Club); Charles Seilheimer (President, Sotheby Parke Bernet Realty); Donald War (Private Islands Unlimited); John Gedney (President, Wagner Pools); Ann Dorfsman (Wallpaper Expert, Cooper-Hewitt Museum); Vic Braden (Vic Braden Tennis College); James Beard (Food Critic); Deborah Szekely Mazzanti (Founder, Golden Door Spa); Gideon Ariel (Biomechanical and Computer Engineer); Giorgio Deluca and Joel Dean (Owners, Dean & Deluca); Murray Klein (Owner, Zabar's); Louis Balducci (Balducci's); Luciano Todaro (Todaro Bros.); Tony Skilton (Director, Orvis Flyfishing School); Harold Swift (Director, Hazelden Foundation); Ralph F. Colin (Administrative Vice-President, Art Dealers Association of America);

Madelein Kamman (Cooking Teacher); Milton Zelman (Publisher, *Chocolate News*); Joel Schapira (Author, *The Book of Coffee and Tea*); Barbara Ensrud (Author, *Pocket Guide to Cheese*); Paul Kovi (Owner, The Four Seasons); Jim Robertson (Author, *The Connoisseur's Guide to Beer*); William Boyd (President, Home News Publishing Co.); Herb Hobler (President, DowAlert); Fong Chow (Expert, Oriental Art); James Nicholas, M.D. (The Institute of Sports Medicine and Athletic Trauma); Diane Darrow (Food Writer); Richard Berry (Editor, *Astronomy* Magazine); John Hart (The Chicago Wine Company); Edward Munves, Jr. (James Robinson, Inc.); Nick Seitz (Editor, *Golf Digest*); Lewis W. Gillenson and Evan Marshall (Dodd, Mead & Co.); Neil Weinstock (Contributing Editor, *Popular Computing*).

INTRODUCTION

AS any top-notch professional athlete or world-renowned artist will testify, rising to greatness in one's profession is only half the battle. Finding the courage and wherewithal to stay there is at least as difficult, if not more of a challenge. So it is with the products and services listed in *The New Book of Bests*. In this newly updated edition we celebrate those which have survived the test of time, and welcome some promising new-comers that have risen through the ranks.

Our format for this edition is the same as before: Eight fact-filled chapters covering a broad range of topics from Arts and Culture to Sports and Travel, each devoted to identifying the recognized bests in every field. These have been updated and revised to reflect the comings, goings, rises and falls that naturally accompany the noble pursuit of quality.

We've also expanded our scope somewhat to include *topics new in this edition:* compact disc players, luxury motorcycles, skiwear, private island resorts, Japanese spas, steak houses, rocking chairs, home gyms, vacation home exchanges, heli-skiing, lounge chairs, toothbrushes, gourmet foods by mail-order.

The New Book of Bests doesn't cover everything, of course, and within every topic there will be plenty of debate about our choices. Clearly, ours is not the final word, but, rather, an educated and carefully considered one. We hope that these pages inform and entertain you, and stimulate thoughts and discussions about our conclusions that will lead you to your own. All the Best!

THE EDITORS
New York City, 1986

Note: For continuing updates on "the world of quality," check out *The BEST Report,* a concise monthly newsletter packed full of information on the best in new products and services, and regular reviews of old standards. Priced at $48 per year from *Best Publishing, Inc., 350 Fifth Ave., Suite 4210, New York, NY 10118.*

ONE

Arts and Culture

ART MUSEUMS: U.S.

WERE a travel agent to ask for a list of the dozen best museums in any country in Europe, it would be a difficult, but not impossible, task to make an interesting and valid selection. But America is another matter. We can proudly say that the United States doesn't have a dozen "best" museums, but, rather, we are blessed with *several* dozen. And how does one determine best, anyway, when judgment of quality is involved? Size of collection has importance only when the quantity has historical and aesthetic significance—to own every lithograph ever printed by Chagall (or even Picasso) could be interesting, but without the inclusion of at least several paintings and a few drawings such a collection could prove to be dull to most viewers. On the other hand, for an institution to possess only two canvases by the seventeenth-century master Georges de La Tour could mean that they alone would make that museum one of the most important in the land.

One startling example of quantity and quality giving a little known institution importance is the Greenville, South Carolina, County Museum of Art where Arthur and Holly Magill have deposited their extensive collection of works by Andrew Wyeth. Nothing comparable can be seen anywhere else except for Wyeth's

1

hometown museum itself, the Brandywine River Museum at Chadds Ford, Pennsylvania. And there is another point: does everyone want to see a great collection of Wyeth, or for that matter, of Jackson Pollock? The enjoyment of museums is an amazingly personal matter.

National Bests

Our focus here is the traditional art-oriented institutions, even excluding the historical type such as Vermont's Shelburne or Virginia's Williamsburg, though they both house worthy specialized collections of paintings. The best, in the broadest sense, are all too obvious. There is no one who hasn't heard of *The Metropolitan* and *The National Gallery,* and *Boston's Museum of Fine Arts* would be quickly followed by *The Philadelphia Museum,* with the *Museum of Modern Art* being uttered in the same breath as the *Art Institute of Chicago* . . . so you see in this very sentence half of our dozen best has already been mentioned. And in one more sentence we can cover the *Cleveland Museum,* the *Los Angeles County,* the *Getty,* Kansas City's *Nelson-Atkins,* Fort Worth's *Kimball,* and, by throwing in the *Indianapolis* and Norfolk's *Chrysler* we've hit a baker's dozen with plenty of room for argument as to choice.

So, indeed, **we'll group our best art museums by the dozen, but we'll do so by region,** enabling the traveler to concentrate on the locale he expects to visit. First, though, it would be wise to eliminate the nation's two museum capitals: New York and Washington, D.C. Both have countless and extensive guides to the scores of museums within their realms. Suffice it here to mention a few names to pique the curiosity enough to prompt consultation of those guidebooks. Apart from New York's *Metropolitan* and *Museum of Modern Art,* special mention must be made of the *Brooklyn, Guggenheim, Whitney, Frick,* and *Asia Society,* in that order. After the *National Gallery* in Washington, the list should read: the *Corcoran, Phillips, Hirshhorn, National Museum of American Art, Freer, National Portrait Gallery,* and *Dumbarton Oaks,* also in that order. Any person who knows those fifteen collections well would have no need to visit any other city in the world. But such knowledge, once possessed, would probably inspire the desire to search on forever. That is exactly what museum-going is really all about.

Regional Bests

For our purposes, the continental United States can conveniently be divided into six major regions: New England, Mid-Atlantic, South, Southwest (including Texas and Oklahoma), Midwest, and the West Coast. A dozen top museums can be listed for each of these sections—with the exception of the Midwest, which (in spite of middle-America being maligned for being provincial) requires a list of two dozen.

New England
- Addison Gallery of American Art, Phillips Academy, Andover, MA

- Bowdoin College Museum of Art, Brunswick, ME

- Sterling and Francine Clark Institute, Williamstown, MA

- Currier Gallery of Art, Manchester, NH

- Harvard University: Busch-Reisinger Museum, Cambridge, MA

- Isabella Stewart Gardner Museum, Boston, MA

- Museum of Art, Rhode Island School of Design, Providence, RI

- Museum of Fine Arts, Boston, MA

- New Britain Museum of American Art, New Britain, CT

- Wadsworth Atheneum, Hartford, CT

- Worcester Art Museum, Worcester, MA

- Yale University: Art Gallery and Center for British Art, New Haven, CT

Mid-Atlantic
- Albright-Knox Art Gallery, Buffalo, NY

- Baltimore Museum of Art, Baltimore, MD

- Carnegie Institute: Museum of Art, Pittsburgh, PA

- Winterthur Museum and Gallery, Wilmington, DE

- Everson Museum of Art, Syracuse, NY

- Memorial Art Gallery: University of Rochester, Rochester, NY

- Munson-Williams-Proctor Institute, Utica, NY

- Newark Museum, Newark, NJ

- Pennsylvania Academy of the Fine Arts, Philadelphia, PA

- Philadelphia Museum of Art, Philadelphia, PA

- Princeton University Art Museum, Princeton, NJ

- Walters Art Gallery, Baltimore, MD

South
- Chrysler Museum, Norfolk, VA

- **Salvador Dali Museum,** St. Petersburg, FL

- **Fort Lauderdale Museum of Art,** Fort Lauderdale, FL

- **Greenville County Museum,** Greenville, SC

- **High Museum of Art,** Atlanta, GA

- **Bob Jones University Collection of Sacred Art,** Greenville, SC

- **New Orleans Museum of Art,** New Orleans, LA

- **North Carolina Museum of Art,** Raleigh, NC

- **Norton Gallery of Art,** Palm Beach, FL

- **John and Mable Ringling Museum of Art,** Sarasota, FL

- **Virginia Museum of Fine Arts,** Richmond, VA

- **Vizcaya Museum,** Miami, FL

Southwest

- **Amon Carter Museum of Western Art,** Fort Worth, TX

- **Dallas Museum of Art,** Dallas, TX

- **Thomas Gilcrease Institute of American History and Art,** Tulsa, OK

- **Kimball Art Museum,** Fort Worth, TX

- **McNay Art Museum,** San Antonio, TX

- **Meadows Museum and Sculpture Court,** Dallas, TX

- **Museum of Fine Arts,** Houston, TX

- **Philbrook Art Center,** Tulsa, OK

- **Phoenix Art Museum,** Phoenix, AZ

- **San Antonio Museum of Art,** San Antonio, TX

- **Tucson Museum of Art,** Tucson, AZ

- **University Art Museum,** Austin, TX

Midwest

- **Art Institute of Chicago,** Chicago, IL

- **Butler Institute of American Art,** Youngstown, OH

- **Cincinnati Art Museum,** Cincinnati, OH

- **Cleveland Museum of Art,** Cleveland, OH

- **Des Moines Art Center,** Des Moines, IA

- **Detroit Institute of Arts,** Detroit, MI

- **Elvehjem Art Center,** Madison, WI

- **Indiana University Art Museum,** Bloomington, IN

- **Indianapolis Museum of Art**, Indianapolis, IN

- **Joslyn Art Museum,** Omaha, NE

- **Krannert Art Museum,** Champaign, IL

- **Milwaukee Art Museum,** Milwaukee, WI

- **Minneapolis Institute of Arts,** Minneapolis, MN

- **Museum of Contemporary Art**, Chicago, IL

- **Nelson-Atkins Museum,** Kansas City, MO

- **Wichita Art Museum,** Wichita, KS

- **St. Louis Art Museum,** St. Louis, MO

- **Sheldon Swope Art Gallery,** Terre Haute, IN

- **Taft Museum,** Cincinnati, OH

- **Terra Museum of American Art,** Evanston, IL

- **Toledo Museum of Art,** Toledo, OH

- **University of Iowa Museum of Art,** Iowa City, IA

- **Sheldon Memorial Art Gallery,** Lincoln, NE

- **Walker Art Center,** Minneapolis, MN

West

- **Crocker Art Museum,** Sacramento, CA

- **Denver Art Museum,** Denver, CO

- **J. Paul Getty Museum,** Malibu, CA

- **Huntington Art Gallery,** San Marino, CA

- **Los Angeles County Museum,** Los Angeles, CA

- **Oakland Museum,** Oakland, CA

- **Portland Art Museum,** Portland, OR

- **Seattle Art Museum,** Seattle, WA

- **Norton Simon Museum,** Pasadena, CA

- **Fine Arts Museums of San Francisco: Brundage Asian Art Museum, M.H. de Young, California Palace of the Legion of Honor, Museum of Modern Art,** San Francisco, CA

- **University Art Museum,** Berkeley, CA

- **Utah Museum of Fine Arts,** Salt Lake City, UT

ART MUSEUMS: INTERNATIONAL

MUSEUMS today house the lion's share of the world's art riches. Treasures which in the past could only be viewed in a queen's boudoir or a count's private gallery are for the most part now available for the public to enjoy. But whether through royal bequest or judicious purchasing, several of the world's leading museums have amassed such an impressive array of wealth that they deserve mention below as truly the art world's *crème de la crème*.

What distinguishes a great museum? First, it must include an extensive art collection in a wide range of periods, nationalities, and styles. Sheer numbers are not deciding factors alone (though they certainly help). A collection of quality maintains a balanced selection of the schools it represents as well as works of top artists. A second consideration is display. The works must be well-preserved and evenly lit. Paintings should be eye level, with plenty of space around them and space to stand back. Sculptures should be accessible from as many sides as possible. Finally, the building itself should provide a pleasant, tranquil environment for thoughtful viewing.

But many museums are so large that art watching can easily turn into a tiresome cultural chore. It needn't. Just because a collection is housed under one roof doesn't mean it can be taken in all in one visit. Museum viewing is tiring: it requires long periods of standing and concentration. Go in the morning when you are fresh (and to beat the crowds), get a floor plan, and head straight for the section that interests you most. When you start feeling droopy, don't push on valiantly! Take a break, either at a cafe in the museum or down the street. (For most of the museums below, your ticket stub is good for reentry all day long.) If you try to see too much, you won't see anything at all. For an overview of the collection, your best bet is a guided tour. Find out the hours in advance. To begin here are the giants (outside of the U.S.) you must see:

The Louvre (Paris)

The granddaddy of the world's museums, the Louvre was originally constructed in 1200 as a fortress on the Seine to protect the weakest spot in the medieval city's new wall. For six centuries France's rulers enlarged, embellished, or ignored the structure according to their whims. The Louvre withstood both neglect (in the early 1700s an artist's colony took over the abandoned galleries) and revolutions (the palace was sacked several times) before Napoleon III decided to "complete" the building in 1852. His additions ranked the Louvre as the world's largest royal palace ever. In 1940 the museum again was emptied—this time systematically— and its treasures dispersed and hidden in the French countryside at the approach of the invading Germans. Today the museum catalog boasts nearly 400,000 entries, which is too much to fit even in its 225 galleries.

The famous works are easy to find, though. In nearly every gallery a sign indicates the direction to the *Venus de Milo* or the *Mona Lisa*. But the famous da Vinci may prove a disappointment in the flesh: smaller than often imagined, it is nearly unapproachable behind its layers of bulletproof glass and the crowd that invariably flocks around it. Leonardo's *Virgin on the Rocks* on its left and the Titians on the opposite wall are easier to see. Other famous names also housed in the Louvre's gray walls: the *Code of Hammurabi* (a black basalt slab) and *Arrangement in Gray and Black* (commonly known as *Whistler's Mother*). Entrance to the Louvre is free on Sundays, but with three million visitors annually, it may be worth the price of admission to go on a weekday when the crowds are thinner. *Musée du Louvre, Place du Carrousel, Paris, France; 01 260.39.26, ext. 3388.*

The Hermitage (Leningrad)

The brilliance of the Hermitage Museum in Leningrad is largely the result of the Russian czars' inferiority complexes. In 1703 Peter the Great began construction of St. Petersburg, his modern new capital within easier reach of Europe than Moscow. Prominent in his plans was the Winter Palace, a baroque turquoise fantasy modeled after Versailles and situated in the center of town on the left bank of the Neva. Still the principal building of the museum complex, its main halls such as the Great Throne Room are among the most fabulous examples of royal excess around. In an effort to catch up with other royal houses, Catherine the Great established the Hermitage's collection by snatching up almost every artwork that was put on the block. It is in part due to her that the museum's Rembrandt collection (thirty, including the lovely *Danae*) is the largest outside Amsterdam. At the time of the revolution, much of the banished or killed aristocrats' collections found their way to the Hermitage, greatly enhancing its richness in early twentieth-century masters. Some of the best Cézanne, Gauguin, and early Picasso are displayed only a few rooms away from the Leonardo masterworks. In fact, with the important Asian collection (including fascinating Mongol and Siberian pieces) the number of works in the museum is listed at a whopping 2.7 million.

Unless out and about Leningrad on your own, you'll probably see the museum on a competent (if tediously socialist) guided tour. *Hermitage Museum, M. Dvortsovaya nab. 34, Leningrad, USSR.*

The Vatican Museums (Vatican City)

While the kings of Europe were stockpiling their palaces with priceless treasures, the Vatican Popes managed some fancy collecting and commissioning of their own. The Vatican holdings originated in Pope Julius II's private collection of antiquities, enhanced through sixteenth-century Papal bequests, forming the basis of the museum's Egyptian and Classical departments. The Apollo Belvedere keeps its nickname hundreds of years after being moved inside from the Belvedere Garden on the Vatican Grounds. But the best art here was commissioned directly. Incorporated into the building itself, it can't be moved at all. The Raphael rooms, where nearly every square inch of wall space is covered by the Renaissance master's hand, the Borgia apartments, and the Vatican library are all wonders not to be missed. The Sistine Chapel is here as well. But be prepared for a sore neck when looking at Michelangelo's famous ceiling. Seating is limited and sitting on the floor strictly prohibited. When your gaze lowers be sure to notice the fine Botticelli frescoes on the wall. The labyrinthine network of buildings that make up the museum are unified by a sweeping double-spiraled entry, built in the 1930s. To avoid confusion (and backtracking) follow one of the suggested routes, labeled A, B, C, D along the entire trek through the galleries. *The Vatican Museums, Vatican City State; 06-698-3333.*

The Prado (Madrid)

The Prado is a more assailable piece of architecture than most other great museums. Perhaps because this dignified neoclassical edifice was originally conceived as a museum (albeit of natural history) and because the additions made to it have been discreet and harmonious. A major expansion program, which will provide the museum with three times more space, began in 1985 and is expected to be completed in 1988. Joining the Prado will be the Villahermosa Plaza and its lovely gardens, located diagonally across the Plaza Canovas, and the El Salon de los Reinos, previously the Spanish Military Museum. Together these three buildings will house the world's most impressive collection of Spanish, Flemish, and Venetian paintings, including great works by Goya, El Greco, Murillo, Velázquez, and Zurbarán, plus masterpieces by Bosch, Van Dyck, Titian, and Varonese . . . the list goes on ad infinitum. *The Prado Museum, Paseo del Prado, Madrid, Spain; 1-4680950.*

The British Museum (London)

England's largest museum is a library as much as an art museum. The painting treasures are elsewhere—in the National Gallery or the Tate—but the art here is staggering nonetheless. The main entrance to this columned colossus is awesome enough to put off all but the most intrepid. Inside, in addition to the library's priceless (and beautifully displayed) manuscripts, miles of corridors lead to ancient treasures from the Far East, from Ur and Persia, and to the basement's Assyrian collection. Other prizes include the Elgin Marbles, gathered from the Parthenon, and such archeological finds as the Rosetta Stone. Open seven days a week. *The British Museum, Great Russell St., WC1 3DG, London; 01-636-1555.*

The Uffizi (Florence)

The treasure house of Italian masterpieces, the Uffizi Palace is a jewel in the midst of a city that exudes art in every alley. The formidable exterior, designed by Vasari for the Medici government, beckons the visitor inside. A sense of awe mounts as you take the elevator or the stairway up to the gallery level, where a vast hallway opens up along the building's inner perimeter. Decorated with tapestries, it is flanked by the galleries that contain the finest Botticelli, Giotto, and Raphael in the world. With an active museum laboratory, some of the Uffizi's works have been recently restored to their original glorious colors. The effect is breathtaking, but the work is slow and delicate, and many more works are slated for future restoration. *Palazzo degli Uffizi, Piazza degli Uffizi, Florence; 055-218-341.*

Kunsthistorisches Museum (Vienna)

Often considered the greatest national gallery in the world, Vienna's Kunsthistorisches Museum is based on the Hapsburg royal collection. The list of German, Dutch, and Italian masterpieces is long enough to fill a telephone book, with *The Painter in His Studio* of Vermeer at the top of the list. Located in the middle of historic Vienna, the museum evokes Old World splendor, with a fine garden and outdoor restaurant. (As in many Germanic museums, the restaurant is quite good and worth a visit in itself.) Also, the works are refreshingly well-displayed and clearly labeled (as in many Germanic museums) but the museum layout is especially confusing, with the collection housed in several buildings. *Kunsthistorisches Museum, 1, Maria-Theresien Platz, Vienna, Austria; 93-25-66.*

The Tate Gallery (London)

The Tate is an old favorite for its pleasant atmosphere and impeccable taste. A short walk from Westminster Abbey, it's a nice place to visit—again and again. Founded in 1897 to house the British collection of the National Gallery, the Tate gained autonomy from its massive parent only in the 1950s. Smaller and more intimate than the National Gallery, the Tate has added a lovely Impressionist collection and made a number of daring twentieth-century acquisitions. But its five centuries of British art and roomfuls of Turner bring it to the fore of greatness. *The Tate Gallery, Millbank, London, SW1P4RG, England; 01-821-7128.*

Museu de Arte (São Paulo)

Established in 1947, the fine arts museum of São Paulo was centuries behind its European counterparts in art collecting. But it made up for lost time quickly and, starting from scratch, has assembled an impressive collection of Italian, French, and modern Brazilian art. The display is one of the most innovative (and oft criticized) ever. Housed in a vast glass box on concrete pillars, the second-floor gallery has neither exterior nor interior walls for hanging. Instead, the paintings are suspended from plate glass panels anchored to the floor. The artwork seems to float in air, giving the museum its distinctive, otherworldly atmosphere. *Museu de Arte, Sao Paulo, Brazil; 11-251-5644.*

The Pergamon Museum (East Berlin)

The Pergamon Museum is a tribute to Imperialist audacity. Here you can see, built into the museum walls, the Gates of Babylon in all their splendor (and in remarkably good condition). You will be surrounded by the Roman market of Miletus, transplanted stone by stone, and you will stand before the famed Pergamon Altar, which gives the museum its name. After the division of Berlin, the Pergamon wound up in the Russian sector. As in other East German museums, the old women guards watch over visitors like Death, and you won't find postcards for sale at the entrance. *Pergamon Museum, Museuminsel, Berlin, East Germany; 20-03-81.*

Museo Nacional de Antropologia (Mexico City)

The finest displayed museum in the world, the Museo Nacional de Antropologia in Mexico City is a beautiful and intelligent building. The simple elegance of its sandstone brick exterior harks back to the ancient American cultures whose art is shown inside. Discreet lighting and tasteful presentation distinguish the galleries that enclose the spacious courtyard. The collection spans centuries as well as civilizations, ranging from pre-Classic exhibits to Teotihuacan and Olmec treasures. The great Aztec calendar stone and Mayan riches are of special interest. *Museo Nacional de Antropologia, Chapultepec Park, Mexico City; 905-553-6266.*

SYMPHONY ORCHESTRAS: U.S.

A MERICA is a Land of Orchestras. Important symphony orchestras can be found literally in every corner of the country. Some of them are among the world's finest, ranking with the best orchestras of Europe. Here is a survey of our "Top Five" orchestras. All have budgets of about $12 million and consist of about 100 permanent, full-time instrumentalists. In addition to the subscription series offered by each organization, tours and run-out concerts form a major part of the performing calendar in each case.

The Boston Symphony

The Boston Symphony Orchestra was founded in 1881 by Major Henry Lee Higginson, a Civil War veteran, philanthropist and amateur musician. In the early years, under a succession of German conductors, the orchestra concentrated on the classical repertoire, which is heavily Germanic. After the First World War, however, anti-German sentiment caused a major shift in emphasis. Three great conductors—Pierre Monteux (1919-24), Serge Koussevitzky (1924-49) and Charles Munch (1949-62)—were largely responsible for molding the style of the orchestra in the French and Russian repertoire, for which it has since become justly famous. Today the outstanding reputation of the Boston Symphony Orchestra as one of America's greatest symphonic ensembles rests on the precision and color the orchestra brings to this music. Programming for the orchestra's approximately 100 yearly concerts reflects the importance of this repertoire.

Boston's Symphony Hall (capacity 2,600), built by architects McKim, Mead and White and opened in 1900, is one of the finest concert halls in the country. Its design strikes a balance between the hall's serious intent and the need for comfort and visually pleasing surroundings. The acoustical warmth of Symphony Hall contributes in no small way to the quality of the performances. For that reason it is particularly rewarding to hear the Boston Symphony Orchestra on home turf. Just about every seat in the hall is good, but the sound in the rear of the second balcony is truly outstanding. A trip to Tanglewood, the orchestra's summer home in the beautiful Berkshire mountains, is also a must.

The New York Philharmonic

The New York Philharmonic Symphony Orchestra—that's the somewhat awkward official name—is America's oldest orchestra of its kind in continuous existence and the third oldest in the world. It traces its origins to the Philharmonic Society, founded in 1842 by a group of musicians under the leadership of Urelli Corelli Hill. Their aim was to bring to New York City the same standard of music making that was current in the great cities of Europe. When the Philharmonic was founded, Beethoven and Weber were modern composers while Berlioz, Wagner, and Verdi were considered the avant-garde. Nevertheless the tradition stayed with the orchestra, and more recently, with tenureship of composer Pierre Boulez (1971-77), the orchestra's commitment to modern music was forcefully renewed. Since Zubin Mehta became Music Director in 1978, the repertoire has begun to focus more heavily on nineteenth-century music.

For seventy years the New York Philharmonic made its home in Carnegie Hall, from the year the hall opened, 1891, until the Philharmonic's move in 1962 to its permanent home, Philharmonic Hall (capacity 2,700) at Lincoln Center. In 1973 the building was renamed Avery Fisher Hall in recognition of a substantial gift toward the building's maintenance and improvement. The reconstruction of the auditorium, undertaken in 1976 to improve its inferior acoustics, was only partially successful. Acoustically, seats in the mid-orchestra or in the top tier are the music lover's best bet.

The Chicago Symphony

The Chicago Symphony Orchestra, America's third oldest ensemble of its kind, was founded in 1891 by the German-born conductor and violinist Theodore Thomas. Thomas served as Music Director for the first fourteen years and was succeeded by Frederick Stock. During his dynamic and innovative thirty-eight-year tenure, Stock established many of the most important traditions of the ensemble: the youth concerts; the Civic Orchestra of Chicago, America's first training orchestra for young musicians; regular pops concerts; frequent commissioning of works from major composers. The current Music Director, Sir Georg Solti, is one of the world's great conductors and, in Chicago, follows in the footsteps of such greats as Fritz Reiner, Rafael Kubelik, and Jean Martinon. Solti has been largely responsible for making the Chicago Symphony one of the foremost recording orchestras of today. Under his direction, the orchestra has won over twenty Grammy Awards for its recordings.

The Chicago Symphony is universally recognized as one of the world's top virtuoso ensembles. The orchestra is particularly renowned for its brass section. The bravura and precision of its playing are unequaled in the world. The symphony performs throughout its subscription season of about 100 concerts at Orchestra Hall (capacity 2,500). The building opened in 1904 and is another of America's acoustical miracles. (The sound in the lower balcony is particularly good.) The unique oval shape of the stage corresponds to the elliptical shape of the auditorium. Along the stage's back wall are built-in stands for chorus (another unique feature), and the shell-shaped stage ceiling is rounded directly into the ceiling of the hall itself. Orchestra Hall also houses the Chicago Symphony Orchestra Library, one of the largest and most comprehensive collections of scores and parts in the world.

The Philadelphia Orchestra

In 1900 the success of a series of concerts by the German-born conductor Fritz Scheel, combined with the great civic pride of Philadelphians, led to the creation of the Philadelphia Orchestra. Today the Philadelphia Orchestra, under Riccardo Muti, is the most recorded and most widely traveled orchestra in the world. The orchestra's high place among the great orchestras of this country is the result of the guidance of two former Music Directors— Leopold Stokowski (1912-36) and Eugene Ormandy (1936-80). Stokowski was a flamboyant conductor and a champion of new music and young composers. He was responsible for the orchestra's important relationship with contemporary composers, a tradition maintained by Ormandy, who is credited with the evolution of the "Philadelphia Sound," characterized by smoothness, homogeneity, and balance.

The subscription series of about 100 concerts forms the nucleus of the Philadelphia Orchestra's season at the Academy of Music (capacity 2,900). The building ranks among the most beautiful and acoustically excellent concert halls in the United States. Built in 1857, it is the oldest concert hall in the country still in use for its original purpose. (Seats in the amphitheatre offer the best sound but are notoriously uncomfortable. Second best sound is in the first balcony.)

The Cleveland Orchestra

The Cleveland Orchestra is today America's finest all-round orchestra, combining the best qualities of the other major ensembles: the virtuosity of Chicago, the warmth and coloristic brilliance of Boston, the richness and balance of Philadelphia. The Cleveland Orchestra, the youngest of America's top symphonic ensembles, was founded in 1918 by Adella Prentiss Hughes. Under the leadership of George Szell, Music Director from 1946 to 1970, the orchestra had its period of most dramatic and sustained growth; the size of the ensemble, the length of its season, and its recording and broadcasting activities were all greatly expanded. Moreover, under Szell, the orchestra reached a level of excellence it has maintained ever since, thanks, in great measure, to the work of Szell's successor, Lorin Maazel.

During the season, The Cleveland Orchestra offers about eighty subscription performances in its permanent home, Severance Hall, the ornate, partly Georgian, partly Art Deco structure (capacity 2,000) opened in 1931. The hall was renovated in 1958 to incorporate the latest in acoustical innovations, and today it is one of the finest symphonic halls in the country. (Some of the best seats in the house are in the dress circle.) A special and rather unique feature of The Cleveland Orchestra is the practice its members have of dividing themselves up into smaller groups—a String Quartet, a Woodwind Octet, a String Orchestra, etc. These groups offer their own concerts alongside the regular performances by the full orchestra.

Other Important U.S. Orchestras

- **Pittsburgh Symphony Orchestra**
- **National Symphony Orchestra (Washington, DC)**
- **Detroit Symphony Orchestra**
- **Minnesota Orchestra (Minneapolis)**
- **Los Angeles Philharmonic**
- **Baltimore Symphony Orchestra**

• **Buffalo Philharmonic Orchestra**

• **San Francisco Symphony Orchestra**

SYMPHONY ORCHESTRAS: INTERNATIONAL

MANY of Europe's great symphonic ensembles were products of the nineteenth-century's "democratization" of the arts, which makes them not much older than many of America's great orchestras. Through their touring programs and, especially, the long-playing disc, Europe's top orchestras have become familiar to millions of Americans who have never set foot in a foreign concert hall. Here is a brief look at the European competition to American orchestras.

The London Symphony Orchestra

In the course of its eighty years, the London Symphony Orchestra has developed a tradition of working with celebrated conductors, and its roster of principal and guest artists has included such greats as Weingartner, Mengelberg, Koussevitzky, Beecham, Monteux, Stokowski, and Walter to name only a few. The reputation of the London Symphony Orchestra is based not only on the level of technical excellence it has maintained since the late 1960s but also on its dedication to living composers: it has given more British premiers than any other English orchestra. This outstanding record includes works by composers of all nationalities.

For most of its life, the London Symphony Orchestra, though the pride of its native city, has not had a permanent home of its own. At long last, in March, 1982, the orchestra took up residence in the new Barbicon Centre in the financial district of London. Barbicon Hall (capacity 2,025) is the site of the London Symphony's approximately sixty annual subscription concerts. The new hall allows the ensemble, for the first time in its history, to rehearse and perform regularly in the same acoustical environment. The attractive, natural wood interior provides warm acoustics.

Concertgebouw Orchestra of Amsterdam

In the case of the Concertgebouw Orchestra of Amsterdam, we have the peculiar case of an orchestra being founded for a hall rather than a hall being constructed for the use of an already existing orchestra. The Concertgebouw, the building, was inaugurated in 1888. Later that year the Concertgebouw Orchestra was established. Soon after its founding, the Concertgebouw Orchestra took its place as one of Europe's premier ensembles and, over the years it has been the choice of many of the world's most important composers: Strauss, Schoenberg, Debussy, Ravel, and Grieg, for example. The orchestra's second full-time conductor, Willem Mengelberg (1895-1938) was almost singularly responsible for shaping the Concertgebouw Orchestra into a virtuoso ensemble and for solidifying the international reputation it enjoys to the present day. The Concertgebouw Hall is noted not only for its rich and tastefully grand interior and its excellent acoustics, but also for the tall, steep staircase leading from backstage to the podium. It makes for spectacular, though unnerving, entrances.

Vienna Philharmonic
The Vienna Philharmonic Orchestra was the first completely self-governing orchestra in the world. It has been known, almost continuously since its founding, as one of the finest bodies of players in the world. For the beauty and warmth of its sound it is still unmatched. The woodwinds produce a mellow, homogeneous tone and the brass attack is never aggressive. The strings are famous for their warmth and flexibility, and the ensemble as a whole is capable of an incredible range of dynamic and tonal nuances.

The Grosser Musikvereinsaal is, according to most well-traveled music lovers, the most beautiful concert hall in the world. It is also probably the finest hall in the world acoustically. The warmest sound is to be found in the first rows of the balcony. For those who like their orchestral sound loud and powerful, we recommend the side balcony toward the back. (Also, the string sound is richer on the right side of the house.) Since the Vienna Philharmonic is the ensemble for the Vienna State Opera House, it has time to play only about twenty orchestral concerts a year in its native city. These are scheduled (because of opera commitments) only on Saturday afternoons and Sunday mornings. Tickets are very difficult to come by.

The Berlin Philharmonic
The Berlin Philharmonic Orchestra gave its first concert on October 17, 1882. Early guest conductors included Tchaikovsky, Grieg, Brahms, and Richard Strauss. It is Herbert von Karajan, Music Director since 1954, who has been responsible for the orchestra's current honored status among the world's great symphonic ensembles. No other orchestra—and the latest digital recordings show this quite clearly—can claim, as the Berlin Philharmonic

can, that it is an orchestra of virtuosi. Its solo instrumentalists are the finest in the world, and ensemble work displays an unearthly degree of precision and balance. The Berlin Philharmonic is at once the most disciplined and thrilling orchestra of our time.

The orchestra's original home, the "Philharmonie," was destroyed, along with most of Berlin, in World War II. A new permanent home was not finished until 1963, and it is in this hall that the Berlin Philharmonic now performs its 100 annual subscription concerts. The new "Philharmonie" (capacity 2,400) is a very modern, acoustically excellent hall built "in the round," i.e., audience surrounds the performance area on all sides. This construction makes the "Philharmonie" particularly well-suited for modern music. Unfortunately for the traveling music buff, there is a tremendous waiting list for subscription tickets.

The Dresden State Orchestra

In a very broad sense, the Dresden State Orchestra, founded in 1548, is the oldest group of its kind still functioning in Europe. Early in this century it attracted several important conductors who helped shape its character and reputation: Fritz Reiner, Fritz Busch, and Karl Böhm. As the ensemble for the Dresden State Opera, it became the orchestra of choice of opera composers and in this century is particularly linked with the music of Richard Strauss. Nine of his operas, including *Salome, Elektra,* and *Der Rosenkavalier,* were premiered here. Since World War II the Dresden State Orchestra has been without a permanent home and has performed in the very large, cold, and unattractive auditorium of the Cultural Center. In 1985, reconstruction was completed on the beautiful old opera house, and the orchestra once again has a comfortable and acoustically ingratiating hall.

Other important European orchestras:

• **(East Germany)** Leipzig Gewandhaus Orchestra

• **(USSR)** Leningrad Philharmonic Orchestra

• **(France)** Orchestre de Paris

MUSIC FESTIVALS: U.S.

Ravinia Festival

1985 marked the fiftieth annual Ravinia Festival. Located twenty-two miles north of Chicago, Ravinia has one of the longest and most varied seasons of all the summer festivals in the United States and runs from late June to mid-September. Performances by the Chicago Symphony Orchestra form the core of the Festival's activities, which also include performances by visiting orchestras, chamber music concerts, recitals, ballet, dance, young people's programs, and a jazz/pop/folk series. *Ravinia Festival, 1575 Oakwood Ave., Highland Park, IL 60035; (312) 433-8800.*

Hollywood Bowl

For over fifty years the Hollywood Bowl has been the summer home of the Los Angeles Philharmonic. Each year the Hollywood Bowl Festival offers about ten weeks of superb music-making by some of the world's greatest artists. The Bowl itself is a 117-acre park, which has picnic grounds, fountains, and several perform-ance areas, the most important of which is a huge acoustical shell built into the side of a hill. The natural amphitheater provided by the hill and its extraordinary acoustics make perfect listening for as many as 17,000 patrons. Evenings are pleasant and it never rains! The Festival usually runs from early July to mid-September. *Holly-wood Bowl Office, P.O. Box 1951, Hollywood, CA 90028; (213) 850-2000.*

Aspen

Since its inception in 1949, the Aspen Music Festival has been the festival for those who combine love of music with love of the outdoors. Aspen, Colorado, is situated at an elevation of 8,000 feet in a valley of the Rockies. It is surrounded by breathtakingly beau-tiful peaks of over 14,000 feet. Along with the sheer beauty of the area, there are ample opportunities for hiking, fishing, rafting, and a variety of other invigorating sports and activities. Beginning in late June, the Aspen Festival features nine weeks of symphonies, chamber music, choral, opera, and jazz performances by world-renowned conductors and performers. Jorge Mester is the Festival's music director. *Aspen Music Festival, P.O. Box AA, Aspen, CO 81611; (303) 925-3254.*

Pacific Northwest Wagner Festival

A recent addition to the roster of festivals is Seattle's Pacific Northwest Wagner Festival. Begun in 1975, this series, sponsored by the Seattle Opera Association, presents two complete and uncut performances of Wagner's *Der Ring der Nibelungen,* in German with English supratitles. Performances take place in the Seattle Opera

House and are given during the first and second weeks of August. Lectures on each opera will be offered on the days of the performances. *Seattle Opera, P.O. Box 9248, Seattle, WA 98109; (800) 426-1619.*

Tanglewood

The town of Lenox, situated in the lovely Berkshire Hills of western Massachusetts, is the site of the oldest major music festival in the United States—The Tanglewood Music Festival. Concerts by the Boston Symphony are held on Friday and Saturday evenings and on Sunday afternoons in the Shed, an enormous, open-sided wood and steel structure. The Shed seats over 5,000 and there is additional seating for literally thousands on the lawn. The festival offers recitals in its Theatre/Concert Hall on Thursday evenings and several open rehearsals with a modest entrance fee. Special "Prelude" concerts precede the regular Friday evening programs. Tanglewood runs from late June through late August. *Festival Ticket Office, Symphony Hall, Boston, MA 02115; (617) 266-1492.*

MUSIC FESTIVALS: INTERNATIONAL

SUMMER is the season when Europe's top music festivals take place, providing a chance to see a wide range of artists and repertoire in a relatively short period of time. In addition to the musical performances themselves, lectures, films, exhibits, and tours are part of the program at most festivals. So diverse and rich are the offerings, in fact, that a music lover could easily spend an entire vacation at a single festival; extended visits to several different festivals could constitute the itinerary for an entire summer in Europe.

The Bath Festival

Bath, a resort city known for its graceful Georgian architecture, hot springs, and Roman baths, hosts one of Britain's most important musical events of the year—the Bath International Festival of Music and the Arts. Since 1948, when it was founded, the festival has grown into a seventeen-day celebration. The finest chamber musicians in the world have made frequent appearances. Concerts are held in various music halls and churches in Bath and the surrounding countryside. *The Bath Festival Society, Linley House, 1 Pierrepont Place, Bath BA1 1JY, England; (0225) 62231.*

The Glyndebourne Festival

In 1943 John Christie and his wife Audrey Mildmay decided to build an opera house on the grounds of their estate in Sussex Downs, near Lewes, about fifty miles south of London. Their 800-seat theater has since become the site of the most prestigious opera festival and musical social event of Europe, the Glyndebourne Festival Opera. At first the festival concentrated on the operas of Mozart. Now the summer season is drawn from the entire operatic repertoire, but still includes at least one opera by Mozart. The festival generally offers about sixty performances from May to August. Performances usually begin in the late afternoon to allow time for a lengthy intermission during which patrons can dine and stroll around the lovely grounds. Since the beginning, opera-goers have been encouraged to bring picnic baskets and to dine casually on the lawn. This custom, however, belies the formality of the festival in general: patrons are expected to wear evening dress, and many attend in formal attire. *Glyndebourne Festival Opera, Box Office, Lewes, E. Sussex BN8 5UU, England; Ringmer (0273) 812411.*

The Edinburgh Festival

Described by *The London Times* as "arguably the most important cultural event in the world," the Edinburgh Festival always has a lively and varied program to offer. What began as a primarily musical event in 1947, has grown to include theater productions, dance concerts, a film festival, and even marching pipe and drum bands. The season stretches from August to September. Be sure not to miss Military Tattoo, a spectacular performance by the pipes and drums of the Scottish regiments on the floodlit heights of Edinburgh Castle. *The Edinburgh International Festival, 21 Market St., Edinburgh, EH1 1BW, Scotland; (031) 226 4001.*

The Aix-en-Provence Festival

The city of Aix-en-Provence (pop. 90,000), located in the south of France, was founded in about 100 A.D. by Romans who enjoyed its thermal waters (still a tourist attraction). Situated just twenty miles north of Marseilles, it is also noted for its annual music festival. Since its inception in 1948, the festival has built its season around three opera productions each year, including one by Mozart. Performances are staged in the festival's 1,200-seat outdoor Theatre de l'Archeveche from July to August. *The Festival de Musique d'Aix, Palais de l'Ancien Archeveche, 13100 Aix-en-Provence, France; (42) 23 37 81.*

The Bayreuth Festival

Because of its reputation as one of Europe's most important music festivals, the Richard Wagner Festival in Bayreuth, West Germany, is one of the more difficult festivals to get tickets for. (Hotel accommodations also must be arranged well in advance.) Founded by Wagner himself in 1876 as a vehicle for his music dramas, this event is the undisputed mecca for Wagnerites. To stage his elaborate operas, Wagner secured the backing of a patron, King Ludwig II of Bavaria, and built the Festspielhaus, which remains the festival opera house today. It opened with a performance of *Das Rheingold. Bayreuther Festpiele, Postfach 2320, D-8580 Bayreuth 2, West Germany; (09 21) 2.02.21.*

The Salzburg Festival

The Salzburg Festival holds a preeminent place among all the music festivals spread over the summer period. Salzburg is the city of Mozart's birth; it sets aside one month each summer to pay tribute to him by assembling the world's top artists and ensembles for performances of the highest caliber. Annual Mozart festivals in Salzburg began in 1843. The Salzburg Festival as we know it today was founded in 1919 by composer Richard Strauss, poet Hugo von Hofmannsthal, and stage director Max Reinhardt. At first the musical offerings concentrated on the works of Mozart. Today, each day of the month-long festival offers an almost overwhelming choice of music representing all periods and genres and many different composers, featuring the Vienna Philharmonic Orchestra and the finest contemporary conductors. The festival runs from mid-July to the beginning of September. A smaller Mozart Festival is held for one week at the end of January each year, celebrating Mozart's birthday. *Salzburger Festpiele, Kartenburo, Postfach 140 A-5010, Salzburg, Austria; (06222) 42 5 41.*

JAZZ CLUBS/FESTIVALS

EVEN though a lot of big-name jazz artists perform in vast auditoriums these days, the best place to listen to jazz is still in a club. The seats may be uncomfortable, the air smoky, but the atmosphere is always looser than in a posh concert hall. A great jazz club needn't be posh—in fact, a kind of reverse snobbery often dictates Spartan decor for a truly "authentic" atmosphere. Nor is efficient service a requirement for greatness, though some clubs offer fine cuisine. But a great club has a certain ambience that

attracts the top musicians and the crowds alike. It has the best
piano and sound system affordable, and its management is dedicated to making good music. The clubs listed below feature the best
in mainstream, modern jazz and have consistently offered a variety of top artists.

Clubs

• **The Village Vanguard (178 Seventh Ave. South, New York,
NY; (212) 255-4037)** The Vanguard has been a classic almost
since the day Max Gordon opened it in 1937. His dedication and
perseverence kept the club going through the early 1970s when
many others were forced to close. The subterranean 135-seat haunt
has produced many classic recordings, and what it lacks in creature
comforts it makes up for in top-notch music. Three sets nightly,
seven nights.

• **Blues Alley (1073 Wisconsin Ave. NW, Washington, DC
20007; (202) 337-2338).** The differences between Blues Alley and
the Vanguard are like the differences between Washington and
New York. Located in a historic red-brick building in the center of
Georgetown, Blues Alley offers an excellent dinner menu in a comfortable, supper club atmosphere. With two decades' experience,
this 150-seat club offers top jazz seven nights a week. Several live
recordings have been made at Blues Alley, including the award-
winning LP by pianist George Shearing, simply titled "George
Shearing Live at Blues Alley."

• **Sweet Basil (88 Seventh Ave. South, New York, NY; (212)
242-1785)** Since 1974, this elegant seventy-five-seat club has
offered good food and great jazz seven nights a week in a tasteful,
intimate atmosphere.

• **Jazz Showcase (636 S. Michigan Ave., Chicago, IL; (312)
427-4300)** Joe Segal's Jazz Showcase moved here to the Blackstone
Hotel in 1981, where it continues to present top weekend jazz in this
spacious (yet surprisingly intimate) 200-seat club.

• **Rick's Cafe Americain (644 N. Lake Shore Drive, Chicago,
IL; (312) 943-9200)** Styled after its namesake in the movie *Casa-
blanca,* Rick's, one of the country's largest clubs (seats 350), serves
name jazz five nights a week at the Holiday Inn.

• **Baker's Keyboard Lounge (20510 Livernois, Detroit, MI;
(313) 964-4000)** Still the best place to hear Betty Carter.

• **Pasquale's (22724 Pacific Coast Highway, Malibu, CA; (213) 456-2008)** Spectacular setting, overlooking the beach.

Festivals

• **Monterey Jazz Festival.** The Monterey Jazz Festival has continued at this California peninsula town since 1957. With performances held in the fairgrounds arena, this nonprofit festival maintains its commitment to young jazz artists as it attracts the top established performers. It's truly a festival atmosphere that overtakes Monterey every third weekend in September, with nearly every arena concert a sure 7,000-seat sellout. For information, write: *411 Alvarado St., Monterey, CA 93940; (408) 649-4499.*

• **Chicago Jazz Festival.** Held in Chicago's Grant Park, the Chicago Jazz Festival is billed as the largest free jazz festival in the world. Since its inception in 1978, the event now spans six days at the end of August, attracting about 250 musicians and nearly 300,000 spectators. Breadth distinguishes this festival—from avant-garde to Count Basie, there's something for everyone at Jazztown's summer happening. For information, write: *Mayor's Office of Special Events, City Hall Room 609, 121 N. La Salle St., Chicago, IL 60602; (312) 744-3315.*

• **New Orleans Jazz and Heritage Festival.** Considered the world's largest, this festival attracts 3,000 musicians to the Fair Grounds Race Track in this historic jazz town. Combining traditional Southern food with more kinds of jazz than you can shake a stick at, for the first two weekends in May there are nine stages featuring simultaneous continuous music from dawn to dusk. A real Dixie jamboree, since 1970. For information, write: *P.O. Box 2530, New Orleans, LA 70176; (504) 522-4786.*

• **Montreux International Jazz Festival.** This breathtaking Swiss town is the site of Europe's longest and most respected jazz festival. Since 1967, Montreux has featured the best of many styles of jazz, and the list of recordings "Live on Montreux" keeps growing. For three weeks of July, big names highlight the evening shows at the casino, with smaller afternoon performances and free "Festival Off" concerts throughout the day. For information, write: *Montreux International Jazz Festival, P.O. Box 97, CH 1920 Montreux, Switzerland; (21) 63 12 12.*

• **Nice Grande Parade du Jazz.** The gardens of Roman ruins outside of the French Riviera town of Nice are the setting for the

Grande Parade du Jazz. For two weeks in early June, three stages operate simultaneously from 5 p.m. to midnight, featuring a string of top names. It's a glamorous affair in spectacular surroundings. For information, contact: *Hotel Mercure, 2 rue Halevy, F-06000 Nice, France; (93) 85.09.35.*

• **Molde International Jazz Festival.** One of the oldest festivals around takes place in this tiny Norwegian community on the west coast of the North Sea. For twenty-three years Molde has played host to many greats of jazz in the last week of July. The street parade kickoff, the numerous jam sessions, and free jazz films lend an authentic festival atmosphere to this out-of-the-way event. For information, contact: *Molde International Jazz Festival, Parkveien 42, N-6400 Molde, Norway; (72) 53779.*

MUSICAL INSTRUMENTS: ORCHESTRAL

BUYING an orchestral instrument is not just a question of walking into a store and choosing the prettiest model. If a quality instrument is what you are after, whether for making music or for investment, it pays to consult not only the dealers, but also instrument makers and musicians themselves, to find out just what your money will buy. Take violins, for example:

Violins/Cellos
Violin making began in Italy around 1520; the art reached its first stage of excellence with the craftsmanship of the Amati family in Cremona toward the end of that century. The work of *Antonio Stradivari* (1644-1737) and *Giuseppe Guarneri* (1687-1745) brought the art of violin making to a level of excellence which remains unduplicated to this day. *Jacques Français Rare Violins* in New York specializes in the sale, restoration, and repair of these historic instruments, of which the extant examples number only in the low thousands. (There are approximately 800 violins, violas, and cellos by Stradivari still in existence, about half of his total output.)

Most of Jacques Français' clients are important solo artists, although he does sell many instruments to top orchestral string players around the world. According to Mr. Français, whose business dates from 1797 in Paris, the least expensive Stradivarius would cost around $250,000. Prices as high as $1 million and above have been reported recently for the finest instruments. The 1716 model played by Nathan Milstein, for example, is considered a "peak period" Strad. With the value of rare violins rising at the unbelievable annual rate of about 25 percent for some of the lower priced specimens, these instruments are increasingly sought after purely as investments.

A string player uses two basic criteria in evaluating an instrument: volume and quality. Volume can be easily measured; quality is naturally much more subjective. A soloist must be able to cut through heavy orchestral textures, and even orchestral players must be able to hear themselves within the orchestra. The age of an instrument is an important factor in determining this kind of quality in the tone it produces. Most serious musicians will seek an instrument that has mellowed enough to have proven itself.

In general, the more recently a violin was made, the lower its price. A good nineteenth-century or early twentieth-century Italian instrument would run anywhere from $5,000 to $20,000 and up. A better French or Italian violin dating from late-eighteenth to mid-nineteenth century could cost from $25,000 to $100,000. Of course, in all of these cases, we are talking about handmade instruments. Even today, **the best stringed instruments are still entirely handmade.** Each instrument is the work of one artisan and represents anywhere from two months of work for a violin to six months or more for a cello. A contemporary handmade violin from Germany costs about $1,500. Leading companies producing them include Heberlein, Kaiser, Wagner, and Kraus and Fuchs.

In addition to selling rare instruments, string shops like Jacques Français or *William Moennig and Son, Ltd.,* in Philadelphia—there are only a handful of such shops in the country—also make instruments in their own workshops. A new violin or viola produced in Mr. Moennig's atelier costs somewhat under $5,000. Prices for new cellos would begin around $5,000. A reproduction of a rare eighteenth-century violin, commissioned from the shop of Jacques Français, would cost between $12,000 and $20,000. For a cello, prices would begin at $15,000.

There are machine-made stringed instruments available at prices considerably lower than handmade ones. Chances are, however, that most dedicated amateurs would want to spend more to get an instrument with better tone. Fairly good machine-made instruments are manufactured by Paesold, Jusek, or Schroetter in Germany and cost from $1,500. The Japanese company Suzuki produces good machine-made miniature strings for children. These range in price from $350 for violins and $450 for violas up to about $800 for small-sized cellos.

Flutes

The most prestigious name in flutes is Powell. *Verne Q. Powell, Inc.,* in Arlington, Massachusetts, produces only about 200 a year. Their exquisitely crafted instruments are the choice of orchestral and solo flutists (flautists, if you prefer) around the world. In quality of tone, precision fit of keys and joints, beauty of design, and exactness of intonation, Powell flutes are unrivaled. Prices range from about $4,300 for a sterling silver model (92.5% silver, 7.5% copper) to between $10,000 and $20,000 for gold or platinum models. (Gold flutes are almost exclusively the domain of soloists since their darker, huskier timbre does not blend well in an orchestra with the timbre of silver flutes.)

Though Japanese flutes (Muramatsu, for example) have been praised for their accuracy of intonation, most musicians continue to prefer the richer, more exciting French-type sound of the Powell instrument. Muramatsu flutes are comparable in price to Powell models of similar composition. Another important name in flutes is Haynes. Haynes' silver models run a bit lower than Powell's: $3,000 to $3,500. Haynes' flutes are the second most common choice of flutists in American orchestras. Somewhat below the top two, in both price and quality, are the numerous brands of flutes for students and casual amateurs. Companies like Armstrong, Artley, and Gemeinhaart each turn out thousands of flutes a year. Prices range from about $200 for a nickel-silver model (actually not silver at all but a nickel brass) to about $1,000 for a silver model (usually "coin" silver: 90 percent silver to 10 percent copper).

Clarinets

French clarinets are still the choice of many serious clarinetists. Most players feel that the best instruments were made about a century ago, but finding one of these usually calls for quite a bit of detective work in shops and odd places around the world, and playing it can be problematical. These old instruments were often pitched at a level not usable for most of today's music. Good instruments are still being produced in France, and for some time the top name has been Buffet. A standard model costs about $850, a Prestige model with silver-plated keys, about $1,500. Selmer—the French parent company, not its American subsidiary—also makes excellent clarinets, as does Leblanc. Their prices are comparable to those of Buffet. Germany and Austria also have a long history of clarinet development and performance and their best brands are Wurlitzer and Hammerschmidt. Their keywork, bore size, and other features are different from the French instruments and result in a darker, woodier tone that the Germans have long preferred. Professionals are also using Yamaha clarinets, made in Japan, which are held in high regard. Student clarinets from companies like Artley, Armstrong, and American Selmer cost about $200, or approximately one quarter the price of a professional instrument.

Oboes

Though oboes by the English company Howarth remain popular in England, American oboists prefer the darker-sounding French instruments. Of these, the most prestigious is the *Lorée,* by far and away the leader among French brands. The French Selmer, at a price of $900 to $2,000, has a less rich and penetrating sound than the Lorée, which costs about $2,300. Lorée also makes excellent English horns. (An English horn is not a horn at all but a lower pitched member of the oboe family.) A Lorée English horn costs about $2,800. As with the clarinet, student model oboes from such companies as Linton, Artley, and Armstrong run approximately one quarter of the cost of professional models.

Bassoons

Bassoons fall into two basic categories: French and German. The German instrument has a wider bore, and the keys lie closer together. A player with a small hand will find the German system easier to play than the French system. The German instrument has, in turn, a somewhat duller sound than its French counterpart. Over the years, however, the French bassoon has lost some ground; today, most professional bassoonists play the German instrument, either a *Heckel* or a *Puchner.* The Heckels are the most expensive, beginning at around $10,000. Bassoons made by Puchner cost from $3,000 to $5,000 but have a high reputation among professional players. An American company, Fox, (in Elkhart, Indiana, the musical instrument capital of the United States), has a small but steadily growing following among bassoonists. Fox bassoons are priced from $1,500 all the way to $7,000. Prices for student models made by Artley, Linton, or Armstrong begin at around $800.

Saxophones

Saxophones *made in France by Selmer* are still the finest in the world. (The saxophone was invented in 1946 by the Belgian Antoine—known to intimates as Adolphe—Sax.) The two most popular sizes, alto and tenor, are priced by Selmer at around $1,500 and $1,700 respectively. In the United States, saxes are manufactured by several companies: King and Conn sell their models for about $950 (alto) and $1,150 (tenor). The cost of student models will run approximately one third that of professional models. Saxophones, along with virtually all of the woodwind and brass instruments, are also manufactured by the Japanese giant, Yamaha. They make a complete line of saxophones from student models to professional instruments. Though until now Yamaha instruments have been less accepted than the top brands, dealers like Robert Giardinelli in New York insist that Yamahas compare very favorably with the finest American- and European-made brands. Their prices, in most cases, are only slightly lower than those of the American and European competitors.

French Horns

Conn is the most popular brand of French horns, particularly among American players. Holton, a subsidiary of Leblanc (the clarinet maker), offers a very good horn for about the same price as the Conn instruments: $1,100. But the most prestigious French horn is *the Alexander, from Germany.* The sound is somewhat lighter than the American-made horns, and the instrument demands a bit more of the player to secure proper intonation. The reputation and quality of Alexander horns are reflected in their price: $2,000 to $3,000. Student horns made by American companies such as Conn, King, Holton, Bundy, and Signet cost about one third the price of professional instruments.

Trumpets/Trombones

Most professional trumpet and trombone players in this country use instruments manufactured by *Bach.* Bach trumpets give what players consider ideal results: a big, full, open sound that blends well both with brass and full orchestra. They are priced at about $500. Another trumpet manufacturer with a very high reputation but small production is *Schilke* in Chicago. A Schilke trumpet costs about $800. Student brass instruments by Conn and Bach or companies like Signet, Bundy, or American Selmer are priced at one third to one half the price of professional models.

Since both price and quality vary widely, it is essential to consult not only with an instrument dealer, but also with those in a position to know best—orchestral players who do it for a living.

MUSICAL INSTRUMENTS: PIANOS

A piano is remarkably versatile. It is a dazzling solo performer as well as the epicenter of concerti. Though a percussive instrument, the piano can produce subtle pastels of sound and great orchestral swells. Aside from its musical breadth, the piano is an ingenious machine, comprised of thousands of moving wooden parts and strings under 34,000 pounds or more of pressure.

However fantastic or plain its outer appearance, **the heart of the piano is its action,** the soul the sound produced. Sound is created by a felt hammer striking against a string, which vibrates according to its pitch. The so-called "double-escapement action" of the modern piano involves the hammer hitting the string and, as long as the key is pressed, being checked in an intermediate position: it thus cannot rebound onto the string accidentally and stop the sound; but the key, traveling only a third of the way up, can be replayed in quick repetition. When the key is released, another checking device immediately dampens the string. Though these principles were built into the first piano (born when Bartolomeo Cristofori, keeper of the instruments for the Medici Court, invented the *gravicembalo col piano e forte,* "harpsichord with soft and loud"), they were forgotten for a time by later piano makers and not given final form until 1821 when Erard Brothers of Paris made the piano action known today.

American piano makers are credited for other major innovations. In 1825 one Alpheus Babcock patented the cast-iron frame, making the piano the durable workhorse it is. And in 1857 the *Steinway* firm arrived at a definitive form for overstringing, in which the bass wires fan out over the treble strings and toward the center of the grand's wing-shaped case, producing a powerful bass sound.

By 1900 the U.S. produced more than half the world's pianos. Since 1950 Japan has become the world's leading consumer and producer of pianos, with an average of 400,000 per year. *Yamaha,* the largest manufacturer, makes over 200,000 a year. They range from mass-produced, quite serviceable uprights to concert-level grands. *At the other end of the spectrum are the small atelier-like firms,* which produce essentially handmade instruments in small numbers. These include *Bösendorfer,* which makes almost 800 pianos a year, *Bechstein* from Berlin (700 a year), *Hamburg Steinway* (2,500), and *U.S. Steinway* (3,500). At the prestigious Van Cliburn piano competition, U.S. and Hamburg Steinway, Baldwin, Bösendorfer, Bechstein, and Yamaha are the concert grands on hand. Though Steinway far and away dominates concert hall stages, it represents only about three percent of the American piano market.

Bösendorfer: The Making of a Grand Piano
Bösendorfer is rare to the point of exoticism. Only about 100 are sold in the U.S. each year, and their cost, $30,000 to $70,000, is

more than twice that of the comparable American concert grand. In 1977 the little Viennese firm, financially ailing, was bought by Kimball International of Jasper, Indiana, a manufacturer of inexpensive, pedestrian pianos. There was a fear that the gorgeous instrument beloved by Liszt, lauded by composers and musicians for 150 years, would be downgraded into a "Kimballdorfer." Those fears were unfounded. According to Bösendorfer's Managing Director Roland Rädler, Kimball's effect has been all to the good. Bösendorfer's Vienna factory is in a converted monastery. The sense of dedication is unmistakable. Bösendorfer workers have gone through mandatory three-and-one-half-year apprenticeships and passed state exams to become licensed piano makers. At present, twenty young people, ages seventeen to early twenties, are learning all aspects of piano building. Those with special aptitudes will be trained as tuners and regulators.

From forest to salon, a Bösendorfer piano requires three to five years of seasoning and sixty-two weeks of manufacturing. (The firms boasts it is the world's "slowest piano maker.") The cast-iron frame, the armature of the piano, is sprayed with several layers of resin and lacquer and hand-sanded to silken smoothness. Meanwhile in the wood area, a spruce soundboard is tapered precisely to fit its iron plate. The piano is eighty-five percent spruce. Both the soundboard and most of the inner and outer rim of the cabinet are made from the same fine solid spruce, which is considered crucial to the piano's special resonance. After buying costly woods, about forty percent is disqualified for the sake of appearance or acoustics. And for the maple bridges some eighty percent is rejected. With the felt, too, which is bought from a Stuttgart factory, thirty to forty percent is scrapped, and the rest cut and shaped by craftsmen to accommodate each piano individually. Felt is a hot issue among piano makers. Like wine, it has its vintage years, and in recent times more bad ones than good.

Technicians make piano strings by standing at a lathe and hand-wrapping copper wire around a revolving bass string. Other workmen hand-buff the shiny black cabinets that house the inner works and give added gloss to this pampered piano.

The shiny finish is one tip-off that a new piano is European rather than homegrown. European grands usually are shiny black, while American ones generally are satin ebony. Pianos also can be ordered in wood finishes and, at least theoretically, in Day-Glo yellow or flamingo pink. But black is the traditional and preferred color. Secondly, in Europe piano keys are still made of African elephant ivory, while U.S. firms years ago switched over to plastic. Bösendorfer ivory, about $700 worth per piano, is certified as legal, which is why it is allowed into the U.S. despite the elephant's threatened status. Many musicians swear by ivory. They argue that it grows smoother over time, is warmer to the touch, and, in the heat of performance, absorbs perspiration whereas plastic becomes slippery.

From the moment the Bösendorfer plate and soundboard are fitted together and the bridge chiseled, each piano is an individual creation. Its sound is a product of the qualities and idiosyncracies of the materials and the talents and tastes of the artisans who build the piano, regulate the action, voice the hammers, and tune the strings. The end result is a room full of finished Bösendorfers, literally hundreds of thousands of dollars worth of pianos. All are astonishingly different, yet each has a singing quality characteristic of the Bösendorfer.

Buying a Grand Piano

To buy a piano is to accept the basic sound and feel of the instrument. But a few modifications can be made. If the action is too light, it can be weighed to increase the keys' resistance and give the pianist more of a workout. An overly bright or shrill piano can be voiced; the hammers are pierced with a needle to loosen the felt. Before calling a technician, however, an owner should let the piano "rest" in its new environment, to adjust to the temperature and humidity. Don't be shocked if the instrument sounds different in the home than it did in the showroom. Walls, curtains, rugs, the size of the room, the height of the ceiling, all affect sound. If your dreams tend toward the grandiose, remember that a nine-foot, six-inch Imperial Bösendorfer, the glory of the concert hall, can be overwhelming in a room at home.

Pianos are sensitive: Don't place them near radiators, open windows, air conditioning vents, or on top of humidifiers, although in winter a room humidifier is good for both piano and pianist. Indeed, the standard reason Steinway gives for not selling its Hamburg brethren in the U.S. is that the piano materials are seasoned for European climates, not for overheated American homes. Musicians who are Hamburg Steinway partisans retort that this is merely an excuse and that U.S. Steinway doesn't wish to show off its more brilliant German counterpart. All this amounts to sibling rivalry within the same great piano family.

Pianists have a kind of platonic sound they carry around in their heads. And they choose a piano that approaches their ideal.

As Mr. Steinway himself says, "We just put them in a room with ten pianos and let them choose. To try to tell a pianist which sound is better—that way lies madness."

When purchasing a used Steinway, it may be possible to track down its history through the parent company. Steinway Hall keeps a record book noting the serial number and year of every piano manufactured and subsequent work the factory performed. *Buying an old piano can be dicey.* You may end up with a spectacularly beautiful instrument—or one that is only good for firewood. A once-great piano is as good as the care it has received over the years. Fine rebuilt pianos are not necessarily a monetary bargain. If you're in doubt about an old piano's soundness, hire a technician to examine it before buying. For information:

• **Bösendorfer.** There are about thirty authorized Bösendorfer representatives in the U.S. CONTACT: Vic Geiger, V.P. International Sales, Kimball World, 1600 Royal St., Jasper, IN 47546; (812) 482-1600.

• **Bechstein.**
C. Bechstein Pianoforte Fabrik
Reichenberger Strasse 124
1000 Berlin 36, West Germany

• **Steinway.** U.S. Steinway has over 225 dealerships. For the one closest to you, contact:
Steinway Marketing Coordinator
Steinway & Sons
Steinway Place
Long Island City, NY 11105
(212) 721-2600

• **Hamburg Steinway.**
Steinway & Sons
Colonnaden 29
2 Hamburg 36, West Germany

• **Baldwin.** There are approximately 600 dealers who carry the Baldwin piano. If you do not have one locally, contact the main office for information.
Baldwin Pianos
1801 Gilbert Ave.
Cincinnati, OH 45202
(513) 852-7000

• **Yamaha.** There are over 350 Yamaha dealers. They are listed in the Yellow Pages as "authorized dealer." Yamaha suggests the Yellow Pages as the best guide to a dealer in your area.

OPERA COMPANIES: U.S./INTERNATIONAL

OPERA is both a musical and theatrical art. There are numerous companies around the world but only a handful can be labeled major. **A major opera here is defined as one which:** 1) features a balanced selection of those operas (traditional and contemporary) which represent the finest of this art form, 2) includes performances by major operatic stars of today, and 3) sustains a sufficiently long season. For a list of other worthy companies see the list at the end of this article.

Covent Garden (London)

There have been three Covent Garden Opera Houses. The first opened in December, 1732, and was completely destroyed by fire in 1808; the second, sporting fluted columns modeled on the temple of Athene on the Acropolis and said to be the largest in Europe after those of St. Peter's in Rome, was also destroyed by fire in 1856. The third and present opera house opened its doors in 1858. In 1982 the Royal Opera House celebrated the 250th anniversary of the opening of the first house in 1732 with a new production of Handel's *Semele,* an opera which was commissioned by the first Covent Garden house. Its repertoire is on the traditional side, yet well-balanced.

The season opens in September and is long enough to give early summer travelers a chance to enjoy outstanding opera. For information: *Royal Opera House, P.O. Box 6, London WC2E 7QA, England; 240-1200.*

Vienna State Opera

The enormous budget of the Vienna State Opera is provided by taxes which the Austrian Government levies on the entire nation. The high standard of performance owes a great deal to the flexibility ensured by this immense and unique subsidy. The high level of performance is also maintained by the employment of the Vienna Philharmonic, one of Europe's great orchestras, as the regular ensemble for opera performances. No less important has been the impressive succession of outstanding musical minds who have directed the opera house and made it the finest in Europe: Gustav Mahler, Felix Weingartner, Richard Strauss, Clemens Krauss,

Karl Böhm, Herbert von Karajan. The Vienna State Opera has never been a company noted for experimentation. Though a fair number of operas have had their premieres there over the years, the house's reputation rests rather on the high quality and great variety of its offerings from the more standard repertoire. For information: *Bundestheaterverband, Goethegasse 1, A-1010 Vienna, Austria.*

La Scala

La Scala still retains its prestigious position among the world's greatest opera companies, and its audiences still enjoy their reputation as the most severe and exacting to be found anywhere. A singer's performance at La Scala is today, as it was 100 years ago, the supreme test of his or her artistry. A successful debut in this house is considered, for better or for worse, an artist's baptism to a major international career. Beginning with the first appearance of Rossini's name on the roster in 1812, the annals of the house read like an encyclopedia of nineteenth-century opera with premieres and commissions of works by such composers as Rossini, Bellini, Donizetti, Verdi, and Puccini, all of whom consolidated their own fame at this house. It was also here that Arturo Toscanini, in his several tenureships as director and many guest appearances, made his reputation as the foremost operatic conductor of his time. Under the leadership and influence of Toscanini, La Scala experienced a period of brilliance, integrity, and excitement unmatched in its history. For information: *Teatro alla Scala, Via Filodrammatici 2, Milan, Italy; 809129.*

The San Francisco Opera

Over its sixty-three-year history, the San Francisco Opera has built an impressive reputation for high performance standards and innovative planning. In its history it has presented 134 operas in all, including twenty American premieres and several world premieres. Hundreds of major artists—singers, conductors, directors, designers—have made their American debut on its stage. The company has also been in the forefront in opera broadcasting: San Francisco offered the first live telecast by an American opera company via satellite to Europe in the 1979 performance of *La Gioconda.* Of all the opera companies in the United States, the San Francisco Opera today can boast what is perhaps the most satisfying, well-planned, and balanced combination of far-reaching repertoire, world-class artists, and attention to production values. For information contact: *San Francisco Opera, War Memorial Opera House, San Francisco, CA 94102; (415) 861-4008.*

The Metropolitan Opera

The first Metropolitan Opera House owed its existence to a curiously American set of circumstances. Beginning in the 1850s, the Academy of Music at 14th Street and Irving Place in Manhattan had been the fashionable home of opera in New York City. The nine boxes of the Academy were held season after season by the same individuals who had first subscribed to them or by their descendants. In 1880 a group of wealthy New Yorkers finally grew tired of this arrangement, banded together, and decided to build their own opera house. The list of the disgruntled patrons reads like a "Who's Who" of American millionaires: Vanderbilt, Astor, Morgan, Roosevelt. The new house opened on October 22, 1883, and had no fewer than 122 boxes. Located at 39th Street and Broadway, the building was scarcely adequate for opera production even by the standards of 1883. Almost a century of planning finally produced the new Metropolitan Opera House, located at Lincoln Center, which opened on September 16, 1966. The present house is as technically well-equipped to meet modern production demands as the old house was ill-equipped to meet the demands of 1883. The Metropolitan's recent seasons have been a (very often exciting) mixture of standard and unusual repertory items. Its range includes major production revivals like *Boris Gudunov, Don Carlo, La Gioconda, Lucia di Lammermoor,* and *Parade* and extends to more offbeat presentations like Mozart's *Idomeneo* and Strauss' *Arabella.* The 1983-84 season was the 100th anniversary of the Met and an entire year was given over to the celebration of this milestone. For information: *Metropolitan Opera, Lincoln Center, New York, NY 10023; (212) 362-6000.*

Dress Circle

The following is a list of other very fine companies around the world:

• **Opera Company of Boston**
539 Washington St., Boston, MA 02111, (617) 426-5300

• **Bolshoi Opera**
Bolshoi Theatre, Moscow

• **Dallas Opera**
3000 Turtle Creek Plaza #100, Dallas, TX 75206, (214) 528-9850

• **Deutsche Oper Berlin**
Bismarck Str. 34-37, 1000 Berlin

* **Hamburg State Opera**
  Fremdenverkehrszentrale Bieberhaus am Haupphahnhos,
  2000 Hamburg

* **Lyric Opera of Chicago**
  20 North Wacker, Chicago, IL 60606, (312) 346-6111

* **Munich State Opera**
  Max-Joseph-Platz 2, D8000 Munich 2

* **Sydney Opera Company**
  GPO Box 4274, Sydney, 2001

* **Theatre Colon**
  Cerrito 618, Buenos Aires

* **Theatre La Fenice**
  Campo S. Fantin, 30124 Venice

BALLET AND DANCE COMPANIES
U.S./INTERNATIONAL

WITHOUT question the two best ballet companies in the United States are the New York City Ballet and American Ballet Theatre, and there are many who would contend they are the best in the world. This does not mean there are not many other excellent ballet and modern dance companies worth everyone's attention. Each tours the country and abroad throughout the year giving people all over an introduction to the various styles and dancers.

New York City Ballet
During the last 100 years there was no more creative a choreographer than George Balanchine, who founded the *New York City Ballet* with Lincoln Kirstein and Edward M.M. Warburg in 1934. He created some of the most beautiful ballets the world has ever seen. Among his many masterpieces are "Four Temperaments," "Agon," "Apollo," "Symphony in C," "Serenade," "Union Jack," "Stravinsky Violin Concerto." Upon his death, Balanchine left the New York City Ballet not only his collection of great works, but also the resources—training and moral energy—necessary to

maintain itself, and even grow, in his absence. Jerome Robbins and Peter Martins now choreograph for the company, which is in New York for two seasons a year: Winter—November through February, and Spring—April through June. The dancers people look for are Suzanne Farrell, Patricia McBride, Merrill Ashley, Heather Watts, Darci Kistler, Ib Anderson, and Mel Tomlinson. Their New York headquarters are: *State Theatre, Lincoln Center, New York, NY 10023.*

The American Ballet Theatre

First launched as Ballet Theatre in 1939, the ABT is, in the best sense, a museum of classical ballet. Its forte is traditional works such as "Giselle," "Swan Lake," "Coppelia," but its repertoire also includes ballets by Anthony Tudor, Frederick Ashton, George Balanchine, and Jerome Robbins. Mikhail Baryshnikov is artistic director, and the company numbers among its principal dancers Martin van Hamel, Cynthia Gregory, Natalia Markova, and Fernando Bujones. Its offices in New York are at: *890 Broadway, New York, NY 10003,* and home theatres are the Metropolitan Opera House, New York, and the John F. Kennedy Center, Washington, D.C.

The Joffrey Ballet

Founded by choreographer Robert Joffrey in 1954, it is most distinguished for its revivals of classics such as the German choreographer Kurt Joos' "The Green Table," Agnes deMille's "Rodeo," and Massine's "Parade." Big favorites include "Viva Vivaldi," "Trinity," "Pineapple Poll," and "Deuce Coupe." The company also performs other choreography of Gerald Arpino, Twyla Tharp, Laura Dean, and Anthony Taylor. Although it is now based in Los Angeles, the company usually has one season in New York, where it maintains offices at: *City Center, 130 W. 56th St., New York, NY 10019.*

The Dance Theatre of Harlem

This company was started by former New York City Ballet dancer Arthur Mitchell and Karel Shook in 1969. Because of his background, Mitchell was particularly interested in presenting Balanchine ballets—but with black dancers who he felt had too little chance to dance with traditional ballet companies. His group continues to do a large selection of Balanchine ballets but have added to their repertoire many more theatrical pieces. They usu ally have one season in New York and travel throughout the year. Their headquarters are: *466 W. 152nd St., New York, NY 10032.*

The Alvin Ailey American Dance Theatre

This company is also primarily black, but its tone is modern and jazz. Alvin Ailey started the company in 1957. Among audience favorites are "Blues Suite," "Knoxville, Summer 1915," "Revelations" (which always brings down the house), and "Cry." Their headquarters are: *1515 Broadway, New York, NY 10036,* and when they perform in New York it is at the City Center.

The Feld Ballet

Started by former American Ballet Theatre dancer Eliot Feld in 1974, combines classical and modern styles. His style is unusual and among the composers he uses are Mahler, Bach, and Ives. There is a little bit of Robbins, Tharp, and even Ashton in his dances. Favorites include, "At Midnight," "Harbinger," and "Play Bach." Their offices are: *890 Broadway, New York, NY 10003,* and their theatre is the Joyce on Eighth Ave. and 19th St., New York.

Jose Limon Dance Company

Founded by Jose Limon in 1945; since his death it has been managed by Carla Maxwell. It is a modern company with classically trained dancers. Limon's best known work is "The Moor's Pavane." The company has headquarters at: *38 E. 19th St., New York, NY 10003.*

The Paul Taylor Company

Another modern company with classically trained dancers. Mr. Taylor started the group in 1954, and they have had almost annual runs in New York since then. Probably the best known work of Taylor is "Orbs," set to the final quartets of Beethoven.

Other Leading U.S. Companies

There are many other good dance companies in the United States. They include the ballet companies of Boston, Washington, D.C., San Francisco, Houston, Chicago City Opera, Ballet West (Salt Lake City), and Pacific Northwest in Seattle. All have repertoire and dancers worth seeing.

International Companies

The foreign companies to watch for are the Russians (Bolshoi and Kirov); the Royal Danish Ballet; the Stuttgart (of Germany); the Royal Ballet (of London); all of who perform the traditional ballets. The Netherlands Dance Theatre and the Cullberg Ballet (of Sweden) perform modern works and are highly professional and innovative.

TWO

Collecting

COLLECTING: A BEST GUIDE

COLLECTING seems to be a universal urge. Julius Caesar collected coins, fine books, and silver; according to a recent survey more than half of all children in this country collect something—rocks, shells, butterflies, and baseball cards are among the favorites; twenty-two million Americans collect stamps; and there are organizations of collectors of such disparate items as baby bottles, thimbles, and barbed wire which boasts no fewer than five collectors' associations.

Collectors range from the very part-time hobbyist who picks up a few pieces of Depression glass at flea markets for the sake of the recreation to such ardent big spenders as Malcolm Forbes who, with his children, operates as a kind of collecting conglomerate searching out (and almost always acquiring) the finest examples of such treasures as Fabergé Easter eggs (one-of-a-kind pieces created for the czars of Russia), Lincoln manuscripts, toy boats, photographica, and toy soldiers which he houses in their own museum in Morocco.

For the collector of more moderate proportion, *specialization is the byword. And there is literally a world full of collectibles from which to find that specialty:* everything seems to be collectible. The ticket you throw away from a Broadway show might well be of interest to an ephemera collector, patent mousetraps that capture but don't kill have their fanciers, some people collect railroad spikes (called date nails because they were dated so they could be replaced at regular intervals), there are collectors of telephone line insulators, gas station maps, Cracker Jack toys, spittoons, even cigarettes (and of course others who collect only cigarette packs). The big money can be found in the main line collectibles such as antique furniture ($860,000 for a Queen Anne bureau bookcase in 1981), or stamps ($135,000 for a single 1918 U.S. airmail invert error in 1979) but the less regal collectibles can bring some surprising prices: in 1981 a single antique golf ball brought $1,790 and the same year a 1931 pedal car toy (a Packard, naturally) brought $5,700.

As collections grow, collectors gain knowledge of their field of specialization. *If there is a single general rule for collecting anything, it is to start at a modest level and not to buy beyond the level of one's knowledge*—a sure invitation to get taken. Seek out the dealers who are most reputable in your field of specialization, develop a relationship of trust, and, as you gain confidence, plunge into the auction game where your discernment can bring you bargains (or where your ignorance can unburden a dealer of a dud). The main sources of quality collectibles and antiques are dealers and auctions; flea markets are sometimes good sources for antiques—but be careful that you know what you are about before you buy expensive items in such a hurly-burly setting; and garage and tag sales, for the adventurous, are occasional sources of the collector's favorite purchase, the buried treasure. Prices for any collectible, be it Judy Garland's slippers from *The Wizard of Oz* ($12,000 in 1982) or a hand-printed Roycrofter book ($2 at a rural general antique shop in upstate New York) vary with demand, just like anything else, so *always consult the numerous price guides available* for almost any imaginable collectible—*before* you buy.

AUCTION HOUSES: U.S./INTERNATIONAL

THE auction business is just that: a business. While the social patina may be genteel and the accents of the primary players distinctly upper crust, the day-to-day competition in this industry is intense. The auction firms of Europe and the U.S. vie with one another constantly for the rights to sell top-grade merchandise. Consequently it's almost impossible to predict where the next great piece in a particular collecting specialty is going to turn up.

Truly great works of art and antiques are never plentiful, and as more and more masterpieces become permanently sequestered in museums, the supply dwindles further. Hence the enormous competitiveness among the leading auction houses. Executives of these firms (in company, of course, with dealers and museum directors) spend substantial amounts of time courting wealthy collectors—and their potential heirs—in hopes that their firm will have the inside track when the collections are eventually sold off. When a *really* fine collection is known to be ripe for dispersal the competitive lust can be so unbounded that even Karl Marx would have been shocked. All kinds of deals, such as cut-rate commissions and guaranteed purses, are proffered as inducements.

What all this means is that at any given time a great piece may surface just about anywhere. A small-time country auctioneer with a companionable personality and good terms may snare the collection that seemed naturally destined for one of the big-city prestige houses. This is not as odd as it may at first seem when you realize that dealers and collectors will go anywhere when they hear that great items are going to be on the auction block. Most collecting fields tend to be ingrown and the trade is always looking for "fresh" goods from estates and private collections that haven't been seen recently in dealers' shops, antique shows, or other auctions. It's not unheard of for great pieces to reach world-record levels at little auction houses out in the boondocks. In fact, it happens all the time.

The ease with which money moves across international borders also adds a note of unpredictability to the auction scene. Take the case of fine eighteenth-century French furniture. For years the landmark auctions in this most expensive of all furniture styles have been held by Sotheby's in Monaco. In recent years, however, much of the auction action in this field has migrated to New York. Why? Because that's where the money is. The field of Chinese art has been even less geographically predictable. As soon as you're convinced that all the great pieces in this field are showing up at Christie's and Sotheby's Hong Kong sales, along comes a record-shattering London sale. Having dispersed with all these caveats, here are our nominations for the best bets in the auction field:

Christie's and Sotheby's
Any time you're listing the world's great auction galleries, you've got to give special attention to these giants. They are the Macy's and Gimbel's as well as the Nieman-Marcus and Saks Fifth Avenue of the auction world. Between them they've got offices in

(at last count) eighteen countries. In some countries—especially outside of Europe and North America—their offices are the only links to the international auction market. Both handle an enormous range of material; they run specialized sales in some thirty to forty collecting specialties. Despite the impression that their high-powered publicity operations might give you, not all this merchandise is great and much of it is very affordable (in the under $2,000 range). Still, these two firms undeniably sell more masterpieces than any other auction house.

When it comes to setting world records the two houses stand on relatively equal footing. Take the field of Americana, for instance. Christie's was the first to break the $100,000 mark for a piece of Federal furniture while Sotheby's was the first to break that price barrier in American silver. While Christie's has been snaring more record-breaking *individual* pieces of American furniture, Sotheby's has proved more adept at landing the great private collections, such as Joseph Hirshhorn's accumulation of American furniture and Stewart Gregory's folk art collection. In recent years Sotheby's has been doing about twice the dollar volume of Christie's, but at Christie's the price of the average lot sold has been higher. Sotheby's, chastened after its over-expansion during the hot, speculative art market of the 1970s, has been seeking a higher price-per-lot average by cutting back on the amount of low-end merchandise it sells.

Christie's remains extremely strong in Impressionist drawings. It sold one Degas pastel for a record auction price exceeding $900,000. (Record auction prices announced with great hoopla by the auction houses must be taken with a grain of salt. They are *auction* records. Often works of equivalent quality move quietly between dealers and collectors at greater prices.) The best Impressionist painting sales in the world are generally held each spring at the New York galleries of these two firms. And since both are London based, they regularly offer great English pieces. The best sales of English furniture, paintings and decorative arts are held each year in mid-November at the London salesrooms.

Both firms (along with most of those listed below) offer limited guarantees on the merchandise they sell: Sotheby's for five years; Christie's for six. Basically they guarantee the accuracy of the *bold* print descriptions in their catalogs, nothing more. Exact coverage and terms of sale are spelled out in the front of every catalog. Both charge a ten percent buyer's premium which is added to the hammer price (although in London and New York dealers have been seeking—so far unsuccessfully—to overturn the practice). Sotheby's main London gallery is at *34/35 New Bond St., London W1A*

2AA; phone (01) 493-8080. Its New York headquarters are at: *1334 York Ave. (at 72nd St.), New York 10021; (212) 606-7000.* Christie's main London salesrooms are at: *8 King St., St. James's, London SW1 Y6QT; phone (01) 839-9060.* The New York gallery is at: *502 Park Ave. (at 59th St.), New York 10022; (212) 546-1000.*

International

• **Antwerp.** Leys, 46 Kipdorvest; phone 03/231 6361. One of the more active of the dozen or so Belgian auctioneers; general line.

• **Bonn.** Wichert's, Bonner Talweg 75, D 5300, Bonn 1, phone 02 28/21 99 47. General line; strong on Old Master paintings and antiquities.

• **London.** The third largest English auction house (behind Sotheby's and Christie's) is Phillips Son & Neale, 7 Blenheim St., London W1 Y0AS; phone (01) 629-6602. Phillips has always tended to deal in middle-level goods and has always been strong in the provinces, but it gets its share of fine merchandise as well. Harmers of London is one of the great stamp auctioneers. 91 New Bond St., London W1A 4EH; phone (01) 629-0218.

• **Milan and Rome.** Christie's and Sotheby's both have active Italian offices (the former in Milan and Rome; the latter in Florence and Rome). The local opposition is led by the fine general-line house, Finearte which, as one might expect, is particularly strong in Old Master and Italian paintings. Finearte S.P.A., Piazzetta Bossi 4, 20121 Milan; phone (02) 877041; also, Via della Quattro Fontane 20, Rome; phone (06) 463564.

• **Paris.** There are some sixty auctioneers in Paris, but all auctions are held at the Hotel Drouot, 9 rue Drouot, 75009 Paris; phone (01) 246 1711. That's headquarters of the Compagnie des Commissaires-Priseurs de Paris to which they all belong. The best way to find out what's coming up at the Drouot is to buy the tabloid *Gazette de l'Hotel* which comes out weekly and is sold on French newsstands. When you find what you're interested in, you can then contact auctioneers for catalogs and information. Among the best Parisian auctioneers: Ader, Picard, Tajan, 12 rue Favart; phone (01) 261 8007; Audap, Godeau, Solanet, 32 rue Drouot, (01) 770-6768; Couturier, Nicolay, 51 rue de Bellechasse, (01) 555-8544; Delorme, 3 rue de Penthievre, (01) 265 5763; Laurin, Guilloux, Buffetaud, Tailleur, 12 rue Drouot, (01) 246.61.16.

• **Stockholm.** An active, if somewhat provincial, auction market. AB Stockholms Auktionsverk, founded in 1674, can lay claim to being the world's oldest auction house. Address: Jakobsgaten 10, Box 16256 S-103, 25 Stockholm; phone (08) 14 24 40. Bukowskis, also based in Stockholm, has offices throughout Scandinavia and has recently opened a branch in Zurich, Switzerland, to do battle for the lucrative continental market. Bukowskis, Wahrendorffsgatan 8, S-111, 47 Stockholm; phone (08) 202 672. In Goteborg, Goteborgs Auktionsverk AB also handles a broad range of high-quality goods. Address: Tredje Langgatan 7-9, S41303 Goteborg; phone (03) 12 44 30.

• **Vienna.** The Dorotheum may not be the world's greatest auction house, but it's one of the most interesting. Everything from used car parts to priceless heirlooms shows up there. Dorotheum, Dorotheergasse 17, A-1010 Vienna; phone (0222) 52 85 60.

• **Zurich.** Switzerland is the most active auction market on the continent and Koller in Zurich may be the best full-service auction house on the continent. It is extremely strong in a broad range of collecting specialties. Its continental furniture sales are outstanding. Since Switzerland is a leading market for antiquities, fine clocks, and jewelry you are likely to find the best of these showing up at Koller as well. Galerie Koller Zurich, Ramistrasse 8, 8024, Zurich; phone, (01) 47 50 40. Germann Auktionhaus is another fine Swiss firm; especially strong in paintings of modern masters. Address; Zeltweg 67, 8032 Zurich; phone (01) 251 8358. In Geneva, great stamp auctions are held at David Feldman S.A., Case Postale 81, 1213 Onex, Geneva; phone (022) 57 25 30.

United States

• **Bolton, Massachusetts.** Robert W. Skinner, Route 117, Bolton, MA 01740; (617) 779-5528. Bob Skinner ran one of the most respected regional auction houses. He was known for his discriminating taste and fresh consignments. After his death in 1984 his wife, Nancy Skinner, became president of the firm and has continued in the same tradition. Skinner is still especially strong in American folk art, as well as formal and country furniture. There are regular major auctions of paintings, Indian art, arts and crafts furnishings, bottles, European and Victorian furnishing, dolls, and toys. Skinner also has an outlet in Boston: 2 Newbury St., Boston, MA 02116; (617) 236-1700.

• **Delaware, Ohio.** Garth's Auctions, P.O. Box 315, Delaware, OH 43015; (614) 362-4771. Like Skinner's, Garth's is a key regional marketplace for Americana.

• **Detroit.** DuMouchelle's, 409 E. Jefferson Ave., Detroit, MI 48226; (313) 963-6255. The major general-purpose auction gallery for the upper Midwest.

• **Encino, California.** Joel L. Malter & Co., P.O. Box 777, Encino, CA 91316; (213) 784-7772. An important West Coast outlet for numismatics and antiquities.

• **Hillsborough, New Hampshire.** Richard Withington, Hillsborough, NH 03244; (603) 464-3232. Known as having a fine eye for Americana, Dick Withington's draws top collectors and dealers because his merchandise is unusually fresh and distinctive. Recently, he's been holding some of his sales in Andover, Massachusetts.

• **Hyannis, Massachusetts.** Richard A. Bourne, Co., P.O. Box 141, Hyannis, MA 02647; (617) 775-0797. A decent general-line auction house whose real claim to fame is its great sales of hunting decoys. These have been going on for more than twenty years, and the catalogs of these sales have become standard references in the field.

• **New York.** William Doyle Gallery, 175 E. 87th St., New York, NY 10028; (212) 427-2730. In terms of dollar volume, Doyle is third largest in the U.S. (behind Sotheby's and Christie's). While this house has never particularly concentrated on top-of-the-line goods, it gets its share and is always worth a check.

Phillips, 406 E. 79th St., New York, NY 10021; (212) 570-4830. This is the New York outpost of the London-based Phillips Son & Neale. While nowhere near as established in the U.S. as its larger English rivals, Phillips—a full-line house—has held some interesting sales of toys, posters, and works of American illustrators.

John C. Edelmann, 523 E. 77th St., New York, NY 10021; (212) 628-1700. The leading American specialty house for fine Oriental and European rugs.

Robert A. Siegel, 160 E. 56th St., New York, NY 10022; (212) 753-6421. An important stamp auction house.

Swann Galleries, 104 E. 25th St., New York, NY 10010; (212) 254-4710. The best and biggest U.S. firm specializing in rare books and manuscripts. Also handles maps and photographs.

• **Philadelphia.** Samuel T. Freeman, 1808 Chestnut St., Philadelphia, PA 19103; (215) 563-9275. A fine, general-line house that is sometimes overshadowed by its aggressive competitors in nearby New York.

• **Portland, Maine.** Barridoff Galleries, 242 Middle St., Portland, ME 04104; (207) 772-5011. A relatively small house that does extremely well with American paintings, particularly those of the nineteenth-century. Auctions held two or three times yearly.

• **San Francisco.** Butterfield & Butterfield, Showplace Square, 501 15th St., San Francisco, CA; (415) 673-1362. The West Coast's leading auction house and the largest full-service auction house outside of New York, Butterfield holds four major auctions annually and Victorian auctions on a monthly basis. It recently moved its operations to a vibrant new design area of San Francisco called Showplace Square, while maintaining a Los Angeles office as well. Particularly strong in Oriental art and Western art.

California Book Auction Galleries, 358 Golden Gate Ave., San Francisco, CA 94102; (415) 775-0424. The leading West Coast book auctioneer.

• **Washington, D.C.** C.G. Sloan & Co., 919 E Street, NW, Washington, DC 20005; (202) 628-1468. In the capital since 1853, Sloan's always gets an interesting mix of American and foreign merchandise.

Adam A. Wechsler & Sons, 905-9 E. St. NW, Washington, DC 20004; (202) 628-1281. A range similar to Sloan's.

• **West Brookfield, Massachusetts.** Bruce Smebakken, Main St., West Brookfield, MA 01585; (617) 867-8967. This little local house between Worcester and Springfield seems to attain world-class status whenever it sells Shaker material. In 1982 it established world auction records in two Shaker sales: A small, five-drawer curly maple chest from Connecticut fetched a record $34,100, and a little Shaker fingered box with wonderful painted decoration commanded $5,775.

ANTIQUE DEALERS: U.S.

THERE are specialist dealers for all of the top value collectibles, from the traditional period furniture dealer (the usual image of an antiques dealer) to houses specializing in scientific instruments or folk art or music boxes. Dealers and collectors sometimes find themselves in an adversary relationship because collectors feel the dealer is inflating prices or trying to fob off shoddy goods (both occur), but the dealer, in fact, should be the collector's best friend and greatest aid: the dealer has knowledge of his field and can protect a collector, the dealer has sources for acquiring items that are beyond the collector's means to develop, and a dealer with a special relationship with a client will often offer to buy back what he sells at the price paid when the client wants something else.

There are no hard, fast rules about how to pick a dealer, but one rubric will stand you in good stead: *choose a dealer as if you were choosing a doctor.* Check his references with fellow collectors and curators, if you can. Find out his policy on authenticating items—if he's good, he will refund your money for anything discovered to be not genuine. One good place to shop for a dealer is at major antique shows, where the organizers keep a watchful eye on the trade and not only weed out the disreputable, but actively seek out the good new specialist. When you travel, you can't check dealers you run across as carefully as you can those in your hometown or large cities, but you should consult regional guides for the area, and, among other periodicals, *The Antiques Quarterly* listing of dealers state-by-state.

Top Antiques Dealers
Some of the best known and most respected dealers in the U.S. include:

• **Israel Sack, Inc.** 15 E. 57th St., New York, NY 10022; (212) 753-6562. American antiques.

• **Frederick P. Victoria & Sons, Inc.** 154 E. 55th St., New York, NY 10022; (212) 755-2581 or 2549. English and French antiques.

• **Didier Aaron.** 32 E. 67th St., New York, NY 10021; (212) 988-5248. Specialized decorative French antiques. Late nineteenth-century.

• **Bernard & S. Dean Levy Inc.** 981 Madison Ave., New York, NY 10021; (212) 628-7088. American antiques.

• **James Robinson.** 15 E. 57th St., New York, NY 10022; (212) 752-6166. Silver.

• **Stair & Co.,** Inc. 59 E. 57th St., New York, NY 10022; (212) 355-7620. Eighteenth-century English furniture.

• **Alfred Bullard, Inc.** 1604 Pine St., Philadelphia, PA 19103; (215) 735-1879. Eighteenth-century English furniture and looking-glasses.

Top Antiques Shows

In recent years, antiques shows have proliferated with the abandon of dandelions after a spring rain. Which ones are the best? We consulted a number of sophisticated dealers, collectors, and show managers to compile a selection of top shows. Our **criteria for the best:** 1) The show is strong in many areas of collecting—paintings, Orientalia, continental furniture, Americana, silver, etc.; 2) Dealers hoard their best items to exhibit at the show, creating an aura of freshness, excitement, and anticipation for the collectors who attend; 3) The show attracts collectors from around the country. Collectors are willing to travel to these shows precisely because they know the dealers will be presenting their best goods.

• **The Winter Antiques Show.** (January). Seventh Regiment Armory, Park Ave. and 67th St., New York, NY. For information: *East Side Settlement House, 337 Alexander Ave., Bronx, NY 10454; (212) 292-7392.*

• **Sotheby's Americana Sales.** (October and January). 1334 York Ave., New York, NY 10021; (212) 606-7130.

• **Christie's Americana Sale.** (January, June, September). 502 Park Ave., New York, NY 10022; (212) 546-1181.

• **The Fall Antiques Show.** (September). Passenger Terminal Pier at 54th St. and the Hudson River, New York, NY. Contact: Museum of American Folk Art, 49 W. 53rd St., New York, NY; (212) 581-2475.

• **The Maryland Antiques Show and Sale.** (February). Baltimore Convention Center, 1 W. Pratt St., Baltimore, MD; (301) 659-7000.

• **Ellis Memorial Antiques Show.** (October). The Cyclorama, Boston Center for the Arts, 539 Tremont St., Boston, MA; (617) 426-5000.

• **Western Reserve Antiques Show.** (October). Crawford Auto Museum, 10825 East Blvd., Cleveland, OH; (216) 721-5722.

• **Atlanta High Museum Antiques Show and Sale.** (November). Atlanta Apparel Mart, Spring St. at Harris, Atlanta, GA; (404) 681-1222.

• **The Delaware Antiques Show.** (December). The Soda House at Hagley Museum, Wilmington, DE; (302) 658-2401.

• **The Burlington House Fair.** (March). Royal Academy of Arts, Piccadilly, London, England.

• **Chelsea Antiques Fair.** (September). Chelsea Old Town Hall, London, England.

Compute-Antique

Romantics who worry that computer technology is going to replace, or even destroy, traditions of the past should look to London for an example of the past recovered. A young company called Compute-Antiques has cataloged and programmed more than 10,000 antiques from 500 dealers and made them available to any interested collector anywhere in the world. Each day proprietors David Edkins and Justin Nahum receive 300 inquiries, half by phone and half by mail. The goal of Compute-Antique is to match prospective buyers and sellers. It allows people to find the one piece in a million that they might never locate on their own. When they do, they have the option of traveling to inspect it personally or completing the transaction by mail. For information: *Compute-Antique, 204-6 High St., Bromley, Kent, England; 01-290-0033.*

ART: PURCHASE AND APPRAISAL

PLACING yourself in the hands of an established, reputable dealer is the best start toward making a good purchase. Such a firm will always be willing to sign an agreement to accept the work back, giving you full credit toward another or a future purchase, but that route is still hazardous. You risk damaging the work (or its frame if it's a painting), and repairs can be costly. You also may never find another work which pleases you, and your credit either will stand indefinitely or you have to make a compromise at a loss. The best dealers will always be helpful and they are more interested in cultivating your collection than they are in making a one-time killing. Not all dealers fall into that category, which is why you must know who are the best and those who are the best would not send you to another dealer they didn't respect. Remember, never grovel but always be honest about your knowledge, because the dealer can size you up in a flash. There are many cases where such honesty leads to the dealer becoming a teacher, resulting in the building of a worthwhile collection. The dealers make more money over a longer period and the buyers become specialists respected by museum men and prominent among the citizenry of their own communities. That's what collecting is about.

Investing is something else, generally considered distasteful by the more serious dealer and collector. Any collection by nature is an investment, but if you can't really "turn on" over an artwork without the dollar sign vision, then you might wonder why you want something you really don't like hanging on the walls of your home or office. Art for investment has inflated the market and at long last these games are starting to become suspect, with a negative reaction already visible in the auction area. You don't have to spend big to collect, however. All you really need is a little sensible study and a particular interest—many a collection has grown from modest purchases of good drawings, prints, or watercolors.

It's always good advice to buy only if you have confidence in your own ability to know correct values, aesthetic as well as economic—or consult an honest and knowledgeable advisor. Only a fool sets out to buy great art without a background of extensive study . . . or, once again, a professional advisor. There is no reason why you can't look, take notes, and even ask for a photograph if you are serious; but, never buy unless you honestly consider yourself a specialist in the area of purchase, or have that outside guidance (often willingly provided by your local museum director or curator). One of the best ways to verify the quality of your purchase is to use an art appraisal service.

Art Prices: Art Index/Art Scan

Two of the best resources on the price of paintings are the Art Sales Index and Art Scan. Art Sales Index, Ltd. is an English company that publishes a variety of serial works which track the world auction market and record prices for hundreds of thousands of paintings, watercolors, and drawings. Among the most useful works:

• **Annual Art Sales Index.** 65,000 prices of pictures by 20,000 Old Masters, nineteenth- and twentieth-century artists. Published annually in October, $160. (The same material is also available on microfiche as *The Monthly Art Sales Index*. Nine issues through the auction year cost $120.)

• **American Artists.** 10,000 painting prices; 2,300 artists. Published biennially. Current edition costs $60, softcover. (An earlier edition containing prices from 1970 through 1978 is available for $65.)

• **Impressionist and Twentieth-Century Art, 1970-1980.** 154,000 prices; 12,000 artists. Two volumes, $180.

• **Old Masters, 1970-1980.** 80,000 prices; 12,000 artists. One volume, $175.

• **Nineteenth Century Art, 1970-1980.** Published May, 1982. 160,000 prices; 20,000 artists. Two volumes, $95. For details: *Art Sales Index, Ltd., Pond House, Weybridge, Surrey KT13, England. Phone: (923) Weybridge 42678. Telex: 929476 Apex G (ASI).*

If you want even quicker—almost instantaneous—quotes on a possible purchase, one of the best—and by far the fastest—ways to get a handle on an artist's market value is to call *Art Scan*. This Albany, New York, service, which top auction houses, museums, dealers, and collectors belong to, keeps track of auction price data on more than 100,000 artists. While you're on the phone, the Art Scan computer will summon up a decade-long list of prices realized by a particular artist at any of 200 auction houses around the world. Basically, the firm breaks down a library full of art reference price guides into data bank form.

Say, for example, you're interested in a painting by the contemporary American, Eric Sloane. Within a minute or two of your phone call, the Art Scan computer will tell you that five auction houses (Christie's and Sotheby's in New York, Wechsler and Sloan's in Washington, and Butterfield's in San Francisco) sold twenty-two Sloane paintings since 1971. Title or short description of subject matter, size, and price are given for each. This chronological record also gives you an idea of how an artist's work has been appreciating. (In Sloan's case the printout shows that his stock has not particularly soared.) *Art Scan offers two levels of membership:* 1) An annual fee entitles you to unlimited phone inquires. Mail inquiries and requests for the physical computer printout on a given artist cost $3 each; 2) For a smaller annual fee you can make phone and mail inquiries and be charged by the inquiry. For information: *Art Scan, 310 State St., Albany, NY 12210; (518) 869-1777.*

Art Collector's Seminar

The best way to quickly immerse yourself in the financial aspects of collecting art is by attending the World Art Conference sponsored annually by *ARTnews* magazine. Top collectors, curators, tax accountants, estate planners, auctioneers, artists, critics, and editors converge to discuss their specialties in dozens of seminars and workshops. All periods and forms of art are discussed, plus seminars in corporate collecting, donating to museums, tax strategies for collectors, developing an eye for quality, fakes and forgeries, buying and selling at auction, getting accurate appraisals, and laws affecting collectors and art tax shelters. *ARTnews World Art Conference, 122 W. 42nd St., New York, NY 10168; (212) 599-6060.*

Art Appraisal Services

There are several appraisal organizations where the collector can be sure to find quality professional service. They vary in terms of membership requirements for their appraisers and cost to the collector. While most associations demand a certain amount of appraisal experience, not all require a certification examination. Regarding financial terms, appraisers may work for flat fees, hourly rates, or percentage fees.

• **Appraisers Association of America (AAA).** Membership: 1,100. Membership Requirements: Five years professional experience; prospective members must submit an application, references, and samples of appraisals which are reviewed by the AAA Membership Committee. The AAA allows each member to set his or her own terms; may be flat or hourly rates as well as percentage fees. *Appraisers Association of America, 60 E. 42 St., New York, NY 10165; (212) 867-9775.*

• **American Society of Appraisers (ASA).** Membership: 6,500. Membership Requirements: All members must have a four-year college degree or the equivalent. All prospective members must submit two recent (within the last six months) appraisal reports as well as take a certification examination which concentrates on ethics, theory, and specialty. As part of the ASA's code of ethics, members are forbidden to charge percentage fees. *American Society of Appraisers, P.O. Box 17265, Washington, DC 20041; (703) 620-3838.*

• **International Society of Appraisers (ISA).** Membership: 1,800. Membership Requirements: The ISA demands a minimum of five years of appraisal experience or the equivalent in an educational or business setting; there is no certification test. Members charge on an hourly basis; the ISA does not permit percentage fees. *International Society of Appraisers, P.O. Box 726, Hoffman Estates, IL 60195; (312) 885-2480.*

• **The Art Dealer's Association of America.** Provides a service specifically geared to appraisals of donations for tax write-off purposes. Contact: *Mr. Ralph F. Collin, ADAA, Inc., 575 Madison Ave., New York, NY 10022; (212) 940-8590.*

Art Investment Resources
• **Citibank Loan Program.** Citibank in New York has an art investment service for its customers with $1,000,000 to invest in art. There are two art professionals on staff to advise interested customers. For more information contact: *Citibank, 399 Park Ave., New York, NY 10022; (212) 599-1000.* Or send for a booklet "Art As An Investment" from: *Private Banking Division, One Citicorp Center, 153 E. 53rd St., New York, NY 10043.*

• **The Antiques Trade Gazette**
Expeditors of the Printed
Word
527 Madison Ave.
New York, NY 10022

• **Art & Auction**
Auction Guild
250 W. 57th St.
New York, NY 10019
(212) 582-5633

- **Art As Investment**
  The Intelligence Unit
  75 Rockefeller Plaza
  New York, NY 10019
  (212) 541-5730

- **Art In America**
  Publishes two newsletters:
  The Art Letter published 12
  times per year, $25 yearly.
  The International Art Market
  published monthly, $60
  yearly.
  850 Third Ave.
  New York, NY 10022
  (212) 593-2100

- **ARTnews**
  Has three publications:
  *The Insider's Guide to the Art
  Market; ARTnewsletter; The
  Investor's Guide to the Art Market*

  All these available from:
  5 W. 37th St.

New York, NY 10018
(212) 398-1690

- **The Gray Letter**
  A weekly published by
  Horizon Magazine. $90 a year.
  1305 Greensboro Ave.
  Tuscaloosa, AL 35401
  (205) 345-0272

- **The Primitive Art
  Newsletter**
  Charges $50 a year for 12
  issues.
  P.O. Box 536
  Ansonia Station
  New York, NY 10023

- **The Print Collector's
  Newsletter**
  Published bimonthly, $35.
  16 E. 82nd St.
  New York, NY 10028
  (212) 628-2654

ART PROTECTION: INSURANCE AND THEFT

CONSIDER this shocking statistic: art has been named second only to drugs as the world's most trafficked illicit merchandise. Annually, there are an average of more than 3,000 *major* art thefts in the U.S. and Canada, with 45,000 thefts worldwide.

Art Insurance

If you are a serious collector of art, you'll want an insurance policy that adequately protects your investment. An insurance broker who specializes in insuring art can provide you with a number of services. First, of course, he can determine the specific insurance policy best suited to your collection, and can find the best price for that policy. Second, a broker is the source of valuable advice on security; he can recommend a system to protect the place where you keep your collection, or direct you to a security analyst for consultation. In the event of theft, he knows what steps should be taken to recover stolen art, and how to obtain the most favorable settlement from your insurance policy, should you not recover the work. A note about settlements: if you accept a cash settlement for a stolen artwork, you effectively pass ownership of the work over to the insurer. If you still want the artwork back in the event that it is recovered, get an agreement in writing at the time of the settlement stating that you reserve the option to buy back the artwork at the settlement price, or the settlement price plus interest. Settlements tend to reflect the last appraised value of the work; if the work has not been appraised for a number of years, it could be worth a good deal more today.

The following insurance brokers all have extensive experience in the field of art insurance:

• **Fred S. James and Company,** 3435 Wilshire Blvd., Suite 2700, Los Angeles, CA 90010; (213) 385-0545.

• **Frenkel & Company,** 123 William St., New York, NY 10038; (212) 267-2200.

• **Great Northern Brokerage Corp.,** 950 Park Ave., New York, NY 10022; (212) 371-2800.

• **Huntington Block,** 2101 L St., NW, Washington, DC 20037; (800) 424-8830

• **Penn General Agencies of New York, Inc.,** 355 Lexington Ave., New York, NY 10017; (212) 682-7500.

Art Theft

If you've been robbed of precious artwork, Bonnie Burnham, executive director of the International Foundation for Art Research, recommends a number of steps to follow.
• Contact the police and your insurance agent immediately.
• The police may tell you not to do anything for the first few days following the heist, since they don't want to risk having the work go underground. Your insurance agent, on the other hand, may want the robbery announced on the evening news. The right course of action depends on the particular artwork involved and is a decision best left to the police and the insurance company.
• If the stolen art is worth upwards of $50,000, contact the FBI; they look into thefts involving items of that value, even if there is no evidence of their being transported across state lines.

• If you have reason to believe that the art may have been carried out of the country, ask the police to contact Interpol, an inter-governmental liaison with foreign law enforcement agencies. *Interpol, Room 6649, U.S. Dept. of Justice, 9th St. and Pennsylvania Ave., NW, Washington, DC 20530; (202) 633-2867.*

• Contact the *Stolen Art Alert,* a newsletter now regarded as the fore-most showcase for information related to stolen art. If the matter is especially urgent, the *Alert* will consider doing a special mailing to all their principal sources, providing that you are willing to pick up the cost of postage—a bargain, of course. *Stolen Art Alert, 46 E. 70th St., New York, NY 10021; (212) 879-1780.* It is important to contact the various people to whom the stolen art might be offered for sale. In each case, send photographs and as much detailed information about the art as possible. The following steps will put you in contact with the network of people who buy and sell art:

• Contact the major auction houses nationwide, and those that are located in your general area. A list of auction houses, with addresses and phone numbers, can be located in any issue of *Art & Auction Magazine,* available from *Auction Guild, 250 W. 57th St., New York, NY 10019; (212) 582-5633.*

• Contact the *Art Dealers Association of America, 575 Madison Ave., New York, NY 10022; (212) 940-8590.* The association consists of 117 gal-leries nationwide and circulates the *Art Theft Index* monthly to deal-ers, museums, and government agencies.

• If the artwork is a piece of Americana, place an ad in the *Maine Antiques Digest.* The magazine has become known as a clear-inghouse for information of this kind and has helped get some stolen goods returned. The ad also informs the antiques commu-nity of the theft. *Maine Antiques Digest, Box 358, Waldoboro, ME 04572; (207) 832-7534.*

ART: PRESENTATION, PRESERVATION, RESTORATION

Lebron: The Man Behind the Paintings

Eloise Ricciardelli, the Registrar at the Museum of Modern Art, knows that contemporary paintings "with lightbulbs and odds and ends emerging from every crevice" demand new methods of specialized attention. She is referring specifically to a field where craft merges with art: the field of painting preparation and hand-ling. Ricciardelli also knows that MOMA and many of the biggest and best art institutions in the country can depend on "the man behind the paintings"—James Lebron.

Lebron and his associates perform myriad unseen functions: crafting stretchers for canvas, designing crates for transporting, folding delicate and valuable works, and ensuring safe passage to and from the walls of homes, galleries, and museums all over the world. Lebron is a man aware of the discretions necessary as a participant in the comings and goings of the art world. But beyond his work with the big names, Lebron is equally willing to prepare, transport, and hang paintings for the person with a more humble collection. You won't find Lebron Bros., Inc. in the phone book; he never has and never will advertise. The simple excellence of his work has made his name a household word in the contemporary art world. *Lebron Bros., Inc., 31-36 58th St., Queens, NY 11377; (212) 274-0532.*

Painting Restoration

The American Institute for Conservation (AIC) can provide information concerning restoration and conservation throughout the United States. If you have a specific question, you can call them for information. For a small fee, the AIC will send you a copy of their directory. The AIC has not yet set up a certification system. Thus, they cannot guarantee the services of the people and organizations listed. Lacking a certification system the listings are by geographic area and alphabetically, rather than by specialty. However, the directory does identify which restorer and conservateurs are Fellows of the AIC. Contact: *The American Institute for Conservation, 3545 Williamsburg Lane, NW, Washington, DC 20005; (202) 364-1036.*

Most major art museums in the country have their own laboratory facilities for their collections. However, the conservation departments can recommend private individuals who do restoration and conservation work. The Metropolitan Museum of Art sets time aside for the public on Fridays when individuals can receive expert advice about the value of an art object and whether it's worth restoring. Please call or write to the museum's conservation department for an appointment. *The Metropolitan Museum of Art, Fifth Ave. at 82nd St., New York, NY; (212) 879-5500.*

ART GALLERIES: NEW YORK/INTERNATIONAL

B Y all counts, New York is the art capital of the world. New York is the focus of an international art market that has become a billion-dollar business. It was not always so. Before World War II, Paris was the center which drew artists and collectors alike. But during the War, many European artists fled to New York. The Abstract Expressionist movement was born in the early 1950s, and New York became the capital. There are at least 600 galleries in Manhattan. Every season (which begins in September and goes through June) new galleries open, others close. An exhibition usually is up three to four weeks; thus, a gallery has about eight to nine shows a season. *What, then, are the criteria that make a top gallery?*

• First, the *quality* of the art shown. A gallery is only as good as the artists it represents. Some galleries develop new talent; others show artists already recognized. A true "art dealer," rather than merely a dealer in "pictures," makes a substantial contribution to the cultural life of the city, by the quality of the works offered for sale, by worthwhile exhibitions, and informative catalogs or other publications.

• Second, *integrity.* A top gallery is honest and reliable—a client can depend upon the provenance of a work he is considering. (*Provenance:* where the work comes from, previous owners, major exhibitions.)

• A collector can often return a work to the dealer as a credit against another acquisition if he decides that he does not wish to continue owning it. This of course is not possible with an auction house.

Most of the galleries listed below are members of the Art Dealers Association of America. A member of this Association has to be in existence for at least five years. There are over eighty members in New York. These galleries show paintings, sculpture, drawings, some graphics, and some photographs. New York's important galleries are located in three general areas: first, *57th St.,* East and West; then, *Madison Avenue,* from the 50s to the 80s; and finally, the *SoHo* (south of Houston St.) area.

New York

• **Blum-Helman.** Irving Blum and Joseph Helman show Contemporary American Painting and Sculpture and share artists like Lichtenstein, Stella, Kelly with Leo Castelli; share Diebenkorn with Knoedler. They also show younger artists: Donald Sultan, Bryan Hunt. *20 W. 57th St., New York, NY 10019; (212) 245-2888.*

• **Leo Castelli Gallery.** Considered by many to be the Dean of New York art dealers, Leo Castelli is a gentleman with Old World charm who for more than a quarter of a century has shown top American artists: Oldenburg, Johns, Lichtenstein, Stella, Kelly, Rosenquist, Warhol. *420 W. Broadway, New York, NY 10012; (212) 431-5160 and 142 Green St., New York, NY 10012; (212) 431-6279.*

• **Andre Emmerich Gallery.** First, in 1954, a dealer in Pre-Columbian and Ancient art, now shows Contemporary American and European artists: Sam Francis, Al Held, Helen Frankenthaler, Beverly Pepper; British artists David Hockney, Anthony Caro. Also antiquities. *41 E. 57th St., New York, NY 10022; (212) 752-0124.*

• **Zavier Fourcade.** A Frenchman who has, since 1972, snared Willem de Kooning, Malcolm Morley, Georg Baselitz, Joan Mitchell, Dorothea Rockburne among other twentieth-century European and American artists. Gallery located in a discreet townhouse around the corner from the Whitney Museum. *36 E. 75th St., New York, NY 10021; (212) 535-3980.*

• **Michael Knoedler & Co.** Lawrence Rubin directs this long-established gallery founded in 1846 and the second oldest in America that shows Old Masters as well as nineteenth- and twentieth-century European and American art. *19 E. 70th St., New York, NY 10021; (212) 794-0550.*

• **Pierre Matisse Gallery.** Son of Henri Matisse, Pierre opened this gallery in 1932. Shows European masters: Balthus, Giacometti, Miro, Dubuffet, and Matisse. *41 E. 57th St., New York, NY 10022; (212) 355-6269.*

• **Marlborough Galleries.** The largest 57th Street gallery (space), where you find work by European and American masters: Henry Moore, Tamayo, Botero, Alex Katz, Lipchitz, photographers Brandt, Brassai, Penn. *40 W. 57th St., New York, NY 10019; (212) 541-4900.*

• **Robert Miller Gallery.** Robert Miller opened his own gallery in 1977 after a stint at Emmerich and quickly began to show important twentieth-century painters and sculptors: Alice Neel, Louis Bourgeois, Georgia O'Keeffe, Larry Rivers, Lee Krasner, and younger artists Jedd Garet, Louisa Chase, Gregory Amenoff. *724 Fifth Ave., New York, NY 10019; (212) 246-1625.*

• **Pace Gallery.** Since 1960, this large 57th Street gallery has been showing twentieth-century artists: Nevelson, Agnes Martin, Dubuffet, Steinberg, Samaras, Brice Marden, and Estates of Rothko, Reinhardt. *32 E. 57th St., New York, NY 10022; (212) 421-3292.*

• **Paula Cooper.** Credited with being the first gallery to settle in SoHo in 1970, Paula Cooper shows Contemporary and Advanced

American artists: Borofsky, Joel Shapiro, Lynda Benglis, Jennifer Bartlett. *155 Wooster St., New York, NY 10012; (212) 674-0766.*

• **Wildenstein & Co.** Family-owned gallery since 1902, Wildenstein shows European Masters and Old Masters—Impressionist and Post-Impressionists. Most exhibitions are benefits (small charge). Elegant townhouse in the East 60s reflects Old World charm. *19 E. 64th St., New York, NY 10021; (212) 879-0500.*

• **Zabriskie Gallery.** A dealer for more than thirty years, Virginia Zabriskie is known for rediscovery of early twentieth-century American artist Elie Nadelman, as well as showing sculptors Mark Frank, Stankiewicz, Kenneth Snelson, William Zorach, and photographers Callahan, Friedlander, and the Estate of Paul Strand. *724 Fifth Ave., New York, NY 10019; (212) 307-7430* and *521 W. 57th St., New York, NY 10019; (212) 245-7568.*

In addition to the above galleries, there is a growing number of avant-garde dealers, mostly located in SoHo, who are promoting emerging *New Expressionist* artists—American, Italian, and German. They are:

• **Mary Boone Gallery.** Americans: Julian Schnabel, David Salle; German: Rainer Fetting. *417 W. Broadway, New York, NY 10012; (212) 431-1818.*

• **Marian Goodman Gallery.** German: Anselm Kiefer. *24 W. 57th St., New York, NY 10019; (212) 977-7160.*

• **Annina Nosei Gallery.** American: Jean Michel Basquiat, Keith Haring. *100 Prince St., New York, NY 10012; (212) 431-9253.*

• **Tony Shafrazi Gallery.** American Keith Haring. *163 Mercer St., New York, NY 10012; (212) 925-8732.*

• **Sonnabend Gallery.** German: A.R. Penck, Baselitz, Georg. *420 W. Broadway, New York, NY 10012; (212) 966-6160.*

• **Sperone Westwater.** Italian: Sandro Chia, Francesco Clemente, Enzo Cucchi. *142 Greene St., New York, NY 10012; (212) 431-3685.*

• **Edward Thorp Gallery.** American: Eric Fischl. *103 Prince St., New York, NY 10012; (212) 431-6880.*

Paris
• **Galerie Maeght Lelong S.A.** Arakawa, Bonnard, Braque, Pol Bury, Calder, Chagall, Derain, Giacometti, Kandinsky, Kienholz, Klapchek, Leger, Lindner, Matisse, Miro, Steinberg, Tapies. *13 Rue de Teheran, 75008 Paris; (14) 563.13.19.*

• **Karl Flinker.** *25 Rue de Touron, 75006 Paris; (1) 325.18.73.*

• **Daniel Templon.** *30 Rue Beaubourg, 75003 Paris; (1) 42.72.14.10.*

• **Claude Bernard.** *5-9 Rue des Beaux Arts, 75006 Paris; (1) 43.26.97.07.*

West Germany
• **Galerie Rudolf Zwirner.** *Albertusstrasse 18, 5 Koln 1; 23587/38.*

• **Galerie Gmurzynska.** Twentieth-century avant-garde. *Obenmarspforten 21, 5000 Koln 1; (0221) 236621/22.*

Japan
• **Gatodo Gallery.** Owner, Shigeru Yokota. *3-7-9 Nihonbashi, Chuoku, Tokyo; (271) 75-71.*

• **Tokoro Gallery.** Owner, Akiyoshi Tokoro. *Kyodo Building, 1-5 Hon-cho, Nihonbashi, Chuo-ku, Tokyo; 03-242-6695.*

ART GALLERIES: BEST IN THE REGIONAL U.S.

WHEN you're looking for the best art to buy, New York City is the preeminent place to find it. Today, the art market is a highly specialized and highly limited market. Regionalism existed before World War II, but is no longer a potent force. *Thus, eighty percent of the best art in the nation, consequently, is in New York City. The remaining twenty percent is found in a half-dozen major cities*—Boston, Chicago, and Los Angeles, followed by Philadelphia, San Francisco, and Washington. There are also serious dealers in other cities—Dallas, Houston, Miami, Palm Beach, and maybe New Orleans. And, of course, if you're crossing the Canadian border, there is only one true star—Toronto. That's about it, but experts also have friendly feelings toward Atlanta, Minneapolis, and Santa Fe/Taos.

Limiting our quest to the best art outside New York City, there are a number of suggestions, ideas, and clues for the uninformed as well as informed gallery-goer. Recognizing the need to compete with New York City as well as to broaden client awareness, dealers outside New York deliberately buy at auction to satisfy local needs, making it wise to "look in" on the best galleries, no matter where they are.

The following list of dealers outside New York should be valuable to anyone who is interested in art, but the experienced buyer will already know most of the names. Keep in mind that there are primarily two kinds of dealer: the traditionalist and the contemporary, though some dealers touch both areas. The method here is to describe them as simply as possible and to stress their strongest area. To aid the reader who may be traveling, we have drawn as broad a set of criteria as possible, so as to include dealers who may not have as large a stock or as prestigious a stable as the Madison Avenue shop but who are of good reputation and are the best show in their town. As with that awe-inspiring list of twenty-eight ice cream flavors, the tried and true chocolate, vanilla, and strawberry still come out on top, but a few of us can't resist butternut crunch. So, your search for fine art needn't be limited to this list.

Atlanta

• **Aronson Gallery**
56 E. Andres Drive (30305)
(404) 262-7331
Nineteenth-century and modern masters plus regional of quality.

• **Fay Gold Gallery**
3221 Cains Hill Place (30305)
(404) 233-3843
Avant-garde masters and regional contemporaries.

• **Heath Gallery**
416 East Paces Ferry Road NE
(30305)
(404) 262-6407
Atlanta's oldest dealer in first-rate nationally-known contemporaries with a fine local stable too.

• **Jacobson/Bernard Gallery**
1197 Peachtree St. NE (30361)
(404) 875-1438
Sound contemporaries, original home of NYC 57th St. outlet.

Baltimore

• **Grimaldis Gallery**
928 N. Charles St. (21201)
(301) 539-1080
Mainstream contemporaries plus regional.

Boston

• **Alpha Gallery**
121 Newbury St. (02116)
(617) 536-4465
Top contemporaries—international and especially local name artists.

- **Childs Gallery**
169 Newbury St. (02116)
(617) 226-1108
One of the oldest and most
respected; traditional art of
high quality, American and
European.

- **Impressions Workshop**
27 Stanhope
(617) 262-4114
One of the great contemporary print workshops.

- **Nielsen Gallery**
179 Newbury St. (02116)
(617) 266-4835
Painting and sculpture of recognized international
contemporaries.

- **Vose Galleries of Boston**
238 Newbury St. (02116)
(617) 536-6176
America's oldest art gallery
(proper but very friendly),
eighteenth- to twentieth-
century American masters of
highest reputation, superb
American Impressionists.

Chicago
- **Barbara Balkin Gallery**
120 S. LaSalle
(312) 372-0160
Where new local names are
important.

- **Jan Cicero Gallery**
221 W. Erie
(312) 440-1904
Pioneers promising Chicago
talent.

- **Dart Gallery**
212 W. Superior

(312) 787-6366
Established national
moderns.

- **Marianne Deson Gallery**
340 W. Huron
(312) 787-0005
Experimental, adventurous
avant-garde, mostly local.

- **Fairweather-Hardin Gallery**
101 E. Ontario St. (60611)
(312) 642-0007
Long-established, prestigious
national and regional
moderns.

- **Richard Gray Gallery**
620 N. Michigan Ave. (60611)
(312) 642-8877
Top-flight internationally
famous contemporaries.

- **Hokin Gallery**
210 W. Superior
(312) 266-1211
Famous names in the international contemporaries.

- **B.C. Holland**
222 W. Superior
(312) 664-5000
Dean of Chicago dealers,
ancient and modern in any
area.

- **R.S. Johnson International**
645 N. Michigan Ave. (60611)
(312) 943-1661
Traditional works plus quality
drawings and prints.

- **Phyllis Kind Gallery**
313 W. Superior
(312) 642-6302
Chicago's own school, "The

Hairy Who," and other
national contemporaries.

- **Worthington Gallery**
620 N. Michigan
(312) 266-2424
Specialist in German
Expressionists.

Cincinnati
- **Tony Birckhead Gallery**
342 W. 4th St. (45202)
(513) 241-0212
Stimulating regional
contemporaries.

- **Carl Solway Gallery**
314 W. 4th St. (45202)
(513) 621-0069
Regional discoveries pep-
pered with nationally known
contemporaries.

Cleveland
- **New Gallery of Contemporary Art**
11427 Bellflower Road (44106)
(216) 421-8671
This nonprofit operation is
about the only show in town.

Dallas
- **Delahanty Gallery**
2611 Cedar Springs (75201)
(214) 744-1346
This once-bold discoverer is
now established with national
quality contemporaries (with
New York City branch).

- **Nimbus Gallery**
1135 Dragon St. (75207)
(214) 742-1348
Encourages talented regional
contemporaries.

- **Carol Taylor Art Gallery**
2508 Cedar Springs (75201)
(214) 745-1923
Balance between regional and
national contemporaries with
traditional nineteenth- and
twentieth-century masters.

Detroit/Birmingham
- **Feigenson Gallery**
310 Fisher Building, Detroit
(48202)
(313) 873-7322
The one voice in the city promoting regional talent.

- **Sheldon Ross Gallery**
250 Martin St., Birmingham
(48011)
(313) 258-9550
Some good contemporary and
German Expressionists.

Fort Lauderdale
- **Carone Gallery**
600 S.E. Second Court
(33301)
(305) 463-8833
The only show in town, with
regional and national
contemporaries.

Houston
- **Janie C. Lee Gallery**
2304 Bissonnet (77005)
(713) 523-7306
Established contemporaries
from the 1950s onward.

- **Meredith Long Gallery**
2323 San Felipe (77019)
(713) 523-6671
Broadest range in town, fine
nineteenth- and twentieth-
century masters to national

and regional contemporaries of import.

• **Moody Gallery**
2015 W. Gray (77019)
(713) 526-9911
Top regional contemporaries, some with national fame.

• **Robinson Galleries**
1200 Bissonnet (77005)
(713) 521-9221
More traditional contemporaries.

• **Texas Gallery**
2012 Peden St. (77019)
(713) 524-1593
National and regional contemporary, names of consequence, some international and national avant-garde.

• **Watson/De Nagy**
1106 Berthea (77006)
(713) 526-9883
Regionalists supplemented with important contemporaries from New York gallery.

Los Angeles
• **James Corcoran Gallery**
8223 Santa Monica Blvd. (90046)
(213) 656-0662
Good contemporary locals and avant-garde.

• **Flow Ace Gallery**
8373 Melrose Ave. (90069)
(213) 658-6980.
Area's home for international avant-garde stars.

• **Janus Gallery**
8000 Melrose Ave. (90046)
(213) 658-6084
Contemporaries from both coasts.

• **Ulrike Kantor Gallery**
801 N. Canon Dr.
Beverly Hills
(213) 273-5650
Challenging contemporary local stable.

• **Margo Leavin Gallery**
812 N. Robertson Blvd. (90069)
(213) 273-0603
Sound contemporaries, known and unknown.

• **Jack Rutberg Fine Arts**
357 N. La Brae Ave. (90036)
(213) 938-5222
Modern masters, European and American.

Miami/Bay Harbour
• **Hokin Gallery**
1086 Kane Concourse
Bay Harbour Island (33154)
(305) 861-5700
Chicago stable plus important international names.

• **Gloria Luria Gallery**
1033 Kane Concourse
Bay Harbour Island (33154)
(305) 865-3060
Broad and impressive list of American contemporaries.

• **Barbara Gillman**
270 NE 39th, Miami
(305) 573-4898
Outstanding regionalist with

nationally-known contemporaries.

New Orleans

• **Bienville Gallery**
1800 Hastings Place (70130)
(504) 523-5889
Avant-garde and contemporary, national and local, sometimes with an international surprise.

• **Arthur Roger Gallery**
3005 Magazine St. (70115)
(504) 895-5287
A most respectable stable of local and nationally known contemporaries.

• **Galerie Simonne Stern**
518 Julia (70130)
(504) 529-1118
Local contemporaries, occasionally of national fame—all high quality.

• **Tahir Gallery**
823 Chartres St. (70116)
(504) 525-3095
Abe Tahir is one of the nation's half-dozen dealer-authorities on nineteenth- and twentieth-century American prints.

Minneapolis

• **Peter M. David Gallery**
430 Oak Grove St. (55403)
(612) 870-7344
Good regional contemporaries.

• **Dolly Fiterman Art Gallery**
12 S. 6th St., Suite 238
(55402)

(612) 338-5358
Standard national contemporaries along with regional talent. Appointment recommended.

• **Barry Richard Gallery**
10 S. 5th St. (55401)
(612) 333-7620
Predominantly regional.

• **John C. Stoller Gallery**
400 Marquette Ave. (55401)
(612) 871-7060
Major blue chip Americans.

Philadelphia

• **David David Art Gallery**
260 S. 18th St. (19103)
(215) 735-2922
Traditional blue chips from Renaissance to present.

• **Marian Locks Gallery**
1524 Walnut St. (19102)
(215) 546-0322
Lively and experimental for regional avant-garde as well as nationally known contemporaries.

• **Makler Gallery**
1716 Locust St. (19103)
(215) 735-2540
Another powerhouse for regional talent plus blue chip contemporaries.

• **Newman Galleries**
1625 Walnut St. (19103)
(215) 563-1779
One of the oldest in Philadelphia handling important eighteenth- and nineteenth-century European and Amer-

ican masters with occasional contemporary figurative shows.

• **Frank S. Schwartz & Son**
1806 Chestnut St. (19103)
(215) 563-4887
Nineteenth-century masters with particular emphasis on Philadelphia.

Phoenix/Scottsdale
• **Elaine Horwitch Galleries**
4211 N. Marshall Way
Scottsdale (85251)
(602) 945-0791
Good regional with some national names.

• **O.K. Harris West**
4200 N. Marshall Way
Scottsdale (85251)
(602) 941-1284
The western division of the SoHo avant-garde gallery with promising regionalists.

St. Louis
• **Okum-Thomas Gallery**
1221 S. Brentwood Blvd. (63117)
(314) 725-7887
Contemporary Americans, regional and national names.

San Francisco
• **John Berggruen Gallery**
228 Grant Ave. (94108)
(415) 781-4629
Blue chip contemporaries, international and regional— possibly the city's most important dealer.

• **Fuller Goldeen Gallery**
228 Grant Ave. (94108)
(415) 982-6177
Promising regional contemporaries with some national names.

• **Harcourts Gallery**
535 Powell St. (94108)
(415) 421-3428
High-powered with established international moderns plus Latin-American contemporaries.

• **Pasquale Iannetti Art Gallery**
575 Sutter St. (94102)
(415) 433-2771
Especially strong in fine prints from the Renaissance to the present.

• **Maxwell Galleries**
551 Sutter St. (94102)
(415) 421-5193
Nineteenth- and twentieth-century European and American traditional art; one of the city's most established.

• **William Sawyer Gallery**
3045 Clay St. (94115)
(415) 921-1600
Local and national contemporaries, occasional avant-garde and often a worthy discovery.

Washington, DC
• **Adams Davidson Galleries**
3233 P St., NW (20007)
(202) 965-3800
Traditional nineteenth- and twentieth-century masters, conservative, top quality.

- **Franz Bader Gallery**
1701 Pennsylvania Ave. NW
(202) 659-5615
One of the Capital's first galleries, contemporary regionalists, augmented by special exhibitions.

- **Fendrick Gallery**
3059 M St. NW (20007)
(202) 338-4544
Important names of the American contemporary scene. Excellent stock of prints.

- **Jane Haslem Gallery**
2121 P St., NW (20037)
(202) 638-6162
A source roster of contemporary Americans, local and otherwise.

- **R.R. Kornblatt Gallery**
406 7th St. NW (20004)
(202) 638-7657
Americans of the 1950s, plus the present avant-garde.

- **Mickelson Gallery**
707 G St., NW (20001)
(202) 628-1736
Washington's oldest, from frames to contemporary Americans with a sprinkling of discoveries from abroad.

- **Osuna Gallery**
406 7th St., NW (20004)
(202) 296-1963
A sound stable of contemporary North Americans with Latin American overtones.

FLEA MARKETS

IT'S a few minutes before 6 A.M. on a Friday morning in the middle of May near Brimfield, Massachusetts. In a large field off U.S. 20 some 700 dealers in antiques and collectibles are unpacking and setting up their wares—barber poles next to Federal furniture, trays of antique jewelry next to tables of early jazz 78's—and outside the enclosure a milling crowd of eager buyers waits impatiently fingering rolls of hundred dollar bills. At exactly six, the gates open and the former meet the latter in a flurry of wild buying and selling. So starts The Reid Girl's Famous Flea Market, also known simply as the Brimfield Flea Market, a three-times-a-year event that combines elements of an antique show, old-fashioned country market day, and county fair.

Flea markets, or fleas as they are called by regular habitués, are like shopping centers without walls between the stores. Some are indoors, some not; some are huge, some small; some are weekly, or even daily, affairs. Some, like the big ones in Brimfield, take place only a few times a year. At heart, *a flea market is an impromptu bazaar where sellers rent space to show merchandise,* do their business, and, when the market is over, pack up and go home. Starting in the early 1960s, these markets began to take on importance for collectors when antiques dealers started coming to what had previously been second-hand swap sessions. Now, at the larger markets, dealers queue up to rent space years in advance.

The markets listed below are all large ones where the emphasis is either exclusively or mostly antiques and collectibles—if you go to any of these, you can be sure you won't find the booths selling most snow tires, discount anti-freeze, or newly discarded children's clothes. But the nature of antiques flea markets is such that the "better" the market, the less likely it is that you will find that buried treasure that is every collector's dream. Dealers at antiques flea markets are canny and usually have their goods priced at, or above, market value. If you want to go treasure hunting, try the smaller, out-of-the-way markets that spring up and disappear by the hundreds every year. *At the large markets it is always best to arrive as early as possible:* the crowd waiting for Brimfield to open walks off with the pick of the market; dealers do thousands of dollars worth of business on Friday morning, only hundreds of dollars worth on Saturday and Sunday. Also, don't be shy about bargaining; some dealers set 'firm' prices, most do not and it never hurts, and often saves money, to find out which are which. The following flea markets all feature antiques and collectibles and all have several hundred dealers. **Call ahead to find out exact dates and admission prices.**

Major Flea Markets

• **Englishtown Auction Sales,** Englishtown, NJ; (201) 446-9644
  Held: Saturday and Sunday.

• **Adam's Antiques and Collectibles Market,** Route 272 North, Denver, PA 17517; (215) 267-4547
  Held: Sundays, year round.

• **The Atlanta Flea Market and Antique Center,** 5360 Peachtree Industrial Blvd., Chamblee; (404) 458-0456
  Held: Friday through Sunday, year round.

• **Super Flea Flea Market,** Coliseum Greensboro, NC,
  Held: Saturday and Sunday, monthly.

CONTACT: Smith-Tomlinson Corporation, P.O. Box 16122, Greensboro, NC 27416.

• **The Springfield Antique Show and Flea Market,** Clark County Fairgrounds, Springfield, OH
Held: First weekend every month.
CONTACT: Bruce Knight, Box 2429, Springfield, OH 45501; (513) 325-0053.

• **Rose Bowl Antiques Flea Market,** Rose Bowl, Pasadena, CA
Held: Second Sunday every month.
CONTACT: R.G. Canning Enterprises, P.O. Box 400, Maywood, CA 90270; (213) 587-5100.

• **The Reid Girls Famous Flea Market,** Route 20, Brimfield, MA
Held: Friday through Sunday, May, July, and September.
CONTACT: J&J Promotions, (413) 245-3436.

• **Farmers Flea Market,** 9919 Pulaski Highway, Baltimore, MD
Held: Saturday and Sunday, April through November.
CONTACT: Ken Hill, (301) 687-5505.

• **Canton First Monday Trade Days,** Highway 19, Canton, TX
Held: Weekend ending in first Monday of each month.
CONTACT: Gerald Turner, Box 245, Canton, TX 75103; (214) 567-4300.

• **Salisbury Flea Market,** Route 44, Salisbury, CT
Held: Saturday after Labor Day.
CONTACT: Russell Carrell, Salisbury, CT 06068; (203) 435-9301.

• **The Great Chautauqua Antiques Market,** Chautauqua County Fairgrounds, 1089 Central Ave., Dunkirk, NY
Held: Last weekend in June.
CONTACT: Dick Taylor, 135 Salan Road, Chagrin Falls, OH 44022; (216) 247-8319.

• **Appalachian Trade Festival,** Appalachian Fairgrounds, Gray, TN
Held: Last weekend in May.

CONTACT: Jim Cornell, P.O. Box 1406, Kingsport, TN 37662; (615) 246-4500.

• **Caravan Antiques Market,** St. Joseph County Fairgrounds, Route 86, Centerville, MI
Held: First Sunday in June, second Sunday in July and August.
CONTACT: J. Jordon Humberstone, 2995 Iroquois, Detroit, MI 48214; (313) 571-0452.

THREE

EDUCATION &

Scholarship

HIGHEST MARKS: FELLOWSHIPS

FOR the academically and artistically inclined, the fellowship has always been a special treasure. It rewards achievement, recognizes promise, and provides a seldom-matched opportunity to reflect and create. The availability of fellowships is often contingent on the economic situation. Yet the real problem for the applicant has never been only funds but competition. Applicant-to-recipient ratios of ten to one aren't at all unusual; as an example, the Visual Arts program of the National Endowment for the Arts attracts roughly 10,000 applicants for 500-odd grants. Nevertheless, the lure of the fellowship remains. And for those with talent, imagination, and skill at framing a proposal, the prize is still attainable. Here are several of the nation's most eminent fellowships:

Rhodes Scholarship

Named after and funded by Cecil Rhodes, a key figure in the economic and political development of southern Africa, this has become the best-known fellowship in the world. It enables an elite of U.S. college and university graduates to undertake further studies at Great Britain's Oxford University. The U.S. is allotted thirty-two scholarships, three times as many as any other country. They are awarded by means of a painstaking process involving a selection committee in each state. The numbers can be dazzling: the California committee has received as many as ninety names for the two nominees it can pass along. (One can apply from his state or the state in which he's attended school.)

Whoever you are and wherever you study, Rhodes will provide four standards by which ye shall be judged: literary and scholastic attainments; fondness for and success in sports; truth, courage, devotion to duty, and similar qualities; moral force of character and instincts to lead. Most scholarships are for two years of study, although a third year is possible. The Rhodes Trust pays all expenses plus a "maintenance allowance." Apply through the secretary of your state selection committee. Committees are listed in the application form, available from the central Rhodes office at: *Pomono College, Claremont, CA 91711.* Applications due by October 31 of the year prior to selection.

Guggenheim Fellowship

Guggenheims go to serious artists, social and natural scientists, and students of the humanities "who have already demonstrated an unusual capacity for scholarship or an unusual creative ability. . ." Of the approximately 330 awards made, the great majority have gone to people associated with a university.

Roughly one-third of the Guggenheims fall into the general category of creative arts; other major categories include the sciences, history, and several areas of the humanities. In the arts, the emphasis is always on research or production of works, not on performance. "We fund the choreographer, not the dancer, or the composer rather than the pianist," says a Guggenheim spokesman. Grants usually run for one year and pay in the $18,000 range. They cover overseas travel, if it's an integral part of the project. WRITE: *John Simon Guggenheim Memorial Foundation, 90 Park Ave., New York, NY 10016.*

MacArthur Foundation Prize Fellows Program

If the fellowship world contains a pot of gold, this is it. In 1981, Chicago-based MacArthur began giving large sums to what it calls "exceptionally talented" people. Amounts run according to the recipient's age, ranging from $24,000 for a thirty-year-old historian of ancient science to $60,000 for the distinguished seventy-six-year-old poet Robert Penn Warren.

The money is intended to provide time to think and create over a five-year period, in the hope that "this freedom will lead to discoveries or other significant contributions to society that might otherwise not have been made." But don't rush to your typewriter. The program does not accept applicants. "We'll call you" is how a MacArthur spokesman puts it. If they do, it will be at the behest of anonymous "talent scouts." For more information—but not an application—address: *John D. and Catherine T. MacArthur Foundation, 140 S. Dearborn St., Chicago, IL 60603.*

Woodrow Wilson Fellowship

The Wilson may be unique in its approach, which brings to the Wilson Center in Washington about forty-five men and women of "intellectual distinction." Program officials describe their aim as generating "scholarship at the most advanced level," dealing not just with academic subjects but also with "projects that include consideration of the enduring, if intangible, questions of artistic form, moral value, and higher belief."

The fellowship is open to so-called practitioners as well as to scholars—but the list of recipients shows only a handful of non-academics among the winners. Their topics run heavily to economics, politics, and history. A large proportion of Wilsons go to foreigners. Stipends are based on the fellow's normal income. Deadline for the annual awards is October 1. WRITE: *Assistant Director for Fellowships, Woodrow Wilson International Center for Scholars, Smithsonian Institution Building, Washington, DC 20560.*

Rockefeller Foundation Humanities Fellowship

The Rockefeller program has sometimes been less academically inclined than others of its type, in terms of topics if not grantees. The program's aim is "to support humanistic scholarship intended to help illuminate and assess contemporary social and cultural issues." Rockefeller primarily seeks proposals in such "traditional" humanistic disciplines as literature and philosophy but is also open to suggestions in other subject areas, "if the humanistic implications are clear and substantial."

A significant trend in the awarding of Rockefellers calls for approximately half of the forty annual fellowships to be given to applicants "in the early stages of their careers." Grants range up to $25,000. The application deadline is October 15. WRITE: *Rockefeller Foundation, 1133 Avenue of the Americas, New York, NY 10036.*

NEH/NEA Fellowships

The Fellowships of the National Endowment for the Humanities and National Endowment for the Arts are federally funded programs and thus subject to the vagaries of politics. In 1986, the

NEH still offered its ongoing Fellowships for Independent Study and Research, Fellowships for College Teachers, and special summer seminars for secondary school teachers. The first is open to anyone, with maximum awards of about $25,000; the last, to teachers, scholars, or others in the humanities.

Both NEH and NEA fund institutions as well as individuals. Grants may be outright or "matching"; that is, they may require the grantee to raise an equivalent amount from other sources. Deadlines vary according to the program involved. For NEH, write to the Program Office for the program in which you're interested (or, if you're not sure, to the Fellowship Division) at: *National Endowment for the Humanities, Room 402, 1100 Pennsylvania Ave. NW, Washington, DC 20506.* For NEA, write to the Visual Arts or Literature program at: *National Endowment for the Arts, 1100 Pennsylvania Ave. NW, Washington DC 20506.*

"Artists Colony Fellowships"

For writers, musicians, and fine artists, such "colonies" as MacDowell and Yaddo offer no money but a congenial working environment, food, and lodging. All are located in quiet surroundings, mostly in rural areas. Typically, they provide fellows with a small studio for working and living, all meals (lunch brought to the door), and companionship when, and if, desired. In most places, however, family visits are discouraged, on the grounds that the resident artist should be getting away from his or her everyday environment. Stays normally range from one to several weeks and can be repeated.

State or local arts organizations can point you to a number of the colonies. The two mentioned above are among the most prominent. (MacDowell's past fellows include Thornton Wilder, Aaron Copland, and William Rose Benet—and, if you don't know who they are, don't bother applying.) INQUIRY ADDRESSES: *MacDowell, 100 High St., Peterborough, NH 03458; Yaddo, Box 95, Saratoga Springs, NY 12866.*

Nieman Fellowship

The Nieman Fellowship was one of the first established to provide sabbaticals for working journalists and media professionals. Awarded for a full academic year, the fellowship enables journalists to study in a variety of areas at Harvard University (which does not have a journalism school) in order to deepen and broaden their intellectual horizons. Each year, twelve American and between four and seven foreign students receive the fellowship which includes a stipend providing for their living expenses. The fellowship is self-initiating; candidates are not nominated. Applications due by February 1 each year. CONTACT: *Program Director, Nieman Foundation, 1 Francis Ave., Cambridge, MA 01238; (617) 495-2237.*

• **Best Scholarship Resources.** Three computerized scholarship search services go beyond the obvious sources of financial aid which any bursar's office can list for concerned parents (and some services charge to tell you about). They concentrate on lesser-known, privately financed student aid from corporations, professional groups, foundations, and individuals with a cause. For example, if your name is Anderson, Baxendale, Borden, Bright, Pennoyer, or Murphy, there are possible fellowships at Harvard. Sons and daughters of fishermen qualify for a scholarship at Tufts. If you have high grades and can rope cows at rodeos, you have a shot at the Kenneth Gunther Fellowship at the University of Arizona.

• **The National Scholarship Research Service, Box 2516, San Rafael, CA 94901** charges $45 for a search of its 200,000 listed grants after the applicant has filled out a thirty-two-question form. It turns up an average of thirty-five to forty leads within two weeks.

• **The Scholarship Clearing House, P.O. Box 36745, Los Angeles, CA 90036** charges $39 for a computer printout of five to twenty-five sources of private aid from its databank containing 250,000 financial aid sources.

• **Campus Consultants, Inc., 338 E. 67th St., New York, NY 10021** offers its computerized financial aid analysis service for $65 per search.

TOP SCHOOLS: INTERNATIONAL

TIME was when studying at a foreign university was more socially than educationally appropriate: the "junior year abroad" functioned as a sort of finishing school for generations of well-to-do American college students. Foreign study has grown up now, in scope, purpose, and value. That's partly because the quality of foreign universities—beyond the traditional bastions of western Europe—has improved. There are more choices to complement the American student's increased sophistication and purposefulness.

Rating educational institutions, even at home, is a highly subjective matter. After consultations with American educators and administrators who deal with them firsthand and on a regular basis, we offer the following selection of foreign universities. With a few obvious exceptions, such as Oxford and Cambridge, the schools are not outstanding in every academic area; but they all have strengths that make them standouts in an international context.

Two caveats are in order. These institutions are listed primarily as a guide to students looking for long-term study, and probably a graduate or undergraduate degree, rather than for a single year's "experience." Language can be a barrier; before committing yourself to any university located in a non-English-speaking country, you should make direct inquiries to determine what facility is needed in the native language and whether some courses are taught in English or in another language in which you're fluent. Our selection, by geographical area:

England

• **Oxford and Cambridge.** Known throughout the world as citadels of learning, Oxford and Cambridge enroll few Americans—aside from the Rhodes Scholars who attend the former. Their high degree of competitiveness is a principal reason; as Britain's elite institutions of higher education, they are very difficult to get into. For individualized, demanding, traditional instruction, there is no finer undergraduate education anywhere. Students become part of specific, history-laden residential colleges (i.e., Trinity at Oxford) and receive virtually all of their instructions from tutors or "supervisors." "Whatever academic specialty you choose there," says an American professor who specializes in foreign study, "you'll do very, very well." Yet the two universities do have their special strengths: Oxford, the classics, humanities, and social and political sciences; Cambridge, modern literature and especially the physical sciences.

• **The University of London.** While far less known abroad, this is an outstanding collection of thirty-five or forty colleges. The prestigious London School of Economics may be the most famous of them; the LSE remains excellent at the graduate level, but its undergrad programs have become, in the view of one qualified observer, "crowded and generally overrated." University College offers a very good undergraduate education and medical program. Its School of Oriental and African Studies may well be the best of its kind in Europe. One major U. of London advantage: it is not difficult to get admitted to, partly because many of its colleges are hurting financially.

• **University of Sussex.** A sleeper is the University of Sussex. "It's been having some troubles with curriculum and enrollment," says a source, "but it remains a good and interesting place. For one thing, Sussex is a much more 'American' school in style and approach. It has almost a liberal-arts flair."

• **Richmond College.** London's independent Richmond College has a strong American connection. It operates under the aegis of the American Institute for Foreign Study and, although only a decade old, is fully accredited in the United States. An official of the institute describes Richmond as "truly international. It's multicultural and operates basically on the American system. Many world leaders are sending their children there."

Europe
• **The University of Paris.** Completely overhauled after the student riots of 1968, it remains a large and prestigious institution. The Sorbonne, most famous of its colleges, retains a certain romantic appeal. But, says an American critic, "It's overrated nowadays. You can get just as good an education at plenty of other places in France, such as the **Universities of Poitiers, Lille,** and **Strasbourg.**" Those who wish to fine-tune their academic specialties should note that Poitiers has an excellent program in Medieval French history.

• **University of Freiburg.** West Germany's University of Freiburg is rated superb in the humanities. Highly esteemed is its Institute for European Studies; in case you still want that junior year abroad, the institute has a program geared to it.

• **The University of Salzburg.** Located in Austria, Salzburg has nothing to do with the celebrated Salzburg music festival, but it is tied in with the local Mozarteum, a scholarly institution devoted to the life and work of the great composer. Music aside, Salzburg gets high marks from educators.

THE GLOBAL SCHOOLHOUSE

E VERY year more than 10,000 American college students engage in some form of study abroad. These young people spend $700 to $7,000 for courses that include language and academic studies, usually for one or two semesters. Each one will find something different, based on his or her own expectations, needs and, most of all, the type of academic program he or she selects.

Three Resources
• **Council on International Educational Exchange.** The Council on International Educational Exchange (CIEE) is best for undergraduates. A nonprofit organization with offices in New York and California, CIEE coordinates a host of programs, including several language centers in Europe, a film study center in Paris, a Russian language program in Leningrad, and reciprocal work-abroad programs. It helps individual students with study programs, transportation, accommodations, tours, and insurance, and also issues the very useful International Student Identity Card which entitles a student to discounts.

• **Institute of International Education.** The second group, Institute of International Education, administers the predoctoral Fulbright scholarship and some other scholarship programs, and handles applications for the British University Summer School program. It offers helpful information about these programs, and a variety of general publications on studying overseas, including the extremely useful *Study Abroad.*

• **Experiment in International Living.** A third avenue for exploring European study is the Experiment in International Living, a private, nonprofit institution that has been a leader in international education exchange for almost fifty years. The Experiment has Summer Outbound programs in thirty-one countries and a College Semester Abroad program in sixteen countries.

For a broad range of information and advice, CONTACT: The Council on International Educational Exchange, The New York Student Center, William Sloan House, 356 W. 34th St., New York, NY 10001; (212) 659-0291; Institute of International Education, 809 United Nations Plaza, New York, NY 10017; (212) 883-8269. Experiment in International Living, Brattleboro, VT 05301.

TOP PROFESSIONAL SCHOOLS: U.S.

FOLLOWING are selected professional areas and those schools judged, in the opinion of educators and practicing professionals, (over the last ten years) as offering the best programs and opportunities for career advancement.

The Best Law Schools
During the past decade several rigorous surveys of law schools have appeared in such specialized and prestigious journals as *The Chronicle of Higher Education, Juris Doctor,* and *Change.* In some studies, law school deans were asked to rank the best; in others, faculty members were queried. And in still others, objective measures— such as the ratio of students to volumes in the law school's library were used. No matter what the methodology, Harvard is the nearly unanimous first choice, with Yale a close second. University of Michigan, Stanford, Columbia, and University of Chicago usually vie in some order for the third, fourth, fifth, and sixth positions. When it comes to the bottom group of the Top Ten (positions seven to ten), there is much less agreement. There are about fifteen "second-best" schools of almost equal quality that could fill these slots. University of Pennsylvania and University of California, Berkeley are most frequently mentioned. Other candidates include: University of Virginia, UCLA, New York University, Cornell, Duke, University of Texas at Austin, and Georgetown.

1. Harvard University (Cambridge, MA)
2. Yale University (New Haven, CT)
3. University of Michigan (Ann Arbor, MI)
4. Columbia University (New York)
5. University of Chicago
6. Stanford University (Stanford, CA)
7. University of California (Berkeley, CA)
8. New York University (New York)
9. University of Pennsylvania (Philadelphia)

The Best Business Schools
1. Harvard University (Cambridge, MA)
2. Stanford University (Stanford, CA)
3. University of Chicago
4. University of Pennsylvania (Philadelphia)
5. Carnegie-Mellon University (Pittsburgh)

6. Massachusetts Institute of Technology (Cambridge, MA)
7. University of California (Berkeley, CA)
8. University of California at Los Angeles
9. University of Michigan (Ann Arbor, MI)
10. Columbia University (New York)

The Best Engineering Schools

1. Massachusetts Institute of Technology (Cambridge, MA)
2. University of Illinois (Urbana, IL)
3. Stanford University (Stanford, CA)
4. University of California (Berkeley, CA)
5. California Institute of Technology (Pasadena, CA)
6. University of Michigan (Ann Arbor, MI)
7. Purdue University (West Lafayette, IN)
8. Georgia Institute of Technology (Atlanta)
9. University of Wisconsin (Madison, WI)

The Best Medical Schools

1. Harvard University (Cambridge, MA)
2. Johns Hopkins University (Baltimore)
3. Duke University (Durham, NC)
4. Stanford University (Stanford, CA)
5. Yale University (New Haven, CT)
6. University of Chicago
7. Washington University (St. Louis)
8. University of California (San Francisco)
9. University of Washington (Seattle)
10. Columbia University (New York)
11. Case Western Reserve University (Cleveland)

The Best Nursing Schools

1. Case Western Reserve University (Cleveland)
2. University of Washington (Seattle)
3. University of California (San Francisco)
4. New York University (New York)
5. University of Colorado (Denver)
6. Wayne State University (Detroit)
7. University of California at Los Angeles
8. Boston University (Boston)
9. University of Maryland (Baltimore)
10. Catholic University of America (Washington, DC)

The Best Schools for Social Work
1. Columbia University (New York)
2. University of Chicago
3. University of Michigan (Ann Arbor, MI)
4. Brandeis University (Waltham, MA)
5. University of California (Berkeley, CA)
6. University of Southern California (Los Angeles)
7. Case Western Reserve University (Cleveland)
8. University of Wisconsin (Madison, WI)
9. University of Maryland (Baltimore)
10. Washington University (St. Louis)

Best Journalism Schools
1. Columbia University (New York)
2. Northwestern University (Evanston, IL)
3. University of Missouri (Columbia, MO)
4. University of North Carolina (Chapel Hill, NC)
5. University of California (Berkeley, CA)
6. University of Michigan (Ann Arbor, MI)
7. Marquette University (Milwaukee, WI)
8. University of Illinois (Champaign, IL)

SPECIALTY DEGREES: U.S.

AS every college student, and tuition-suffering parent, knows, the plain old B.A. degree has suffered a serious deflation of marketplace value. Specialty education has become highly popular and profitable, and the more specialized, it seems, the better. With this in mind, we considered seven specialty education areas, in both graduate and undergraduate studies. Herewith, a consensus selection of the leading institutions for the study of mining and metallurgy, forestry, ecology and environment, computer science, oceanography, hotel management, and diplomacy ("foreign service").

Mining and Metallurgy
• **The Colorado School of Mines** (Golden, CO) is, after Columbia University's Krumb School, the nation's oldest institution of this type. It remains very near the top in quality, for undergrad and grad work. Colorado has 3,000 students and ten different departments, plus an unusual graduate department in the burgeoning

field of "mining economics." Its strongest areas are widely considered to be in mining engineering, particularly such sub-specialties as geology and geo-petroleum.

Other leading schools, all of which have both undergraduate and graduate programs, with their emphases or strong areas:

• **New Mexico Institute of Mining and Technology** (Socorro, NM)—uranium and "hard rock" mining.

• **South Dakota School of Mines and Technology** (Rapid City, SD)—mining oriented, especially toward gold and silver.

• **University of Arizona College of Mines and Metallurgy** (Tucson, AZ)—mining oriented.

• **University of Idaho College of Mines and Earth Resources** (Moscow, ID)—"hard rock" mining, particularly lead and silver.

Forestry
• **Syracuse University** (Syracuse, NY)—excellent work in basic forestry.

• **Utah State** (Logan, UT)—several outstanding professors, strongest in such sub-specialties as turbulence and diffusion in timber stands.

• **Colorado State University** (Fort Collins, CO)—known as a "ranger factory" years ago, now oriented toward fire prevention hydrology and reclamation of mining areas.

• **University of Washington** (Seattle, WA)—has had tough financial problems, yet retains an excellent faculty.

Ecology and Environment
"Environmental Engineering," as the discipline is often called, has gained a firm hold at American universities, and new programs continue to appear.

• **Penn State.** Among the more established schools, Penn State ranks very high. At the undergraduate level, ecological studies are blended with numerous academic disciplines: wildlife management, biology, and so on. At the graduate level, where M.A.'s and

Ph.D.'s are granted in Ecology, the emphasis is on interdisciplinary work in such specialties as aquatic biology, population ecology, and forest ecology. Penn State's program has pioneered in a number of areas, including waste water reclamation.

• Other well-regarded programs are located at: Philadelphia's **Drexel Institute,** Washington, D.C.'s **George Washington University,** and **Colorado State's Department of Earth Resources. Johns Hopkins University** pays particular attention to the public health side of environmental concerns.

Computer Science

A degree in computer science may be the hottest academic ticket around—the M.B.A. of the eighties and beyond. At the graduate level, specialization has taken over. **Where you will go depends heavily on what sub-specialty appeals to you.** Among the outstanding institutions and the programs for which they're highly esteemed.

• **Carnegie-Mellon** (Pittsburgh)—artificial intelligence.

• **Stanford** (Palo Alto, CA)—artificial intelligence, computer science theory.

• **MIT** (Cambridge, MA)—hardware, artificial intelligence, theory.

• **Harvard** (Cambridge, MA)—theory.

• **Cornell** (Ithaca, NY)—theory.

As in many other disciplines, schools with strong graduate programs are not necessarily the best for undergraduate studies. Almost every university worthy of the name has built or is building a computer sciences undergrad department. Our sources recommend enrolling in a broad-scale, wide-ranging program, which will provide a solid basis for either the workplace or grad-school admission. Two of this type are highly regarded: **Columbia University** and the **State University of New York at Stony Brook. The City University of New York** offers excellent value. It is one of the nation's largest, cheapest (especially for New York City residents), and best. The Ph.D.-level graduate program, operated in Manhattan by a consortium of CUNY institutions, includes all of the sought-after sub-specialties.

Oceanography

Sub-specialization has invaded this field, too, and so have a handful of good new institutions to challenge the long-established leaders. Among the best of the new are:

• **University of California at Santa Barbara** —strong in biology, zoology, and botany (the marine versions).

• **Texas A&M** —which emphasizes shrimp farming.

• **University of Rhode Island** —which has earned a fine reputation in ocean law.

The leaders are **Scripps, Woods Hole,** and **Rosenstiel.** They offer an admirable geographic as well as curricular spread.

• **Scripps Institute of Oceanography,** University of California at San Diego; **Woods Hole Oceanographic Institute** at the southern extremity of Cape Cod. Both have very broad-based curricula that explore physical, chemical, geological, and geophysical—as well as biological—aspects of the field. By most measures, Scripps remains preeminent. It has the largest faculty and operates some 250 research projects simultaneously, with a total annual budget (heavily funded by government contracts) of some $68 million. Scripps's special collections of oceanographic specimens and other materials attract researchers from around the world. Its academic "fleet" boasts four research vessels and two research platforms.

• **The Rosenstiel School of Marine and Atmospheric Science** is attached to the University of Miami, and, as one might expect, its forte is tropical oceanography; an interesting sub-specialty: aquaculture keyed to the marine resources of developing countries.

Hotel Management

• **Cornell. The traditional leader in this field has been Cornell University's School of Hotel Administration.** Cornell still leads, but it has plenty of competition. The number of hotel-management institutions has roughly doubled in the past decade, with some eighty four-year and even more two-year schools now operating. The increased numbers have brought considerable diversity in terms of academic approach. Some institutions maintain a formal tie with a business school; others, like Cornell, avoid that. Some enroll students directly in hotel courses; others have them take liberal arts or business courses for a year or two, then begin their hotel-management concentration. **The Universities of Denver and New Hampshire** are two schools that take the latter approach. Cornell itself has expanded to meet the hotel-management demand. It now enrolls more than 600 undergraduates but remains highly selective, with several applicants rejected for each one accepted. Cornell has the largest faculty of any school in the field, and its strongly supportive alumni often provide useful contacts when new graduates go job hunting.

• **Michigan State.** Cornell's traditional rival, Michigan State, remains an excellent four-year hotel school. It differs from Cornell in one important way: it is connected to the university's business school.

• **Among the other institutions** that have gained increasing prominence in the field are: the **University of Houston,** the **University of Nevada at Las Vegas, Florida International University, Penn State,** and **Washington State.**

Diplomacy ("Foreign Service")

In the field of international relations education, there have been numerous changes in what is studied and how—but very few in *where* the studying takes place. The schools that headed a short list a few decades ago still head a list that's grown only modestly; together they turn out a substantial majority of the new recruits who enter the U.S. government Foreign Service.

By almost any reckoning, the leading institutions are: **the Woodrow Wilson School of Public and International Affairs at Princeton; the Fletcher School of Law and Diplomacy at Tufts; and the School of Advanced International Studies at Johns Hopkins.** Not far behind are Columbia's School of International Affairs, Georgetown's Walsh School of Foreign Service, and a small and relatively new program at Yale. All of these institutions grant the standard two-year master's degree, while Yale and one or two others also award Ph.D.'s. Almost all are firmly committed to the idea that they should produce not specialists in a region or culture but generalists with good analytical abilities.

In addition, the top schools have embraced business education and downplayed foreign language requirements. The first step reflects the fact that increasing numbers of their graduates are being sought by international banking and business firms; the second, that "operational" language skill, rather than to-the-letter proficiency, is considered a sensible objective.

• **Princeton.** Princeton, for example, no longer has any language requirement. This is partly because the school has followed another new trend: a tendency to incorporate domestic studies—of politics and economics in particular—into the international program. Yet Princeton remains "traditional" in one important way: it still has as its objective "a rigorous preparation for careers in public life," in an era when competitors are sending as many grads into business as into the Foreign Service.

• **Tufts.** Tufts offers an especially strong program in international law. It is one of the few schools that doesn't require the study of "core" courses. Instead, it has designed its curriculum so that each student can choose freely yet get a good sampling of the major subject categories.

• **Johns Hopkins.** Johns Hopkins, on the other hand, sticks with a core curriculum and requires students to pass exams in three of its four divisions. Hopkins is known for its excellence in Asian studies.

TOP UNDERGRADUATE SCHOOLS: U.S.

CHOOSING—and investing in—an education is fraught with intangibles and subjective elements. Nevertheless, the following four approaches to evaluating U.S. undergraduate programs do provide a starting point for picking a top school.

HERI Pilot Study
A pilot study published in the education journal *Change,* it ranks the top undergraduate departments in six academic fields: economics, history, English, chemistry, sociology, and biology. The Higher Education Research Institute of Los Angeles (HERI) and the Council on Learning, a nonprofit foundation for improving higher education, asked 15,000 college educators to rate undergraduate departments in their field at colleges nationwide, evaluating overall quality of education, faculty excellence, innovativeness of curriculum, and preparation of students for employment and for graduate school.

It was no surprise that the traditionally top-notch schools—**Harvard, Yale, Princeton, Stanford, the University of Chicago, and the University of California at Berkeley**—all received top ranking in six fields. Winning top rankings in five of the six fields studied were departments at **Cornell** (only the history department fell short) and the **University of Michigan** (strong in everything but chemistry). Both schools also boast renowned graduate departments. But some smaller schools, not noted for superb graduate programs, also received high marks in five of the six departments. **Amherst, Dartmouth, Williams, Bryn Mawr, Carleton, Haverford,** and **Pomona** all offer outstanding undergraduate instruction, according to the HERI survey.

Other colleges rated highly in the HERI report include the following (the figure in parenthesis indicates the number of departments, of the six evaluated, that received high ranking in the poll): **University of Wisconsin, Madison** (4), **Reed** (4), **Brandeis** (3), **Columbia** (3), **Johns Hopkins** (3), **Middlebury** (3), **Northwestern** (3), **MIT** (3), and **Smith** (3). The study also heaped praise on some lesser known institutions: **the University of California at Irvine** and **Macalester** for their economics departments; the **U.S. Naval Academy** for biology and history; **Hamline University** and **Rose-Hulman Institute of Technology** for chemistry; and the **University of Alabama** and the **University of Massachusetts** in Boston for sociology.

The Gourman Report

Some of the results of HERI's exhaustive study were mirrored in the report issued by Dr. Jack Gourman, a California researcher whose quality ratings of universities are frequently cited. Gourman assessed American undergraduate institutions on the basis of admissions, enrollment, staff, facilities, curriculum, research, and finances.

Gourman ranks the nation's leading undergraduate schools as follows:

1. Princeton
2. Harvard
3. University of Michigan
4. Yale
5. Stanford
6. University of California, Berkeley
7. University of Wisconsin, Madison
8. Cornell
9. University of Chicago
10. UCLA
11. MIT
12. California Institute of Technology

Profile of Freshman Class

The degree of selectivity a school exercises in choosing students is another popular measure of quality. The authors of the *Comparative Guide to American Colleges* group colleges by selectivity, based on the average test scores of recent classes, the percentage of applicants accepted, the ranking of recent freshmen in their high school classes, and other statistical data. The *Comparative Guide* is edited by James Cass, former director of research at the National Council for Better Schools, and Max Birnbaum, professor emeritus of human relations and sociology at Boston University. They maintain that a university is no better than its student body.

Cass and Birnbaum's list of "Most Selective" schools, their highest classification, included many of the schools already mentioned here, as well as **Cooper Union School of Engineering and Science, Georgetown University School of Foreign Service, Harvey Mudd College, Rice University, St. John's College in New Mexico, St. John's College** in Maryland, **Wellesley College,** and **Wesleyan College.**

Profile of Alumni

Other raters look at the later achievements of a college's graduates, reasoning that it is the education an institution confers, not the caliber of students it accepts, that proves a school's worth. Gene Hawes, in his *Comprehensive Guide to Colleges,* examines graduates' success in business, industry, education, science, government, the professions, and the arts. Using tallies of where the persons listed in *Who's Who* went to college, Hawes compiled a ranking of American colleges based on the social achievement of their graduates. It should be noted, however, that his raw data does not include any per-capita adjustment to offset the impact of larger schools, nor any compensation for possible regional biases in *Who's Who* listings.

1. Harvard
2. Yale
3. Princeton
4. Columbia
5. University of Michigan
6. University of California, Berkeley
7. Northwestern
8. University of Illinois, Urbana

9. University of Minnesota, Minneapolis-St. Paul
10. University of Wisconsin, Madison
11. Dartmouth
12. City College of New York

FOUR

FINE TASTING

DE GUSTIBUS

OF all the "bests" in the world, judging food may be the most subjective and therefore most varied. The range, subtlety, and potential for permutation and combination produces an unending choice for the person who places a high value on eating and drinking well. Sophistication in the enjoyment and preparation of fine food and drink is, for the most part, an acquired art. Acquaintance and familiarity with the finest examples of foodstuffs, recipes, restaurants, vintages, and brews is really the only way to develop standards of taste. Literally speaking, we mean the education of the palate and all those attendant senses which let us appreciate the best of nature's consumable bounty. Following are some starting points for those who want to know more about the art of fine tasting.

GOURMET SOCIETIES

THE range of gourmet societies around the world is broad, diffuse, and imprecisely defined. Any self-appointed group, congregating on a regular basis, primarily to enjoy good food and fellowship, would qualify. Down in one of Mississippi's bayou towns there is, for instance, the Dirty Dozen, organized in the late 1960s. The D.D. consists of twelve good ole boys who convene at 6 P.M. on the first Thursday of every month—except in July and August when it's so hot that "jest the sight of a plate o'barbecue would give even a mule the sweats." The menu during the other ten months is rooted in tradition: heaping platters of barbecued beef, black-eyed peas, grits, cornbread, and collard greens plus a full keg of *Dixie* beer. In Paris the Club des Cent, which meets weekly at Maxim's for lunch, would seem a far cry from the Dirty Dozen. Basically however, the two organizations are not so dissimilar. Both were founded for the simple, unassailable purpose of enjoying good food and good company. That one group hunkers down around a well-scrubbed pine board table, attired in freshly laundered overalls, while the other draws up to a table set with crystal, silver, and gold-bordered china wearing the inevitable three-piece dark business suit that is the uniform of the male Parisian are *differences not of principle but only of degree.*

• **Club des Cent.** Like the delta dwellers across the sea, the Club des Cent is jingoistic in the extreme. Non-French guests may, though only on rare occasions, be invited to share a single repast but even the suggestion of having so alien a creature as an actual dues-paying member is enough to trigger severe heartburn in those close-knit Gallic ranks. The Club des Cent consists of exactly 100 members, each of whom has been invited to join because of his superior knowledge in all matters related to food and wine. Of equal importance is his skill as a witty, or at least a cheerful conversationalist and, of course, his ability to pay his share of the weekly tab which, at Maxim's, is no small consideration.

• **Commanderie des Chevaliers du Tastevin.** Founded in 1934 the Commanderie des Chevaliers du Tastevin, headquartered in New York at 445 Park Avenue, is undeniably French in origin. The parent organization is grandly lodged in the Chateau de Clos de Vougeot, 1 Rue de Chaux, Louis St. George in the very heart of the French countryside which annually tramples out the world's finest Burgundies. Here in the U.S. this honorary society boasts about 1,200 well-fed, well-read, well-heeled members. Its chapters are scattered across the U.S. in major cities.

• **Commanderie de Bordeaux.** Smaller in membership but no less closely tied to France is the Commanderie de Bordeaux des Etats-Unis with offices at 99 Park Avenue, New York. Its 650 U.S. members (many of whom also belong to the Tastevin) have pledged heart and checkbook to the promotion of the wines of Bordeaux, the area that surrounds the ancient seaport, perched on the coast were the Garonne empties into the Atlantic. This elitest group, founded in the years immediately after World War II, today has branches in fifteen U.S. cities as well as in Canada. A regional head is known as a Grand Maître. Qualifications for membership place heavy emphasis on an intimate knowledge of wine in general and Bordeaux in particular.

• **Confrerie de la Chaine des Rotisseurs.** Confrerie de la Chaine des Rotisseurs with offices at 300 East 59th Street in New York. Similar in that a bang-up good dinner plus a bang-up good time is a top priority. Different in that it lays as much emphasis on the enjoyment and knowledge of food as of wine. Different also in that, unlike all the societies listed above, only La Chaine des Rotisseurs admits the gentler sex to its privileged ranks. Worldwide it claims 35,000 well-wined and dined members. In the U.S. it has no fewer than eighty-five branches and, in order to accommodate its members, holds monthly meetings at which only a portion of the membership attends at one time. The Chaine also publishes a beautiful semi-annual journal called *Gastronome*.

• **Wine and Food Society.** More purposeful, and some might say more serious, than any of these is the Wine and Food Society Inc. of New York at 50 East 42nd Street. This society has grown from London where it was founded in 1934 until today it counts 9,000 members worldwide with ninety-eight branches in the U.S. and Canada.

• **Les Amis d'Escoffier.** Based at 220 East 72nd Street, New York, Les Amis is, like the Wine and Food Society, a serious minded organization that originated through the C.I.A.—the Culinary Institute of America in Poughkeepsie, New York. Membership is by invitation only.

GOURMET GUIDES/RATINGS

CONSULT the laden shelf of guidebooks in your local bookstore, and from that impressively large inventory remove those books which concern themselves primarily with sightseeing and places to stay and only secondarily with places to eat. Behold— you'll discover the list of reliable and unbiased restaurant guides is all too short. Titles come and go, not many exhibiting the staying power that identifies a truly authoritative reference.

The Guide Michelin

So saying, it's comforting to state that there is, of course, one towering exception to such caveats: the *Guide Michelin, Red Edition*. In those countries for which a red Michelin is compiled (Great Britain and Ireland, Spain and Portugal, Italy, Germany, Benelux countries, Greater London, France and a separate edition for Paris alone) this annually issued guide carries all the solemn authority of the Bible and the Koran combined.

Unlike other guides which content themselves with comprehensive listings and descriptions of restaurants, the red Michelin rates the restaurants, indicating its omnipotent preference by means of the coveted stars. A star from Michelin is not easily come by. Of the more than 3,600 restaurants listed in France, 533 rate one star "very good cooking," sixty-five rate two stars, "excellent cooking, worthy of a detour," and only nineteen restaurants have earned the highest accolade of three stars, "superb food, the epitome of French cooking."

To make their coverage as thorough as possible, as accessible as possible, Michelin employs a system of symbols, clearly visible in the margin, and intelligible to anyone regardless of lingual proficiency. Pleasant surroundings, comfort and ambience, excellence of wine are all judged and noted in a single entry. *Michelin Guides and Maps, P.O. Box 3305, Spartanburg, SC 29304; (803) 599-0850.*

Gault-Millau

Although Michelin has not yet tackled the admittedly awesome project of reviewing U.S. restaurants, another publisher of first-rate restaurant guides, Gault-Millau does rate U.S. establishments. Having published their findings and ratings of the restaurants of France and Italy with boundless courage, they have now produced *The Best of New York* ($12.95), an English translation of their own French language guide to the Big Apple. Descriptions of New York restaurants are provided, accompanied by a rating which, the authors say, ranges from zero to twenty.

Best U.S. Series

A San Francisco publisher, 101 Productions, offers nine Best Restaurants guides: San Francisco, Washington, DC, Philadelphia, Hawaii, Los Angeles, Chicago, Southern New England,

San Diego, and Orange County. All are in paperback for $4 and $5. The series shows some artistic flair, with replicas of menus and delightful woodcuts scattered throughout each book. Apart from the descriptions of each restaurant, the only rating affixed to each concerned not the quality of the fare but the cost. One, two, or three dollar signs $$$, appear beside the establishments where entrées fell into specified price ranges, i.e., under $5, under $15, and over $15. Also publishes *Country Inns* guide books of regional bed and breakfasts. *101 Productions, 834 Mission St., San Francisco, CA 94103; (415) 495-6040.*

New York Guide

As the admitted restaurant capital of the continent, New York City alone rates a larger share of city-wide guides than any other North American metropolis. Updated every other year, *The Restaurants of New York* by Seymour Britchky (Simon & Schuster, $9.95) has earned a devoted readership through successive editions. Britchky prides himself on trying out personally every restaurant listed, a practice followed too seldom by authors of supposedly reputable guides. In accordance with his findings, he then ascribes a rating which starts at the lowest end of the scale, deemed Unacceptable, and rises to four stars, Excellent. More than one chef or owner has winced under the Britchky adjudication.

TOP RESTAURANTS: INTERNATIONAL

FOR the globe-girdling gourmet the world is an endless feast. One could, if trying to list the world's best restaurants, find 100 that might qualify. Possibly more depending on your own criteria. Ours are: 1) culinary excellence; 2) service; 3) setting; and 4) orchestration, a term we've coined to cite the integrating skill which melds the physical with the intangible to create that rare event—a great meal.

Some of our choices are as grandly impressive as *La Tour d'Argent* in Paris or the *Jockey* in Madrid. Others are as modest in appearance as *Campana* in Rome or *Comme Chez Soi* in Brussels. We've included samplings of exotica of which Tokyo's *Ten Ichi* is a fine example. Yet as disparate as our choices may appear, they hold in common a pride in preparing the very finest food with skill, imagination, and delicacy—and they do this with consistency. May you have the pleasure of dining in every one of them.

Forty Top International Restaurants

- **Aubergine** (Munich)
- **Café de Paris** (Biarritz)
- **Campana** (Rome)
- **Chez Max** (Zurich)
- **Chitpochana** (Bangkok)
- **Comme Chez-Soi** (Brussels)
- **Connaught Grill** (London)
- **Diao Yu Tai** (Beijing)
- **Fang Shan** (Beijing)
- **Frères Troisgros** (Roanne/ Loire)
- **Gualtiero Marchesi** (Milan)
- **Jockey** (Madrid)
- **Jockey Club** (Buenos Aires)
- **Kronenhalle** (Zurich)
- **La Ciboulette** (Paris)
- **L'Archestrate** (Paris)
- **L'Auberge de L'Ill** (Illhoeusern)
- **L'Oasis** (La Napoule/Cannes)
- **Lasserre** (Paris)
- **La Tour d'Argent** (Paris)
- **Le Grand Vefour** (Paris)
- **Le Vivarois** (Paris)
- **Maison du Cygne** (Brussels)
- **Maître** (Berlin)
- **Maxim's** (Paris)
- **Mayflower** (Singapore)
- **Michel Guérard** (Eugenie Les Bains/Landes)
- **Operakallaren** (Stockholm)
- **Passetto** (Rome)
- **Paul Bocuse** (Lyon)
- **Pic** (Valence)
- **Ranieri** (Rome)
- **Red Pepper** (Hong Kong)
- **Restaurant Girardet** (Crissier)
- **Rivoli** (Mexico City)
- **Salle Empire** (Monte Carlo)
- **Savini** (Milan)
- **Taillevent** (Paris)
- **Ten Ichi** (Tokyo)
- **Walterspeile** (Munich)

TOP RESTAURANTS: U.S.

UNLIKE Europeans who can find gastronomic certainty in the red Michelin guide (cf. above, *Gourmet Guides*), Americans must often fend for themselves in search of a memorable meal. There is no single arbiter of excellence among U.S. restaurants. Whether this is impossible, or even desirable, is something for after-dinner debate. Like most of America, the variety and quality of its eating establishments prohibits neat definition and categorization.

As in other areas, America's culinary self-respect grew slowly, essentially under the tutelage of the French masters of haute cuisine, then and now. Simultaneously, its appreciation of native culinary arts is really only now coming to the fore. By which we mean that Southern cooking or coastal seafood dishes are seen not only as "interesting" regional counterpoints to the refined creations of the Continent, but as fine eating in their own right.

Our list of top U.S. restaurants represents some of America's best practitioners of the well-prepared meal. You may quarrel with the choices but then, isn't that the fun of lists? Both to make and to read. All of them should provide happy memories of places where people really try to "do it right"—and succeed.

Twenty-five Top U.S. Restaurants

* **Cafe des Artistes**
1 W. 67th St.
New York, NY
(212) 877-3500

* **Cafe Chauveron**
9561 E. Bay Harbour Drive
Bay Harbour Island, FL
(305) 866-8779

* **Chez Panisse**
1517 Shattuck Ave.
Berkeley, CA
(415) 548-5525

* **Commander's Palace**
1403 Washington Ave.
New Orleans, LA
(504) 899-8231

* **Ernie's**
847 Montgomery St.
San Francisco, CA
(415) 397-5969

* **The Four Seasons**
99 E. 52nd St.
New York, NY
(212) 754-9494

* **Jean-Louis**
2650 Virginia Ave., NW
Washington, DC
(202) 298-4488

* **La Caravelle**
33 W. 55th St.
New York, NY
(212) 586-4252

* **La Grenouille**
3 E. 52nd St.
New York, NY
(212) 752-1495

* **Le Bec-Fin**
1523 Walnut
Philadelphia, PA
(215) 567-1000

* **Le Cirque**
58 E. 65th St.
New York, NY
(212) 794-9292

* **Le Français**
269 S. Milwaukee Ave.
Wheeling, IL
(312) 541-7470

* **Le Lion D'Or**
  1150 Connecticut Ave. NW
  Washington, DC
  (202) 296-7972

* **Le Perroquet**
  70 E. Walton Pl.
  Chicago, IL
  (312) 944-7990

* **L'Ermitage**
  730 N. La Cienega Blvd.
  Los Angeles, CA
  (213) 652-5840

* **Le Ruth's**
  636 Franklin St.
  Gretna, LA
  (504) 362-4914

* **London Chop House**
  155 W. Congress St.
  Detroit, MI
  (313) 962-0277

* **Lutèce**
  249 E. 50th St.
  New York, NY
  (212) 752-2225

* **Maisonette**
  114 E. Sixth St.

Cincinnati, OH
(513) 721-2260

* **Ma Maison**
  8368 Melrose Ave.
  Los Angeles, CA
  (213) 655-1991

* **The Mandarin**
  900 North Point
  San Francisco, CA
  (415) 673-8812

* **The Mansion**
  2821 Turtle Creek Blvd.
  Dallas, TX
  (214) 559-2100

* **The Palace**
  420 E. 59th St.
  New York, NY
  (212) 355-5150

* **Rancho Del Rio Tack Room**
  2800 N. Sabino Canyon Road
  Tucson, AZ
  (602) 298-2351

* **Tony's**
  826 N. Broadway
  St. Louis, MO
  (314) 231-7007

RESTAURANTS: GRAND CELLARS

IN 1981 *The Wine Spectator,* a national bimonthly newspaper devoted to wine, initiated an annual Grand Award to be given to American restaurants whose wine lists meet stringent criteria for overall breadth, quality and depth, actual inventory on hand, storage and service. The Grand Award is given for a three-year period. Thus far the following restaurants (listed alphabetically) have been honored:

* **Ambrosia Restaurant**
  (Newport Beach, CA)

* **The American Hotel**
  (Sag Harbor, NY)

- **Anthony's Pier 4**
  (Boston, MA)

- **Bern's Steak House**
  (Tampa, FL)

- **The Beverly Wilshire Hotel**
  (Beverly Hills, CA)

- **Blue Boar Inn**
  (San Francisco, CA)

- **The Breakers**
  (West Palm Beach, FL)

- **Brennan's Restaurant**
  (New Orleans, LA)

- **The Carnelian Room**
  (San Francisco, CA)

- **Charley's 517**
  (Houston, TX)

- **The Chronicle**
  (Pasadena, CA)

- **The Colony**
  (Longboat Key, FL)

- **Die Ente vom Lehel**
  (Wiesbaden, West Germany)

- **The Dining Room**
  (Chicago, IL)

- **Doros**
  (San Francisco, CA)

- **The Down Under**
  (Fort Lauderdale, FL)

- **Elario's**
  (La Jolla, CA)

- **Enoteca Pinchiorri**
  (Florence, Italy)

- **Ernie's**
  (San Francisco, CA)

- **Five Crowns**
  (Corona Del Mar, CA)

- **Flagstaff House Restaurant**
  (Boulder, CO)

- **The Forge**
  (Miami Beach, FL)

- **The French Room**
  (San Francisco, CA)

- **George Badonsky's Maxim's
  on Astor**
  (Chicago, IL)

- **Gidleigh Park**
  (Chagford, Devon, England)

- **Heritage Hotel**
  (Englewood, CO)

- **Hermitage Inn**
  (Wilmington, VT)

- **Imperial Dynasty**
  (Hanford, CA)

- **Italian Village Restaurant**
  (Chicago, IL)

- **Jean Louis**
  (Washington, DC)

- **La Bella Fontana**
  (Beverly Hills, CA)

- **Lahiere's**
  (Princeton, NJ)

- **La Petite Auberge**
  (Cresskill, NJ)

- **La Rive Gauche**
  (Palos Verdes Estates, CA)

- **Laurent**
  (New York, NY)

- **Le Pavillon**
  (Washington, DC)

- **Le Tastevin Restaurant**
  (Seattle, WA)

- **Lutèce**
  (New York, NY)

- **Madison's**
  (Greensboro, NC)

- **Mr. Stox**
  (Anaheim, CA)

- **Narsai's**
  (Kensington, CA)

- **The 95th**
  (Chicago, IL)

- **Pierce's 1894 Restaurant**
  (Elmira Heights, NY)

- **The Ranch House**
  (Ojai, CA)

- **Ritz Carlton Hotel**
  (Chicago, IL)

- **Rosellini's Other Place**
  (Seattle, WA)

- **Salishan Lodge**
  (Gleneden Beach, OR)

- **The Sardine Factory**
  (Monterey, CA)

- **Scandia**
  (Los Angeles, CA)

- **Silverado Restaurant**
  (Calistoga, CA)

- **Spark's Steak House**
  (New York, NY)

- **Spinelli's**
  (St. Cloud, FL)

- **La Strega Ristorante**
  (Los Angeles, CA)

- **Taillevent**
  (Paris, France)

- **Tan Dinh**
  (Paris, France)

- **Top O' The Cove**
  (La Jolla, CA)

- **Valentino**
  (Santa Monica, CA)

- **White Horse Inn at Chilgrove**
  (Near Chichester, England)

- **Windows On The World**
  (New York, NY)

- **Yankee Silversmith Inn**
  (Wallington, CT)

TOP RESTAURANTS: STEAKHOUSES

THERE are those who would have us believe that gourmets and gourmands the world over are feasting only on warm duck breast salads, pasta primavera, and mesquite-broiled Alaskan fresh salmon served with crisp infant vegetables. Not so. Lovers of good food around the globe still find a bit of heaven in a great steak, and even closet carnivores seek out a slab of succulent steer, broiled to perfection, for a special meal.

What makes a steak great? We have interviewed chefs and restaurateurs, food experts and restaurant critics across the country and around the world to determine not only what makes a steak great, but also where to find the best. First, a truism: a fine chef in an award-winning restaurant will prepare for you a great steak. This capability is an important part of his training—indeed one of the most demanding skills. One noted chef, a young man who has recently been inducted as one of twelve chefs and restaurateurs into France's "hall of fame" in the Order of Fine Arts and Literature, confessed that he prayed fervently he would not draw "bifteck et pommes frites" as his graduation exercise. "You can fool around a little with *supremes de volaille* or *blanquette de veau*," he explains, "but a steak must be perfect."

Top International Steakhouses

Hotel Okura (Tokyo, Japan)
The most pampered beef in the world is that of Kobe and Matsuzaka in Japan. Here a calf must be born of prize-winning parents, and then leads the next three years of his life on a farm where climate, water, and optimum grazing conditions help transform him into a perfect steer. He is curried daily, just as though he were a thoroughbred horse, and has a hand massage with *shochu* (Japanese gin) to knead the accumulating fat gently through the muscles to impart the "marbled" look of fine meat. He eats rice, bran, and beans, and just before his third birthday, is given beer to round out his diet. His final months of pampering assure that he will become *shimofuri* ("fallen frost"), ranked by connoisseurs as the best beef in the world. In the United States there are a few restaurants which on occasion will have Kobe or Matsuzaka beef, but for the real thing in the proper setting go to Tokyo's Hotel Okura. A steak dinner in this beautiful restaurant will cost over $100 per person. *1-10-4 Toranomon Minato-ku, Tokyo; 03-582-02-11.*

Pierre Cardin's Maxim's (Tokyo, Japan)
Another great steakhouse serving Kobe and Matsuzaka beef, located in Tokyo's Sony Building. This restaurant has pleasing decor and marvelous service, and steak dinners, once again, will cost over $100 per person. *5 Chome-chu-ku, Tokyo; 03-572-36-21.*

Winston's (Toronto, Canada)
In Canada, we recommend John Arend's famed Toronto restaurant, which recently celebrated its fiftieth anniversary. The decor is magnificent, and one of the world's finest wine cellars complements some of the best steaks in the country. *104 Adelaide St. West, Toronto; (416) 363-1627.*

Restaurant Les Halles (Montreal, Canada)
Noisy and fun, patterned after the old marketplace of Paris. Customers personally select their steaks, which are then weighed and grilled to order. *1450 Rue Crescent, Montreal; (514) 844-2328.*

Black Beard's (Acapulco, Mexico)
Cary Sinclair and Carlos Medoza serve the best steak in the country. Located on the beach, where the rolling surf and swaying palms will complete the euphoria. The decor is that of an ancient pirate ship, enhanced by magnificent drinks of pineapple and rum. *Condesa Beach, Costera M. Aleman; phone Guerrero 4-25-49.*

Delmonico's (Mexico City, Mexico)
Offers spectacular chandeliers and amber glass ceilings above rooms designed with modern interpretations of traditional Mexican arches. Here Nick Noyes offers prime steaks from the best beef in Mexico, served impeccably. *Londres 87; (905) 514-7003.*

Brazz (Puerto Vallarta, Mexico)
Offers prime steaks from pampered Hereford steers, grilled to order as guests enjoy music from strolling musicians. Open daily for dinner. Prices moderate. Morelos y Gajeana; (322) 2-03-24.

Peter Langan (London, England)
Traveling Americans have created a demand for good steaks in Great Britain and fine restaurants in which to find them abound. Peter Langan, described by the *London Times* as "a garrulous, pear-shaped roisterer," runs a brasserie where you can have an excellent steak. The downstairs is informal and noisy, upstairs is pleasant and quieter. *Stratton Street W1; 493-6437.*

Dorchester Grill (London, England)
Under the supervision of chef Anton Mosimann, offers an impressive menu and luxurious surroundings. Expensive. *Park Lane W1; 629-8888.*

Guinea Grill (London, England)
Informal and fun, with competent service and good steaks cooked to order; moderately expensive. *30 Bruton Place W1; 629-5613.*

Rowley's (London, England)
For $25 for two, try Rowley's. The lone specialty is grilled entrecôte in Café de Paris sauce, with french fries, salad and dessert, and wine served from magnums. *113 Jermyn St. W1; 930-2707.*

Champany Inn (Linlithgow, Scotland)
For first-rate steaks in Scotland, try the Champany Inn at the junction of route A904 and A803, about a thirty-minute drive from Edinburgh. Here, an array of steaks including rib loin, Pope's eye (no American equivalent, but an exceedingly tender cut), sirloin, and filet are cooked—over a massive charcoal grill—black on the outside and dark red on the interior. The restaurant, tastefully appointed with hunting prints on the walls, mahogany tables, and green velveteen-upholstered chairs, boasts an impressive wine selection. Prices moderately expensive. *Phone 683-4532.*

Abbey Tavern (Dublin, Ireland)
Offers a pub downstairs where spirited ballad singing attracts visitors. Upstairs in an intimate setting generous, well-prepared steaks are served. Prices are moderate. *Howth; phone 322006.*

Guinea Pig (Dalkey, Ireland)
Enjoy both steaks and game dishes in this charming restaurant in a quaint fishing village. *Dalkey, County Dublin; 859005.*

Paris Hilton (Paris, France)
While it's more likely that you will be sampling fresh foie gras and *homard à l'absinthe* during your stay in Paris, if you do hanker for the simplicity of a well-prepared steak, try the Paris Hilton, which offers pleasing, American-style selections. In a saloon-like setting, cowboy-attired waiters offer sirloin, porterhouse, and T-bone steaks (the beef is flown in from the U.S.), as well as barbecued spare ribs, chili, Mexican black bean soup, Caesar salad, and cheesecake. *18 avenue de Suffren, Paris; 273.92.00.*

Le Procope (Paris, France)
Just a few steps off boulevard St. Germain is one of the world's oldest cafés, founded in 1686. (Ben Franklin was a guest . . . as were Voltaire and Robespierre.) There is a $15 fixed-price menu with superb *steak au poivre. 13 rue de l'Ancienne-Comédie, Paris; 326.99.20.*

Monsieur Boeuf (Paris, France)
Opened in 1972 and a success ever since. The steaks are excellent, service fine, and there is a list of good little wines. *31 rue St. Denis, Paris; 508.58.35.*

Restaurant La Réserve (Nice, France)
In Nice, we have recommendations from one of France's top chefs. "The best steak in all of France," he claims, "is that pre-

pared by Louis Bertho!" It is served at Restaurant La Reserve, better known as "Chez Loulou" at the boulevard de la Plage. *Cros de Cagnes s/mer.*

Tredici Gobbi (Florence, Italy)
One of the city's more deluxe restaurants, serving succulent *bistecca Fiorentina*—Florentine steak—in giant slabs, accompanied by a rich and velvety Chianti. *Via del Porcellana 9; 29-87-69.*

Le Fonticine (Florence, Italy)
Where *bistecca Florentina* as well as homemade pasta dishes and other Tuscan specialties are commendable. *Via Nazionale 79/r, Florence; 28-21-06.*

Papa Giovanni (Rome, Italy)
One of the most romantic restaurants in Rome. Small and intimate, but the wine list offers more than 700 labels. Prices expensive. *Via dei Sediari 4, Rome; 6565308.*

Al Chianti (Rome, Italy)
Run by the same Tuscan family for sixty years, and serves excellent Florentine steaks. Also called "Ernesto & Mario," there are only fourteen tables, and sometimes service is hectic. *Via Ancona 17/19, Rome; 86-10-83 and 85-67-31.*

Girarrosto Toscano (Rome, Italy)
Offers an open grill. Great salamis and cheeses as hors d'oeuvres. Save room for the thick sizzling Florentine steak, grilled to perfection. Steaks are priced according to weight and are moderate for the quality. *Via Campania 29, Rome; 4933759.*

Cuatro Estaciones (Madrid, Spain)
Very much in vogue at the moment, small menu, but extravagant decor and service. The *entrecôte Villagodio* is excellent, and there is a salad bar. Good wine list. *General Ibaniz Iberis 5, Madrid; (91) 253-63-05.*

Casa Botin (Madrid, Spain)
Located in the heart of the old quarter, next to the Plaza Mayor. This restaurant has been owned and managed by the same family for 250 years, and consists of three rooms, one above the other, connected by an open staircase. Most diners prefer the roast baby lamb or suckling pig, but steaks are fine here. Proprietor

Antonio Botin speaks excellent English and is a genial host. *Cuchilleros 17, Madrid; (91) 266-42-17.*

Casa Paco (Madrid, Spain)
A fine old tavern that offers excellent steaks—and convivial atmosphere. *Puerta Cerrada 11, Madrid; (91) 266-31-66.*

La Cabaña (Buenos Aires, Argentina)
The city's single most famous restaurant. Here, enormous steaks are grilled to perfection, and the atmosphere is turn-of-the-century Spanish. Excellent service; fairly expensive. *436 Etre Rios, Buenos Aires; 37-26-39.*

Top U.S. Steakhouses

Canlis (Honolulu, Hawaii)
Authentic Polynesian designs, wooden beams, and lava walls brilliant with orchids and tropical foliage, waterfalls and Koi pools set the scene for prime steaks cooked over Keawewood charcoal. Popular and offering an extensive menu of island delicacies, Canlis is open for dinner nightly, closed on major holidays. Prices are moderate. *2100 Kalakaua Ave., Honolulu; (808) 923-2324.*

Jack's Restaurant (San Francisco, California)
This brightly lit restaurant has been doing everything right for no less than 121 years. It has a beautiful atmosphere, with gold garlands on the walls, snowy linens, and comfortable chairs. Open for lunch and dinner, closed major holidays. Prices moderate to expensive. *615 Sacramento St., San Francisco; (415) 421-7355.*

Pacific Dining Car (Los Angeles, California)
A favorite with Southern California steak lovers, this restaurant has been serving marvelous steaks since 1921, and is still run by the same family. The finest of Eastern beef is personally chosen by the owner, and then shipped to the restaurant to be aged in their own curing box. Succulent, juicy, and grilled exactly to order, these are as good as steak can get. Open twenty-four hours a day, seven days a week, with valet parking and one of the best wine lists in the state. Prices moderate. *1310 W. 6th St., Los Angeles; (213) 483-6000.*

Ruth's Chris Steak House (Beverly Hills, California)
A newcomer which has already gathered a host of fans. A clone of Ruth's in New Orleans, this steakhouse run by Paul Flem-

ing uses the same Iowa dry-aged beef as the original, shipped fresh in refrigerated trucks. The smallest steak is an eight ounce filet at $13, and the largest a two-and-a-half pound porterhouse, which serves four, at $76. *224 S. Beverly Drive, Beverly Hills; (213) 859-8744.*

Monti's La Casa Vieja (Tempe, Arizona)

Once the home of former Senator Carl Hayden of Arizona. Here in a series of thirteen rooms, each decorated with memorabilia of the Old West, a thousand diners can be seated for some of the best steaks in the country. Prices are modest, ranging from $9.95 for an eleven ounce sirloin to a two pound sirloin-for-two at $19.95. *First St. and Mill Ave., Tempe; (602) 967-7594.*

Golden Ox (Kansas City, Missouri)

Located in the heart of the old stockyards, this is the best place for steak in Kansas City. Informal and easy, with Western decor. *1600 Genessee Ave.; (816) 842-2866.*

Morton's (Chicago, Illinois)

A basement restaurant, very handsome, expensive, and crowded. There is no menu, but items are presented on a large silver tray; the steaks are superb, grilled before your eyes in the open kitchen at one end of the large room. Open for dinner every evening but Sunday and major holidays. *1050 N. State St., Chicago; (312) 266-4820.*

London Chop House (Detroit, Michigan)

Acclaimed as one of our top twenty-five U.S. restaurants, and new owners Max and Lanie Pincus are intent on keeping it that way. Elegantly informal with fabric-covered tables, concerned and expert service, this cellar is a meeting place for epicures around the country who dote on the succulent steaks and fine wines. Open daily, except Sunday, for lunch and dinner at moderate prices. *155 W. Congress, Detroit; (313) 962-0277.*

K-Paul's Louisiana Kitchen (New Orleans, Louisiana)

Yes, they do eat steak in New Orleans. Owner-chef Paul Prudhomme did it first with redfish, but his blackened steak is considered terrific by one and all. First the tender steak is coated in a special combination of hot spices, then seared quickly on both sides of a blazing hot cast-iron pan. Black on the outside, moist and tender and rare inside, the meat is wonderfully accented by the spices. No reservations are accepted, and there is usually a long line outside the little restaurant, but it's worth it. Rather expensive. Open Monday through Friday for dinner only. *416 Chartres St., New Orleans; (504) 524-7394.*

Palm (New York, New York)
In New York City, our experts chose the venerable Palm, where the steaks—recited along with the rest of the menu—are pronounced flawless. Decor consists of sawdust-covered floors and walls decorated with celebrity cartoons, and we hear tell that the bartender, John, makes a splendid Bloody Mary. *837 Second Ave., New York; (212) 687-2953.*

Spark's (New York, New York)
Located on Manhattan's "Steak Row," owner Pat Cetta describes the house specialties as being grilled prime sirloin; filet mignon; and steak fromage, a generous portion of butterflied steak topped with Roquefort butter. Spark's wine list is formidable. Open Monday through Saturday for lunch and dinner. *210 E. 46th St., New York; (212) 687-4855.*

Peter Luger Steakhouse (Brooklyn, New York)
This homey, German-style landmark restaurant has remained in the same Brooklyn location since 1887. Their hefty broiled porterhouse steaks weigh about one-and-a-half pounds per serving, and the classic side dish, sliced tomatoes with red onion, makes an excellent accompaniment. *178 Broadway, Brooklyn; (718) 387-7400.*

Bern's Steak House (Tampa, Florida)
Florida boasts just one steakhouse worthy of the name, but what a steakhouse! Bern Laxer entitles his menu "Art in Steaks," and offers eighty-three different steaks, butter-basted and broiled over charcoal. In Bern's you not only have a choice of sizes from a one-inch thick six ounce filet to a three-inch thick four-and-a-half pound sirloin strip (which feeds six), but also eight degrees of doneness. Bern uses prime meat, aged two months, trimmed and cut to order. Other enticements of this fine restaurant are the exceptional salad greens and fresh vegetables, grown on Laxer's own organic farms and delivered each morning fresh to the restaurant. The wine list is gargantuan: with more than 500,000 bottles described, it contains 2,000 pages and weighs eight pounds. Another treat is the coffee, blended from fourteen kinds of beans,

roasted individually, and then ground and brewed to order. *1208 S. Howard St., Tampa; (813) 251-2421.*

CLASSIC COOKBOOKS

EVERYONE'S childhood home had at least one or two cookbooks sitting high on the kitchen shelf. Maybe it was the brown covered Boston cookbook or a battered copy of Fanny Farmer. Whatever its title, it came into use largely to determine the roasting time of the Christmas turkey or perhaps to yield up secrets for pie crusts or bread dough. Chances were it was rarely if ever consulted to supply new menu ideas. Why should it? Before World War II, America's home menus were pretty well determined: hot soup, meat, one green vegetable, one starch, dessert, and coffee. Today a cook of even modest abilities and aspirations is at home with many imported dishes from manicotti to stir-fry vegetables, from duck á l'orange to Irish soda bread—each nourishing, but also varied and interesting. And so are cookbooks. A shelfful of cookbooks can provide a library of good reading. The collection that follows represents a library of basic bests and is divided into three sections.

Section I will give an interested neophyte a sound start in the fascinating world of gastronomy. Section II assumes mastery of the basics and an interest in going on to somewhat more complicated food preparation. Section III introduces the reader to the subtleties and endless variations that characterize a few ethnic schools of cooking.

At this point the collector's own tastes and preferences should guide any further acquisitions. We stress however that handsome as many of these books may be—with glorious mouth-watering, full-color illustrations—*they are essentially manuals of instruction,* intended to be used and not simply displayed.

I—Primers
• **The Joy of Cooking** by Irma Rombauer and Marion Rombauer Becker (Bobbs Merrill, deluxe edition $23.95). This is the basic of the basics. It not only clearly explains how to prepare food, it also provides a good deal of information about buying food. It discusses equipment, utensils, and even touches on various aspects of kitchen layout. Recipes are sound if a trifle uninteresting but the current edition has been expanded to include many non-American dishes that were not covered in earlier editions. An ideal wedding present.

• **The James Beard Cookbook** (Dutton, $15.95). Less complete than *Joy*, it still gives simple recipes that, by interesting touches, are made to sound more difficult than they actually are. Perfectly accessible to the novice.

• **The New York Times Cookbook** by Craig Claiborne (Harper & Row, $18). First edition. The second edition acquired a more complicated format than the first which we here recommend. Easy-to-follow recipes are presented with just enough sophistication to keep them interesting to both the cook and the cooked-for.

   II—Fine Food
• **Mastering the Art of French Cooking,** Volumes I and II by Julia Child and Simone Beck and Louisette Bertholie (Vol. I) and Julia Child and Simone Beck (Vol. II); (Knopf, $45 boxed set). Certainly the best-written introduction to this highly developed national school of cooking.

• **The Art of Fine Baking** by Paul Peck (Simon & Schuster, $7.95).

• **The Complete Book of Breads** by Bernard Clayton, Jr. (Simon & Schuster, $18.95). Both of these provide comprehensive but not overly complicated instruction in straightforward baking minus unnecessary frills.

• **Simple French Food** by Richard Olney (Atheneum, $10.95). Exactly what the title says.

• **The Food of France** by Waverly Root (Random House, $6.95). Not a how-to book, but rather a history and discussion of French food and its evolution from the days of Henry II to the present.

• **The New Larousse Gastronomique** (Crown, $35). An invaluable, altogether comprehensive encyclopedia of ingredients, utensils, recipes, and history.

   III—A World of Food
• **The Classic Italian Cook Book** by Marcella Hazan (Knopf, $18.95).

• **The Fine Art of Italian Cooking** by Giuliano Bugialli (Times Books, $19.95).

• **Classic Indian Cooking** by Julie Sahni (Morrow, $19.95).

• **Japanese Cooking: A Simple Art** by Shizuo Tsuji (Kodansha, $18.75).

• **The Chinese Cookbook** by Craig Claiborne and Virginia Lee (Barnes & Noble, $9.95).

• **A Book of Middle Eastern Food** by Claudia Roden (Knopf, $16.95).

• **The Original Thai Cookbook** by Jennifer Brennan (Putnam, $14.95).

• **The World of Cheese** by Evan Jones (Knopf, $12.50).

• **Cooking the Nouvelle Cuisine in America** by Michele Urvater and David Liederman (Workman, $12.95).

• **Elizabeth David Classics** (Knopf, $15.95). A collection of French recipes presented with exceptional literary expertise and charm.

COOKING SCHOOLS: U.S./INTERNATIONAL

I N the last decade, as interest in cooking has mushroomed, the number of cooking schools and courses has also grown dramatically. Not surprisingly, the quality of these schools varies greatly. But the best cooking schools have certain traits in common:

• **Technique and fundamentals.** Rather than just teaching a recipe, a good teacher points out the underlying principles or techniques, thus allowing adaptation of any recipe. As Marcella Hazan says, "I would want a person who could teach me not just to prepare a certain dish, but how to fix a dish that's gone wrong, how to adapt a dish to do what you have available."

• **Quality ingredients.** The best teachers avoid shortcuts based on processed foods.

• **Adequate preparation.** When a dish can't be completed within the class time, the teacher should prepare a sample in advance so students can taste it.

• **Good facilities.** The kitchen should be clean, fully equipped, and large enough to permit maximum visibility.

In Europe
• **Le Cordon Bleu.** One of the most famous cooking schools in the world, Le Cordon Bleu teaches students to prepare classical French dishes by demonstrating cooking techniques. In addition to a degree program (six or twelve-week courses), classes open to the public are conducted in French each afternoon. *24 rue de Champ de Mars, 75007 Paris, 33-1-555-0277.*

• **Giuliano Bugialli Cooking Classes.** Well-known cooking teacher and author, Giuliano Bugialli, offers a series of classes in the kitchen of the luxurious Grand Hotel e La Pace in Montecatini. The program is limited to twelve to fourteen participants and costs $1,650 per person, which covers double occupancy accommodations, cooking classes, a day trip to the famous Carrara marble quarry, dinners at local restaurants, and many extras. *Audrey Berman, 2830 Gordon St., Allentown, PA 18104; (215) 435-2451.*

• **Marcella Hazan's School of Classic Italian Cooking.** Marcella Hazan, author of *The Classic Italian Cook Book* and one of the stars of Italian cooking, offers an eight-day course ($1,950) in Bologna, Italy, that includes five demonstration/participation classes, a pasta workshop, field trip and banquet in Parma, restaurant meals, trips to the wine country, and accommodations. She also offers a one-week course ($1,150) in Venice at the Hotel Cipriani each autumn. *P.O. Box 285, Circleville, NY 10919; (914) 361-3503.*

• **Cordon Bleu Cookery School London Ltd.** Founded thirty-five years ago by graduates of Le Cordon Bleu, this school has no official relationship with its Parisian counterpart, but its standards are equally high. *114 Marylebone Lane, London W1M 6HH; 44-1-935-3503.*

• **École de Cuisine La Varenne.** This school has become one of the best-known in Paris. Courses are conducted in English and are tailored to the American student. *34 Rue St. Dominique, 75007 Paris, 33-1-705-10-16.*

• **Gourmet's Oxford.** A week-long, in-depth program devoted to the study and enjoyment of British cuisine. Participants attend daily demonstrations by High Table menus conducted by Oxford University's distinguished chefs. *Jean Dickens, Templeton College,*

Kennington Road, Kennington, Oxford OX1 5NY, England; tel (collect) (0) 865 (Oxford) 735422.

• **La Varenne in Burgundy.** The preparation, study, and enjoyment of Burgundy's elegant cuisine are the objectives of a one-week course hosted by Anne Willan, founder of Paris' prestigious La Varenne Cooking School. Participants prepare classic dishes, visit local markets, vineyards, and three-star restaurants. Accommodations at the restored seventeenth-century Chateau du Fey. Course is repeated six times per year; $1,980 per person double occupancy, airfare not included. *P.O. Box 15574, Washington, DC 20007; (202) 337-0073.*

Around the U.S.
• **Peter Kump's Cooking School.** Classic cooking techniques with no particular ethnic label. Full participation in once-a-week lessons, twenty-five sessions to a course. Also offering special Weekend Workshops. François Dionot, Marcella Hazan, Diana Kennedy, Paula Wolfert, and Jacques Pepin are but a few of the notables who have turned up as guest teachers. *307 E. 92nd St., New York, NY 10128; (212) 410-4601.*

• **The China Institute.** Here Florence Lin, author of *Florence Lin's Chinese Regional Cookbook,* teaches one of the most authentic Chinese cooking classes around. Limited to fifteen students, the course includes two demonstration workshops and a banquet. *125 E. 65th St., New York, NY 10021; (212) 744-8181.*

• **The Postillion School of Culinary Arts.** Madame Liane Kuony is called extremely demanding by some, harsh by others, but no one questions her abilities as a teacher of French cooking. She offers a 400-hour certificate program for people seriously interested in careers in food, as well as one-day seminars on selected subjects: soups, crepes, omelettes, etc. *615 Old Pioneer Road, Fond du Lac, WI 54935; (414) 922-4170.*

• **Chez Mimi Cooking School.** Mimi Gormezano offers a program called "Techniques and Theory of French Cuisine" culminating, after 160 hours, in a certificate. Full preparation classes on individual stoves limited to twelve students. *621 Holt, Iowa City, IA 52240; (319) 351-4071.*

• **Richard Grausman.** As a student of the Cordon Bleu in Paris in the late 1960s, Richard Grausman so impressed Madame Brassart, the school's owner, that she made him the Cordon Bleu's exclusive U.S. representative. He continued in that capacity, giving demonstration classes around the country, until 1984, when the Cordon Bleu changed ownership. Today Grausman regularly tours major cities of the U.S. teaching French cooking. *Richard Grausman, 155 W. 68th St., New York, NY 10023; (212) 873-2434.*

CHILI WISDOM

LYNDON B. Johnson once said, "Chili concocted outside of Texas is a weak, apologetic imitation of the real thing." L.B.J.'s statement adds presidential authority to the great debate about the best chili, and his use of the verb "concocted" accurately notes the elusively eclectic nature of this Tex-Mex dish. What, after all, is chili? Similar question marks abound after every ingredient used in the individualized and inventive mixing and matching that has come to be known as chili. What kind of meat? What kind of tomatoes? Should there be beans? What kind of spicing? The controversy continues unabated.

Chili Rules

However, there are those who scoff at the very existence of a differing opinion. One such folk hero was the late Frank Tolbert, who became a Texas institution. "I don't understand the fuss," he once said. "Chili should be very simple. It started as just pepper and meat." Tolbert literally wrote the book on chili, *A Bowl of Red* (Doubleday, 1967), one of the all-time classics on the subject. Tolbert's rules for chili:

• **Beans.** If you like beans in your chili, that's fine, just don't cook them in with the rest of the ingredients. And don't overdo them. The main ingredients in chili are meat and gravy. Anything else comes under Tolbert's criticism as being "silly chili" that approximates soup, salad, or hash, rather than chili.

• **Meat.** The meat should be bite-size pieces of braised or seared steak; ground meat is merely "mush or gruel" in Tolbert's candid words.

• **Spices.** The spicing of the tomato gravy is not quite so simple. Variations abound, but if one rule can be set, it is, don't overwhelm; not too much oregano (or it will be like spaghetti sauce), not too much cayenne or Tabasco or hot pepper (who wants to be a fire-eater?). And subtle flavors are never going to be found in that commercial blend called "chili powder." Use unblended, fresh spices to your own taste and satisfaction.

For those interested in making their own chili powder, there are instructions and several recipes in Bill Bridges' book, *The Great American Chili Book,* available in the U.S. for $9 postpaid from Bridges at *P.O. Box 284, Ventura, CA 78250.*

• **Chile pods.** Fresh chile pods require time and energy, both to find them and to prepare them for cooking, but the control they allow over spicing is worth the effort (they are also full of vitamins, particularly Vitamin C). The heat of the pods is *not* found in the seeds, but in the veins, or placenta, where the oils flow. Removing the veins produces a mild, sweeter flavor; if you want the hotter or more bitter flavor, chop the veins and skins into your gravy for both a full flavor and a smooth texture.

When buying fresh chiles be aware that generally the more sharply pointed the chile the hotter it is. The rounder tips indicate a more mild flavor. To retain their freshness you may freeze them after peeling and chopping.

Ristras, or ropes of chile pods, can also be bought by the foot and hung in your kitchen to dry naturally. Drying takes from two to five months, but you'll have pungent, fresh spicing at your fingertips. Note that the only difference between a green and red chile is its degree of ripeness. Dried chiles turn a dark, brick red. Chile ristras as well as excellent chile *molido* (ground peppers) and other native New Mexican foods such as blue corn are available by mail from the following companies. Most have price lists and catalogs available:

• **Spanish Trail Spice Company**
P.O. Box 279-D
5025 S. Eastern #16
Las Vegas, NV 89119

• **La India Packing Company**
520 Marcella Ave.
Laredo, TX 78040

• **El Jalapeno Chili**
2440 Canal
Houston, TX 77003

• **Mexican Chili Supply Co.**
304 E. Belknap
Fort Worth, TX 76102

Chili Cook-offs

Chili cook-offs have become major culinary events, but behind the fun of thousands of people cooling their palates with Lone Star beer are some pretty serious cooks who compete for the world championship chili award.

• The most popular cook-off has been held the first weekend of November for twenty years in the ghost town of Terlingua near the Rio Grande, but not much nearer to anything else (700 miles from Dallas; 300 miles from El Paso). CONTACT: *The Goat Gap Gazette, (713) 667-4652 or 523-2362.*
• *The Chilympiad,* the Texas State Men's Chili Cook-off, is held the third Saturday in September every year in San Marcos, with as many as 400 teams—not limited to Texans—competing. CONTACT: *Helen Schofield, (512) 396-5400.*
• *The Texas Women's State Cook-off* is held in Luckenbach each year during the first weekend in October. CONTACT: *Luckenbach General Store, (512) 997-3224.*
• But these are only a few of hundreds. One publication exists which keeps track of all the chili cook-offs around the country, as well as barbecue events, and includes rules and regulations as well as listings of winners. It's called *The Goat Gap Gazette,* edited by Jo Ann Horton and published by Judy Wimberly. The cost is $11 for 11 issues. CONTACT: *The Goat Gap Gazette, 5110 Bayard Lane #2, Houston, TX 77006; (713) 667-4652 or 523-2362.*
• An organization that gives a broader range of information on chile is the International Connoisseurs of Green and Red Chile. Affiliated with New Mexico State University, the members include professionals from restaurants and agriculture as well as chili-hobbyists. CONTACT: *Jeanne Croft, P.O. Box 5600, New Mexico State University, Las Cruces, NM 88003; (515) 646-1939.*

TOP DOGS

SEARCHING for the perfect hot dog may strike some people as a mundane exercise. They've obviously never tasted the best. While just about any frank tastes good when you consume it at a ballpark or at the state fair, there are substantial differences between the average commercial hot dog and a carefully produced "gourmet" wiener.

• **Usingers.** If we were forced to pick just one "great" hot dog we'd probably go with Usinger's of Milwaukee. Usinger's line of cold cuts reaches heights of quality and flavor rarely achieved in this country. A Usinger's wiener spends three hours in the smoker; a commercial frank may only get a ten- or fifteen-minute smoking. The entire process for making a Usinger's frank takes two days. A commercial hot dog is generally produced and packaged in about an hour. Like all of the best hot dogs Usinger's have natural casings and exhibit a subtle blend of spices. They pop in your mouth as you bite into the slightly resilient casing. Natural-casing franks can't be packaged. They are shipped in bulk and sold loose. Usinger's wieners show up throughout the Midwest and are sold in some specialty food stores and gourmet delis in other parts of the country. For a list of stores that carry Usinger's, contact: *Usinger's Sausage Co., 1030 N. Third St., Milwaukee, WI 53203; (414) 276-9100.*

• **Slotkowski's.** In a class with Usinger's are Leonard Slotkowski's wieners from Chicago. This firm has a strong—and justified—following in Chicago and also ships substantial quantities to Tennessee, Kentucky, and Florida, but it's little known on the East and West Coasts. The company can tell you if any stores near you carry its franks. (The best sausage makers prefer not to do any mail-order business because it's difficult to adequately refrigerate small quantities of the perishable franks.) *Slotkowski Sausage Co., 2013 W. 18th St., Chicago, IL 60608; (312) 226-1667.*

• **Nathan's.** Our third favorite frank is Nathan's, sold at restaurants of the same name in New York City.

Because of their perishable nature, the best franks are those that are freshest. Ask your butcher if he knows of any local sausage maker producing natural casing franks. A good perfectly fresh hot dog may taste better than a great one that's had to travel a thousand miles in a refrigerated truck.

• **Homemade.** If you want to make your own hot dogs—thereby getting the freshest possible product—you must get one of the free catalogs from Richard Kutas in Buffalo, New York. He deals largely with farmers and hunters who stuff their own sausages, but he's happy to send his catalog to anyone. It contains the home smokers, natural casings, spices, and everything else you need to create the perfect homemade hot dog. *Richard Kutas Sausage, 177 Military Road, Buffalo, NY 14207; (716) 876-5521.*

And which is the best of the everyday, commercial frankfurters in your local supermarket? We left that decision to Consumers Union, since they've researched and tested some 200 commercial nationwide brands. Their choices for best: **Hebrew National, Oscar Mayer,** and **Eckrich.**

OYSTERS OPTIMUM

O NE of the classic "best" ways to start an important meal is oysters on the half shell, gleaming on a platter of crushed ice and garnished with lemon wedges. Contrary to the folk wisdom, you don't have to give up oysters for the months that don't have an R in them. The problem of oysters "going off" in summer heat has been solved by refrigerated shipping and handling techniques. In fact, raw oysters are a near-perfect hot-weather dish. They're cool, moist, light, and refreshing, packing a lot of nourishment into very few calories. Eating oysters raw is the best way to savor the oysters' very delicate distinctions in flavor.

American vs. European

With a few exceptions, mentioned later, all oysters that come from American waters are of the same species. (And it's a different species from all European oysters.) American oyster fanciers think European oysters taste thin, sharp, and metallic—"coppery" is the usual word. Europeans find American oysters slack and insipid. The differences in appearance and flavor of the various-named oyster types all come from the environment the oyster lived in— what kind of microorganisms flourished in the water and how salty it was. There's a range of water salinity that oysters can tolerate; and where they fall in that range is what makes the biggest difference in flavor.

Saltwater/Freshwater

Mostly-saltwater oysters have an oceanic tang to them. You taste the salt as a counterpoint to the mainly sweet meat. Mostly-freshwater oysters tend to reflect more of the minerals present in their water, and taste a little sharper, acidic, or even earthy.

If you like the saltier style, the oysters to have are: Chincoteagues, from the Atlantic Ocean side of Chincoteague Island off the coast of Virginia—and Cotuits, or Chathams, both from northern Nantucket Sound, off Cape Cod. (Wellfleets are another famous Cape Cod oyster, reputedly the favorites of Diamond Jim Brady.) Next down the saltiness scale are two Long Island oysters: Box, from Gardiner's Bay near the easternmost tip of the island, and Blue Point, from the Great South Bay about half way along the island's Atlantic coast, behind the barrier beach.

If you prefer freshwater oysters, look out for Appalachicolas, from the mouth of the river of that name on the Florida panhandle, or Kent Island Oysters, from that island in Chesapeake Bay just opposite Annapolis, Maryland.

Taste Differences

Within these broad categories, taste differences from one type of oyster to another are easier to perceive than describe: no one has yet developed the equivalent of a wine-tasting vocabulary for oyster-tasting. Besides, much of one's impression of an oyster depends on how fresh, cold, and large it is. Sizes can vary even among oysters taken from the same bed, though if you like really big ones, Box oysters should be your choice, probably followed by Blue Points.

Both size and coldness are very much a matter of individual taste. Some people like oysters thoroughly iced; others say that kills their flavor. Those who make it a test of freshness that an oyster ought to writhe when you squeeze lemon juice on it obviously don't want their oysters numbed with cold.

Taste differences are more noticeable, however, in a couple of other types of oysters available in some U.S. markets. In Maine they've recently started cultivating Belons, one of the European oyster species, in waters that closely resemble those of their native Atlantic coast of Brittany. For most French oyster fanciers, Belons are *the* oyster. Americans who like the European oyster style find them superb. To others, they're just ho-hum. Puget Sound in Washington is home to two varieties of a Japanese species of oyster. Olympias are one—tiny, rare, and prized by connoisseurs. Golden Mantles are the other—huge oysters with deep, gorgeously fluted and tinted shells and a strong, clear, astonishingly rich flavor.

CAVIAR: CASPIAN IS BEST

CAVIAR—moist, lustrous black pearls heaped in a crystal dish, nestled on a bed of crushed ice—is still the epitome of luxury at the dining table. For caviar devotees, the only caviar worthy of the name comes from the sturgeon, and *more precisely from one of the three varieties of sturgeon that live only in the Caspian Sea.*

The Caspian Sea is the world's largest inland sea, bounded three-quarters by the U.S.S.R., one-quarter by Iran. Caviar fanatics unalterably believe that it has a magic combination of salinity, temperature, and biochemistry to produce the huge fish—some up to 2,000 pounds—whose tiny eggs become those precious black pearls. Caspian caviar has never been cheap and over the past several years its prices have soared at a rate that makes inflation look mild. And yet despite the strong advances in quality that American sturgeon caviar has made recently, caviar connoisseurs are still willing to pay for "the real stuff" from the Soviet Union.

This passion is hard to understand if your exposure to caviar has been limited to pellets of lumpfish roe or pea-sized over salty salmon eggs. These lesser caviars have their uses, but they aren't in the same league as first-rate sturgeon caviar.

• **Ideal caviar is fresh and moist.** With every individual egg softly intact. When you take a spoonful in your mouth and gently press the grains against your palate, they should briefly resist and then burst to release a vivid flavor—savory, sometimes faintly nutty, with a whiff of the sea but never heavily "fishy" or salty. Caviar like this should be eaten all by itself, or only with lightly buttered toast—not with the hard-boiled egg and minced onion used to disguise the defects of lesser caviars. Add a glass of icy vodka or brut champagne and you have one of the truly great gastronomic experiences of a lifetime.

For all its cachet, the cost of caviar is dictated at least as much by hard facts as by its mystique. Dwindling sources, labor-intensive methods, and the perishability of the product are reasons why beluga caviar—the most prized variety—can cost $25 to $35 an ounce.

• **The beluga is the rarest** of the three caviar-producing Caspian sturgeon. A single fish weighs up to a ton and can yield 200 pounds of roe—once in its lifetime. And it takes twenty years for a beluga sturgeon to mature enough to produce eggs. The osetra sturgeon, half the size of the beluga, matures in about twelve years, and the much smaller, relatively more abundant sevruga sturgeon produces eggs at the age of seven.

Beluga caviar has the largest grains, the softest texture, and the palest pearly hues. While neither size nor color affects the flavor, you pay a premium price for glamor. Sevruga caviar tastes very much like beluga, only slightly stronger, is darker gray or black, and has smaller and firmer eggs. Osetra caviar is the most different, with medium-sized eggs, a rich, nutty flavor and a warm brownish tint. When crushed, it exudes a clear golden oil as opposed to the dark gray of the other two. Osetra usually commands seventy to seventy-five percent of the price of beluga, and sevruga sixty to sixty-five percent.

• **Another important price factor is freshness.** The fish are netted twice a year when they swim upriver to spawn. Entirely by hand, their egg sacs are removed, sorted, and sieved to clean and separate the eggs. Varying amounts of salt are mixed in to enhance flavor and improve keeping qualities. The process is simple but the caviar is so fragile and perishable that speed, skill, and delicacy are needed at every stage.

The more mature the eggs when taken from the fish, the better they will taste—but also the more easily they can be damaged, like ripe fruit. The ripest eggs are mixed with very little salt so as not to mask their flavor—which means, however, that they remain more perishable. They are then packed in two-kilo tins and kept under constant refrigeration, to be sold as fresh as possible. This type of caviar is called molossol, a word that means "little salt." Less ripe eggs need more salt to bring up their taste, thus they keep better but never have the delicate flavor of molossol.

The best non-molossol caviars are also sold fresh; the rest are pasteurized. Pasteurized caviar can be kept without refrigeration as long as the container is unopened. It usually tastes saltier than fresh, and its grains are invariably toughened somewhat by pasteurization—but it costs perhaps only sixty percent what the equivalent fresh caviar costs.

• **Buying caviar has its pitfalls.** The complex politics of Soviet trade contracts has created a huge secondary import market. (The Iranian caviar industry has been in disarray since the revolution and is now a negligible presence in the U.S.) Major buyers from all nations resell to other importers, who in turn sell to restaurants, wholesalers, and gourmet shops—many of whom repack under their own labels. Nomenclature can be very confusing.

The most important thing an aspiring caviar fancier needs is a good supplier. The spring catch arrives in the U.S. around late July, and the fall catch usually in time for Christmas. A good supplier will usually gauge his needs and be able to start selling the fresh catch as soon as it is available. In restaurants that serve caviar, turnover is important because the longer a tin of caviar is opened the more it deteriorates.

Brands To Buy
Here are some recommendations among the major brands:

• **Romanoff.** Romanoff is probably the name in caviar most familiar to the American consumer. The company's numerous pasteurized sturgeon and non-sturgeon caviars are carried by supermarkets and gourmet shops across the nation. Its top-grade pasteurized beluga sells for around $20 an ounce. Romanoff also does a large business in more-expensive fresh caviar (mostly beluga and sevruga), much of which is repacked under private labels.

• **Petrossian.** Petrossian, the premier French caviar firm, has long been supplying U.S. importers, restaurants, and gourmet shops. It now has a retail store in New York (182 W. 58th St.) and is opening another in San Francisco. Petrossian offers only fresh caviar and only one grade of each. Quality is consistently high—particularly the osetra, which other suppliers seem to de-emphasize. Prices are competitive: about $30 an ounce for beluga, $25 for osetra, $20 for sevruga.

• **Poriloff.** Poriloff is a relatively small importer whose business is mostly wholesale. You may not see the Poriloff label often, but when you do you can trust it. The firm purchases all types of caviars with great care. Its Caspian molossols are particularly fine and even the smallest quantities are packed in tins like those in which caviar is shipped from the U.S.S.R. (Caviar seems to keep better in tins than jars.)

A large mail-order business is done by *Caviarteria* (29 E. 60th St., New York, NY 10022; (800) 221-1020). It carries all kinds of caviar and makes definite quality distinctions—for example, four kinds of beluga molossol at prices ranging from $16 to $30 an ounce. The catalog descriptions can be confusing and the lower grades are sometimes disappointing, but some very good buys are also possible.

THE BEST PASTAS

YOU don't have to be Italian to love pasta, but you do have to *buy* Italian to get the best-tasting pasta. Pastas imported from Italy taste different from those made in the U.S. because of the kind of wheat used for the flour. The imports (which cost only a few cents more per pound) are made entirely of semolina, which is flour from durum wheat, the hardest-kerneled variety of wheat there is. American pastas are made from softer wheat varieties, which have less gluten and more starch. (Some American pastas claim to be made "with" semolina, but the proportion can be very small.)

• Top brands to look for are: *De Cecco* and *Del Verde,* both made in Fara San Martino, in the southern Abruzzi region, said to produce the best pastas in Italy; *Mennucci,* made in Lucca, further north in Italy; *Gerardo di Nola* brand from Naples (another region famed for excellent pasta-making); and *Dino Martelli* of Lari, Italy.

HERBS AND SPICES

THE fact is that no one particular combination of soil and climate is optimum for every variety of herb or spice plant—and (sad to say) most of the U.S. isn't optimum for any of them. As a solution to this problem a company called *Select Origins* believes that "for every herb and spice growing there is not only a season but a place where that season is best." It seeks out the finest Turkish bay leaves, Egyptian marjoram, French tarragon, Sumatran cinnamon, Malabar ginger, Greek oregano, and so on. (American patriots, take heart: its dillweed is Californian.) It sells only the current year's crop, handsomely packaged in jars suitable for refrigerator storage—the best way to preserve freshness—together with an intelligent booklet of instructions for getting the most out of "the influential quarter teaspoon" in cooking.

• Select Origins is available largely through mail order, but is gradually expanding into fine department and food specialty stores across the country. Before long it will be offering other types of premium-quality cooking ingredients. Many of its spices are linked thematically. There are the French Essentials—tarragon, thyme, and rosemary; the Mediterranean Collection—oregano, bay leaves, and marjoram; and the Christmas Spices—cinnamon, ginger, and nutmeg. *Select Origins, 670 West End Ave., New York, NY 10025.*

SAFFRON: THE WORLD'S MOST EXPENSIVE SPICE

SAFFRON, the world's most expensive spice, imparts a rich golden color to the food it seasons: it's the saffron, for example, that makes Spanish paella yellow and gives bouillabaisse its characteristic orange-gold hue.

• **The best saffron is *red* in its raw state.** Saffron is actually the dried stigma of the *crocus sativus,* a relative of the lily. The stigma is dark yellow at the base, and gets gradually deep red at the top. It's the red portion that is most precious, so top grade *mancha superior* saffron will be ninety-five percent red with only a few yellow filaments remaining. Stigmas from about 70,000 flowers must be gathered by hand to produce one pound of saffron, a delicate task that explains saffron's price tag of $5 to $7 a gram.

• It's best to buy saffron in whole "threads" rather than ground. Ground saffron is less expensive mainly because the manufacturer doesn't use a top quality product for grinding. These leave a lot of yellow filaments and, in addition, it may be cut with a product like safflower.

• Although saffron is also grown in Mexico and Iran, *the best comes from Spain*, specifically from the province of Murcia, where it has been harvested for over 2,000 years.

PAPRIKA WITH A PUNCH

THE best paprika in the world comes from Hungary. Originally, the pepper pods from which paprika is derived came from South America and Asia. Today the best Hungarian paprika will come from one of two cities: Kalocsa or Szeged. In these areas, the growing conditions are nearly perfect. To grow properly, the pepper pods require rich soil, torrential rainstorms in the late spring, very sunny summer days, long crisp autumns, and great flowing rivers nearby. Much of the paprika found in America is simply a color enhancer for food. However, in Hungary it is an essential part of the cuisine which adds a zesty flavor as well as an appealing color.

• **Grades.** There are eight grades of Hungarian paprika. Not all, however, are available in this country. Most common in the U.S. are the sweet and the hot paprikas. Quality and freshness are important. If you buy from a good place, you will certainly get quality. (The package should say "Hungarian" or "Magyar" to be true Hungarian paprika.) Source to contact: *Paprikas Weiss, 1546 Second Ave., New York, NY 10028; (212) 288-6117.*

WHITE TRUFFLES

NOVEMBER and December are the two months of the year when fresh white truffles from Alba, in the Piedmont region of northern Italy, are available. Although canned or bottled truffles can be purchased year round, they don't match the marvelous perfume of their fresh counterparts. "The overwhelming thing is the bouquet," says Giorgio Deluca, partner in Dean & Deluca, the New York gourmet shop that stocks white truffles in season. "When we open our containers of truffles in one corner of the store, which is 3,000 square feet, the whole store smells like a forest."

Fresh truffles should never be cooked; rather, they are sliced paper thin and sprinkled over warm, delicate dishes like risotto, pasta, or even potatoes. The warm food releases the aroma of the truffle. Although Mr. Deluca admits that, at $25 to $30 an ounce, fresh white truffles are hardly everyday fare, he advises, "With such intense goodness, a little goes a long way." A one-ounce truffle can be shaved over six dishes of pasta. Mr. Deluca also suggests storing white truffles in a cold, dry place with uncooked rice or eggs, which will pick up the truffle bouquet. When you cook the eggs or rice, you'll get the taste of the truffle without actually consuming any of the precious commodity—a little bonus to you from your truffles.

OLIVES WORTH EATING

ALTHOUGH martini drinkers may not care much, serious olive eaters know that **you can't get a decent olive out of a jar or can. The reason:** those olives have been cured by a process that removes most of the olive's characteristic flavor.

A much tastier olive is one that's been packed in dry salt to draw out the bitterness while leaving the flavor of the flesh intact. Such "dry-cured" olives are sold loose, by the pound, in specialty food stores. **Look for these top varieties,** all of which come from the countries around the Mediterranean Sea. They are priced between $3 and $7 per pound.

• **Nicoises.** These firm-fleshed, black-to-brown olives from Provence are tiny (one-half to three-fourths inches long), though with rather large pits in proportion to their size. They have a rich savory taste, not notably salty.

• **Picholines du Gard.** Also from Provence, these are dark green, small-pitted olives with a strong, bright, "vegetably" flavor.

• **Calamatas.** An off-center point at one end and a pale purple matte finish distinguishes these olives from Greece. Their flesh is soft, the flavor delicate; length is about one and one-fourth inches.

• **Napthlions.** Also from Greece and also soft-fleshed, these are smaller, pale green, slightly wrinkled olives with a pungent, earthy flavor.

• **Moroccans.** About seven-eighths inches long, these olives from the western shore of the Mediterranean are very wrinkled and glisten deep black from their oil cure. They have a meaty pure flavor that is as close to sweetness as an olive ever gets.

• **Gaetas.** Italian, smooth and less shiny than Moroccans, but similar in size, color, and flavor. Both Moroccans and Gaetas are good to try on people who aren't sure they like olives at all.

GOURMET VINEGARS

SALAD fanciers rarely agree on the perfect dressing for a bowl of greenery. But one strong candidate for the world's best salad vinegar would certainly be *aceto balsamico,* the rich, dark and fruity product made for over 800 years in the small region around Modena, Italy. What makes balsamic vinegar special is its elaborate production process. The fresh juice of selected grape varieties is cooked down and subjected to carefully controlled alcoholic fermentation; then the new vinegar is lengthily aged in a succession of wooden barrels: oak, chestnut, cherry, locust, ash, mulberry, juniper. The vinegar picks up the aromatic "balsams" from the particular combination of woods and the resulting flavor is sweeter and subtler than that of ordinary vinegars.

• The most renowned name in balsamic vinegar is *Giuseppe Giusti,* whose products are a rarity in the U.S. The firm's 1972 vintage vinegar has sold for as much as $25 a pint, and its 1930 for $75 a half-pint. More easily come by in this country are the balsamics of *Monari Federzoni* or *A. Grosoli* (the latter under the name of Duke of Modena Reserve), both of which sell for about $4 a pint.

TASTES OF HONEY

NATURE often has its own processing mechanisms that allow a food its full vitality. Honey is no exception: let the bees do the work. As one beekeeper puts it, "sugar is the man-made substitute for honey." The bees' enzymes break down the complex sugar known as sucrose, so that all that remains are the simpler sugars, fructose and dextrose, which can be quickly taken up by the human digestive system—a definite health plus.

Honey's Variety

The variety of honey flavors is enough to inspire a collection. Flavors range from strong and dark through the spectrum to light and bland. Deciding on the best honey for a particular use requires experience and an acceptance of seasonal variations. An all-purpose honey just doesn't exist. Generally, blander types are best for multiple purposes.

But to help you realize the full richness of honey flavors some recommendations are in order: Cream honey is purposely crystallized to provide a thicker, pasty spread. Try it on your little finger out of the jar or on hot toast and you may never go liquid again. English Heather is a rare find; its dark color and strong flavor are well worth searching out when in England or via importers. Similarly, Sourwood, a mellower honey from the trees most common in North and South Carolina, has its own fan club. Buy Sourwood in quantity as soon as you see it in stock, since it has a short season and is quickly snapped up by people in the know.

Buying the Best Honey

If you wish to buy close to home, contact your local Beekeepers' Association for the names of reputable neighborhood producers. Although honey has its seasons, year-round mail order is a viable alternative to a local producer. Some flavors with short seasons may not be available and crystallization may be more common since the honey may be older, but mail order can generally be taken with confidence.

• **Ed Weiss Apiaries** sells under the Wilton Gold label, producing exceptional natural creamed honey. Also offers wildflower, comb, and chunk honey. Mail orders on entire line of products. *3 Whipstick Road, Wilton, CT 06897; (203) 762-3538.*

• **Crabtree & Evelyn and Scarborough & Co.** products are available at specialty food shops and department stores throughout the United States.

• **Thousand Island Apiaries** sells cream comb and liquid honey mostly in clover flavors. They will mail anywhere in the U.S. *1000 Islands, Clayton, NY 13624; (315) 654-2741.*

• **Bob Cole** is a source for Sourwood honey. *Route 1, Box 175, Blowing Rock, NC 28605.*

• **Whistle Creek Apiaries** also sells Sourwood honey, as well as five other flavors: Tulip Poplar, Thistle, Locust, Wildflower, and a Tulip Poplar/Sourwood blend. *Route 6, Box 43, Lexington, VA 24450; (703) 463-4202 or 463-2928.*

ANTIQUE APPLES

A SK your grandmother about the Duchess of Oldenburg and you'll likely inspire a mouth-watering vision of a symbol synonymous with American democracy—apple pie. You see, the Duchess of Oldenburg is a variety of antique apple, not a rusty, dusty souvenir from the attic, but an alive and growing fruit with little resemblance to the homogenized McIntosh or Red Delicious dominating the supermarket. In a business rampant with standardization, where ninety-nine percent of all commercial apple trees produce only four or five varieties, the fact that there are well over 200 varieties of antique apples available indicates how little we know about the apple.

When it comes to choice you can't beat the antiques: one is particularly good for pies, one for apple sauce, one for dessert. Lewis Hill, a "collector" of old varieties and author of *Fruits and Berries for the Home Garden* (Knopf, 1980) is critical of commercial apples simply because they are multipurpose. "An all-purpose apple ends up being a no-purpose apple," he says. Different uses bring out the best in an apple. So do different pickings. An early crop of Red Astrachan is excellent for cooking, while later in the fall it is best for eating. A commercial apple will have only one picking per season which prevents uniform ripeness and ignores subtle flavors that change throughout a season. Another advantage that antique apples have over the commercial ones is their relative immunity to disease. Developed before chemicals came into use, most of these apples have acquired a strong and natural resiliency toward many of the plagues affecting commercial varieties.

The suppliers who raise these old-fashioned delicacies cater mostly to home orchards. They sell young trees or scion wood for grafting. The rest is up to you. If you're in the neighborhood you may be able to coax an apple or two out of them, but most orchards limit the number of mature trees. The orchards we found are concentrated in the New England area but watch for an increasing number of new orchards in the Midwest.

- **Worcester County Horticultural Society**
  30 Tower Hill Road
  Boylston, MA 01505

- **J.E. Miller Nurseries, Inc.**
  5060 West Lake Road
  Canadaigua, NY 14424
  (716) 396-2656

- **Hillcrest Nursery**
  Greensboro, VT 05841
  (800) 533-2609

- **Grand Isle Nursery**
  South Hero, VT 05486
  (802) 372-8805

CHEESES

ANYWHERE that dairy animals are kept by mankind, from ewes to yaks, there is probably some form of cheesemaking still going on that began in prehistory. It obviously did not spring up full-blown as the result of a strong gourmet influence in the Bronze Age marketplace. But the quality of concentration of nourishment and flavor of fresh dairy products into a substance that not only does not spoil but often improves with age is what gives cheese its fascination and mystique.

As with any food process involving active biochemistry, local techniques, local raw materials, and local bacteria are the prime determinants. *Great cheese will always be a local product, produced in limited quantities.* Cheese does tend to acquire a reputation in direct proportion to the amount of age it can take before being considered prime, but time alone means nothing. A cheese aged rock-hard for twenty years in a Swiss mountain village is only suitable for grating into a dish to lend subtleties; its effect cannot be compared to the absolute jolt to the palate that a classic, blue-veined English Stilton, French Roquefort, or Italian Gorgonzola will deliver after only some months' actual processing.

Good cheese is not hard to find, and, thus, takes on the qualities of a commodity—e.g., the government distributes surplus quantities to the needy. Cheese that rises above being merely "good" is usually a product that reflects a certain amount of tradition. There are plenty of examples here, as well. The cheddars of England and the U.S. (notably, Wisconsin and Vermont) have graced many a humble table; versatile cheeses in the same category include Emmenthaler and Gruyère as produced in four northern European countries, the Gouda and Edam of Holland, and the excellent, firm Scandinavian variants of all the foregoing. In a different vein, the aged Italian hard cheeses add both substance and piquancy to a variety of ethnic dishes.

But for sheer ascension into the realm of epicurean experience, one country still maintains a near monopoly on the cheeses that really count as menu items. Not even French wines maintain the degree of gourmet primacy that French cheeses still enjoy. There is some logic here: The country is a vast dairy land and has been for centuries; from this natural resource, employed in myriad locales with a profound *savoir faire* (not to forget the airborne microorganisms), flows *la crème de la crème.*

For the American seeking France's best cheeses, never before have so many been available in the U.S. And quality is up, too.

Most of the larger and more serious American cheese merchants now travel to Europe reguarly.

Especially exciting is the presence in American shops of cheeses virtually unknown here a few years ago: highly perishable unpasteurized specialty cheeses made by small French farmers. It is well known that cheeses made from unpasteurized milk have more definitive character and more complexity than those made from pasteurized milk; the differences are especially noticeable in soft-ripened cheeses like Brie and Camembert, or in washed rind cheeses like Pont-l'Evêque. But unpasteurized cheeses cannot be legally sold in the U.S. unless they are aged at least sixty days. Since raw milk Brie and Camembert are usually ripe and ready to eat within six to eight weeks, one now finds legal sixty-one-day-old Brie in U.S. stores. Obviously, it is at peak ripeness the moment it goes on sale, and will remain so for no more than a day or two. Better containers for the cheese and improved air shipments have also contributed to the availability here of relatively fragile cheese. And the sixty-day aging requirement seems to have been somewhat relaxed.

What the Labels Say
There are certain terms found on the labels of some French cheeses that provide a good deal of information about their origins:

• **Appellation d'origine controlée.** About forty French cheeses are protected by laws (similar to those applied to French wines) that restrict the use of the name, and guarantee origin and traditional production methods.

• **Fermier.** Indicates that the cheese is farm-made from unpasteurized milk in limited quantity.

• **Laitier.** Signals that the cheese was made in a creamery or small factory; cheeses made at larger factories are not marked *laitier.* the *laitier* cheeses may or may not have been made with unpasteurized milk.

• **Affiner.** *Affiner* means "to finish"; the term indicates that the cheese has been acquired young and ripened by a specialist, called an *affineur,* prior to marketing. Some *affineurs* have excellent reputations and their names appear on the labels; look for *Robert Goussin,* who handles Brie de Meaux and *fermier* Camembert, or *Comte Robert-en-Brie.*

Some French cheese shops also act as affineurs, ripening young cheeses in their own cellars or ripening rooms. There are two excellent ones in Paris: *La Ferme Saint Hubert,* at 21 Rue Vignon, just off the Place Madeleine, offers over 160 different cheeses, many farm-produced; *Pierre Androuet* is the doyen of French cheese merchants, with a world-renowned fromagerie and restaurant at 41 Rue Amsterdam in Paris.

France's Leading Cheeses

Nearly 400 different cheeses are produced in France, the largest variety of any country in the world. Here are some leading categories, many of which have been widely imitated by other countries.

• **Soft-ripened.** Examples here are Brie, Camembert, double and triple creams. Soft-ripened cheeses are soft; smooth and creamy in texture, though not necessarily runny. They develop white, downy (or bloomy) rinds that form a thin crust on the exterior of the cheese and ripen it from the outside to the center, a process that takes from six to nine weeks. Brie is the most popular cheese in this category, but in fact most Brie is factory-made and rather bland; the white rind of factory-made Brie will be thicker, and may not develop the reddish-brown flecks that are the indication of natural ripening.

Brie de Meaux and Brie de Melun are the leading types of *fermier* Brie. They have richer color and more complexity of flavor than factory-made Bries, and they are correspondingly more expensive. Not all cheese labeled Brie de Meaux is authentic, however, since the name is not protected. Once cut, Brie does not ripen further. A thin, white, caky line in the center means that the cheese has not ripened fully; though it may taste good, it won't have the full complex of flavors for which the best Brie is noted. Brie that is hard or dark or exudes the smell of ammonia is past its prime.

Good Camembert is equally hard to find, since, like Brie, much of it is factory-made. There are 500 brands produced in Normandy alone, where the cheese originated. Some of the better brands that come from small factories are Vallee, Le Rustique, La Normandie. Best of all are those from Normandy's Pays d'Auge region; look for such names as Sainte-Mère, Reo, Lanquetot, Antegnac and Robert Goussin. The best season for Camembert is November through January. Whole, small (4 and one-half inch) Camemberts are preferable. They should not be hard or dried out.

Many double and triple creams are also soft-ripened, with bloomy rinds, including Boursault, Brillat-Savarin, Saint-André,

Corolle. These rich, creamy cheeses are quite luscious, though they lack the complexity of fine Brie and Camembert. Double creams contain sixty percent butterfat; triple creams contain seventy or seventy-five percent.

• **Washed Rind.** Examples: Pont-l'Evêque, Reblochon, Muenster, Livarot, Chaumes, Maroilles, Epoisses cheeses are highly prized by connoisseurs for their assertive, intriguing flavors. These cheeses are also soft-ripened but the rind is washed with brine or other flavored liquids to foster a reddish bacteria on the outer surface that ripens the cheese. Most develop pungent aromas but their interiors are milder in taste than their smell would suggest. *Best brands for Pont-l'Evêque and Livarot* are Graindoge or Lanquetot; Le Bastard for Reblochon, Ermitage for Muenster.

• **Chèvres.** (Banon, Ste. Maure, Clochettes, Crottins, Pyramide Chabichou, Montrachet, Lézay, and others) have soared in popularity. These goat's milk cheeses come in an astonishing variety of shapes: pyramids, cones, cylinders, logs, trapezoids, bells, domes, and loaves. Many have bloomy rinds; others are coated with edible vegetable ash. Chèvres are rarely pasteurized, since goat's milk has less bacteria to begin with and does not spoil easily. At perfect ripeness they should have a moist, smooth, chalk-white texture. Though some cheese lovers prefer them slightly overripe, they are over the hill if overly ammoniated, discolored or distorted in shape. They are made in every region of France, but because goat's milk is seasonal and lower in yield, chèvres made of 100 percent goat's milk *(pur chèvre)* are becoming rarer. *Michèvre* on the label indicates that fifty percent cow's milk was used.

• **Blues.** (Roquefort, Bleu de Bresse, Bleu d'Auvergne). Roquefort is made from ewe's milk. Its provenance and production are strictly enforced and protected by *appellation d'origine.* Each cylinder of white Roquefort is injected with spores of mold and ripened for three months in the caves of Mount Combalou in south-central France near Rouergue, where the special atmosphere develops its unique character. The mature cheese is white, marbled with blue veins, moist and creamy in texture, rich, salty, and piquant in flavor. It should not be bitter, overly salty, or dried out.

Other French blues are also quite good; sample the creamy, milder ones like Blue de Bresse or Pipo Crem' or those with a tangier blue accent such as Bleu d'Auvergne or Fourme d'Ambert.

CHOCOLATES

SAMPLING the world's finest chocolates is a pleasure everyone can enjoy. While most of us do it for fun, the expert editors of *Chocolate News,* the leading American publication devoted to chocolate, would argue that the pursuit of chocolate is serious business, a process of developing a discerning palate that distinguishes the many nuances chocolate masters build into their creations. Before reading their recommendations one should understand the meaning of the following terms:

• **Ganache.** Filling made of reduced cream, butter, and chocolate.

• **Gianduja.** Filling prepared of nuts (usually almonds), sugar, milk, and chocolate cream.

• **Nougat.** Whipped egg whites, boiled sugar, honey with almonds, and occasionally candied fruit.

• **Marzipan.** Melted sugar mixed with finely grated almonds.

• **Truffle.** A paste blended of chocolate, butter, sugar and cream, traditionally rolled in cocoa or powdered sugar.

• **Fondant.** Sugar, glucose, and flavorings, whipped to a paste.

• **Ballotin.** French word for box.

With these terms in hand, try the following and see if they measure up to your palate's criteria for a "best" chocolate.

Best Bars

Most chocolate connoisseurs prefer dark to milk chocolate, which can range from a dry and pungent extra-bittersweet to a cream-enriched semisweet. *Suchard Bittra* is very rich, very creamy, very bittersweet, very luxurious. If you like a slightly sweeter bar, *Tobler's Tradition* is exceptionally well-balanced—flavor, texture, and aroma are all superb. If you insist on eating milk chocolate, try *Suchard de Luxe;* it's actually a bittersweet bar with additional milk, but no additional sugar. It's also more sensual than silk. *Sarotti,* a German company, makes the ultimate overdose bar. The dark chocolate is so creamy it verges on oily, and it is intensely flavorful. Almost more than the mouth can handle, it is not for casual munching. Purge with *Lindt Extrabittersweet:* light, dryish, it's quite bitter and leaves a clean taste—great for summer. Or try *Maillard's Eagle Sweet,* the only American in the lineup, which, despite its name, is a semisweet of pleasingly creamy texture and gentle flavor.

Best Domestic Boxed Chocolate

• **Andre Bollier.** In this category Kansas City's Andre Bollier gets highest marks. Born and apprenticed in Arrau, Switzerland, Bollier left his job as head pastry chef at Singer's pastry shop in Basel to bring his art to the U.S. in the early 1950s. The chocolates he created were not for the timid and upon his death, in 1985, he left behind a family dedicated to carrying on the tradition of quality which he built up over three decades. Bollier's chocolate flavors are strong and rich; moka (sic) ganache tastes decidedly of fine coffee, while the hazelnut gianduja with crushed nougat bursts with nutty goodness. Orange butter fondant flavored with curacao rolls ingratiatingly across your tongue, the curacao lingering. The marzipan creations are, quite simply, magnificent. Exceedingly fresh and tender, they are worthy of any Swiss confiserie. Bollier's truffles have become increasingly popular, especially the Truffle Monsieur, a bittersweet ganache dusted with cocoa. *(Note that Bollier's will not ship between April and September due to the heat; this is a common practice among fine chocolate makers.) Andre Bollier, Ltd., 5018 Main St., Kansas City, MO 64112; (800) 892-1234.*

Best Fudge

Forced to choose only one we nominate a Los Angeles firm, *See's Candy,* which recently celebrated its sixty-fifth anniversary. Not for aficionados of the gooey kind that clings to the roof of your mouth, *See's* fudge is the kind your grandmother might have made if she really knew her way around the kitchen. Light and creamy, studded with generous chunks of walnut, this ambrosial confection is rich, but not too sweet. Indeed, it's possible to polish off one half-pound or so of the celestial stuff at one sitting. *See's* is an old-fashioned firm, with no-nonsense values: their creamery butter and pure chocolate are top quality, the candy is made in small quantities to ensure absolute freshness and they only make fudge with nuts. Fans with an antipathy to nuts have been known to try and eat around them. *See's* Candies are sold at 218 company-owned stores, primarily in western U.S. states, but also in Hong Kong and Disney World. *See's Candy Shops, 3423 La Cienega Blvd., Los Angeles, CA 90016; (213) 559-4911. For toll-free orders call (800) 448-7337.*

Best Packaging

Godiva. There's simply nothing more romantic than those beautifully etched gold ballotins featuring the lovely lady astride her horse. Although the chocolates presently manufactured in the United States are a shade too sweet, Godiva has probably been the major force behind American interest in fine chocolates. You can feel quite luxurious treating yourself to anything from a one-ounce mini-ballotin for about $2.25 to the impressive three-pound ballotin for $56 plus. Godiva also offers the prettiest seasonal packaging, festooning its shimmering boxes with roses, ribbons and whatever for the holidays, and tucking your purchase into smart taupe and buff striped bags. Nothing could be finer. Available from better department stores across the country or order directly from *Godiva Chocolatier, 701 Fifth Ave., New York, NY 10022; (800) 223-6005.*

Best Ice-Cream Topping

The Silver Palate fudge sauce is so thick it borders on chewy. Heat it up and revel in the luxurious commingling of chocolate, cream, butter, sugar, and vanilla that makes this the finest topping available. For serious dark chocolate lovers only, the bittersweet flavor is the ultimate in sophisticated decadence. So, unfortunately, are the prices, about $8.50 to $9.00 per sixteen-ounce jar of plain fudge sauce, with the more exotic Grand Marnier or raspberry-flavored jars also around $9.00. But if you're fond of *blanc de blancs* and beluga, you owe it to yourself to try this concoction. *The Silver Palate, 274 Columbus Ave., New York, NY 10023; (212) 799-6340.*

Best Imported Boxed Chocolates

It is more difficult to choose "best" in this category than in any other, because of the significant variations in national tastes. Overall, however, the Swiss sacrifice rich flavor for smooth texture, the British like both their chocolate and their fillings entirely too sweet, and the French have an inflated idea of the value of their offerings.

This leaves the Belgians as clear choice for makers of the finest boxed chocolates in the world: theirs have a richness and sophistication that is unequaled. And of the many companies currently extant, none are finer than *Neuhaus, Corne de la Toison d'Or,* and *Le Chocolatier Manon.* The selections from *Neuhaus* are spectacular; beautifully molded chocolates are filled with ganaches so rich, creams so delectable, and flavors so fresh and sophisticated that they rank with foie gras as a gourmet experience. *Corne de la Toison d'Or* makes a more subtle product; the chocolates of the shells housing the various exquisite fillings is creamier and richer. The nougats, giandujas, and fondants are of a superior quality that more than justifies the price. *Manon* offers a wide selection of milk and dark chocolates, combined with some unusual fillings. Its antique molds and cream from specially fed cows also distinguishes these fine creations.

Also worth trying: *Mary* and *Wittamer.*

Best Truffle

Teuscher truffles are absolutely nonpareil; these lust-inspiring nuggets are nearly obscene in their buttery richness. Of the ten varieties, the most decadent is the popular Champagne truffle—made with butter, chocolate, cream, and champagne—which is an absolute must for the aspiring chocolate connoisseur. All of Teuscher's truffles are made from fresh cream and butter with no preservatives, additives, or artificial flavors. Air-shipped each week from Switzerland, they arrive wonderfully fresh. *Teuscher Chocolates of Switzerland, 25 E. 61st St., New York, NY 10021; (212) 751-8482.*

MAPLE SYRUP

THE state of Vermont produces the highest quality maple syrup in the world. Vermont's cool mountain climate and special soil conditions are particularly well-suited to the production of maple syrup and over many generations, Vermont sugar makers have refined and perfected their art. Syrup making is akin to wine making in that no two days' production tastes exactly the same. All Vermont maple syrup is made entirely from the sap of the maple tree, but the syrup made from one grove of maple trees will have a different flavor from that made from another grove of maple trees. It takes about forty quarts of sap to make one quart of syrup, which is the amount of sap that comes from an average maple tree during the entire sugaring season.

Vermont has a Mandatory Maple Syrup Grading Law (the first state to have such a law) and its maple syrup is required to have a heavier density than the U.S. standards and to be free of preservatives. Maple Inspectors rigidly enforce this law and assist the producers in maintaining the highest quality product. In recent years, the grading standards have changed so that all syrup passing inspection is "Grade A," with the following color descriptions used to differentiate between syrups:

• **Medium Amber.** A medium amber color and a more pronounced maple flavor makes this syrup very desirable for pancakes, waffles, French toast, and cereals. A great all-purpose syrup.

• **Dark Amber.** A dark amber color and more robust maple flavor makes it the choice for buckwheat pancakes and whole wheat waffles.

• **Cooking Syrup.** A very dark amber color with a pronounced carmel flavor and the strongest maple flavor. Used primarily for cooking purposes, although some people prefer it on their pancakes.

For a complete price list and order form, write: *Henry and Cornelia Swayze, Brookside Farm, Tunbridge, VT 05077; (802) 889-3737.*

GOURMET-BY-MAIL

IMAGINE sampling Atlantic crab claws when the mercury hits 100 degrees on a Palm Springs patio or garnishing an aperitif with fresh-cut mint on a blustery snowy night in a Vermont ski lodge. Today, some of the finest regional gourmet specialties are available to customers around the country through top-flight suppliers who ship their products via priority mail services. The following is a listing of superior delicacies available by mail:

Meats & Charcuterie
Pâtés. Rich, buttery versions including black truffle, wild cèpe, duck with orange and pistachios, all-vegetable. One-pound loaves are $12 to 14, plus shipping. *Balducci's, 424 Avenue of the Americas, New York, NY 10011; (212) 673-2600 or (800) 228-8028, ext. 72.*
Virginia Hams. Authentic hickory-smoked. Traditional accompaniments are biscuits, grits, and fried apple rings. Available in quantities as small as one pound presliced ($14.98) on up to fourteen-pound whole hams ($3.55 a pound, uncooked). Shipping included. *Wallace Edwards & Sons, P.O. Box 25, Surry, VA 23883; (800) 222-4267 or (804) 294-3121.*
Quail, Pheasant, Smoked Capon. Available from a famous purveyor of American caviars. Shipping via Federal Express. For prices and information: *Michael Nelson, California Sunshine Fine Foods, Inc., 144 King St., San Francisco, CA 94107; (415) 543-3007.*

Seafood

Florida crab claws. So large that three of them weigh one pound. Caught and shipped by air within twenty-four hours. Three to five pounds are $15.75 per pound; over five pounds, $12 a pound. Surcharge for overnight delivery, $15. *Smith Knaupp's Catch of the Day, 3309 NE 33rd St., Fort Lauderdale, FL 33308; (800) 327-7723 or (305) 565-6619.*

Live Maine lobsters. The real McCoy. Prices vary between $3.75 and $5.75 per pound. Next-day air delivery costs about $30. *Phillips Seafood Co., P.O. Box 350, 35 Union Wharf, Portland, ME 04112; (207) 774-3953.*

Petrossian Caviar. Hand-packed in beluga, osetra, sevruga, and pressed types. Five ounces ranging from three and a half ounces to two-pounds three-ounces, $39 to $800. Caviar samplers cost $69 to $223. Express shipping is $24. *Pamela Krausmann's Notebooks, 496 La Guardia Place, Dept. 183, New York, NY 10012; (212) 473-8002.*

Produce & Preserves

Tomatoes. Sun-dried homegrown Ohio tomatoes packed in garlic-infused oil—marvelous with pastas, pizzas, and seafood. Three eight-and-a-half-ounce jars are $21, plus $3 postage. *Genovesi Food Co., P.O. Box 5668, Dayton, OH 45405; (513) 277-2173.*

Fresh-cut herbs. Direct from the farm to you via UPS air service. Twenty-five types ($2 each, plus shipping); potted herb plants and herb vinegars, too. *Fox Hill Farm, 444 W. Michigan Ave., P.O. Box 7, Parma, MI 49269; (517) 531-3179.*

Dried wild mushrooms. Morels, cèpes, fairy rings, and matsutake are $12 to 14.50 per ounce. Includes shipping. *American Spoon Foods, Inc., 411 E. Lake St., Petoskey, MI 49770; (616) 347-9030.*

Baked Goods

Chocolate mousse cake. Also available in orange and espresso flavors. A one-pound cake is $17.95, plus $12.95 for overnight express delivery. *Desserts by David Glass, Dept. BR, 140-150 Huyshope Ave., Hartford, CT 06106; (203) 525-0345.*

Savannah pralines. Made from an original French recipe. Available in one-pound jars and bags. Hazelnuts are $8.95, almonds $9.20, pecans $11, macadamias $16.50; plus $1.75 for shipping. *Gaston Dupre, Inc., 1515 Bull St., Savannah, GA 31401; (912) 236-9223.*

WINE: BEST GUIDE

TO the person in pursuit of the best, wine offers a happy hunting ground, a whole world of bests. For the informed palate, each great wine—and happily there are many, many great ones—is unique, irreplicable. Is Château Lafite better than Château Margaux? The question is absurd, unanswerable. Is the Empire State Building better than the World Trade Center? Just as you can say that the World Trade Center is measurably taller than the Empire State Building, you can describe Margaux of a given year as softer or harder, lighter or heavier than Lafite. But better? At those heights, *de gustibus non est disputandum:* the best wine is the one you like best—as long as you know why.

Pursuing the best narrows the focus at least a bit. The areas that are of greatest interest to knowing wine drinkers are portions of the western United States and several locales in western Europe—scattered valleys and ridges in California, Bordeaux and Burgundy in France, the provinces of Piedmont and Tuscany and one or two other isolated spots in Italy, the Rhine valley in Germany, the Iberian peninsula. Following are detailed looks at some of the world's great wines.

THE GREAT HOUSES OF BURGUNDY

THE fabled Burgundian Côte d'Or, the golden slope that follows highway N74 south from just below Dijon to just above Chagny is about forty miles long—but at some points is scarcely 100 yards wide. Within this narrow band grow the dry white wines universally acknowledged to be the premier dinner whites of the world and the soft, fruity reds with a polish and elegance uniquely their own. The best of these famous wines of Burgundy (Puligny-Montrachet, Vosne-Romanee, Nuits Saint-Georges, Gevrey-Chambertin) currently stand on a pinnacle of prestige—and of price. Are they worth it? In good years, resoundingly yes. One has only to drink a properly aged Burgundy of a good vineyard and year to understand why perfectly sane people will pay the requisite prices. The problem for most people is buying Burgundies intelligently. The Burgundy zone may be small, but it encompasses more than thirty townships whose names may appear on wine labels. Those names are multiplied in turn by many more precise *cru* and vineyard designations. And some of the vineyards are owned by upwards of thirty-five individuals or firms, each tending a plot that may range downwards in size from several acres to half an acre; any of those growers may or may not sell wine under their own names.

To simplify your quest for the best Burgundies you must be familiar with a small but important group of wine houses. These *negociants* usually, but not always, own properties in their own right in the important vineyard areas, but a large part of their activity consists of buying grapes of wine from small growers and either vinifying the grapes or aging the wine in their own cellars for distribution and sale under their own house name. The reputation and integrity of a Burgundian *negociant* can often be a surer guarantee of a decent wine than is an impressive place name. There are five Burgundian wine houses that play a major role in the wine market. Here is a report on some of their specialties.

Bouchard Père et Fils

Bouchard Père et Fils (the full name is important since there are other Bouchards) looms large on the Burgundian scene. The 250-year-old family firm is one of the largest landowners in the Côte d'Or. Its headquarters, like those of many other *negociants,* is situated in Beaune, a charming medieval and modern city that for all practical purposes divides the northern half of the zone, the Côte de Nuits, from the southern half, the Côte de Beaune (the north is usually more esteemed for its reds and the south for its whites, but that rule is not unbendable). The firm's whites include well-made and reliable Chablis and Puligny-Montrachet, especially a charming example of the latter from the vineyard called Les Pucelles, a wine worth any enthusiast's attention.

For all that, the firm's heart seems most deeply committed to its red wines, which it vinifies in the old-fashioned way for power, polish, and long life. Bouchard is the sole proprietor of the vineyard L'Enfant Jesus in Beaune Greves, and the wines from there and from its holdings in Beaune Teurons and Beaune Marconnets make a trinity worthy of any wine lover's admiration. Incidentally, they also prove that the reds of the Côte de Beaune, properly treated, can measure up to those of the Côte de Nuits. Not that Bouchard Père et Fils neglects the latter—it is the sole distributor for La Romanee, Vosne-Romanee Aux Reignots, and Nuits-Saint-Georges Clos Saint Marc. But of its own properties, it is the trio of Beaune wines that bear away the laurels. Bottles of Beaune Marconnets 1961, Beaune Teurons 1959, and L'Enfant Jesus 1929 have been judged uniformly great.

Maison Louis Jadot

When American wine drinkers see the name Jadot, they probably think first of Beaujolais, since Maison Louis Jadot in fact ships us large quantities of usually excellent Beaujolais. The firm, however, is much more than that: it is among the best all-around Burgundy houses, with an enviable reputation in France and abroad for consistent quality. Founded in 1859 and still family-owned, Jadot has holdings in some of the most prized areas of the Côte de Beaune—in the commune of Beaune itself, in Corton, in Pernand-Vergelesses, in Montrachet. Its reds are normally soft wines of great elegance and complexity, wines which well reward long aging. Jadot's white wines though fewer in number than its reds do not fall below them in quality: some experts in fact think them superior. Two single-vineyard wines form the stars of the line-up: a Chevalier-Montrachet from Les Demoiselles and a Corton Charlemagne, from the fields legend claims were once owned by Charlemagne.

Maison Louis Latour

The name Latour is equally strongly linked in the American mind with Beaujolais—and probably with high prices as well. Maison Louis Latour—founded in 1797 and now headed by the fifth Louis—has been the most prestigious name in Burgundies for some years, and its wines have drawn premium prices in both the retail and auction markets. In some respects, Maison Latour is a twin of Maison Jadot: both are medium-sized Burgundy houses; both market a full line of Burgundian wines, red and white; both are also important Beaujolais shippers. They even share ownership of the vineyard Les Demoiselles in Chevalier-Montrachet, as well as priding themselves on their respective Corton Charlemagnes. *Latour's red wine estates are a bit more varied than Jadot's:* in addition to holdings in Beaune (Greves, Perrieres, Clos du Roi) and Corton (Pougets, Grancey), Latour has good estates in Aloxe-Corton, Volnay, and Romanee-Saint-Vivant.

Maison Joseph Drouhin

The century-old firm of Maison Joseph Drouhin has recently undergone something of a rebirth. A disastrous fire in 1972 consumed a large portion of the firm's stock, and wines under its label for the next few years were uncertain quantities. Beginning approximately with the 1976 vintage, however, the house's wines once again justified its high reputation—but surprisingly in a style very different from that with which it had been previously asociated. Where before Drouhin had made softer, "feminine" wines (wine language is hopelessly chauvinistic), it now produces firmer, "masculine" wines of greater depth. Drouhin differs from previously mentioned houses in that its greatest holdings are in the Côte de Nuits, where powerful red wines are made the norm than in the Côte de Beaune. However that may be, it is certain that Drouhin bottles some of the most glorious reds of the entire Côte d'Or.

Maison Prosper Maufoux

Maison Prosper Maufoux functions more nearly like a pure *negociant* than any of these other firms. Founded in 1860 by the mayor of Beaune whose name it still bears, the house of Maufoux has very few actual holdings of its own, and most of those cluster around Santenay in the extreme south of the Côte d'Or. Its high reputation for quality and consistency has been built by the canniness of its buying and by the uniform care it expends on the wines it purchases. Like other *negociants,* Maufoux carefully tends its wines in its own cellars, maturing them in its own fashion so that they are truly its wines when they go on sale. The results are consistently successful, especially with white wines, which seem to be the firm's forte.

BORDEAUX SUPERIEUR

T HE section of the universe that wine lovers know as Bordeaux encompasses much more than the city of that name. For oenophiles, the city is only the dockyard from which the wine they cherish is shipped, and the real Bordeaux consists of the shallow hills and slopes that run down to the Gironde and its two tributaries, the Garonne and the Dordogne. *That* Bordeaux forms one of the largest fine wine areas in the world and is home to wines of legendary status and prestige.

Important as the name Bordeaux is in wine lore, in law it is the least of the region's *appellation controllée* designations. Simple red or white Bordeaux are at best everyday table wines. Above them rank the wines of more precise regional designation—Médoc or Entre-Deux-Mers for instance. Above those stand wines from individual townships, like Margaux or Pauillac or St. Emilion, and beyond those, rising in tiers like the Alps, lies the whole range of château or estate wines, from the foothills of *cru bourgeois* up to the exalted summits of the five *premiers crus* of the famous 1855 classification:

Château Lafite, Château Latour, Château Margaux, Château Haut Brion, and Château d'Yquem—a roll call of princes of the vine.

Big as the wine-producing area of Bordeaux is, it falls into readily intelligible units. The river Gironde and its two tributaries form an inverted Y flowing northward to the Atlantic. On the west bank of the Gironde, north of the city of Bordeaux, lie the great châteaux and communes of the Médoc: Margaux, Pauillac, St. Julien, and St. Estèphe. Starting right at the edges of the city and running south along the west bank of the Garonne (the western leg of the Y), the great estates of the Graves district stretch right up to the beginnings of the communes of Barsac and Sauternes, from which come some of the world's finest dessert wines. Almost straight north of these last two (across both legs of the Y) the estates of St. Emilion and Pomerol occupy a low plateau above the east bank of the Dordogne. All the areas between make wines, both red and white, that range in quality from drinkable to respectable, but the Médoc, the Graves, Sauternes and Barsac, and St. Emilion and Pomerol unquestionably produce the highest quality wine of the region and some of the finest wine in the world. All of these are what most wine lovers today mean when they speak of Bordeaux wine.

Bordeaux wine is not cheap, but it is less expensive than Burgundy, and there is much more of it. *The canny oenophile buys his Bordeaux as futures whenever he can,* since at that point its prices are generally as low as they will ever be. Since red Bordeaux is above all a *vin de garde,* a wine for laying down and keeping, its market price increases with every year of bottle age. To buy a fully mature Bordeaux, if you can find one in the first place, can be quite an expensive undertaking. Better to buy young, keep them yourself, and only drink them when they are ready. Most people in this country—and in France also, alas—consume Bordeaux far too young and thereby lose one of the greatest pleasures wine can offer.

At the present, the 1970s are only now coming ready and will certainly give pleasure for years yet, but there are next to none of them in the shops and precious few in restaurant or private cellars. 1970, 1975, 1978, 1979, and 1982 are also years that promise long life and excellent quality.

The Sauternes and Barsac wines are superb dessert wines with a luscious, uncloying sweetness. They also take bottle age well, and in some superior years are capable of almost Biblical life spans. Most of the other Bordeaux white wines are quite frankly negligible. Even the Graves, most of whose châteaux make both red and white, does not produce a single white wine to measure up to the standards of Burgundy. Dry white Graves can be very, very good, but it is rarely great.

That is no handicap to the region's reputation, however. Its red wines amply sustain it, and for the real wine lover the fascination of Bordeaux is endless—vintage differs from vintage, commune from commune, chateau from chateau. One estate plants more cabernet sauvignon, another a higher percentage of merlot. One harvests early, another late. One vinifies in steel, another in wood. One macerates the musts on the skins for a week, another for two weeks or more. Each small variation affects the wine and makes each chateau's wine a totally different product from its neighbors, a personal expression of each owner's care and style. That intense individuality is the essence of Bordeaux.

VINTAGE RHONE

FOR those who love French wines but tremble at the prices of the famous estates of Bordeaux and Burgundy, the wines of the Rhone Valley represent a godsend. Big, robust, and long-lasting, they can, at their best, offer the elegance of fine Burgundy combined with a very individual authority of their own. And they do that at prices well below the sale of either Bordeaux or Burgundy.

The Rhone is a long, picturesque, and sometimes dangerous river frequently given to flooding. Below Lyons, where the Saone joins it, it flows relatively straight south to the sea. On its way it waters two separate wine areas: a northern zone lying between the ancient Roman legionary towns of Vienne and Valence, and a much larger southern zone around the colorful city of Avignon. Rhone wines come in every range, from simple blended Côtes du Rhone—some of which offer excellent value, like Jaboulet's Table du Roy—to regional A.C. *(Appellation Controllèe)* wines, like Crozes-Hermitage and Châteauneuf-du-Pape, up to individual estate bottlings. The northern zone contains many names famous in wine lore—names like Condrieu and Côte Rotie, St. Joseph, and Hermitage. For most wine lovers, these are destined to remain names only. Production is small—in some cases only sufficient to supply shops and restaurants in adjacent towns, rarely more than enough to supply France. *Travelers should seek out the Côte Rotie and St. Joseph, since they are the finest products of the region.*

Hermitage and its neighboring, but lesser appellation, Crozes-Hermitage are, however, regularly shipped to the United States in significant quantities, which is a blessing. Hermitage is a wine for people with patience. Like many Rhone wines, it is harsh, tannic, and unyielding when young. A badly made Rhone wine, young, looks like mimeograph ink. A good one is dark, deep and not forthcoming. In a fine year like 1978—one of the best vintages the Rhone has seen in a long while—the wines will take between five and ten years to come around. Production in this zone will never be significantly larger than it is now. The hillsides are steep and stony, the climate harsh. The narrow terraces of vines are painstakingly maintained, but in many fields the work can only be done by hand because of the pitch of the land. So perhaps it's just as well Hermitage is not a popular wine—that leaves enough of it to satisfy the patient few who love it.

The southern section of the Rhone produces a great number of different wines in large quantities—everything from simple Côtes-du-Rhone table wines up to the most famous name of the area, Châteauneuf-du-Pape. Most of the lesser appellations tend to be fruity, medium-bodied, dry and charming, not unlike a Beaujolais with a bit of spunk. Châteauneuf, however, rises well above that level, and while it rarely, if ever, challenges Hermitage, a good Châteauneuf can provide pleasures aplenty: warmth, roundness, soft generous fruit wedded to fairly intense vinosity—in short, the epitome of the best qualities of southern wine.

The wines of Châteauneuf offer the charms of variety and surprise as well. With wine making growing more and more regulated (to our benefit, no doubt), Châteauneuf remains one of the few areas where viticultural free spirits can express themselves. The *Appellation Controllée* legislation (which was the first in France and the model for later French laws) permits a total of thirteen different grape varieties to be used in making Châteauneuf-du-Pape. No growers use all thirteen. Most, in fact, restrict themselves to a few, choosing them carefully to suit their soil and climate. But this still means that there can be great differences in the style of wines made even on neighboring estates. So there's always a chance to learn something new about Châteauneuf, or to happen on an unknown gem of a wine. In line with current trends, much Châteauneuf-du-Pape is being vinified lighter to be drunk younger: most will be ready to drink at five years old, though a vintage like that of 1978 might take longer. To a slightly lesser degree than Hermitage, Châteauneuf enjoys a long bottle life without deterioration.

SHERRY DISTINCTIONS

SHERRY has more than its share of mysteries, which may be why Edgar Allan Poe chose a cask of it to star in his little chiller.

But the appetite for Amontillado that led Poe's victim to his doom is, in contemporary America at least, exceptional, and the biggest mystery about sherry is why, with all the habits we've borrowed from Britain, the taste for it hasn't become as widespread here as there. Perhaps if the *Mayflower* had carried some of its usual cargo—it was a sherry transport, making regular runs from Cadiz—we might all be sherry sippers right now, celebrating Thanksgiving with a Fino or an Amontillado. It would certainly be our gain, since the pleasures of sherry are among the most varied and affordable in the wine spectrum.

Distinguishing Sherries

It doesn't take the deductive powers of Sherlock Holmes to see that one of sherry's problems on the American market is the mystery of its names—plural. There are five major kinds of sherry, and each sherry house may have a separate brand name for its examples (plural) of each kind, so there is a great multiplication of labels for essentially similar products. The few sherries that have succeeded in the United States are those that have achieved brand identification—drinks like Williams & Humbert's Dry Sack and Harvey's Bristol Cream, which are happily drunk by thousands of people who probably are blissfully unaware that they are sipping sherries at all, much less anything as recondite as an Oloroso or a Palomino and PX blend. Their success shows at least that Americans do have a palate for sherry, if they can once be brought to taste it.

All true sherries are fortified wines made under precisely regulated circumstances within a zone of 50,000 acres in Spain, the most important town of which is Jerez de la Frontera: the name sherry is a corruption of Jerez. The predominant grape in Spanish sherry is the Palomino, with some Pedro Ximenez—usually just called PX—mixed on occasion for sweetness. All genuine sherries are vinified in the same way, in an elaborate system known as the solera. This involves the regular blending of fresh wine with older, so that vintage distinctions are eliminated and a consistent house style can be perpetuated year after year as the older sherries "educate" the younger ones.

These few facts remain constants for all sherries. Beyond them is where the differences and the major mysteries arise. The fact is that human control over the making of sherry is very limited. Sherry differs from almost every other wine in the world in that each and every separate butt of young wine chooses its own style. No one knows why or how, but two barrels of wine standing side by side, stored under identical conditions and filled with the same juices of the same grapes from the same harvest, can develop in radically different ways, one growing light and pale and dry and heading towards the Fino class, the other darker, fuller, heavier, ending up as Oloroso. Whatever brand name or names the sherry bottle may bear, its label will also give you all the essential information you need to know about the general style of the wine, since the five basic types of sherry conform to consistent standards.

Fino

Fino normally is the driest of the sherries and the most popular as an aperitif or cocktail wine. Once upon a time there was even a fad for sherry martinis (about an ounce of Fino to two of gin) in the United States. Fino is the kind of sherry most drunk by the Spanish themselves and the kind most familiar on the market here. Such familiar brands as Gonzalez Byass's Tio Pepe and Pedro Domecq's La Ina are good, representative Finos, distinguished from each other largely by house style. Fino should be pale, often straw colored; it should be dry and crisp, with a pronounced aroma. Serve it chilled and keep opened bottles in the refrigerator. And don't keep them too long: Fino is the most fragile of the sherries, and once opened it will oxidize. Drink a bottle in two weeks if you can, in a month at most, or re-cork into smaller bottles if you take only an occasional sherry.

Manzanilla

Manzanilla is the sherry Spaniards prize above them all, but it comes from a very small area within the sherry zone and is very difficult to find in the United States. Particularly suited to seafood, manzanilla is pale, very light-bodied, and tangy: according to sherry lore, you should be able to smell and taste the salt breezes of its oceanside home in it. In most areas of the United States, you will be lucky to be able to taste it at all: it is included here largely for the sake of completeness.

Amontillados

Amontillados are darker than Finos: they can run the whole range of ambers, from light to dark, and that color spectrum reflects their textures as well. They tend to be fuller, with varying degrees of dryness, though never really sweet. The characteristic flavor of Amontillado can usually be described as nutty: think of toasted almonds and you're in the right area. Amontillados make good apertif or simple sipping wines. They are very versatile and can be served at almost any temperature. They also keep better than Fino once opened. Byass, Domecq, Hartley & Gibson, Sandeman, and Wisdom & Warter all market good Amontillados.

Oloroso

Oloroso can be the most rewarding of all sherries to the wine lover. Whether dark gold or dark amber or some shade between, Olorosos characteristically show a beautifully burnished golden edge when held against the light. Oloroso has great body and softness; it runs from fully dry to medium sweet. These wines are the most complex and interesting of the sherries. The dry ones make superb aperitifs and after-dinner drinks; the sweet ones should open new vistas to cordial drinkers. Particularly fine dry Olorosos are made by Williams & Humbert and Sandeman; the latter also makes a lovely sweet one. With this class of sherries it is particularly important to pay attention to all the information the label provides, since each house tries to indicate whether its style of Oloroso is mellow or fully dry, and even to differentiate further if it makes several Olorosos.

Cream Sherries

Cream sherries usually achieve their high degree of sweetness by blending some Pedro Ximenez or, more rarely, Moscatel grapes with the basic Palomino. People blessed or cursed with a sweet tooth drink cream sherries any time, anywhere, at any temperature, but they really show best as dessert wines or cordials, served at room temperature after dinner. Bristol Cream is the most famous of these, but there are many other interesting ones. Especially good are Wisdom & Warter's Delicate Cream and Hartley & Gibson's Cream. These sherries and Olorosos do not need refrigeration after opening; they keep quite well for relatively long periods of time.

PX Sherries

There is one final wine to mention, though it falls outside the regular categories. PX sherries, made largely or entirely from Pedro Ximenez grapes, are relatively rare but, oddly enough, easier to find in the U.S. market than Manzanilla. They are always very dark, often almost syrupy in texture, and frequently very long aged. Their flavor marks them off from other sherries, and even for confirmed sherry drinkers it is something of an acquired taste— though definitely one worth acquiring if you have the chance.

BRANDY: COGNAC/ARMAGNAC

BRANDY can be a satisfying drink on many other occasions, but it belongs at the end of a meal. Brandy sends you away from table convinced, at least for the moment, that you are a fine fellow, the world a decent place, and that civilization has a chance after all, despite taxes, typhoons, and baseball strikes. This wonderful elixir comes in many varieties. Strictly speaking, the term brandy covers any spirits distilled from fruit. Grapes, pears, plums, apples, cherries, peaches—all can yield a brandy. But more commonly brandy means a distilled wine—cognac and Armagnac are the prime examples—and the other sorts are usually indicated by an additional adjective, such as the blackberry brandy that used to figure in American households as a cure for childhood colic.

Those fruit brandies can be exquisite. The French, for instance, make a whole range of them that they call *alcools blancs* (because they are colorless) from fruits as diverse as strawberries (Fraise), raspberries (Framboise), pears (Poire), and several varieties of plums (Prune, Mirabelle, Qvetsch). Like the related Slavic plum brandy, Slivovitz, none of these is ever sweet and, depending on their maker, they can range in quality from crude to marvelously elegant.

But for all that, the true brandies for connoisseurs remain the grape brandies. More exactly even, hard-core brandy lovers use the word to mean only spirits derived from wine—and most of the time they are referring only to the most famous of those, cognac and Armagnac. The most common error about brandy is to think that cognac means brandy and brandy cognac, which is simply not the case: cognac is just one kind of the many brandies possible.

Cognac
Cognac is a regional name for a brandy made by the distillation of wine in the Charente region of west-central France, a bit northeast of Bordeaux. The wine cognac originates from is undistinguished at best, and the process of distillation and aging that it undergoes seems to purify and refine it as well as concentrate and subtilize it. Certainly no one tasting the base wine would ever expect it to result in a drink as polished as cognac.

The Charente district which produces the wine for cognac has been carefully divided up into zones that yield brandies of greater or lesser quality. The most prized area is the Grande Champagne, the next Petite Champagne (it's important to note in this case that Champagne here means simply 'field' or 'countryside': it has nothing to do with sparkling wine). After that comes Borderies, Fins Bois, Bons Bois, Bois Ordinaires. Most commercial Cognacs are blends of distillates from several districts, but the major distilleries also sell Cognacs labeled "Champagne" or "Fine Champagne" or "Grande Champagne;" by law the first two can contain only brandies from the two best areas, and the latter must contain brandy from the Grande Champagne zone exclusively. Some smaller makers will also sometimes produce a labeled Borderies or Bons Bois, but that is very rare even on the French market.

VSOP on a cognac label stands for Very Special Old Pale. French law requires that any cognac so named must be aged minimally four years. Since cognac is a blend, this means that the youngest spirit in the bottle will have aged at least four years, while the other components of the blend may be considerably older. The varying proportions of the blend are closely guarded house secrets, but it is no secret at all that the different price levels of a single distillery's several cognacs reflect the increasingly higher percentages of old spirits in them. Each cognac firm maintains in its cellars barrels of older brandy from different districts and different vintages. These are almost never bottled straight, but are instead reserved exclusively for blending. Some few very fine cognacs may contain individual brandies from turn-of-the-century harvests, or even older. The house of Hennessy is reputed to have the largest reserves of old cognacs in the world.

Despite its meaning, a VSOP is not very often pale. Cognac emerges from the still completely colorless and only gradually takes on tone from the oak barrels in which it ages. The older the spirit, the darker it gets, ranging from a pale gold in comparative youth to deep reddish amber in venerable old specimens. VS or VSOP, the name of the zone, a specific claim of age—these are the significant parts of a cognac label. The name of Napoleon or Lafayette or any other real or fictitious Frenchman has absolutely no legal standing and establishes nothing at all about the brandy in the bottle.

Good cognacs are widely available in the United States. Probably the best known is Courvoisier, whose VSOP is a sound, representative cognac: pale amber-brown, with a rich, mellow flavor marked by great smoothness. Remy Martin, also widely distributed, tastes more smokey, with almost a hint of peat, and while still smooth—that is cognac's great forte—possesses a more distinctive character. Martell's stands about midway between those two, while Hennessy's VSOP seems fuller and weightier than either. Also interesting is the less known Bisquit: it is darker than most of these, elegant and harmonious, with a decidedly nutty flavor.

Armagnac

Though most connoisseurs consider cognac the world's supreme brandy, a small but vocal group of heretics would award the crown to Armagnac. The two brandies have been rivals for several centuries now, and many brandy drinkers have happily spent their lives trying to determine which one they preferred, so the issue does not demand immediate resolution. Happily so: this is one case in which the thirst for knowledge is really its own reward.

Armagnac too is a true brandy made from distilled wine. As with cognac, the grapes that go into Armagnac produce a very undistinguished wine. Once again it is the process of distillation that performs the magic and transforms mediocre wine into magnificent brandy. Most Armagnac makers function on a much smaller scale than cognac distillers, and even the few larger houses carefully preserve the traditional, regional manner of making brandy. Even the Armagnac still is distinctive: an old-fashioned contraption of gleaming copper and tubing that looks like an alchemist's dream, it differs markedly from the pot still used in cognac, which Armagnac traditionalists claim puts out a brandy that does not age well or last as long as that from their apparatus.

Armagnacs are generally speaking darker than cognacs in color and fuller in body. If the outstanding features of cognac are smoothness and elegance, the great virtues of Armagnac are warmth and generosity. Armagnacs are light on the palate, warm, with just the slightest touch of sweetness in the finish, and they often show a tiny, pleasing rasp that reminds you of their hearty Gascon origins. They range in color from pale gold to deep reddish amber, even sometimes shading into warm brown, depending on their barrel age. Their aromas are among their chief attractions: as they open in the snifter they reveal successive layers of scent— wood and prune and earth and truffle.

A really fine old Armagnac's perfume will linger almost a day in the emptied glass. In Gascony, Armagnac professionals never drink or even taste the brandies they are buying for blending: they simply rub a few drops between their palms to warm and evaporate them and then make their decisions by scent alone. A fine old Armagnac is one of the highest pleasures the world of wines and spirits affords. Vintage dated Armagnacs are not common because like cognac most Armagnacs are blended from several vintages, but when they can be found they are invariably worth their hefty price tags.

For everyday drinking, or for those who have never tried any Armagnac, several widely distributed brands are highly commendable: Marquis de Caussade, Marquis de Montesquiou, Larressingle, Sempé—all are first-rate, absolutely representative Armagnacs. Three of them—Caussade, Larressingle, and

Sempé—also make truly lovely older Armagnacs which, though not always available, are always worth asking after.

CHAMPAGNE IN EXCELSIS

THERE are probably as many misunderstandings about true champagne as there are imitation champagnes. Most people use the term loosely to mean sparkling wine, but that just isn't so. The real article is a sparkling wine made from the blending of three varieties of grapes only: Chardonnay, Pinot noir, and Pinot meunier. It must be made only by the rigidly regulated and costly process known as the *methode champenoise,* the champagne method. Finally, it is made only in a sharply limited zone in France within the region of Champagne. By French law and European Common Market agreement, only a wine that meets all those requirements can call itself champagne. Everything else is just sparkling wine.

Many people legitimately wonder if the distinction isn't too subtle for the human palate to discern. Is champagne really that different, that much better? Or is it all a matter of swank and PR hype? Even the most rabid champagne fanatic will admit that there are plenty of pleasing sparkling wines in the world, wines whose virtues are describable variously as lightness, fruitiness, charm, vivacity, et cetera. What the true champagne lover prizes in his favorite drink is all of those plus—plus elegance, plus complexity, plus depth, plus breed, plus finesse, plus all the perceptible but indefinable qualities that add up to Character and Style with capital letters. Champagne has them because of its unique combination of soil, grapes, and technique as well as hundreds of years of experience of its makers.

Let's start with soil. First, it has a peculiar composition: a thin layer of loamy black earth over a bed of chalk. Not fat, not rich, this chalky sub-soil keeps the grapes lean and acidic and lends the finished wine some of its austerity and attack. In addition, the Champagne vineyards lie very far north; they are in fact the most northerly in Europe. So the climate stresses the grapes and forces them to develop an intense individuality. The richer soils of Burgundy, Chardonnay, and Pinot noir produce lush vines, big with fruit. In the harshness of Champagne, those same grapes make more acid than sugar, more spine than softness.

People are often surprised to find that red wine grapes go into the making of champagne, but they are in fact a major component of the wine. So important are they to fine champagne that some purists refuse to make or drink a *blanc de blancs* (a white wine made entirely from white grapes) as not being champagne at all. Tasted side by side, the differences between Champagne containing red grapes and a *blanc de blancs* are immediately apparent: the dark grapes give depth and roundness to the wine, while the product of all white grapes tastes more monochromatic. Particularly popular, in fact, is the pink or rose champagne, which is available in vintage, non vintage, and prestige cuvée bottlings. Virtually every major house now produces a pink champagne. *Blanc de blancs* champagnes with their lightness and delicacy make perfect cocktail or aperitif wines and accompany hors d'oeuvre very well. The more traditional champagne blends, having greater body and substance from their Pinot noir grapes, better accompany the more substantial courses of a dinner.

The Methode Champenoise

Champagne represents one of the ultimate triumphs of art over nature. At any point in its making a dozen things can go wrong, and many of them do. Wines sour. Bottles explode as pressures inside them build too high. Wine is spilled in the process of disgorging. At every step wine can be lost—and the steps are numerous. The first stages of champagne making resemble those of any other wine, save for the speed with which the juices are separated from the skins and pulp to prevent the reddening of champagne's characteristic pale gold color. After the initial fermentation, however, champagne undergoes a series of processes that sound like a list of medieval tortures: racking, fining, second fermentation, bottling, riddling, aging, disgorgement.

Most of these processes must be done by hand, and most take a great deal of time. Riddling, for instance, involves placing the bottles neck inwards in what look like large sandwich boards. There they incline at gradually steepening angles until they almost stand on their heads. Every day they are carefully shaken and twisted, one by one, until the sediments thrown off by their second fermentation accumulate against their corks. This single step can take up to three months, at which time they are ready for disgorgement—the extrication of that wad of sediment—and their final topping-up and corking.

All champagnes go through these same processes. What makes one different from another are the whole range of variables at the beginning—the grapes and the vineyards and the vintage—plus the variables introduced by the vintners. All champagnes are a blend—first, of the three kinds of grapes, second, of grapes from different fields (usually from entirely different districts within the champagne zone), and, third, of wine from different years. This is why the great majority of champagnes marketed are N.V.—nonvintage. Those nonvintage champagnes constitute the core of each maker's production, and each has pride in maintaining a distinct and recognizable house style. Just to give some broad examples: Laurent Perrier and Taittinger tend to produce pale wines, light-bodied, with delicate aroma and a tiny suggestion of sweetness in the finish; while Pol Roger and Bollinger are more deeply golden, heavier-bodied, with pleasing toasty aromas and long dry finishes. Achieving this kind of consistency from year to year requires considerable artistry of the master blender, who will sometimes use upwards of thirty separate wines to get the harmony he seeks.

The other common departure from the nonvintage norm is vintage champagne. It is not always better, but it is always more costly. Vintages do not occur in champagne: they are declared. Champagne houses will bottle a vintage only when they think they have a harvest distinctive enough to make a wine superior to, or at least different from and as good as, their normal blended wine. Even in a very good year, not all champagne houses will declare a vintage. In 1973, '75, and '76, most champagne houses made a vintaged wine; in 1978, many houses did so; in 1979, only a few.

Cuvées Spéciales

Most champagne houses also market what are known as *cuvées spéciales*—that is, special blends of wines superior to their normal *cuvée*. For these, each house has a different and jealously guarded formula. In general it is safe to say that the wines going into *cuvées spéciales* will be drawn from the highest rated communes and will occasionally include large admixtures of fine old champagne from the house's reserves. Almost invariably, a champagne firm's *cuvée spéciale* will embody the house's highest levels of the wine-maker's art. These can be really exquisite wines—champagne *in excelsis,* so to speak.

Whether the champagne is nonvintage, vintage, or *cuvée spéciale,* one fact remains true for all: once bottled, champagne does not improve. Bottle age does nothing for it other than, eventually, kill it. You hear tales of remarkable old bottles of champagne that have miraculously retained the sparkle of youth; miracle is what it is. Like most white wines, champagne should be drunk within a few years of bottling—it is emphatically not a wine to lay down for long-term keeping.

D.O.C.G.: ITALY'S BEST

SINCE 1963, connoisseurs of Italian wine have looked for the letters D.O.C. on labels, the Italian guarantee of a wine's authenticity, much like France's *appellation controllée. But quality control on Italian wines reached new heights in 1981 when Italy's more stringent denomination, the D. O. C. G.* (Denominazione di Origine Controllata e Garantita) *was awarded for the first time.* The classification indicates that a wine has been tasted periodically throughout its production by members of the D.O.C. commission and has met their standards for quality. This is in addition to the authenticity requirements of the D.O.C. concerning a vineyard's location, soil composition, type of grape, and cultivation procedures.

Although over 200 Italian wines have won D.O.C. status, only a handful have qualified for D.O.C.G. The 1980 Brunello di Montalcino, a full-bodied Tuscan red, was the first to win the designation. Some others attaining the D.O.C.G. rank are: Barolo, a red from Piedmont; Vino Nobile di Montepulciano, Barbaresco, and Chianti.

In order for a wine to be eligible for D.O.C.G., all of the winegrowers authorized to produce that type of wine must agree to submit their product to the D.O.C. commission. The risks are considerable: if a wine fails the taste test, it loses its D.O.C. status and the right to call itself by its own name for one year. During that year, it can be sold only as "table wine" and will command a considerably lower price. Albana di Romagna has applied for the rank. Albana di Romagna is the first white wine to seek the prestigious classification.

Because of the time required to age the wines after they are bottled, the D.O.C.G. wines were not available to consumers until 1985.

CALIFORNIA: SORTING OUT THE FINEST

CALIFORNIA has become twentieth-century America's dream capital in so many respects that it's hardly surprising that it should be a wine paradise too. Perfect climate, a wide variety of soil types, access to the very latest and finest in agricultural or biochemical technology, even a relatively long-established tradition of viniculture; the only other requirements are a few inspired wine makers to show the way and some passionate palates to follow it, and neither of those has been lacking in recent years. As a result, California wines have captured into the international spotlight.

There are three separate items to sort out for a basic grasp of California wines, and no one of them is simple. First is the amazing number of kinds of wine produced in the state. Where a Bordeaux château of a hundred acres will make one wine, bearing its own name, a California wine maker with half that acreage may turn out six or seven or more different wines—a merlot and a cabernet, a zinfandel and a pinot noir, a chardonnay and a sauvignon blanc, and a gewurztraminer and a chenin blanc. He may make some of them in several styles, dry or sweet, still or sparkling, normal vintage or late harvest—and he may distinguish between different lots of the same wine by vineyard labeling, like the famous Heitz Cellars Cabernet Sauvignon from Martha's Vineyard.

That's only the first difficulty. The second is the variety of California's grape growing regions, from the Napa and Sonoma valleys in the north all the way to San Diego in the south. It's like having every wine climate from the Rhine to Jerez distributed through a single state—and obviously all zones are not equally suited to all wines.

The third complexity, when you get past those two, involves the question of quality. California is blessed in that the weather variations from vintage to vintage are rarely as marked as those in Europe, but not all wine makers are equally talented.

Most wine drinkers approach California wines with some knowledge of European ones. This can stand you in good stead in coming to terms with California wine types. *The premium wines almost unanimously bear varietal names; that is, they are named for the grape that makes the bulk of their contents.* The law requires that this be minimally seventy-five percent, but the best exceed that. One hundred percent varietals are not uncommon, and eighty-five to ninety percent is about average for fine wines. Many vintners give exact proportions on their labels, along with much other useful information—sugar and acid levels, for instance.

Most of the varietals used in California will be familiar from European contexts, primarily French and German. Those of greatest interest and success in California are Merlot, Pinot Noir, and especially Cabernet Sauvignon for red wines and Sauvignon Blanc (Bordeaux), Gewurztraminer (Alsace, Germany), Riesling (Alsace, Germany), and, above all, Chardonnay (Burgundy, Champagne) for white wines.

The grape that may be practically considered a California native, the Zinfandel, has recently been discovered to derive from the southern Italian Primitivo. In the hands of California vintners it makes a pleasing, light Beaujolais-style wine. For the wine enthusiast seeking a taste at once unique to and absolutely characteristic of California, Zinfandel is the grape to watch.

Wine makers in California have simplified for themselves the geographical complexities of viticulture in the state by dividing it up into five climate zones—which only makes things more difficult for the amateur, since a single valley, like Napa, can fall into three separate zones. Useful as those zones are to growers, the serious wine drinker will probably get more real utility from learning a few broad areas and the names of their best vineyards and best grapes. Almost all the really distinguished wine comes from the coastal counties. Sonoma, Mendocino, and Napa are the northernmost, lying north and slightly inland of San Francisco.

These counties are home to some of California's finest vineyards: *Beaulieu* (some consider its Georges de Latour Private Reserve Cabernet the finest example of that variety California produces); *Buena Vista* (the original estate of the "father of California viticulture"—Agoston Haraszthy—and the home base for Zinfandel in California); *Château Montelena; Château St. Jean* (which in its short history has already set benchmarks for white wines, especially for Chardonnay); *Domaine Chandon; Fetzer* (reds, especially Zinfandel and Cabernet); *Gundlach-Bundschuh* (a lovely Merlot plus other reds and whites vinified in a very elegant European style); *Heitz* (Cabernet, especially Martha's Vineyard); *Kenwood* (red wines, and big ones, for laying away); *Louis Martini* (trust the Special Selection varietals); *Mondavi* (greatest success with whites, especially a fine Fumé Blanc); *Stag's Leap* (Cabernet and Merlot); *Sutter Home* (White Zinfandel); and *Trefethen* (Chardonnay).

South of San Francisco, the vineyards of Alameda, Santa Clara, San Benito, and Monterey counties produce some extraordinary wines: *David Bruce* (big, big Chardonnay and Zinfandel); *Monterey Vineyard; Ridge* (some of the finest Cabernets and Zinfandels in California: wines for keeping.).

BEST WINE RESOURCE: U.S.

FOR the professional or serious amateur, the finest single resource in the United States for the world's best wines is The Chicago Wine Company. Started by John Hart and Philip Tenenbaum, out of a shared enthusiasm for fine wines, the firm now holds in excess of $3 million worth of fine and rare wines in inventory which it sells primarily through sealed bid auctions. The company's long-standing policy of accurately describing every bottle listed in its catalog insures purchasers of getting exactly what they are expecting. Their most recent catalog offered 4,397 different lots of red Bordeaux wines from pre-1900s to 1983s. Twice a year the company hosts black-tie, gourmet tasting dinners featuring some of the world's greatest wines. These dinners are timed to coincide with "live" fine wine auctions conducted by Patrick Grubb, Master of Wine. For more information about the company and its auctions, CONTACT: *The Chicago Wine Company, Dept. BR, P.O. Box 48027, Chicago, IL 60648; (312) 647-8789.*

PREMIER WINE EVENTS

THERE is a handful of absolute must-do events in the wine calendar, and they are spread far and wide over the globe and calendar. Here is a short list of the biggest, most prestigious, and the most enjoyable of them.

Los Angeles
The site of the Heublein Premiere National Auction of Rare Wines. Heublein's auctions were the first really important wine auctions held in America, but their future is uncertain and they are being held only every other year at present.

Chicago
The only major U.S. city in which wine auctions are conducted on a regular basis. The Chicago Wine Company conducts eight auctions per year and Christie's holds four per year. The Chicago Wine Company offers insured temperature-controlled storage facilities for out-of-town purchasers.

England
Christie's holds about forty, Sotheby's about thirty, wine auctions every year. The lots offered range from inexpensive wines to collections of fine and rare vintages. There is an auction almost every week in London. In addition to Christie's and Sotheby's, there is a third major fine wine auction company worth exploring—International Wine Auctions. For information, CONTACT: *Christie's Wine Department, 8 King St., St. James', London SW1Y 6QT;*

(01-839-9060); Sotheby's Wine Department, 34-35 New Bond St., London W1A 2AA; (01-493-8080); International Wine Auctions, P.O. Box 760, London SE1 9DG; (01-403-1140).

Paris

There are regular wine auctions at the Hotel Drouot on the Left Bank. See the *International Herald Tribune* for information.

California

The annual Napa Valley Wine Auction. A past version of this charity event presented to the wine world the first offering of the Mondavi-Rothschild wine. Michael Broadbent presides. For information: *Napa Wine Auction, P.O. Box 141, St. Helena, CA 94574.*

The California Wine Experience (held in late October) is a major annual event. Under the sponsorship of *The Wine Spectator,* the event brings together professionals and amateurs of wine for three days of tastings, seminars, dinners, and awards. For information: *The Wine Spectator, Opera Plaza, Suite 2040, 601 Van Ness Ave., San Francisco, CA 94102; (415) 673-2040.*

Champagne

A visit to the cellars of one of the great champagne houses is not to be missed. At most of them, guided tours (in English, French, or several other tongues) are regularly available. Write: *Comité Interprofessional du Vin de Champagne, 5 rue Henri-Martin, 51200 Epernay, France,* or *The Champagne News and Information Bureau, 220 E. 42nd St., New York, NY 10017.*

Burgundy

Every autumn the lovely town of Beaune is the scene of the Trois Glorieuses and the annual auction of the wines of the Hospices de Beaune. Bidding here usually establishes the price level for all Burgundy wines. Many of the activities of the three glorious days are restricted to members of the Chevaliers du Tastevin and to wine dealers (the wines auctioned are the current year's vintage, in bulk), but the spectacle and the excitement is for everybody. For information, contact the *French Government Tourist Office.*

SCOTLAND'S SINGULAR SINGLE MALTS

THOUGH bourbon drinkers may be reluctant to admit it, Scotch fanciers know that the world's best whiskies are the glen whiskies, single-malt Scotches. For decades a treasured almost-secret of British connoisseurs, single malts are at last beginning to make an impression in America: there are about twenty different brands available in retail shops. Scarce, relatively costly, and definitely distinctive in flavor, single-malt Scotches will never be everyone's tipple, but for those with the palate for true and intense Scotch flavor, they are unquestionably the whisky of choice.

Single-malt Scotch is the ancestor of all Scotch whisky, the original form of what is now the world's most popular liquor. The major difference between conventional Scotch and single-malt whisky is the fact of blending; the second distinction is what is used in the blend. All blended Scotches use some single malts in their mix, but the proportion varies greatly from firm to firm. It is very rarely as much as fifty percent, equally rarely less than twenty percent.

Glen whiskies, on the other hand, are completely unblended. They are made exclusively from malted barley—that is, barley that has been allowed or been induced to sprout. The purpose of that is to convert the seed's starches to fermentable sugars, a process that occurs naturally during germination. The green malt, as the sprouted barley is called, is then dried—smoked, almost—over peat fires. This important step imparts a great deal of flavor to the finished whisky, and many of the differences between one glen whisky and another depend on the degree to which the peat smoke permeates the malt. After that, the dry malt is ground and mixed with Highland spring water—the quality and source of the water being another major determinant of the character of the final whisky. Yeast, added to the mash, turns it into a kind of watery beer. This wort, as it is called, requires two distillations to convert it into raw whisky. It will then need anywhere from eight to twenty years aging in oak barrels to complete the process and metamorphose it into one of the world's finest sipping liquors, a single-malt Scotch.

Almost all malt whiskies come from the Highlands of Scotland. Three regions are particularly prized: the eastern Highlands, where the Glen Livet—probably the most famous malt whisky—and the Speyside malts originate; Campbeltown; and Islay. The last two lie on the west coast of the Highlands. The eastern malts are prized for their comparative lightness and great elegance, the western malts for their fuller body and smoky pungency. Those are only the grossest distinctions, however. The single-malt fan soon discovers that the variations from distillery to distillery, even within the same region, are at least as pronounced and important as the regional differences. One malt whisky differs from another in the same way that two adjacent Bordeaux châteaux make distinctive wines.

In blind tastings with very experienced and enthusiastic consumers of single malts, the most popular brand, Glen Livet, finished dead last, while the most exotic, with the strongest, most pronounced peat-and-smoke character, placed first. That was Laphroaig, a ten-year-old from Islay, the area generally reputed to make the fullest glen whiskies. Most non-Scotch drinkers (and some Scotch drinkers) tasting it for the first time find Laphroaig medicinal in flavor; iodiny is the most common adjective. For many single-malt devotees, however, Laphroaig is the ultimate whisky. Glen Livet, on the other hand, is the most easily appreciated of the glen whiskies, in that its comparative lightness of body, gentle, almost subdued peat flavor, and great elegance make it resemble the popular blended Scotches more than the Islay malts. If it is like blended Scotch, however, it is certainly the cream of the crop, and a drink sure to be prized by anyone with a taste for any form of Scotch.

Between those two poles are a whole range of single-malt whiskies that vary from one another in body and flavor and assertiveness. Some particularly commendable examples are Glenmorangie (nice peaty aroma, medium body, nice tang), Glendullan (very full, very smooth), Glenfiddach, Glen Grant, and Glenronach. These are all around ten or twelve years old, which most experts consider optimum age for any Scotch—after that, they begin to fade a bit if left in the barrel. Bottle age of course makes no difference at all, as long as the seal is tight.

BEST BEER: U.S./INTERNATIONAL

AS with wine, there is also an art to brewing, choosing, and tasting a beer. Chemically more complex than wine, beer has somehow been downgraded into that ultra-cold, thin, thirst-quenching liquid that seldom commands the respect given to wine. But knowledgeable beer lovers know there is a fascinating range of fine brews from virtually every country, labels sporting thousands of styles from ale to weizen, stout to pilsener, boks and exports and lights and browns by the score. Understanding the subsets of brewing methods can aid in clearing the froth.

For all the styles of beer the recipe remains deceptively simple: barley, water, hops, and yeast are the main ingredients. First, barley is soaked and heated into malt. This releases fermentable mash known as *wort*. Hops are added and boiled and then yeast is permitted its testy chore of converting the sugars to alcohol and carbon dioxide during fermentation.

There is a certain amount of continuing life in all beers and the debate over additives and pasteurization stems from this fact of brewing. Pasteurized beers are made more stable and thus travel better for larger markets and have a longer shelf life. But there is a subtraction in such additions and most connoisseurs agree that pasteurization alters the natural living complexities of fermentation and carbonation. The Campaign for Real Ale in Britain has successfully prevented their treasures from being pasteurized and the only German beers which are pasteurized are those which are canned or produced for export. You can be sure that most Germans drink from the bottle or the tap of their local *Biergarten*.

Top- and bottom-fermented beers have distinct tastes. The relatively high temperatures employed in the production of top-fermented beers make their flavor best realized without severe chilling. The German cities of Cologne and Düsseldorf, as well as areas of Belgium, produce top-fermented beers. All English ales, porters, and stouts are top-fermented. These beers are marked by a strong, individualistic flavor, although their alcoholic content, body, and color can vary tremendously. Bottom-fermented beers are generally cleaner ones which are thirst-quenching, lighter in body, and less zesty than ales. The German lagers of Munich and Dortmund are bottom-fermented as are all pilseners and most American beers.

But thanks to the brewmaster, excellent tastes abound in beers of all styles and certain standards exist for such tastes. The best beers have a wonderful complexity, a medley of the related yet distinct aroma, taste, and aftertaste. A singular beer is a boring beer; personality and courage are the keys to an outstanding beer. The balanced combination of hops, malt, water, and yeast makes a great beer.

Of the ten experts consulted by *The New Book of Bests* all agreed on one thing: *there is no best beer.* This not only has to do with the subjective element of taste, but also with the immense variety of brewing. As with wine, one beer is particularly suitable for after dinner or a mid-morning snack; then in turn would not be acceptable as an accompaniment with a meal; and, seasonally speaking, the heat of the summer your favorite beer will be quite distinct from the one which warms you on a cold evening. *The expert tasters chose ten beers for their clear representation of a particular style or for their reputation as being in a class by themselves.*

Dortmunder Kronen
From the oldest brewery in the largest brewing city of Europe, Dortmunder is a pale gold, with a clear, slightly toasty, and delicate taste.

CD Pils
A pale pilsener from Stuttgart's Dinkelacker brewery which produces beer in the Munich/Bavaria tradition. More malty than pilseners tend to be, and therefore also less bitter, which some tasters found to be a negative trait.

Mönschof Kulmbacher
Another of the Bavarian style beers, this is also malty, pale yet slightly more amber in color than the Dortmunder or Dinkelacker. It is sweeter and heavy with a nice bitter coming during the finish.

Samuel Smith's Pale Ale
The deep amber of the Pale Ale sparkles with a sweet, caramelized flavor and a fruity, fragrant aroma.

Taddy Porter
The Taddy Porter is a beautiful, foamy black, resembling, in one taster's words, Coca-Cola. It gained consistently high marks for its big, full body and temperate malty sweetness.

Theakston's Old Peculiar Ale
Another British example. This ale is quite unique, brewed in the "old" style which combines light body with dark, rich color and malty flavor. The dark head is filled with small bubbles.

Pilsner Urquell
Czechoslovakia's treasure, this golden lager has a marvelous head whose power extends to its taste—one taster described the first sip as a "hit." It has a pleasant hoppy bitter, more so than the majority of lagers, which keeps it from being syrupy. Pilsner

Urquell is often seen as the epitome of a balanced brew.

Aass Bok
From Norway it is brewed in the bock style, unusual because it is a larger but with a dark, stout color. Slightly sweet and rich, it is a heavy beer with a zesty personality.

Biere de Paris
One find from France is of the rare *biere de garde* style and called Biere de Paris. Its winey qualities are the most pervasive— no surprise from the land better known for grapes than for barley. It is not only bottled like a wine, but is meant to be "laid-down" or conditioned like one also. Its beautiful dark amber shade gives off a fruity and clean aroma.

New Amsterdam Amber Beer
The one example of the United States' brewing, it hails from one of the growing number of "boutique" breweries which are producing the finest American beers. These breweries are recapturing traditional methods in top-quality, specialty beers. New Amsterdam Amber Beer is the infant child of the Old New York Beer Company and an extraordinarily fruity and estery brew. Some tasters compared it to champagne. It has similar complex and subtle flavors as well as tiny amber bubbles that grace the head. Its long taste turns only slightly bitter as it finishes. The real test of New Amsterdam, now sold only on a small scale around New York where it is brewed, will be in competition with the other coast's gold mine micro-brew—Anchor Steam. The steam process of brewing is the only one indigenous to the United States, invented out of necessity because of the lack of refrigeration in the old pioneering days. "Steam" is an exaggerated term referring to the warm temperatures at which this beer is brewed. Both Anchor Steam and New Amsterdam are changing the meaning of beer in the United States.

CREAM OF THE COFFEE BEANS

CHOOSING the best coffee from the wide array available can be confusing. We consulted leading experts including coffee buyer Joel Schapira, author of *The Book of Coffee and Tea,* for advice on selecting the world's finest coffees. Following is a list of some of the best:

Sumatra Mandheling
Grown near Padang, Sumatra, in the Indonesian islands, this is a smooth but heavy, syrupy-rich coffee.

Guatemalan
The hard bean varieties grown above 4,500 feet are the best; look for beans from the Antigua and Cobán districts.

Jamaica Blue Mountain
The 7,000-foot Blue Mountains produce this aromatic, sweet-tasting coffee, one of the world's most famous. Make sure it's the real thing. Other Jamaican varieties don't have its attributes. Its rarity makes it expensive, about $20 per pound.

Kenya AA
The "AA" rating is the highest applied by the Kenyan government; smooth, mild, with a delicate acidity.

Hawaiian Kona
The only coffee grown in the U.S., the tiny crop thrives on the lava-encrusted hillsides of the active volcano, Mauna Loa. It's rare, which tempts some handlers to blend it with less expensive beans. Make sure you're getting 100 percent Hawaiian Kona.

Celebes Kalosi
Another rare Indonesian variety known for the rich flavor and body that characterizes these island coffees. (Note: Celebes island is also known as Sulawesi.)

Yemen (or Arabian) Mocha
The term mocha often designates a chocolate flavor, but that's not the case with this famous, old coffee. It's named for the Red sea port of Mocha, where it's grown, and is uniquely smooth and full of body.

• Not all coffee is labeled with its bean name; some are designated instead by the method which was used to roast the beans. Beans are roasted to different degrees of darkness to bring out their particular flavor; the darkest roasting of all is called Italian roast, traditionally used when making espresso. (Espresso is the way the coffee is *brewed,* not a type of coffee bean.) For the richness of espresso without quite so much bite, try Spanish, Cuban, or French-Italian roasts, which produce a lighter-colored bean than the Italian roast. A French roast is smoother yet, and can be blended with an even lighter Viennese-roasted bean. For just a hint of dark roast flavor, try a Brazilian roast—not to be confused with Brazilian coffee. Other roasting designations that you may encounter are Full City, City, and Light City roasts, each a progressively lighter degree of roasting.

• The world's best coffee beans won't produce the world's best coffee *if they're not fresh.* Be belligerent about freshness. After green coffee beans are roasted, they'll remain fresh only for about two days. Shop around for a specialty store where they roast the beans in small quantities every few days, or every day, ideally. Once the coffee is ground, it will remain fresh for about seven to ten days, if stored in a glass jar in the refrigerator.

READING TEAS

AT 10¢ a cup (for the finest and rarest) the best tea has always been accessible to everyone, from Chinese mystics to British merchant princes—two key groups in its growth as a universal drinking experience. Naming "a" or "the" best tea is silly since "favorites" usually win out, but well-trained taste buds and an awareness of tea terminology can improve one's enjoyment.

Tea Types
Fine tea is ultimately recognized by its taste, attained from quality plants and a careful manufacturing procedure. There are three major tea types:

• **Black tea.** An all-purpose, strong but unbiting tea, it is fermented, allowing a higher concentration of flavor-producing oils to penetrate the leaves.

• **Green tea.** Is completely unfermented and the quality of this delicate light tea is, therefore more dependent on the actual plant rather than the process.

• **Oolong.** Is the half-and-half of teas. It is semi-fermented, producing a nice balance which is often blended with the richer black teas but equally enjoyed on its own as a lighter beverage.

A blend of tea doesn't necessarily mean a compromise in quality; in fact, special blends are specifically created for their superior flavor. However, the excellence of the blend depends not only on regional climate, soil, and growing season but also on the youth and uniformity of the bud size and the "wither" and "twist" of the leaves. Although these qualities are not easily discernible to the average consumer's eye, it is best to buy from merchants who sell loose bulk tea. The advantages include economy—often fifty percent savings over pre-packaged teas—and also the freedom to buy smaller quantities which allows for one's own taste-testing and experimentation in blending. Tea merchants often buy pre-blended teas from wholesale importers, carry a large variety of excellent unblended teas, and/or blend their own varieties.

Blending Teas

When blending your own tea, basic guidelines determine the best combinations of flavors and quantities. Tea experts suggest using a strong, full-bodied black tea (Keemun, Darjeeling, or Assam) as a base to be mixed with smaller quantities of a lighter or uniquely flavored tea such as Oolong, Lapsang, or Jasmine. Gunpowder is generally agreed to be the best of the green teas, although because of the lack of manufactured changes, such quality will be reflected by seasonal ups and downs. Of the Oolongs, Formosa (Taiwanese) is the best, surpassing the Oolongs from China.

Brand names of the larger, more established companies should not be disregarded even if the advantages of buying bulk are many. Prepackaged teas that successfully balance excellence and consistency are Boston Harbor's Darjeeling blend and Fortnum & Mason's varieties. Fortnum & Mason has several blends available in top-quality tea bags as well as a greater variety loose in tins.

Fortnum & Mason's tea buyer especially recommends their Formosa Oolong which is picked from particularly young buds. Many of these blends are more difficult to obtain than loose, bulk teas, but, of the most readily available (some supermarkets are even stocking it now) Jacksons is your best bet. But a word of warning about pre-packaged teas: there is a limited quantity of good tea in the world, and when a company gets too large, their quality is necessarily going to be sacrificed for consistency.

FIVE

PERSONAL GOODS

SHOPPING: STREETS AND STORES

IN one sense, all the world's a store and each of us a shopper who strolls through the merchandise, picking and choosing according to our tastes and our pocketbooks. However, there are some special places where most (or more) of the world's finest personal goods can be purchased. Following is an international listing of shopping meccas, supplemented by a roster of some of the greatest department stores in America.

London

The hub of the finest shopping is Bond Street, which is situated in the heart of Mayfair, the mecca for Britain's royalty, political rulers, and captains of commerce. The spokes (not literally) on this hub are Savile Row, Piccadilly, Regent Street, Dover Street, Jermyn Street, Burlington Arcade, Grafton Street, Curzon Street, and others. A brief listing of the shops, boutiques, and stores offering most of the finest goods in the world would run to the hundreds. A sampler would have to include: *John Lobb* (shoes and boots); *Alfred Dunhill* (tobacconist); *Turnbull & Asser* (shirts); *A. Sulka* (men's clothing); *Spink & Son* (antiques); *H. Huntsman* (men's clothes); *Swaine, Adeny & Briggs* (gloves, umbrellas); *Lock* (hats);

Burberry (coats, rainwear); *Rolls-Royce* (autos); *Henry Maxwell* (shoes); *Hatchards* (books); *Floris* (soaps, perfumes).

London is possessed of what most people consider the ultimate store on earth: *Harrod's* on Brompton Road. The anecdotes about the range of goods and services available (or temporarily out-of-stock) run from elephants to exotic earrings. Over 5,000 employees offer prompt service and direct answers to your inquiries. If they don't have it now, they'll get it for you. Other leading London stores are: *Fortnum & Mason* (Piccadilly), which besides being an exceptional department store also has a legendary food section, one of the world's best; *Liberty's* (Regent Street) with its famous mock-Tudor wall is especially good for its own cotton prints, leather goods, tweeds and velvet coats, Persian rugs, and a huge assortment of scarves; *Marks & Spencer* (Oxford Street) has a number of locations throughout London and rates best for selection of medium-priced wares.

Paris

The glamorous world of Paris shopping revolves, logically enough, around that area between the Champs-Elysees and the Seine, where the *grand couturiers* have their salons—names like Givenchy, Courrèges, Chanel, Balmain, Dior, Lanvin, Cardin, and others. They set the pace for the fashionable, who buy the originals, or the growing group who indulge in the *prêt-à-porter* fashions. The chief shopping thoroughfare is the Rue de Faubourg Saint-Honoré, and its satellites the Avenue Montaigne, Avenue Georges V, et al. A day of shopping in these environs will be very costly, so some time might be best spent simply appreciating the beauty and elegance of the wares. A sampler: *Hermès* (the original atelier sells the world's finest leather goods and includes the Paris branch of *John Lobb,* the London bootmaker); *Alexandre* and *Carita* (hairdressers); *Cartier* (Jewelry); *Chichen-Itza* (rare leathers); *Porthault* (luxury linens); *Baccarat, Christofle, Lalique, Georg Jensen* (glass, silverware, china); *La Civette* (tobacconist); *Le Nain Bleu* (toys); *Galignani* (books); *Francois Villon* (shoes); *Louis Vuitton* (luggage); *Fauchons*—the finest and most famous of Paris's food stores, *Petrossian, Fouquets, Maxims, Lamazere* (gourmet foods).

Among Paris's best department stores are: *Aux Trois Quartiers* (oldest in the city, merchandise generally of very good quality); *Forum des Halles* (the newest—a super modern shopping complex that has great variety but lacks the charm of the *old* Paris); *Galeries Lafayette* (probably the best known, a classic all-in-one emporium).

New York

The maxim is: if you can't buy it in New York, it hasn't been made yet (or isn't made anymore). The bewildering variety of goods offered in the city (and the boroughs) requires weeks to sort out in person and all the good stuff is not just on Fifth Avenue in the 50s (or satellite streets like 57th, Madison Avenue, and Park Avenue). Your *best deal* for diamonds and cameras is on 47th between Fifth and Sixth, top art is housed in the SoHo Galleries, great bargains are available on the Lower East Side, Russian Sable from the wholesalers in the 20s, etc.

But if it's luxurious ambience you want, then the shops and stores along and around Fifth Avenue are your happy hunting ground. A sampler: *Burberry's, Brooks Brothers, Paul Stuart, Ted Lapidus, Armani, Valentino, Pucci, Roberta di Camerino, Ferragamo, Botticelli* (clothes); *Gucci, Mark Cross, Hermès, Mädler, Dinoffer, T. Anthony, Crouch & Fitzgerald* (leather goods, luggage); *Tiffany & Co., Harry Winston, Cartier, Gubelin, H. Stern, David Webb, Buccellati, Bulgari, Van Cleef & Arpels* (jewelry); *Steuben, Baccarat, Scully & Scully, A La Vielle Russie, Tiffany & Co.* (china, glass); *Wally Frank, Nat Sherman, Dunhill* (tobacconists); *Zabars, Balducci's, Dean & Deluca* (gourmet foods); *F.A.O. Schwartz* (toys); *Hammacher-Schlemmer* (unusual gifts); *Rizzoli, Brentano's, Scribner's* (books); *Kenneth* (hairdresser); *Caswell-Massey* (pharmacy).

New York has more good *big* stores than any city in the world. Among them: *Macy's* (the world's biggest and one of the nicest to shop in, if a bit crowded; quality generally good); *Saks Fifth Avenue* (great range of fine items); *Bloomingdale's* (great selection, some unusual items, caters to *au courant* clientele); *Henri Bendel* (known for its jazzy displays and up-to-date merchandise); *Bergdorf Goodman* (a classic store that balances new and old); *Lord & Taylor* (genteel and traditional in its lines and look); *Bonwit Teller* (carries a number of very exclusive labels and logos—*Missoni, Galanos, Hermès, Turnbull & Asser*). The *Trump Tower* is also a place to find some of the world's best names for quality merchandise; and lastly, if you're wondering why *Neiman-Marcus* is not listed, the answer is—they don't have a Manhattan store. They do have one in White Plains, Westchester County, about forty minutes from the city.

Beverly Hills

Although this opulent offspring of Hollywood fortunes has many fine places to shop, its most famous street (and one of the best known in the world) is Rodeo Drive, which attempts to assume all the best names into the most condensed and expensive blocks of retailing in the world. A sampler: *Bijan* (appointment required, men's merchandise for the very rich); *Sassoon* (hairdresser); *Bottega Veneta, La Bagagerie* (leather, handbags); *Carroll & Company* (men's clothes); *Williams-Sonoma* (kitchenware); *Pierre Deux* (country prints); *Don Loper, Fred Joaillier* (men's fashion), *Frances Klein* (jewelry); *Bally* (shoes).

Beyond Rodeo Drive the area defined by Bedford and Canon Drives, Wilshire and Santa Monica Boulevards offers more shopping opportunity. Larger stores include: *Bonwit Teller, Neiman-Marcus, I. Magnin, Saks Fifth Avenue,* and *Bullock's-Wilshire.*

Palm Beach

The magnet here is Worth Avenue, populated by elegant specialty stores where the very rich shop when not entertaining or being entertained in the palatial homes that distinguish Palm Beach society. Whereas other leading shopping bazaars may include people with normal incomes, the odds at Palm Beach are that every fourth person you see has a million to spend. There are 200 shops, plus the Esplanade, a beautiful courtyard with a fountain ringed by more shops. A sampler: *Lilly Pulitzer* (patterns alive with her trademark hues); *Purple Turtle* (children's clothes); *Gucci's* largest U.S. store; a *Bonwit Teller* (specialty shop); *Sara Fredericks, Martha* (formalwear, ball gowns); *F.A.O. Schwartz, Hermès, Valentino, David Webb, Charles Jourdan, Mila Schön,* and many more.

Rome

The Via Condotti is the throughfare most associated with the finest Rome has to offer. Here you will find *Valentino* (premier Italian fashion creator); *Bulgari* (jewelry); *Valentino-pui, Richard-Ginori, Janetti* (furniture, housewares); *Gucci* (the plush home office), among others. More names to seek out: *Brioni, Angelo, Battistoni, Caraceni, Cucco, Cifonelli, Polidori* (clothing); *Ferrara* (silver, porcelain); *Giusti* (sporting goods); *Al Sogno* (toys); *Soria* (coins); *Righini* (luggage). Also: stroll the Via Borgognona, a pedestrian mall with flowers and fine goods.

Milan

The way to walk and see the best merchandise in this city is to start at the lower end of Via Monte Napoleone and then make a U-shaped pattern through the via delle Spigna and the via Manzoni. A sampler of names to look for: *Mila Schön, Baralta, Giorgio Armani, Versace, Fendi, Missoni, Ferre, Krizia* (clothing).

Madrid

The major streets here are the Calle Serrano and Calle Ortega y Gasset. A sampler: *Sanz, Duran* (local style jewelry); *St. Laurent, Courrèges, Celene, Hermès;* generally, the area is dominated by famous brands made in other countries.

Geneva

Rue de Rhone is the place to look for fine things—especially jewelry, watches, and chocolate. Look for: *Bazanger* (cultured pearls); *Gilbert Albert, Gerald Genta* (jewelry); *Max Reby* (furs); *Davidoff* (tobacconist), plus high-fashion boutiques.

Stockholm

If you want to find the best here, start on the Birger Jarlsgatan where you'll find *Svenskt Glas* (markets the leading crystals—*Orrefors, Kosta Boda,* and others—in a Tiffany-like atmosphere); *Gustavsbirg Utstallning* (china, ceramics); *Nordkalott Shopen* (Laplander wear); *Ivan Petersson* (furs); *H. Bukowskis Konsthande, S. Magaliff* (antiques). Elsewhere look for: *Kurt Decker AB, Argentum* (silver and gold).

Dublin

Grafton Street has most everything you'll want in the form of two department stores: *Switzer & Company* and *Brown, Thomas & Company.* Also: *The Fine Arts Showroom* (antique silver); *H. Johnson Ltd.* (blackthorn articles); *Cottage Industries, Ltd., The Dublin Woolen Co.* (handmade Irish clothes); *Kilkenny Design Workshops* (furniture, household items).

Brussels

The shopping tip here is to look for the Belgian specialties: chocolate, lace, tapestries, pewter, and fine shotguns. Names to check: *R. Pompe* (pewter), *Henrion Wolfers Frères* (jewelers); *Vlaminck, Butch* (men's clothes); *Maison du Chasseur & Mahillon Reunis, E.J. Binet, Missiaen, Poliakoff, l'Artisan* (guns); *Val St. Lambert* (crystal, glass); *Chaudoir* (tapestries); *Vinche* (pipes); *Dandoy, Wittamer* (bakeries); *Loix, Dergent, Manufacture Belge de Dentelles* (lace). Best department store: *L'Innovation.*

Munich

Among shopping streets the toney three are: Maximilianstrasse, Briennerstrasse, and Theatinerstrasse. The hub of this superb shopping display is the *Hotel Vierjahrzeiten*. On the Maximilianstrasse you'll find at least a dozen top art and unique dealers. On the Theatinerstrasse look for top fashion designers. A sampler of stores and shops: *Rosenthal, Nymphenburg* (German china); *Kohlroser* (cameras); *Henckels* (cutlery); *Rothmuller, Butschal* (jewelry); *Sohnges* (optical wear); *Loden-Frey* (loden coats, Bavarian wear); *Gert M. Weber* (furniture); *Dallmayr* (gourmet foods). Also, visit the underground shopping center beneath the *Stachus,* Munich's main square.

Moscow

At No. 3 Red Square, the enormous **GUM** department store often offers goods that are virtually unobtainable at any other retail outlet in the Communist bloc countries. Its vastness alone qualifies it for inclusion here, which is not to say that a shopper should expect to find anything like the variety and assortment of goods sold by even modest Western department stores. Displays and marketing techniques have evolved to something approximating U.S. 1930 sophistication. Nonetheless, no one ever visits Moscow without shopping **GUM.**

Montreal

The Paris of North America exudes the Gallic influence that makes it Canada's most stylish city, even with the ascendancy of Toronto as the business center. Shopping is concentrated *underground* in Montreal in a series of 'Places'—*Ville Marie, Bonaventure, du Canada, Westmount Square, Complexe Desjardins*. You'll find most of the top fashion names and myriad other products there. Above ground *Holt Renfrew* is the store of choice, followed by *Ogilvy's, Eatons, The Bay,* and *Simpsons* (Canada's version of Sears).

Toronto

All the money has flowed into Toronto in the last two decades and its shopping areas mirror this. The single best gathering of merchants is *Hazelton Lanes,* over fifty boutiques running from *Chloe* to *Davidoff.* Some fine stores are: *Dacks* (men's shoes); *Birks* (jewelry); *Creeds* (ladies' wear); *Davids* (leatherwear).

Buenos Aires

The *Avenidas Alvear, Arroyo, Quintana,* et al. are the distinguished addresses of some of the best shopping in Argentina's capital city. Many of the names adorning other international boutiques can be found here. In particular, look for native Argentinian items from its earlier colonial periods—silver, leather, and textile artifacts, and *objets d'art*.

Tokyo
As in Hong Kong, the top hotels offer some of the finest choices, i.e., *The Okura, The New Otani*. After visiting these, move on to *Harajuku* and *Motoyama,* and then two department stores— *Takashimaya* and *Isetan.* Some specialties to seek: pearls, computer goods, and native crafts, i.e., lacquered wood creations and textiles.

Hong Kong
The city that rivals New York for its ability to sell almost anything you want to buy—and at a discount in many cases. First stop for men should be one of the many fine tailors, so they can get your measurements, and you can order from home after that. Best general resource for top names are hotels like the *Peninsula, Mandarin,* and *Regent.* Other places to look are the *Landmark Shopping Centre, Lane Crawford, Chinese Merchandise Emporium,* and the *Prince's Building.* For a pleasant open-air shopping experience visit *Stanley Market.*

Sydney
Double Bay is the area to frequent if you're looking for fine stores and, if you desire one-stop shopping then the only place to go is *David Jones,* a 150-year old emporium that has almost everything. Special jewelry stores to remember: *Anne Schofield* and the *Australian Opal Galleries.*

Great American Department Stores (Outside of New York)
• **Bullock's** (Pasadena)
• **Dayton's** (Minneapolis)
• **The Emporium** (San Francisco)
• **William Filene's Sons Company** (Boston)
• **Gump's** (San Francisco)
• **The J.L. Hudson Company** (Detroit)
• **Jordan Marsh Company** (Boston)
• **I. Magnin & Company** (Los Angeles)
• **Marshall Field & Company** (Chicago)
• **Neiman-Marcus** (Dallas)
• **Sakowitz-Gulfgate** (Houston)
• **John Wanamaker** (Philadelphia)

PERSONAL SHOPPERS: STORES

THE "personal shopper" is a convenient, quality service available at many of the finest department and specialty stores. Personal shoppers are on call to streamline your shopping trips, to advise you on your own wardrobe, and to help you find gift items. Following is a list of stores which have personal shoppers, (Note: not every branch of a store has the personal shopper service. Inquire about one in your area.)

- **B. Altman & Co.**
  361 Fifth Ave.
  New York City
  Personal Shopping: (212)
  689-7000, ext. 6942

- **Bergdorf Goodman**
  754 Fifth Ave.
  New York City
  Personal Shopping: (212)
  872-8809
  "Solutions": (212) 872-8772

- **Bloomingdale's**
  1000 Third Ave.
  New York City
  At Your Service (212)
  705-3136
  At His Service (212) 705-3030
  Beatrice Dale (212) 705-2380
  Hope's Corner (212) 705-3375
  Interior Design (212) 705-2592

- **Bonwit Teller**
  4 E. 57th St.
  New York City
  Director of Personal Shoppers: (212) 593-3333, ext.
  4445

- **Bullock's**
  3050 Wilshire Blvd.
  Los Angeles
  Director of Personal Shopping: (213) 382-6161, ext. 304

- **Garfinckel's**
  14th and F St., NW
  Washington, DC
  Director of Personal Shopping: (202) 628-7730, ext.
  207

- **Lord & Taylor**
  424 Fifth Ave.
  New York City
  Director of Personal Shoppers: (212) 391-3675

- **Macy's**
  Herald Square
  New York City
  Macy's Buy Appointment:
  (212) 560-4161

- **Marshall Field & Co.**
  111 State St.
  Chicago, IL
  Director of Personal Shoppers: (312) 781-4444
  Personalized Shopping: (312)
  781-5354

- **Neiman-Marcus**
  1618 Main St.
  Dallas
  Personal Shopper: (214)
  741-6911, ext. 5760
  Silver Key Service: (214)
  748-2539

• **Rich's**
45 Broad St. SW
Atlanta
Director of Shopping Service:
(404) 586-2510

• **Sakowitz**
500 Westheimer
Post Oak Branch

Houston
Director of Personal Shoppers: (713) 877-8888, ext. 204

• **Saks Fifth Avenue**
611 Fifth Ave.
New York City
Fifth Avenue Club: (212)
940-4200

PERSONAL SHOPPERS: INDEPENDENT

WHETHER you are seeking a new image, looking for professional fashion advice, or simply do not have the time to shop
for yourself, *independent* personal shoppers can be an excellent service to contact. They will tailor their efforts and energies to fit your
individual needs (often at your home where they can examine your
present wardrobe and determine what additions or changes would
best suit your lifestyle). The individual style they will create for you
can be your office appearance, social image—whatever you
request. In addition to the consultation, the personal shoppers will
shop for you (charging by the hour). Often, personal shoppers
receive special privileges from the stores not offered to the ordinary
retail shopper. Many personal shoppers also have access to the
wares of wholesale manufacturers, sometimes before the goods are
available at the retail stores. (Note: while the wholesale access can
be very attractive, there are often restrictions, i.e., clothes cannot
be returned.) Most of the personal shoppers will keep ongoing files
(some computerized) about their clientele which allows them to
personalize their services even more. The emphasis is on individual attention, whether you are interested in a complete wardrobe or are simply in town for a visit and want help shopping for a
few hours. Below is a listing of independent personal shoppers
located in New York and Los Angeles. The services they offer will
vary, as will their service fees.

New York City
• **Susan Dresner/Successful Ways and Means.** $255 annual
membership fee (includes at-home wardrobe analysis, a personal
profile, annual wardrobe budget, and referrals to other expert services such as custom dressmakers); $60 per hour to shop thereafter.
Specialty: success dressing for career women; wardrobe coordina-
tion to maximize clothes investment; keeps extensive files; does
some wholesale work. 36 W. 89th St., NY 10024; (212) 877-1417.

• **William Thourlby, Ltd.** $100 per hour to shop, minimum of three hours work; dresses only men; does not keep files. Prepares seminars called "You Are What You Wear" for many top corporations (men and women). 509 Madison Ave., NY; (212) 421-6632.

• **Allison Utsch.** Does wholesale work only. Please call for an appointment. 160 E. 83rd St., NY 10028; (212) 794-8530.

Los Angeles

• **Mary Parks.** $35 per hour of basic shopping service. Familiarity with salespeople at every significant store. Examines wardrobe, assembles selections for you from various stores. Beverly Hills, CA; (213) 559-6300.

• **Pat Smith and Christine Kunzelman/Panache Appearance Studios.** $50 per hour for color draping and figure analysis; $50 per hour shopping and wardrobe work. Specialty: accessorizing fashions. Torrance, CA; (213) 378-8308.

• **Barbara Burak and Linda Camras.** $60 per hour to analyze your wardrobe and to take you shopping. Specialty: women in transition, business women. Beverly Hills, CA; (213) 556-0390.

• **Carolyn Clark.** $150 for a two-and-a-half hour initial visit. Specialty: color tones, fabric, makeup. Beverly Hills, CA; (213) 273-5687.

• **Seasons.** $200 for a three-hour analysis plus color chart; $80 for color chart and makeup advice only; $60 per hour to shop or reorganize closets. Specialty: flattering colors for skin tones, men and women. Beverly Hills, CA; (213) 641-2614.

MEN'S SUITS: SAVILE ROW SAVVY

FOR all who appreciate male finery, the Mecca of tailoring, even for those who cannot afford it and those who have never been to England, is Savile Row, London, W.1. Savile Row today is a generic term, like "Madison Avenue" and "Hollywood." Many fashionable tailors are dotted nearby in other streets of Mayfair. Their showrooms come in all decors, "mod" like Hayward of Mount Street, "trad" like Henry Poole of Cork Street, and outright baroque like Wells of Mayfair, whose Maddox Street shop is a riot of stucco detail, coats of arms set into the wall, whorls, curlecues.

What Makes a Savile Row Suit?

First of all, what is so special about a Savile Row suit and what is so special about the man inside it? Answers: 1) Even the most expensive of American tailors simply sew the sleeve buttons to the sleeve. On a Savile Row suit all three buttons have buttonholes that can be unbottoned (American tailors will supply buttonholes on request; at $10 a buttonhole, that will add $60 to the bill), 2) The sides of the lapel of most Savile Row suits feel nubbled, slightly abrasive to the touch, the result of handstitching. The sides of a machine-finished lapel are smooth to the touch. Some customers and tailors, exaggerate the hand stitches so that they can be seen from a distance. Savile Row tailors frown on this sort of thing. Feel under the left lapel below the buttonhole, and one will find a little loop, to hold down the boutonniere, 3) Back vents, whether single or double, do not separate when one bends or sits. The choice between center or double vents should be left to the tailor. Quietly, Savile Row tailors suggest double for those broad of beam. The checks on a sports jacket or a Prince of Wales suit should form a single, uninterrupted pattern. Like well-hung wallpaper, there should be no break on either side of the back center seam, or on the pocket flaps or the lapels. 4) Pants should just touch the shoe in front, and stop short of the floor behind. The jacket sleeve should be five inches from the thumb-nail, with half an inch of shirt sleeve showing.

The British preeminence in the world of male fashion is sometimes almost subliminal in its evidence. The Japanese word for a jacket is "a Savile". The French word for a Prince of Wales suit is a Prince de Galles. *The Oxford English Dictionary* gives 1297 for the first known use of the word "tailor." The British Tailors' Guild was born three years later, in 1300. Subsequent developments are as applicable today as they were 200 years ago. The basic English cloth was wool, not the velvet favored by the more flamboyant French. England was a rural and a seafaring society. Side vents made for a more comfortable seat on a horse. The commander of H.M.S. *Blazer* smartened his tars by outfitting them in blue jackets with gold buttons, and the word "blazer" was born. The naval blazer incorporated the side vents of the country squire. Thus began the amalgamation of country and ocean into the appearance of the Mayfair gentleman.

Savile Row and Ready-to-Wear

It would be wrong to say that a 100 percent Savile Row bespoke (custom-made) suit is by its existence superior to an off-the-peg suit. There can be few well-dressed men who have not been burned by experimenting with a new tailor, sometimes small and unknown, sometimes the opposite, and finished up with an honestly made suit of no personality whatever. Colin Hammick of *Huntsman's Ltd., of 11 Savile Row,* which is probably the Rolls-Royce of Savile Row houses, considers that *Chester Barrie,* the British r.t.w. (ready-to-wear) firm is superior to many Savile Row houses, as a result of which Huntsman's has joined Chester Barrie in an off-the-peg extension of Huntsman's itself.

About seventy to eighty percent of Savile Row suits go to overseas customers and, of that, fifty percent go to the United States. If you ask plaintively, "I never get to England, so how can I get a Savile Row suit?" the answer is that *Savile Row will come to you.* Tailors travel all over the United States and Europe, telephoning customers. If you say further, "But nobody telephones me," the answer is that you haven't asked. Select the one that appeals to you (see listing below) and soon enough the telephone will ring and an unctuous Arthur Treacher-like voice will say, "Good morning sir. I am from Brown & Smith of Savile Row staying at the Loews Hotel. I have with me a collection of swatches . . . ." That voice, thank heavens, is all that remains of the old pre-World War II tailor who affected a butler's manner and waited a year for his bill to be paid.

Making a Suit

Today Savile Row tailors are a jovial, amusing lot, the social equal of their customers, and more likely to address a customer as "Jimmy" than "Your Lordship." By the nature of their art they are compelled to be advertisements for themselves, and have to be beautifully dressed at all times, even at weekends and presumably even in their pajamas. They consider themselves, rightly, to be artists and divide their work into the psychological and the physical. As a spokesman puts it, "Good cloth and sewing do not of themselves make a good suit. Cutting and design make a good suit. That and mutual trust. The customer is not seeing a suit. All he is seeing is a small square of cloth. So he must trust the tailor, the way one trusts a portrait painter, sight unseen. Tailors want to give the impression they have a care for the quality of life. Through their clothes they care for people."

On the physical side, a suit takes forty man/woman hours of tailoring plus cutting and fitting time (and a tailor, if he is dealing with a customer for the first time, may take up to five fittings). The cutter produces a paper pattern which is filed and kept updated with each new suit for the same customer. Savile Row tailors boast of filing up to 20,000 patterns which they discard only when their owners die. The pattern is laid on the cloth which then moves to the tailoring stages and the first fitting. This is the most alarming part of the procedure. The tailor regards you, makes marks with chalk on you, then rips the whole suit apart to begin all over again. The staff is carefully selected for specialization. Some are best with trousers, others with jackets. Some sew better than they cut. Women are traditionally better at stitching and making button-holes.

Fashions

Savile Row stands or falls by the claim that its suits will never go out of fashion, that they will retain shape and style for the life-time of the cloth itself. They look cautiously ahead to what will be the style for the next season, and even more cautiously to the next five or six seasons. If a recession is forecast, the demand will be for somber clothes, black with chalk stripes, dark grays. The customer wants something safe, something that will last and shore up his sense of security. If the economists declare the recession to be end-ing, there will be a demand for softer, brighter clothes and accessories. So of the scores of Savile Row tailors, who are the happy few that really stand out for fashion, durability, and the certain *je ne sais quoi* which makes people turn round and stare?

Top Tailors

Huntsman is perhaps the most famous. The name is mislead-ing. It sounds like a trendy boutique in Greenwich Village. The first Henry Huntsman came into tailoring in 1849 and in 1866 was appointed tailor and leather-breeches maker to the Prince of Wales, later Edward VII. The tailoring firm of Robert Packer took over from the two sons of Henry Huntsman in 1932. Huntsman is the principal tailor to recognize the continuing influence of the country on city styles, influencing vents, depths, the placement and size of pockets. The Huntsman directors get mildly embar-rassed at the size of their own prices. A worsted coat and trousers will cost around £800 plus VAT (Value Added Tax), total circa £900. A silk jacket and trousers costs £1,000 with tax. Huntsman's clothes are made by a process which has not changed in fifty years. Sleeve linings and pocket casings are done by hand. A sleeve lining takes three and a half hours of work by hand. A machine can do it in three minutes. The machine process is excellent, but it is just not as good.

Henry Poole, the first tailor to move into Savile Row in the 1820s continues to thrive in Cork Street, with a third-generation Henry Poole still at the helm. Poole clients have included the Emperor Louis Napoleon, Charles Dickens, Disraeli, De Gaulle, and Winston Churchill (the last two not necessarily good advertisements for the house). *Wells of Mayfair* is a fashionable name to have on a label, as are *J. Dege & Sons* at 16 Clifford Street, *Anderson & Sheppard* at 30 Savile Row, *Kilgour, French & Stanbury Ltd.* at 33A Dover Street, and *Hawes & Curtis* at 2 Burlington Gardens.

Gieves & Hawkes with the prestigious address of Number 1 Savile Row is perhaps the most international of the big tailors. The Great Room on the second floor was the Map Room of the Royal Geographical Society from 1870 until 1911. The two separate firms, Hawkes and Gieves, were both started in the eighteenth century. Hawkes, founded in 1771 were tailors to the Duke of Wellington. Gieves, founded in 1785 were tailors to Lord Nelson. Gieves & Hawkes have made their modern reputation by moving fast for overseas visitors. David Gieves says, "Some customers are in London only briefly. We need forty-eight hours from ordering the cloth to measuring and fitting—in the customer's hotel room if necessary—and about seven days in all. We enjoy the challenge, but we prefer to avoid it in tailoring for gentlemen."

But the real reason for owning a Savile Row suit, as all Savile Row tailors will tell you, is that you are making an investment. "The suits last," they say. "Prices and costs shoot up. A suit which cost £100 less than a decade ago, may cost £400 now, so better buy because next year it will be £500, or buy three for £1,200 and you will congratulate yourself in a few years."

Savile Row Tailors

Savile Row tailors belong to the Federation of Merchant Tailors, and very high standards must be met to qualify for admission. Thus, you can be assured that you are getting one of the best when you go to a Savile Row tailor. For a list of addresses and phone numbers you need to contact these fine Savile Row establishments, write: *Federation of Merchant Tailors, Admin. House, Market Square, Leighton Buzzard, Bedsminster, England LU7 7EV.*

MEN'S SUITS: U.S. CUSTOM MAKERS

BROADLY speaking, American tailor-made suits come in three styles: traditional conservative; Broadway-Hollywood pizzazzy; Ivy League/natural shoulder. Each shop makes one of these three styles, so choose your tailor according to your tastes.

Traditional Conservative: Dunhill

Representing traditional conservatism to perfection is Manhattan's Dunhill, which is also, in the view of many observers (and of its own management), the top of the American line. "We're the best in this country," says Dunhill executive Norman Block matter-of-factly. "Huntsman [a famed London shop] says so."

No relation to the equally famous pipemaker, Dunhill offers two types of suits. To the uninitiated, the difference between them, except in price, will seem slight. One is "custom made"; the other, "made to order." The prices hover around $1,500 and $800, respectively, per two-piece garment (no vests at these bargain rates). "We cut paper patterns in both cases," explains Norman Block, "but there's a lot more handwork, and overall workmanship in the custom-made one. Some people can recognize the difference and appreciate it: The custom-made suits never lose their shape and can be worn for years and years, until they literally wear out."

Block says there is "no real name" for Dunhill's style: "We call it simply the 'gentleman's cut.' It is not extreme in any way." One hallmark of the cut is a trim silhouette. For the money, the wearer has a right to *look* trim, even if he's not. Dunhill doesn't deign to mention its competition. For the "gentleman's cut," it probably has none.

Broadway-Hollywood

• **Mariani.** Perhaps the closest in that category is Mariani of Beverly Hills, who fashions clothes for the film world's elite. Already the acknowledged best in the West, Mariani gained celebrity as well as success when a regular client named Ronald Reagan was elected president.

• **Fioravanti.** The other top tailors are located in midtown Manhattan. One of them, Fioravanti, is only a couple of blocks from Dunhill, but the distance between their styles could be measured in light years. Fioravanti comes as close to flashy as custom tailoring gets. The head Fioravanti, William, was pictured recently in one of his typical ensembles: a suit with an open-collar shirt whose fulsome cuffs are rolled back over the jacket sleeves. Dunhill patrons would look with disdain at such a get-up.

Ivy League

Finally, the Ivy League entries—**Chipp** and **J. Press.** Their stores stand side by side on East 44th Street. (Actually, Press's headquarters, the place where its suits are tailored, is in New Haven, Connecticut.) Fidelity to the Ivy look—three-button jackets with narrow lapels, etc.—is not all that distinguishes Chipp and Press. They are among the very few purveyors of ready-to-wear clothing who also offer custom services. The two shops have long symbolized success among a large body of aspiring business and professional men, but not, it is instructive to note in the rarefied atmosphere in which Dunhill operates.

For further information, contact: Dunhill, 65 E. 57th St., New York, NY 10022, (212) 355-0050; Fioravanti, 45 W. 57th St., New York, NY 10019, (212) 355-1540; Chipp, 14 E. 44th St., New York, NY 10017, (212) 687-0850; J. Press, 16 E. 44th St., New York, NY 10173, (212) 687-7642; Mariani, Inc., 321 S. Beverly Dr., Beverly Hills, CA 90212, (213) 276-5972.

MEN'S SUITS: READY-TO-WEAR: OXXFORD

UNITED STATES Senators, Cabinet members, governors, past presidents, doctors, lawyers, and actors all share a common "thread"—they wear the Oxxford suit. Among clothing connoisseurs the seventy-year-old Chicago-based Oxxford Clothes company is rated the *crème de la crème* in the manufacture of ready-made garments. It has earned its place principally because of the skilled workmanship of approximately 200 Italian and sixty Chinese tailors, who, Oxxford feels, have a special affinity for needlework. Each is an artisan.

Just as Michelangelo created his David with the most exquisite materials, so too does Oxxford create its classically styled clothing. First, they buy from European mills that make only pure and natural fabrics: woolens, Shetlands, cashmeres, silks, and the like. Buttons made from the horns of African water buffalo adorn their coats and jackets. Second, *each unit is individually hand-cut with shears.* Most clothing manufacturers stack the fabric, lay out the patterns, and then a machine cuts many layers at once, i.e., when you stack layers forty to eighty high, the first four or five will be okay, but after that slippage, and imprecision, occurs.

Next, careful attention is given to matching stripes, plaids, and patterns with precise details. *One hundred percent of Oxxford's garments are hand-sewn with silk thread;* the only machine sewing is on straight-line seams such as pant legs and the back of suit jackets where more strength is needed. In addition, the collar and lapels of their jackets and coats have a total of 2,950 hand stitches. Most ready-made suits have only half that number. Also, the garment undergoes thirty-two underpressings, or preparatory pressings, prior to the final pressing which takes one hour. Conversely, most manufactured suits take about five minutes of electronic pressing.

Oxxford sells its men's suits for an average retail price of $925 (ladies' suits for ten percent less). Overall, prices range about $225 for a pair of slacks up to $4,200 for a Guanaco topcoat (made of a luxurious wool from the South American llama family). Although Oxxford can't state how durable its clothing is (some fabrics wear better than others), wearers interviewed say its garments last for a minimum of eight years to a lifetime.

These ready-to-wears, gray, blue, and pinstripes, are designed for conservative tastes. Suit jackets are the traditional two-and three-button designs with cuffed pants. As Oxxford says, "We do not design for shock value. Instead, we dress gentlemen. We believe in evolution not revolution." The lapels on their men's suits change accordingly—about one-quarter inch per season. Oxxford suits are available at Neiman-Marcus and top clothing stores throughout the U.S. For information: *Oxxford Clothes, Inc. 1220 W. Van Buren, Chicago, IL 60607; (312) 829-3600.*

CUSTOM SHIRTMAKERS

THERE are a lot of department and specialty stores advertising "custom-made" shirts, but they're not quite the real thing. While the stores do offer an extensive variety of styles and quality fabrics, they use standard, pre-cut patterns, rather than making a separate pattern for each customer. These "made-to-measure" or "special order" shirts will more closely approximate your own size than will ready-made garments, because they're sized by the quarter-inch rather than the half-inch. For the best fit, though (not to mention the finest fabrics and detailing), you must go to one of the few shirtmakers who still make shirts from individual paper patterns. From them you can expect the following:

• **A tailor takes about ten measurements** —hip, armhole, wrist, shoulder angle, and shirttail length included—and will usually make one sample shirt from which he'll check and alter the fit a second time. The pattern is kept on file for subsequent orders.

• **All manner of collar and cuff styles are available,** and the tailor is an excellent source of advice for just the right look. "People usu-

ally know their own style and what they want," says Fred Calcagno
of Pec and Co. in New York, "but I try to steer them away from
styles that I know are wrong for them—a high collar on a short
neck, for example, or a wide spread collar that will make a man
look broader than he should."

• **Fabrics are imported** from France, Italy, Switzerland, and
England. Most tailors disdain anything but 100 percent cotton
(Egyptian) or 100 percent silk.

• **The construction is flawless:** mother-of-pearl buttons are held
in place with the finest imported threads (spaced at three-and-a-
half-inch intervals; four inches is standard for ready-made); stiff
collar linings often eliminate the need for starch; the twenty to
twenty-five stitches per inch are strong but delicate-looking; narrow French seams provide durability; hand-embroidered mono-
grams add style.

The shirtmakers' craft is a dying one, but the tailors acknowl-
edge that there's still a market for their goods. "It's a recession-
proof business," says Peter Fiduccia of Fiduccia Custom Shirts in
Fort Lee, New Jersey. "People who want quality goods and can
afford the prices will buy no matter what the cost." Expect to pay
from $75 to $200 for cotton, $125 to $200 for silk. Tuxedo, western,
and sport shirts will be more expensive. *A six-shirt minimum order is
standard practice.* In London, **Turnbull & Asser** *(71 Jermyn St., SW1)*
offers over 800 patterns and stripes, superbly tailored with two- or
three-button cuffs. After an in-person visit, shirts will be mailed
across the Atlantic. A list of custom shirtmakers found in the U.S.
follows:

California
• **Larry's**
1151 S. Beverly Dr.
Los Angeles, CA 90035
(213) 271-8663
CONTACT: Larry Fleishman

• **Nat Wise Shirt Makers**
8504 Sunset Strip
Los Angeles, CA
(213) 652-5870
CONTACT: Mel Wise

Illinois
• **Riddle McIntyre**
175 N. Franklin
Chicago, IL
(312) 782-3317
CONTACT: Frank H. Kang

Missouri
• **Woolf Brothers**
311 Nichols Road
Kansas City, MO 64112
(816) 561-7500
CONTACT: Linda Christianson

New Jersey
* **Fiduccia Custom Shirts**
2024 Center Ave.
Fort Lee, NJ 07024
(201) 592-0595
CONTACT: Joseph DeFelice

New York
* **Pec & Co.**
45 W. 57th St.
New York, NY 10019
(212) 758-0758
CONTACT: Fred Calcagno

* **Poster Custom Shirtmakers**
45 W. 57th St.
New York, NY 10019
(212) 838-4112
CONTACT: Alex Kabbaz

* **Arthur Gluck**
37 W. 57th St.
New York, NY 10019
(212) 758-0610

* **Seewaldt & Bauman**
565 Fifth Ave.
New York, NY
(212) 682-3958

Pennsylvania
* **Barton & Donaldson**
1635 Chancellor St.
Philadelphia, PA 19103
(215) 546-2324

Texas
* **Hamilton Shirt Co.**
5700 Richmond St.
Houston, TX 77057
(713) 780-8222
CONTACT: Mr. Hamilton

* **Rogers Custom Shirt**
1509 Main St.
Dallas, TX
(214) 748-1612
CONTACT: Luther Rogers

TIES

THESE days, the comment "Where *did* you get that tie" is probably uttered with a note of envy rather than disdain. For the tie has truly come into its own, and you can really tie one of the best on by knowing where to find them and what to look for. If there were a Super Bowl of ties (from a quality *and quantity* viewpoint), put your money on New York clothier *Paul Stuart*. This world-famous store offers those lucky enough to shop there a collection of hundreds of ties in every fabric imaginable including linen, cashmere, crepe, and wool. The collection is so vast that it occupies about one-third of the first floor selling area.

Paul Stuart
Stuart offers some experienced tips on how to tell when a tie is tops. Most high-quality ties, are made by hand using natural fiber fabrics and linings, the latter being an important element of the tie as it gives it the body to both hang correctly and afford the best knot. A

quality tie is fashioned from three pieces of material so that it will knot correctly. Another sure mark of the handmade tie is the "slip stitching" which runs along the seam, culminating in *a loose end of thread hanging inside the tie's bottom;* this construction allows the fabric to "give," affording a better knot with no distortion of the pattern. Closer, machine-made stitches don't "give" as well and, thus, they will pose "knotty" problems. Quality ties that are ready-to-wear average between fifty-three to fifty-six inches in length; anything shorter indicates that the maker has been cutting corners.

Stuart says that *the three finest makers of ties are the Italians, English, and, of late, the Japanese.* Paul Stuart offers a vast array of them all, starting at as little as $8.50 for a cotton Madras pattern. Most prices fall into the $20 to $30 range where English mogador stripes happily coexist with Italian silks and shantungs. Bow tie wearers are not to be denied at Stuart, with a wide choice available to them in the $11 to $13 price range.

Exceptional Tie Departments

Other fine stores also provide a superior tie selection. One is the venerable *Brooks Brothers* which has been making its own ties for many years. Prices vary, with the average tie falling in the $20 range. While lacking the panache of the Paul Stuart collection, Brooks's offering is nevertheless awesome. Other stores that maintain exceptional tie departments are: *Saks Fifth Avenue, Bloomingdale's, J. Press, Dunhill Tailors* (all in New York City); *Brittany Ltd.* in Chicago; *Arthur Adler* in Washington, D.C.; *Neiman-Marcus* and *Sakowitz* in Dallas and Houston; and *Wilkes Bashford* in San Francisco. Here, the collected works of such notable American designers as Ralph Lauren, Calvin Klein, and Italians such as Giorgio Armani offer their versions of state-of-the-art neckwear.

Custom Ties

If custom-made clothing is *de rigueur* for you, there are several custom tie makers whose services you can avail yourself of by stopping in or dropping them a line.

• **DeCasi.** Perhaps the finest is DeCasi (37 W. 57th St., New York, NY 10019), an establishment run by the amiable Englishman Henry Stewart. Here the handmade ties are meticulously crafted to order for customers willing to pay on the average of $40 to $50 per tie. DeCasi also offers mail-order service; supply them with your height, neck size, suit size, tie width, and fabric preferences (which you select from the various swatches DeCasi supplies you with upon request), and in a couple of weeks you'll receive a delightful package.

• **A. Sulka & Company.** Not to be forgotten is A. Sulka & Co. (711 5th Ave., New York, NY and also in London, Paris, and San Francisco), whose exclusive top-of-the-line blue silk and eighteen-karat gold lamé tie weighs in at a hefty $125.

• **Rosa Custom Designs** (119 W. 57th St., Suite 1501, New York, NY 10019). Rosa is another custom maker offering mail-order service, albeit without the inimitable style of Mr. Stewart. Offers handmade ties from the finest imported European fabrics, as well as custom-made bow ties, ascots, and cummerbunds. Custom embroidery also available upon request. Ties can be made in one day, but normal delivery time is a week to two weeks.

SHOES: READY-MADE

ELEGANCE, comfort, and style—the benchmarks of fine quality shoes (and boots). When picking the best pair for your feet, knowing what to look for can save you a lot of shoe leather. The three different methods of making shoes are: custom made (all work by hand), bench made (part machine, part hand), and machine made. When looking for the sign of a maker's quality, the first place to look is the "last," which is the basic shape of the shoe. In fine shoes, the last follows the shape of the foot, not vice-versa. "Channeling," a technique of recessing the stitching on the sole of the shoe, is another indication of quality handiwork.

Besides construction, the best shoes are noted for their fine quality leathers. Like prime cuts of beef, prime *quality shoes are cut from one center piece of the leather hide. Thus, both shoes are identical,* a feature less expensive shoes may not always offer. Leathers come in a variety of grades, but the best ones are supple and pliable without being tissue thin. Bending the shoe will give you a good indication of how the leather will perform on your foot. Detail work is another way to separate the better shoe from the best. Sewn leather inner linings, leather and rubber heels, functional yet unobtrusive soles—these indicators of attention to detail really indicate how much loving care the maker has bestowed on the shoe.

Experts agree that *the finest shoes are made by the English and Italians.* Italian shoes are characterized by overall sleekness, without innersoles, and with bottom soles cemented instead of stitched so as not to mar the overall streamline. English shoes are more traditional in construction and appearance; this is more evident in the earlier models which sported thick, unflattering soles. Whichever style you prefer, there is no shortage of fine American stores where you can choose the best of these "lasts."

• **Church's** When considering English men's shoes, the name of Church's immediately comes to mind. Church's famous English shoes (428 Madison Ave., New York, NY 10017.) has been producing traditional English styles since 1873. Their ready-to-wear selection is probably the largest and best in America. Slipping on a pair of their Oxfords is the next best thing to going there. Prices at Church's begin at around $80. And their semi-annual sales are not to be missed.

• **Brooks Brothers.** While offering a limited selection, Brooks Brothers is known for carrying the *Peale* line of shoes, whose famous cap-toe Oxfords begin at around $300.

• **Saks Fifth Avenue: McAfee and Polo.** At Saks Fifth Avenue, English shoemaker *McAfee* is well presented with a line of bench made shoes priced at about $180. And you'll also find the Ralph Lauren *Polo* shoe collection here, English-made to the designer's specifications and priced at about $200 a pair.

• **Artioli.** As for Italian shoes for men, one of the finest collections goes under the Artioli label. Priced at about $300 a pair, they are entirely handmade of the most exquisite leathers available. Other shoemakers of note, for both men and women, include *Ferragamo* and *Bally.* Bally shoes can be bought at numerous department stores or Bally's own stores located in most major cities. Prices average about $200 for men's shoes.

• **Designers.** Besides manufacturers, there are certain designers whose names are synonymous with fine footwear and cater to both men and women. At the top of the charts is *Bennis/Edwards* (440 Park Ave., New York) whose shoes are the favorite of those people whose records and movies are at the top of the charts. Prices vary from exorbitant to outrageous—but the truth is they're worth it. Another cobbler to the stars is *Maud Frizon* (49 E. 57th St., New York, NY), where the latest styles and colors begin at about $230 for men and $180 for women.

• **American Makers.** Finally, let's not forget the American shoe-makers. Companies like *Johnston & Murphy, Cole-Haan,* and *Bass* still offer fine quality shoes at prices far less than their foreign counterparts.

SHOES/BOOTS: CUSTOM

IF the shoe fits, it was probably custom-made: handcrafted by a professional shoemaker who fashioned it for your foot alone. And people continue to seek out custom shoemakers because they can't find shoes that fit elsewhere. Indeed, shoe buyers in department stores including Saks Fifth Avenue, I. Magnin, Neiman-Marcus, and Marshall Field & Co. say it has become too expensive to carry a complete range of sizes because exceptionally long or wide shoes don't sell enough to warrant their cost. But even when size or orthopedics are not a consideration, patrons visit the cobbler simply to obtain the finest shoes available. They want to select from imported leathers and unique designs, experiencing the personalized service they can't get when buying a mass-produced shoe.

United States
• **Vincent and Edgar.** Buyuk Cileli is the new owner of Manhattan's Vincent and Edgar, which has been designing shoes for forty-five years. A first pair of shoes costs about $900, depending on the materials: subsequent pairs start at $700 and can be completed in four weeks. *510 Madison Ave., New York, NY 10022; (212) 753-3461.*

• **T.O. Dey.** Makes about 600 pairs of boots and 2,500 pairs of shoes at a cost ranging from $350 to $1,500. Will work with exotic leathers, make custom ski boots, and alter ready-made boots. Averages eight weeks to complete an order. *509 Fifth Ave., New York, NY 10017; (212) 682-6100.*

• **Imre Nemeth.** One of New York's Upper East Side's best-kept secrets, this master shoemaker offers custom-made dress and walking shoes to international celebrities, as well as individuals interested in quality footwear. Nemeth can make almost any variation requested on the dozens of fashionable and classic models on his shelves, ranging from a men's business shoe to a women's T-strap pump. Prices start at $500 per pair for women, $600 per pair for men. *20 E. 69th St., New York, NY 10021; (212) 737-3984.*

• **E. Vogel.** In business since 1879, it specializes in riding boots, but makes the walking variety too. Normal delivery time is eight to twelve weeks at an average cost of $300 to $500. *19 Howard St., New York, NY 10013; (212) 925-2460.*

• **Bottega Di Fabrizio.** For those who want flair, Pasquale Di Fabrizio offers Hollywood and the world a splashy selection of boots and shoes in patterns and styles he says are limited only by the imagination. Ladies' shoes start at $400, men's at $450, and both can cost as much as $3,000, depending on the materials and the time involved. It normally takes four weeks to four months to get a pair. *8216 W. 3rd St., Los Angeles, CA 90048; (213) 655-5248.*

• **The Hersey Custom Shoe Company.** As anyone who has ever done any running for fitness (a.k.a., jogging) knows, the importance of a good pair of athletic shoes cannot be overemphasized. One of the first to agree is cobbler Bart Hersey, who handcrafts shoes for the jogger with hard-to-fit feet, or the runner who wants a customized pair made from the best possible materials. Hersey Customs cost $130 to $165 a pair, and runners who favor them don't regard the price as a bit too steep, considering what their feet will be snuggling into: soles molded from Goodyear Indy 500 rubber, tops and sides made from the best pigskin leather, and nylon mesh, specially reinforced heel and midsole. *RFD #3, Box 7390, Farmington, ME 04938; (207) 645-3015.*

London/Paris

• **John Lobb, Bootmaker.** This is a 135-year-old shop that holds the Royal appointment to the Queen, the Duke of Edinburgh, and the Prince of Wales. Customers—some of whom have been returning for fifty years—select from a variety of styles and leathers and will be spending at least £300 a pair. According to the founder's grandson, Eric Lobb, that price could double depending on the materials. Lobb maintains a permanent department at Hermès in Paris, and sends his representatives to New York four times a year, as well as Philadelphia, Washington, D.C., Boston, Pittsburgh, Beverly Hills, San Francisco, Chicago, Kansas City, Denver, Dallas, New Orleans, and Houston to take measurements for shoes that will later be handcrafted in London. Delivery time is six to eight months. For information: *John Lobb, Bootmaker, 9 St. James St., London, S.W.1, 44-1-930-3664; Hermès, 24 Rue Faubourg, St.-Honore, Paris; Hermès, 745 Fifth Ave., Room 800, New York, NY 10022; (212) 759-7585.*

• **Maxwell's.** Mr. Louis at Maxwell's is not alone among London shoemakers when he says, "We have no competition; we're the best." The company has been working on its reputation since 1750, and offers shoes and riding boots to both men and women. They can copy your favorite shoes or start from scratch. After the initial fitting the customer returns in eight to twelve weeks to "try on and welt" the shoes. At this stage they have temporary soles and no heels and are easily adjusted if necessary. In total it takes about three months to have a pair made; boots will take a bit longer. Ordinary, lace-up calfskin shoes start at $600. Top hunting boots of hard-wearing waxcalf start at $1,200 and "butcher boots" (minus the tops) are around $1,000. Company representatives visit a number of U.S. cities each year. For more information or to be placed on the mailing list, CONTACT: *Maxwell's, 11 Savile Row, London, W.1.*

• **Poulsen and Skone.** Some of the patrons of this 100-year-old shop have been returning for more than twenty-five years. Shoemaker William Shannon says his customers select primarily from calf and reverse calf (suede); in these materials prices start at $400 for a plain lace-up shoe, $450 for a "casual" shoe and $500 for a full brogue. Prices fluctuate with style and leathers: crocodile starts at $1,200. Hunting boots begin at $700 and can take nine months to complete. For shoes the wait is three months for the first pair and six weeks for subsequent pairs. Company representatives go to Germany and the U.S. twice a year. For information, CONTACT: *Mr. J. Carrera or Mr. G. Glasgow at Poulsen and Skone, 53 Jermyn St., London, S.W.1.*

THE CLASSIC TRENCH COAT

THE classic trench coat, popularized during World War I, has remained fashionable over the last sixty years because of its durability, practicality, and comfort. Although all of the classic trench coat lines offer tie belts, epaulettes, pockets, flaps, and buckles, the individual maker's choice of materials and construction techniques are what distinguish the best from the rest.

First, a trench coat must be water-and wrinkle-resistant. Though 100 percent cotton resists water most effectively, some experts prefer a sturdy wool gabardine that has been treated to resist water. (All trench coats should be waterproofed every other time they are dry-cleaned.)

Second, since trench coats have gradually replaced the need for the in-between coats of spring and fall, the development of detachable linings has become increasingly important in expanding their versatility. *Wool is still the most popular lining because of its durability and warmth.* The principle difference between attaching a lining with a zipper or buttons is style. Zippers create a slightly less bulky appearance by fastening the lining as if sewed to the outer shell, while buttons present a more natural appearance.

Listed below are designers who are the acknowledged leaders in fine trench coats. However, several of our experts maintain that there are a number of lesser known makers who produce truly fine trench coats at reduced cost. The smart buyer should really spend some time going through the racks looking for some of these lesser lights before making a selection.

• **Burberry's.** Excellent and expensive. Three basic models (twelve to fifteen versions) of men's and women's trench coats cost from around $420 to more than $675. The top-of-the-line Burberry "Trench 21" is all-cotton with a button-out, camel wool robe lining, and yoked-cape back wool collar. Burberry, an English company, was the original designer of trench coats for the troops in World War I. It recently reinstituted its patented "tielocken" trench coat made during World War II.

• **Aquascutum.** Makes ten to twelve versions of men's and women's trench coats ranging in cost from about $290 to $690. The best is an all-cotton, full trench with a full button-out cashmere robe lining and overcollar.

• **Brooks Brothers.** The oldest ready-to-wear men's clothing store in the U.S. has been offering its popular English Salisbury trench coat for more than forty years. Made with a yarn-dyed long staple Egyptian cotton twill shell, a cotton plaid lining, and a cotton gauze inner lining, this double-breasted coat is warm in the winter and cool in the summer. Costs about $350 ($55 extra for a button-out wool lining).

• **Issey Miyake.** Collection includes 100 percent nylon double-breasted, belted, and water-resistant poly-cotton oversized beltless coats selling for close to $500. Miyake designs are carried in selected U.S. department stores, such as Bergdorf Goodman and Neiman-Marcus.

• **Giorgio Armani.** Couture collection includes classically styled double-breasted trench of high-grade cotton, with a cotton lining, for about $800. More youthful styles are found in the Emporio line, selling for just over $400.

• **Gleneagles.** This American manufacturer provides excellent trench coats at prices beginning around $200.

UMBRELLAS

THERE is more to an umbrella than providing temporary and portable shelter. Durability and strength are primary considerations. Only the finest umbrellas even attempt to stay right-side-out during a windy storm; only the finest umbrellas will last upwards of twenty years. To find such quality items we looked to those who have learned their skills from the dictates of their climate: the British.

Nowhere in London is there a better or bigger source of umbrellas than James Smith & Sons, a business already twenty-five years old when it moved to its present site at 53 New Oxford Street 130 years ago. This spacious corner store with richly engraved mirrors and rickety stairs leading down to a cellar workshop, stocks a range of several hundred men's (as well as some women's) umbrellas. The slender "City-type" umbrella favored by bankers remains the bestseller to this day. Its curved handle is usually malacca or whangee (Chinese for "yellow cane"), and its nylon fabric is always black. The store does, however, carry numerous styles and "it would be a very unusual customer who wouldn't be able to choose something he wanted," says manager Robert Harvey.

James Smith & Sons' selection includes umbrellas topped with ivory, silver, or ebony crooks; carved wooden heads of dogs or birds; rhinoceros horn handles (a rare amber to green-gray material, costing about £500; even a head of solid gold (price: £1,200). Besides selling from their vast stock, the store will also make umbrellas to order. Prices begin at eight pounds and reach £150 for specially created custom models. Silk, rayon, cotton, and gingham were once the choices of covering at James Smith & Sons, but today, with the exception of a few cotton models, all have been replaced by nylon, which is particularly lightweight and waterproof. For more information CONTACT: *James Smith & Sons, 53 New Oxford St., London WC1A 1BL, England; tel. (01) 836-4731.*

SUPER TOOTHBRUSH

Plaque build-up on teeth is the key cause of pyorrhea, the gum disease that can destroy the bone which supports the teeth. Careful flossing circumvents the problem but studies show that ninety percent of Americans only brush and do not floss. Unfortunately, mere brushing is less than fifty percent effective in removing daily plaque. What's worse, any plaque not brushed away eventually hardens into tartar, a substance that stubbornly clings to teeth, makes gums tender and inflamed, and causes periodontal diseases.

A new alternative to conventional brushing and flossing is the Interplak Home Plaque Removal Instrument, the most advanced electric toothbrush on the market. Most other electric toothbrushes have tufts, or bristles, that can only move together in one direction at a time (up, down, or in a circular movement, depending on which way you guide them). The Interplak, on the other hand, provides continual circular movements. Each tuft not only rotates—it revolves independently of the others. And, to make sure that they reach the especially hard-to-clean spots, the rotating tufts reverse direction every one-and-a-half turns.

A recent Loyola University School of Dentistry study found that Interplak rid more than ninety-eight percent of daily plaque build-up, compared to the hand-held toothbrush's forty-nine percent. It costs $99 and is available by mail direct from the Dental Research Group, or from your dentist. CONTACT: *Dental Research Group, 1726 Montreal Circle, #14, Tucker, GA 30084; (800) 344-4031 or (404) 934-1232.*

JEWELER'S CHOICE

GEMS sparkle, glow, entrance with the kind of magic that is only created deep within the earth. How very extraordinary that they should exist at all. When cut and set for their best effect, they capture the imagination, take us back to our most basic roots. Our choice in jewels reveals us. Antique watch and fob say heritage, breeding. Diamond stud earrings assert contemporary style. A lady's pearl choker declares she is traditionally romantic.

The secret behind such personal statements lies in finding the jeweler whose unique approach to craft coincides with your taste and style. Such jewelers are few and far between. They share in common a keen interest in original design, an absolute fascination for the evocative qualities of stones and metal, and a deep appreciation for tradition tempered by a consciousness of all that is new. Finally, they are all highly respected for the quality of the stones they select and for the craftsmanship that goes into each piece. First, search within yourself and define just what you would like to say. Then examine these jewelers and fasten on the one whose work says you.

Van Cleef & Arpels

Distinguished for using only the finest stones and for their "invisible" setting technique, which creates a velvet-like effect with square-cut stones, Van Cleef & Arpels is the jeweler for people interested in a traditional, timeless, elegant look. With a new "boutique" line aimed at the younger set and priced accordingly and the option to custom design to your specifications if on-hand jewels don't speak to you, Van Cleef & Arpels is one logical choice for spectacular jewels. *Van Cleef & Arpels, 744 Fifth Ave., New York, NY 10019; 300 N. Rodeo Drive, Beverly Hills, CA 90210.*

Harry Winston

America's premier *haute couture* jeweler, Harry Winston is recognized by the knowing public as the single best source of extremely high quality diamonds and precious gem stones. Expert diamond cutters, jewelry designers, and skilled craftsmen all work under one roof in Winston's exclusive salons in New York, Paris, Geneva, and Monte Carlo. In the hushed interiors of the Fifth Avenue salon one can view a selection of exquisitely crafted designs set in platinum with the very large diamonds, rubies, emeralds, and sapphires for which Winston is known. The in-house designer will work with the client to create a custom-made piece. When one is looking for the best in fine jewelry, the house of Harry Winston is one address to remember. *Harry Winston, 718 Fifth Ave., New York, NY 10019.*

Cartier

World-renowned for their Art Deco derived jewelry, Cartier carries on the tradition by continuously seeking inspiration from Louis Cartier's original drawings. The results? Clear, contemporary yet timeless jewels that stun in their simplicity and impact. Custom design is available. *Cartier, 653 Fifth Ave., New York, NY 10022.*

Tiffany

Something for everyone. With prices starting out at $20 and reaching as high as the imagination. Tiffany is very much a jewelry supermarket. Priding themselves on design, quality, and craftmanship, the Tiffany name is so established as to sell diamond engagement rings via their mail-order catalog. If none of the on-hand jewels suit your fancy, custom design is available from Tiffany staff designers. *Tiffany & Co., Fifth Ave. at E. 57th St., New York, NY 10022.*

David Webb

Bold in style, though not necessarily large in size, David Webb jewelry is considered eminently wearable. Studiously avoiding designs that are considered too traditional or too modern, Webb jewels create a strong, clean impression of ease and comfort. With sixty to seventy craftsmen, Webb creates all jewelry in-house. Custom designs can be developed in lieu of on-hand items in both precious and semi-precious stones. In business since 1946, this firm enjoys industry-wide recognition for its tireless effort at excellence. *David Webb, 7 E. 57th St., New York, NY 10022.*

Bulgari

Now in its third generation as stellar jewelers, the Bulgari family is famous for jewelry distinctive for its clearly masculine look. With large, square-cut, often semi-precious stones, these pieces create an impression of eternal strength and dynamism. New to the line and created especially for the young American market are jewels on a smaller scale, more casual in feeling, using such materials as copper and silver as well as the more traditional gold. If nothing on-hand satisfies, custom design is available. *Bulgari, 795 Fifth Ave., New York, NY 10022.*

DIAMONDS

THE evaluation of a diamond focuses on two elements—size and quality. And these, in turn, are measured by the traditional four Cs—Color, Clarity, Cut, and Carat size—particularly as interpreted by the Gemological Institute of America (GIA).

The Four Cs

• **Color.** The common "white" diamond isn't really white. It ranges from colorless through varying degrees of yellow. The less yellow present, or, in other words, the closer it comes to being color-less, the rarer the diamond and the more valuable it is. A "D" color diamond is one with absolutely no trace of color. "E" stones have a minute trace; "F" stones a bit more, and so on down the alphabet.

Diamonds are color graded by turning them upside down and looking through the side (pavilion) of the stone. The color of the stone being graded is compared to that of a set of pregraded "master" diamonds. If the stone being graded is the same color as, say, the "G" master, it is graded as a "G." The layman tends to think of the difference between a "D" and an "E" as being akin to the difference between a piece of white bond paper and a manila file folder. In actual fact, the difference between a "D" and an "E" or even between a "D" and an "F" or a "G" is so very slight that only a well-trained eye can see that there's any difference at all. You can go down as low as "J" or "K" color and the untrained eye still won't spot any color. Once you get down below "L" or "M" though, it doesn't take a gemologist to see the increasing yellow.

• **Clarity.** This is a measure of the number, shape, size, and posi-tion of inclusions within a diamond. Like a stone of "D" color, one with absolutely no inclusions is quite rare. The fewer the inclu-sions, the better the stone. Inclusions are birthmarks left by Mother Nature during the growth process millions of years ago. The vast majority of inclusions seen in gem diamonds present no structural weakness to the stone. The best clarity grade, according to the GIA scale, is flawless. This means that a trained gemologist sees no inclusions or blemishes, either within or on the surface of the diamond, when he examines it under ten-power magnification.

• **Cut.** Cut means two things. First, it defines the basic shape of the stone. Is it round or oval, pear, marquise, or emerald-shaped? Sec-ond, and most important, cut or "make" as it is more commonly called, refers to the proportions of the stone. Cut, perhaps more than any other factor governs the appearance of the stone. Much of a diamond's beauty comes from its sparkle and fire (the flashes of light in rainbow colors that bounce off its surface). And, given decent color and clarity, it is the cut of the stone that determines how much of this sparkle and fire you get. A well-proportioned "J SI_1," for example, can be far more beautiful than an ill-made "D flawless." And yet, cut is the most underrated of the four Cs.

If cut plays such a large role, why aren't all diamonds cut well? It's a matter of economics. Diamonds are sold by weight. The more weight, the more money the cutter gets. Generally, about half the weight of the rough is lost in the cutting process. The cutter tries to minimize this loss; he tries to get as much diamond out of the rough as possible. How well proportioned it is is often a secondary consideration. The actual mechanics of cut are very complicated. Unless the buyer yearns to be a gemologist, he needn't spend the months it would take to understand it. However, if he wants a beautiful stone, the effects of cut must be considered.

• **Carat Weight.** Diamonds are sold by weight. The larger the stone, the more rare it is. So, price increases geometrically rather than mathematically. For example, a half-carat stone costs more than twice what a comparable quarter-carat stone would cost. Likewise, a five-carat diamond costs *considerably* more than five times what a one-carat stone would sell for, all other factors being equal. It's all a function of rarity. There simply aren't as many five-carat stones in existence as there are one-carat stones.

Buying a Diamond

• It's always a good idea to seek out a graduate gemologist from the Gemological Institute of America, or a Fellow of the Gemological Association of Great Britain (FGA) for any jewelry purchase. With diamonds though, this isn't as important as it is with colored stones. Detection of fakes is relatively simple; it doesn't require a degree.

• Once you find a jeweler who's education minded, ask him to show you stones of different qualities. Look at loose stones, not just mounted jewelry. Once you find the right stone you can always find a mounting. Look at different colors, side by side. Do the same with clarity and cut. Ask him to show you how to use a loupe. Look into the stone so you can get a *rough idea* of the difference between a "VVS" stone and an "I" stone, for example.

• Remember, all "D flawlesses" were not created equal. An off make, (less than perfect proportions) will cost considerably less than a finely-made stone. So does one which hovers precariously close to 1.00 carats in weight. A scratch or nick requiring a repolishing could push the stone under that magical 1.00 weight. In so doing its worth would drop tremendously—a drop way out of proportion with the actual weight loss. Here, it's a case of "you get what you pay for." For the buyer who simply wants to say he has a "D flawless," but flinches at the price, an off-make stone, or one that's on the borderline between a "D" and an "E," just may be the answer.

COLORED STONES: THE BIG THREE

EMERALDS, rubies, and sapphires. A very special green, a very special red, a very special blue. Where do they come from, how much do they cost, how can you acquire one? These stones bring out the poetic in all who handle them—the mystique of the gems that came from the now nearly exhausted mines of Burma and Kashmir, the hazards of uncovering emeralds in Colombia. The most brilliant are described as having life, those that are duller are called tired or sleepy, and the one you don't want is said to be dead. Without question, color is all. But dealers talk of cool emeralds, passionate rubies, and peaceful, velvety sapphires. No two colored stones are ever alike and none are perfect. Emeralds, rubies, and sapphires all contain some inclusions—solid, liquid, or gaseous substances trapped inside millions of years ago. These specks may be microscopic or large enough to be seen by the naked eye. If they don't cloud the stone too much, they can add to its beauty. Fine crystals in a sapphire can look as sparkling as a snowstorm.

The best way to purchase one, says Robert Crowingshield, vice-president of the Gemological Institute of America, is with the help of an expert and trusted jeweler. The prospective buyer should never try to buy directly in the countries of the stones' origin; it is too chancy. Although no dealer would give an average price, most good stones, they agreed, would probably cost at least $8,000 to $10,000 per carat. Price, basically, is whatever the traffic will bear.

• **Emeralds.** The finest are mined high in the Andes of Colombia, South America. Once they were used by the Incas and Aztecs for ornaments. Those from the Muzo region are still considered the world's most brilliant. The Egyptians mined the stones as far back as 650 B.C., and in Roman times they were found in the Austrian Alps. At the Smithsonian Institution in Washington, D.C., one can see the thirty-eight-carat O. Roy Chalk stone, and a magnificent necklace of emeralds called the Inquisition Necklace cut over 300 years ago. Tiffany & Co. in New York City, displays the thirteen to fourteen carat Carolina Emerald, now valued around $100,000. It was discovered in 1970 in Hiddenite, North Carolina. However, most emeralds not mined in Colombia, usually come from Zambia, Zimbabwe, Tanzania, and a good supply from Brazil.

• **Rubies.** The most legendary rubies have always come from Burma and Kashmir—those having an intense red often described as "pigeon's blood red." The largest supply of rubies today comes from Thailand—these are often brownish or dark red—and Sri Lanka which has stones of light red or purplish. The star rubies are highly regarded in the United States. Cut as cabochons, they reflect a star when a light is shone directly on them.

• **Sapphires.** These stones range in color from the palest blue to deep midnight blue but many dealers prefer a rich soft, somewhat fuzzy color rather than a translucent one. Angela Cummings, a top Tiffany designer, often uses them with diamonds and platinum to give a watery feel, while Picasso's daughter Paloma, who also creates jewelry for Tiffany, likes to put sapphires together with pearls in her necklaces. This stone is mined primarily in Australia and Sri Lanka. Recently sapphire rings at David Webb's jewelry store in New York City sold for $100,000 and $280,000. Considering sapphires were once worn as amulets against danger and evil, perhaps that's not a very high price to pay.

COLORED STONES: THE LITTLE GEMS

THINK gemstones and what comes to mind? Rubies? Emeralds and sapphires, perhaps? Look a little further. An unusual stone of top quality often carries a price tag that's comparable to, or less than, a well-known stone of only mediocre quality. You'll pay $30,000 to $40,000 or more for the *crème de la crème* in a sizable diamond, ruby, emerald, or sapphire. For a quarter of that price you can get a lifeless stone of ho-hum color. But for that same $7,500 you can own a *tsavorite* so beautiful it will give you goose bumps. For $1,000, a *heliodor* as brilliant as a winter sunrise. The facts are simple. You get a lot more beauty per dollar from the stones whose names aren't household words. And the list of unusual stones whose finest qualities carry reasonable price tags goes on and on. The key phrase is "finest quality." Even familiar stones display a wide range of quality. *Amethyst,* for example. Its finest gemmy quality bears little resemblance to the lilac or pale purple stones you usually see. A fine amethyst is the color of Welch's grape juice.

A logical question to ask is: *if these unusual stones are so beautiful, why aren't they better known?* Answer: because they haven't been promoted. First, unlike diamonds, they're not controlled by a cartel that spends millions of dollars annually to convince you to buy them. Second, it's only lately that the average jeweler has started to sell unusual stones. The Bulgari's, Van Cleef's, Lalique's, and Fabergé's have always adorned their pieces with these unusual stones. Few other jewelers have—at least not in fine enough qualities to make the discriminating buyer look twice. It's easier for the average jeweler to sell a diamond. The consumer knows what they are and he or she wants one. Colored stones are a little harder. And, colored stones with "funny names" are harder still. The average person wants something that he's familiar with—something everyone else has.

Why are they called semiprecious? They're not. The Federal Trade Commission threw that term right out the window. They found it misleading. *Why, the FTC reasoned, should a poor quality sapphire be called precious while a magnificent tanzanite is termed semiprecious?* The fact is, these unusual stones are no less precious than their famous cousins—and some of them are actually much more rare. Tsavorite and tanzanite, for example, come from only two known locations deep within the African continent. Political turmoil there could lock up new supplies at any moment, making existing stones all the more rare.

Buying Wisely

The stock you'll see in most jeweler's cases is mediocre. There are several reasons why: 1) Security—the better stones are in the vault. 2) The jeweler is catering to a mass market. 3) Once a customer sees the best of a particular stone, he'll be unhappy with anything less. If he can't afford the best, the jeweler will be out a sale. The bottom line: window shopping isn't the way to go. Shop around until you find a jeweler with a lot of unusual stones in stock. That's important. The store which has its cases filled only with diamonds and gold isn't the place to go. *If the jeweler doesn't deal with unusual stones on a daily basis, chances are he doesn't have the expertise you need at your disposal.*

Another question: should one buy from an investment company which advertises low mark up? Answer: not really. There are many jewelers who sell fine expensive stones at ten percent and twenty percent over wholesale. Many investment companies sell at 100 percent, 200 percent, and more over the wholesale cost of the goods. There are legitimate investment firms, to be sure, but you're a lot better off with a knowledgeable jeweler.

PEARLS: THE CULTURED JEWEL

IF diamonds are a girl's best friend, then pearls are her secret lover: Pearls announce themselves more quietly than diamonds and should be kept separate from a woman's other jewels to avoid their bumping into one another. A pearl is really the defense an oyster mounts against an irritating particle inside its shell. The oyster secretes a substance called nacre that coats the particle; over a period of years, the layers of nacre form a pearl. *Natural pearls* occur by chance when an irritant wanders inside an oyster's shell. *Cultured pearls* are the result of an irritant planted inside the oyster by man. *Even experts cannot distinguish a natural from a cultured pearl* except by looking at their respective nuclei with the help of an x-ray.

Pearls have fascinated for many, many years. The oldest natural pearl fisheries, in Ceylon, have been worked since the beginning of the Christian era. The first attempt to culture pearls dates back to the twelfth century, in China. But it took until 1896 for Kokichi Mikimoto to develop the technique that led, ultimately, to the Japanese Bureau of Fisheries producing the first wholly spherical cultured pearl in 1909. *Kokichi Mikimoto* was also the founder of the firm by that name which is, today, possibly the world's best known pearl specialist, with their own cultivation areas and stores in Japan, New York, Los Angeles, Zurich, Frankfurt, London, and Hong Kong. Less known, but equally important, is *Tasaki Pearl,* with shops in Japan and Paris.

The effort to control the production of pearls has been so successful that no one bothers to look for natural pearls anymore. *Cultured pearls are sold in the finest jewelry stores; natural pearls are sold only at auction.* Although natural pearl necklaces are valued for their increasing rarity, they are considered less desirable by some people, since the pearls tend to be less than uniform in color and size: before the era of cultured pearls, there were many fewer pearls to choose from when creating a necklace.

The New Book of Bests asked Bonni Selfe, who buys pearls for Cartier in New York, what factors determine a cultured pearl's value. She was quick to point out that *size is most important; the larger the pearl, the more expensive it is.* But given pearls of equal size, several other factors will determine their value:

• **Luster.** The luster or orient of a pearl should be a deep, inner glow; a mere surface shine may indicate that the pearls are fake.

• **Surface.** A premium is placed on the smoothness of a pearl's surface. Although unpitted pearls are rare, pitting that is obvious to the naked eye will lessen the value of a pearl.

• **Shape.** The perfectly round pearl is the most valuable.
• **Color.** This is a highly subjective determinant of value. Among saltwater pearls, "rose pearls are considered the most desirable in the U.S.," says Ms. Selfe, "while Arabs and South Americans prefer a cream color." Black pearls, because of their relative rarity, tend toward the expensive. The adjective "natural" means they are not dyed. But, to be certain, examine the drill hole. A more intense concentration of color is a definite indication of dye. Any suggestion of green, blue, or purple in the black is another telltale dye sign. Black pearls should glow softly, if slightly inconsistently. Good-colored South Sea pearls, which grow to be quite large, are the most expensive pearls because of their rarity and the difficulty in matching them for jewelry.

Because of the tremendous variation in the quality of pearls, the price of a single strand can range from several hundred dollars to the $500,000 price tag of a necklace that Mark Sanne at Wempe Jewelers in New York, called the most beautiful he'd ever seen. "It was made of pearls from Burma that started at ten and one-half millimeters and graduated to sixteen and one-half millimeters in front. The color and quality of the pearls were exquisite. It made you wonder why anyone would buy a diamond necklace." If you're in the market for a nice necklace, any good jeweler can help. But if it's gem quality pearls you're looking for, then consult any of the fine jewelers mentioned in the Jewelers Choice section of this book.

WATCHES: LUXURY

IT used to be quite simple: the best watch was the one that was most accurate. For centuries, Switzerland had dominated the watch industry by making the finest inner workings that resulted in the most precise timepieces. That all changed in 1972 with the introduction of the quartz watch. Electronics replaced mechanical parts and suddenly even the most inexpensive watches achieved accuracy never before imagined, deviating by no more than sixty seconds a year.

The Swiss were wholly unprepared and could not revamp their factories fast enough. In less than five years, the direct U.S. import Swiss watches dropped from twelve million units to six million. Switzerland's foreign trade had been usurped by mass production of quartz watches in the Far East and in the U.S. But while they have been forced to cede large portions of what was once their market, the Swiss have held fast—and still dominate exclusively—the top, luxury line of watches. In fact, exports of luxury, handmade watches are growing at record rates. Watch experts from New York, London, and Geneva pick three names as the very best among handcrafted luxury watches. They are:

The Top Three

• **Audemars Piquet.** Audemars Piquet makes 15,000 units each year. The *Royal Oak,* its most celebrated model, looks like a ship's porthole: it's octagonal and ultra-thin. "The most copied watch in the world," one company spokesman calls it. The most expensive *Royal Oak* prices: men's—$17,000 for the 18K gold model, $18,500 with diamonds; ladies'—$12,500; $14,500 with diamonds. Audemars makes more skeleton watches (with exposed inner workings) than anyone else and also offers a perpetual calendar.

• **Patek Philippe.** Patek Philippe manufactures between 11,000 and 13,000 watches each year and prides itself on being the only company that makes all of its own movements and hand-finishes each part. Its least expensive men's watch sells for $3,850, and, as is the case with each manufacturer, maximum price is determined by the extent of jewelry added to the watch. Although Patek Philippe specializes in traditional, classic designs, its latest model, the *Nautilus,* has a rugged, sporty look. Men's *Nautilus*—$4,000, in steel; $8,000, steel and gold; $16,000, all gold. Ladies'—$3,500 in steel; $5,000, steel and gold; $9,000 all gold.

• **Vacheron Constantin.** Vacheron Constantin is the oldest Swiss watchmaker and maintains a traditional line, with some contemporary models. The company also makes quartz models, but, according to a company spokesman, "Ninety-five percent of our watches are handmade mechanicals." Vacheron makes only 10,000 watches each year, of which there are about 200 standard models. Its least expensive watch is a mechanical watch for ladies selling for $3,000. Vacheron holds the record for selling the most expensive new watch in history. The *Kallista* (Greek for "the most beautiful") was sold in 1980 for $5 million; it was made with 118 emerald-cut diamonds totaling 130 carats.

Two other names are sometimes mentioned along with this august trio: *Piaget* and *Brequet.*

The Second Echelon

Beneath these top three watchmakers, there lies a second, broader tier of quality manufacturers. Among the names most often repeated by experts: *Baume et Mercier, Cartier, Concord, Corum,*

Ebel, Girard-Perregaux, International Watch, Longines, Omega, Rolex, and *Universal Geneve.* Prices vary substantially, beginning at approximately the $1,000 price tag. It's more difficult to make distinctions in this group. *One company of lesser reputation may have a product line or two which is superior to that of another company.* It is safe to say they are all top watch firms of solid reputation. What further obscures distinctions between these companies is that, increasingly, they are all using the same inside parts made by the same Swiss suppliers. Outward design, therefore, is the only difference between many of them.

Watches as Investments

With some watches carrying $1 million price tags these days, people may view them more as investments than as mere timepieces. But watches may prove a disappointment to the person who buys them solely as an investment. *There is, in effect, no investment potential in the expensive watch,* unless someone wants to look far into the future and gamble with current models, or go back fifty years to watches that remain strong on the market, like Art Deco styles.

Another watch specialist adds, "Watches without a clear historical horological value are usually worth only the gold or gems that are in them. Quartz watches, for example, have absolutely no history and are, therefore, definitely only worth their gold content." For those buying watches as investments, the following rules apply:

• Purchase a fine mechanical watch and keep away from the standard circular face in favor of other shapes, such as rectangles or octagons.

• Purchase a watch secondhand. You can get a long-lived timepiece for a better price and the investment potential is greater.

WATCHES: SPORT

SPORTS watches today have become as much a matter of fashion as function. But if you do plan to use a watch during the course of a sport there are still essential features of construction which must be considered. If you're climbing Mount Everest, do you want the same watch that you'd use for diving in the South Seas? To find out what to look for and what to avoid, *The New Book of Bests* talked to watch manufacturers and retailers, and sports experts in various areas.

Almost all watch manufacturers make a so-called "diver's" watch—that is, one that is water-resistant, and has a rugged, sporty look. *Rolex is generally regarded as the top-of-the-line sports watch-maker* because over time they have patented and perfected an immensely water-resistant and durable timepiece. Beneath Rolex are other quality manufacturers (Omega, Movado, IWC, Longines, Tourneau, Tudor, etc.), who usually include at least one sports model. Also notable is *Heuer,* world-famous makers of stopwatches (usually called chronographs), which has now very successfully branched out into diver's and sports watches. The best rule of thumb in choosing a sports watch is to look for the features that best suit your needs, distinguishing between useful features like chronographs, and gimmicks like solar or thermal power. Here are the key elements to consider in a sports watch.

Case and crystal
• **Case.** In a sports watch, the case is of the greatest importance. The thicker the case, the more impervious the mechanism will be to variations caused by shock. Rolex has built its reputation in part on a case made of a single seamless piece of metal, providing a virtually indestructible cover for the works. But the thicker the case, the more bulky the watch will be, which might not be a drawback for a mountain climber but which would prove cumbersome for a runner. The choice of metal—whether a case in stainless steel, gold, or platinum—is purely a matter of individual preference. Gold adds considerably to the price but most manufacturers admit that *since stainless steel is actually harder than gold, it will afford better protection for the watch.*

• **Crystal.** The crystal, which protects the face of the watch, should be made of mineral glass, not plastic. It should be recessed slightly, and flat, not curved, so that it won't scratch so easily. For a durable yet extremely light sports watch consider IWC's titanium Porsche designed chronograph. Titanium is stronger than steel yet lighter; the watch is the lightest chronograph available one and three-quarter ounces. A calendar, stopwatch, and speed indicator are other useful features.

Water-Resistance
The second main feature of sports watches is water-resistance. What was once called "waterproof" must now, under American law, be labeled "water-resistant" (sometimes termed the "water integrity" of the watch), which means that it can withstand water

pressure to a depth of approximately eighty feet. Anyone who is actively involved with water (divers, surfers, windsurfers, water-skiers) or near the water (fishermen, canoeists, sailors) needs a watch that is water-resistant.

Beyond water-resistance capability there are watches made especially for divers to withstand water pressure at extreme depths. In addition to their classic Oyster Datejust Perpetual watch, water-resistant to 165 feet ($2,500 in stainless steel and 14K gold), Rolex makes the Sea-Dweller Oyster Perpetual Chronometer that is water-resistant to 4,000 feet and includes a helium escape valve to prevent build-up of pressure when used in saturation diving ($1,600 in stainless steel).

Heuer makes several diver's watches that are considered by professional divers to be just as good as the Rolex but considerably less expensive. Their Quartz 200-metres model, water-resistant to 660 feet, is $300 in stainless steel; the Quartz 1000-metres (3,300 feet) is also $300. A diver's watch should include several distinctive features: luminous numbers, a large, easy-to-read dial, and a turning bezel—an outer ring around the dial that can be moved to set the immersion time limit. Because the time limit is so important in scuba diving, the bezel should either move only in one direction (counterclockwise), or should be difficult to move, to prevent accidental turning.

Quartz vs. Mechanical

The great revolution that occurred in watchmaking in the last decade—that is, the development of quartz watches that are far more accurate than mechanical models—has affected sports watches as well as luxury ones. Many manufacturers (even Rolex) are coming out with quartz sports watches, though the top-of-the-line ones are for the most part mechanical. Most mechanical sports watches, however, tend to be self-winding (also termed "automatic" or "perpetual"), wound by the movements that you make while wearing the watch. For the sportsman, selfwinding watches make good sense, since it eliminates having to remember to wind it and also the risk that it will wind down. As for a choice between a quartz or a mechanical model, there's not much difference between the two, but, there are two things to keep in mind: 1) If you are going on a long exploration, where replacement batteries would be unavailable, a mechanical watch is preferable; 2) And quartz, while extremely accurate, varies in extreme temperatures (under 14°F and over 122°F), so unless you're planning to wear the watch on your wrist at all times, which will maintain it at body temperature, *don't buy a quartz watch for harsh conditions.*

Where the quartz versus mechanical question *does* make a big difference is in chronograph (or stopwatch) function. Quartz digital readout chronographs have great advantages in timing sports where hundredths-of-a-second accuracy is essential (in sprinting or competitive swimming, for example), or where things like lap function (where the chronograph will record the time of one lap while simultaneously timing the next lap) are needed. Analog stopwatches (ones with hands, which appear on mechanical watches), have advantages in sports where the time still available needs to be ascertained quickly (in timing football or basketball, for example).

Special Functions

In addition to time-telling, other features are often added to watches.

• When a chronograph is needed, whether digital or analog, look for one that records at least twelve hours, like Tourneau's day/date chronograph ($400 in black steel).

• A tachymeter scale on the bezel allows one to time a measured distance and convert the results into miles per hour, or to work from miles per hour over a measured distance to determine estimated time of arival. The Omega "Speedmaster," for example, includes a tachymeter scale, as well as a twenty-four-hour chronograph ($750 in stainless steel).

• IWC makes an unusual watch suitable for anyone who relies on a compass: the face of this automatic watch (with a 24K antimagnetic rotor) flips to reveal a high quality compass underneath ($1,800 in black or olive steel).

• Racing sailors would appreciate a fifteen-minute register on a watch, which marks off three five-minute segments, enabling them to cross the starting line of a race at precisely the right moment. Heuer makes a water-resistant model, with a chronograph and color-coded fifteen-minute timer ($500 in stainless steel). Heuer also makes a calculator chronograph that has a complete slide rule engraved on the bezel, suitable for pilots and navigators.

• Also suitable for sailors is Tourneau's water-resistant Moon Phase chronograph ($3,000 in 18K gold; $750 in stainless steel), which shows, in addition to the day and date, the phases of the moon.

• Runners have a different set of needs from other sportsmen. They require a lightweight watch with a highly accurate stopwatch and lap function, that doesn't need to be particularly shock-resistant. For these reasons, the inexpensive digital watches made by manufacturers like Casio, Seiko, and Pulsar are ideal. Casio in particular is favored by experienced runners, as they have developed watches with runners in mind. Their "jogger," for example has, in addition to split and lap functions, a chronograph and a calculator, a pacer that when set to the length of your stride will tell you how far you've gone ($60).

FOUNTAIN PENS

AN endangered species since the 1950s when cheap ballpoints flooded the market (to be followed by even cheaper felt-tip markers and rolling-ball writers), the fountain pen has made a dramatic and stylish comeback in the luxury field.

Where you buy a fountain pen is most important. In most cases, only large, well-established stationers and art supply houses carry an adequate selection. Department stores seldom offer informed assistance; most likely, the sales clerk was in housewares the day before. Stationers and art supply houses take fountain pens seriously because their clients do. Marilyn Brown, pen manager of Arthur Brown in New York, says, "Our customers not only write with fountain pens, but collect them. Often they come in just to talk about what new models are coming and which old ones are going out of production. We advise, explain, and discuss, but mostly we let the customers play with pens and make up their minds. A fountain pen is a personal instrument. Each customer must find the one that fits him best."

Fit is the operative word: A fountain pen must fit the hand for comfort, ease, and expression. Generally, the larger the pen the better, so long as it fills but doesn't dwarf the hand. Herewith a selection of fine fountain pens from leading American and European houses:

Mont Blanc Diplomat
Designed in 1910 and made only on order until the 1930s, this pen is a hefty instrument. Created primarily for use by men, and thus weighted more toward the back of the pen, the Diplomat has an extra large gold nib and a smooth, consistent flow of ink, even while aloft in an airplane. It is called the Diplomat because, as one devotee says, "it looks like the sort of pen you'd use to sign the Treaty of Ghent." In black, it sells for $250. An 18K solid gold Diplomat is also available, at $6,500.

Waterman de Paris
The revered American name lives on through its thriving

French subsidiary, which celebrated a century of Waterman heritage with its Le Man 100. The model equals the Diplomat in quality, but surpasses it in elegance. With an 18K nib, it comes in black at $225 and limited-edition sterling at $500.

Omas

Little-known in the U.S., Italy's Omas offers the 1930-style Gentlemen's Fountain Pen, a truly remarkable combination of size (larger than medium) and lightness (extraordinary). Its shape is a duodecigon—a twelve-sided cylinder—whose flat panels help position the pen in your hand. Accented by a gold clip and a gold Greek-key frieze surrounded by narrow gold rings, it is $145.

Parker

The "51" model made Parker internationally famous. Now history, the "51" is splendidly succeeded by the sleek Premier in Chinese lacquer at $200, grid-patterned sterling at $175, and 22K plate at $135. *Handsomest is the Premier Pin Stripe* ($150), whose gold plate is inlaid with lacquer stripes. Top of the line is an 18K solid-gold pen, at $2,500.

Shaeffer

Long the "other" American pen, Shaeffer offers an excellent calligraphic pen for under $6, but the class of its line is the 18K solid-gold Masterpiece, $3,500, and the lacquered models, $100 to $120. In-between are its Nostalgia pens, which hark back to the 1920s with jet-black cylinders richly inlaid with scrollery of sterling, $250, and vermeil, $295.

Dupont

La Plume Ultime and Line 2 series offer wide choices in lacquer—seven colors and patterns from Peking black, $280, to poudre d'or, $400. These are classic cylinder pens with 18K nibs.

Cartier

Cartier's fountain pen, topped by its famous rolling-ring symbol, is particularly eye-catching. Available gold-plated at $210, in sterling at $180, or lacquered at $260.

Cross

After decades of ballpoints, Cross had added a fountain pen, a smooth-writing design available in 14K gold at $800. Nicely scaled to medium and small hands.

BOOKS: LIMITED EDITIONS

W HILE paperbacks and computers increasingly threaten the existence of the conventional hardbound book, the demand for long-lasting, handcrafted books for aesthetic as well as reading satisfaction is on the rise. This tradition of quality bookmaking is known as fine printing and includes books primarily put together by hand using the finest materials and methods available.

In the world of high quality fine printing, one press—the Limited Editions Clubs (LEC)—is considered to be in a class alone. An elite mail-order book club, it commissions all its work from outside craftspeople. "We buy more fine typesetting, printing, and handmade paper than anyone else in the world," claims Benjamin Shiff, chief designer and son of owner, Sidney Shiff. All LEC works are richly illustrated, many by such renowned artists as Picasso, Matisse, and Larry Rivers, and made to last for centuries.

The LEC, which only publishes works by recognized literary figures, leans heavily toward literary classics both past and present. Titles include: *The Death of Artemio Cruz* by Carlos Fuentes, with illustrations by Ruffino Tamayo; *The Dubliners* by James Joyce, illustrated by Louis le Brocquy; *Romeo and Juliet* by William Shakespeare, artwork by Giacomo Manzu; *The Sea and the Mirror* by W.H. Auden, illustrated by David Hockney. During the course of the year LEC members will receive eight sumptuously handcrafted literary works like these for an annual membership fee of $2,000.

For more information, CONTACT: *Limited Editions Club, 551 Fifth Ave., New York, NY 10017; (212) 682-7115.*

Publishing Your Own

If you want to commission a quality rendition of your own (or someone else's) work, fine printing may be the answer to your needs. Many smaller presses make it possible for an individual to commission the printing of his or her favorite literary work. Frequently this is done under the tutelage of a printer who combines forces with independent typesetters, binders, craftsmen, designers, and artists to make the project an aesthetic experience.

One small press which prints books commissioned by individuals and organizations is Dan Kelcher's *Wild Carrot Letterpress* in Hadley, Massachusetts. Kelcher says that 300 copies of a forty-page volume of poetry with a high-quality paper cover might cost between $4,000 and $6,000 depending on the paper stock, type, and binding selected.

Most of the small quality printing operations, like Boston's *Heron Press,* employ less than five people, and many shops work closely with each other on projects. Depending on the kind of type, paper, and binding used, a small edition from Heron (100-500 copies) would cost between $3,000 and $5,000. Among its works, Heron Press printed the Leonard Baskin etchings to accompany Limited Edition Club's publication of *Death of a Salesman.*

In most cases, the printer's responsibility for an individual commission ends after printing. The client then takes the printed book and distributes it himself. Small U.S. publishers that do fine printing: *Anthoensen Press, P.O. Box 4726, Portland, ME 04112, (207) 774-3301; Heron Press, 36 Bromfield St., Boston, MA 02108, (617) 482-3615; Vantage Press, 516 W. 34th St., New York, NY 10001, (212) 736-1767; Wild Carrot Letterpress, 47 East St., Hadley, MA 01035, (413) 586-2648.*

STELLAR STATIONERY

FROM rags to riches has always been an American ideal, and, therefore it comes as no surprise that the prime status symbol in American paper is rag. While Europeans and Asians are renowned for their unique use of textural woods, barks, and even gunny sacks in their traditional paper making, the finest U.S. papers are 100 percent cotton rag, the basis for a paper of extraordinary finish: smooth, soft, strong, and lasting. There are two names in American machine-made cotton rag: **Crane** and **Strathmore.** Both are large companies and widely available through fine stationers across the U.S. But giant doesn't mean bad here; in fact, high technology has made both 100 percent cotton paper and the engraving associated with fine stationery very accessible. Cotton paper used to be used exclusively for legal documents, since it will not yellow or become brittle. Today it is used more widely, i.e., for personal stationery, but still remains the most prestigious sheet available.

Fine stores like Cartier and Tiffany make it a mainstay in their stationery departments. Tiffany has been using Crane's 100 percent cotton rag paper for their 140 years in the business. That is all they use and all they sell. Both Cartier and Tiffany also hand-engrave every piece of personalized stationery. A die for such engraving, with any complexity of design, can cost upwards of $200. Most engraving is not done by hand anymore. The process is computerized, cutting costs even over the traditionally cheaper thermographic method of offset printing, yet the process still utilizes a plate which is etched, inked, and printed. The beauty of engraving—i.e., subtle lines in the design and raised lettering—remain.

While cotton rag is a superior paper, fine wood papers are also available. These are mostly from Europe where design and decoration, rather than the paper, is the outstanding quality of the stationery.

• **Lalo from Paris** makes paper from part rag and part wood. Unusual colors are more frequently found in wood-based papers than in cotton rag. Lalo is no exception, designing superb sets in off-pastels or bolder brights.

• **A Florentine company named Pineider** produces an equally fine boxed stationery with a pin-thin border in such color combinations as gray and salmon, and chalky blues and reds.

• **Another Italian company, Fabriano,** makes spectacular handmade wood pulp paper. Their products, like most handmade papers, are difficult to find in commercial establishments. They are available, however, in sheets nineteen inches by twenty-six inches and are well worth cutting into letter size.

• **Japanese papers.** Handmade paper, especially that from Japan, is known for its wonderfully long and silky textures that come from fibers native only to Japan. The length of these strands also produces an incredibly strong paper—often 100 percent stronger than cotton rag paper made in the U.S. Beautiful designs in stencils, silk-screens, collage, and woodcuts adorn paper pre-cut to greeting card and stationery sizes. Aiko Art Materials in Chicago imports hand-designed cards and stationery from the only house in Tokyo still practicing the wood-cut crafts in the manner of their ancestors. *Aiko's Art Materials Import, Inc., 714 N. Wabash Avenue, Chicago, IL 60611, (312) 943-0745;* also, *80 Papers, 80 Thompson St., New York, NY 10012, (212) 966-1491.*

American rag and fine European papers can be ordered from the following stores: *Tiffany and Co., Fifth Ave. at 57th St., New York, NY 10022, (212) 755-8000; Cartier, Fifth Ave. at 52nd St., New York, NY 10022, (212) 753-0111; Henri Bendel's, 10 W. 57th St., New York, NY 10022, (212) 247-1100;* and *Dempsey & Carroll, New York, NY.*

SUNGLASSES: A CLEAR LOOK

THE best sunglasses you can buy offer *defense* (screening out the harmful ultraviolet and infrared rays) and *decoration* for your eyes. And the more you know about the lenses and the frame construction, the easier it is to buy the right sunglasses. *The New Book of Bests,* has asked several expert opticians to provide you with an understanding of the best optical quality sunglasses.

The Lenses
There are several key terms here:
• **Photochromic.** These lenses are light sensitive and light responsive, and grow darker as the sun brightens and lighter as the sun fades. One disadvantage: they require a breaking-in period before they function consistently.

• **Polarized.** With this lens the special crystal structure of the glass itself helps to reduce glare. *Polarized lenses are most effective on a horizontal surface* such as the water or the highway, and not on irregular surfaces.

• **Gradient.** The density of the protecting material in the lens varies; usually it is darker at the top of the lens and then the density decreases until it is almost clear at the bottom. Gradient lenses were first developed for pilots who had glare from above, but needed to see their instrument panel clearly. For the same reason, they are *an excellent choice for driving*.

• **Mirrored.** The lens is coated with a special chrome-nickel alloy that reduces glare and deflects heat. These are *especially good for sports like skiing* where glare from above and below can be a problem. Top quality lenses are usually precision-ground and polished. Ask about this. Make sure also that lenses are impact resistant by FDA regulations.

Lens Color
• **Gray** offers the best protection from the sun. In addition, it has a neutral effect on the colors you see. Thus, the light of every color retains its true value. A dark gray lens is the best protection for a cold bright day.

• **Green and then brown** are the next best choices after gray. The color balance is only slightly shifted. This might have some effect upon your focusing, but it is minimal. Green functions well in bright sunlight. Brown is good for sunny and warm days.

• **Yellow or amber** should be used on hazy, foggy, or cloudy days. It is not for bright sunlight. This shade actually makes objects seem brighter in order to increase contrast which sharpens detail. Shades such as blues, oranges, and pastels are more for fashion and appearance. They are not true sunglasses.

Glass vs. Plastic

Glass lenses are less likely to scratch, usually offer more protection from infrared rays, and tend to last longer. Plastic lenses, however, are lighter. Certainly cheap plastic lenses do not offer the durability and protection of glass. However, there are some top quality plastics, such as the top of the line of the CR (Canadian Resin) 39 plastic.

What Brands To Buy

Our optical experts told us that when you buy a good pair of sunglasses you *should buy the brand and expect to spend at least $30 to $300*. Their recommendations: For glass lenses the best are Ray-Ban® by Bausch & Lomb; choose Zeiss, or Porsche by Carrera for plastic lenses. All three of the above manufacturers produce top quality sunglasses.

• **Ray-Ban.** There are over fifty frame styles in a variety of lens colors. *Lens: all precision-ground and polished glass.* Price range: $50 to $2,000. (For this high price tag: 14K gold frames, lens coated with 24K gold by process called flashing.) Or, the Ambermatic™, an excellent all-weather sunglass; lenses change color and density as the amount of light and temperature shifts. They can turn from amber to brown to gray (suggested retail $75). Available with mirror coating for even more protection. Also available: full lines of photochromic and gradient lenses, women's high-fashion, sport glasses and more. All parts are fully adjustable.

• **Zeiss.** There are approximately twenty different frame styles (metal and plastic). *Lens: all CR 39 plastic in a variety of colors.* Price range: $25 to $75. Adjustable parts. Especially good high protection, lightweight glasses for sports.

• **Carrera (Porsche).** Each pair of sunglasses is handmade (eighteen different soldering steps). They are made in limited editions (serial number, year of manufacture and production sequence number appear at the left temple). *Lens: CR 39 plastic in a variety of colors.* Price range: $125 to $300. Three models: Interchangeable, comes with two sets of lenses; men's collapsible; ladies' collapsible. Frames: black matte, chrome, two-tone gold, or 18K gold plated. For $3,000 you can get 14K solid gold sunglasses (1¼ ounces of gold).

BINOCULARS

FOR the finest quality in binoculars, buy one of three brands: *Zeiss, Leitz,* or *Swarovski Optik.* Zeiss and Leitz are German optical companies, already well known in this country. Swarovski is an Austrian firm whose expertise in manufacturing fine glass is lauded in Europe; it is less familiar to Americans. Each of these companies makes a variety of binoculars in a range of sizes and magnifications for different uses. To choose the best pair for your needs, remember these basics:

• **Magnification.** Standard magnifications enlarge an image six, seven, eight, or ten times, and are indicated on the binoculars as 6X, 7X, 8X, and 10X.

• **Diameter of Objective Lens.** The objective lens is the lens at the outer end of the binocular, closest to the object being viewed. The larger the objective lens, the greater the amount of light that enters the binocular; thus, larger lensed binoculars tend to deliver a brighter, clearer image. This number is marked on the binocular next to the magnification; 8X42, for example, means that the image is magnified eight times and that the objective lens diameter is 42mm.

• **Twilight Performance.** In less-than-ideal light, many binoculars fall short: details disappear and everything begins to look gray. The twilight factor measures the quality of the image in dim light, and is determined by taking the square root of the product of the magnification and the diameter of the objective lens. The higher the twilight factor, the more detail visible under twilight conditions.

• **Diameter of the Exit Pupil.** The exit pupil is the hole you look through in the binocular's eyepiece. It should be at least as large as the pupil in your eye. The size of the exit pupil is calculated by dividing the diameter of the objective lens by the magnification. For daytime use, a 4mm exit pupil is adequate, but in dim light, when your own pupil is opened wider, you need a larger exit pupil in order to see comfortably into the binoculars. Also, in situations where it is difficult to hold binoculars steady (for example, on a sailboat), a larger exit pupil is easier to look through.

• **Field of View.** The size of the area you can see through the binoculars. It is usually expressed as the width in meters visible from a distance of 1,000 meters. In general, the wider the angle the more preferable the binoculars, as long as the field of view is not extended at the expense of image sharpness, as it often is in less expensive binoculars.

TYPE	MODEL	COST
All-purpose	Zeiss Dialyt 8 X 30B C.F.	$1,000
	Leitz Trinovid 7 X 42B	$1,250
	Swarovski Habicht 7 X 42 SL	$1,250
For: stadium sports, sightseeing		
High-power	Zeiss Dialyt 10 X 40B C.F.T.	$1,000
	Leitz Trinovid 10 X 40B	$1,200
	Swarovski Habicht 10 X 40 SL	$1,400
For: birdwatching, hunting		
Compact	Zeiss Mini 8 X 20B	$500
	Leitz Trinovid 10 X 25B C.F.	$600
For: hiking, theatergoing		

CAMERAS

IN a well-stocked camera shop today, you'll find any number of cameras sold under some familiar brand names at between $150 and $250. Mostly 35mm single-lens reflexes (SLR), they are often hawked by salespeople as "professional-model" cameras, primarily because of electronic, automated features. Don't you believe it. Automation is well down on the list of what pros are looking for—and $200 is not going to touch one of the top cameras. When *The New Book of Bests* interviewed industry experts on its quest for the top cameras, two characteristics were mentioned constantly—quality and durability. As this country's preeminent sports photographer, Neil Leifer, says: "There are two things in life I never have to worry about as a photographer. One is Kodak film and the other is Nikon cameras. I've never blown an assignment because my equipment failed to deliver. A professional photographer has enough on his mind so he must have absolute trust in his cameras."

Professional Models

• **Nikon F3.** There is unanimous agreement among all experts that the Nikon F3, a 35mm single-lens reflex, would certainly qualify as one of the best cameras on the market. Ken Hansen, whose New York camera store caters to a clientele that makes its living with a camera, says: "You just can't beat Nikon for reliability. You know it works. The optics are first-rate. The results show it." The Nikon F3 has six interchangeable viewfinders, including an autofocus and high eye-point type and twenty interchangeable focusing screens. The shutter is electronically controlled and uses a quilted titanium foil focal plane with speeds from eight to 1/2000 sec. All of the experts point to the rugged basic camera body which consists of two-piece alloy body casting with a black finish. Marty Forscher, head of Professional Camera Repair Service in New York City, and one of the most respected technicians in the camera industry, says, "Nikon is one of those cameras built like a hockey puck. It's indestructible." Average price: $600.

• **Hasselblad 500 C/M.** Pros agree that the Hasselblad 500 C/M would have to be included in any best camera category. The handmade, medium-format camera, boxier and heavier than any 35mm camera, rolls out at a very slow pace from the Goteborg, Sweden, factory where it is said to take a year to asemble one camera. They are rugged and reliable and constructed on a "box within a box" principle. Forscher calls the camera "a workhorse" and points to its "guts and weight"; the Zeiss lens gives it "the best optics of any medium-format camera." Average price: $1,100.

• **Deardorff.** Best for portraits and landscape photography—Deardorff's precision hand-crafted wooden view cameras deliver some of the sharpest and most detailed pictures possible. Prices range from $1,800 for a 4x5 camera to $5,600 for an 11x14 model. Numerous accessories are available.

• **Alpa Rotocamera.** One of the more spectacular of the panoramic cameras, this electrically operated seventeen-pound bruiser costs about $6,000 and can cover up to 360 degrees in a single photograph. It is a mite inconvenient, however. Its tripod alone is too heavy for most people

• **Panon Widelux F7.** It looks like an ordinary 35mm camera, but this panoramic camera has a kind of turret when you would expect the lens to be. The lens is inside the turret, mounted on a pivot and rotated by a clockwork drive. When you press the shutter, the lens assembly goes into action, sweeping from left to right and "painting" a 140-degree view onto the film. The Widelux uses ordinary 35mm film, but gives only about half as many shots per roll. Average price: $500.

• **Linhof Technorama.** Another panoramic camera, using 120 and 220 roll film. Its wide angle of view is equivalent to a 21mm lens on a 35mm camera, but without the distortion of the smaller format. Average price: $3,600.

Automatic and Compact Models
• **Minox 35GT.** The smallest of the world's full-frame 35mm cameras uses a four-element lens and German optical glass to produce the sharpest pictures in the compact class. Since picture quality is the primary concern of any photographer, the Minox is an excellent buy. It measures 4 by 2.4 by 1.2 inches and weighs 6.7 ounces, barely enough to cause a sag in the pocket. Average price: $350.

• **Olympus XA.** The XA's aperture performed like the Minox. The difference in the two cameras is the XA's range finder, which you can focus by merging two lines in the viewfinder. Controlling focus is a plus for the XA, but in practice the Minox zone focusing gives just as clear a picture. One advantage the XA does have is its flash, which mounts on the side rather than on top, and so fits more easily in the pocket. Average price: $300.

• **Mamiya U.** The compact Mamiya U broke with black camera tradition and brought out a sleek futuristic looking silver finish model. The Mamiya U boasts built-in flash and a warning beep and light indicating when to use it. Average price: $180.

• **Polaroid 600 SE.** Until the introduction of the 600 SE, a Polaroid camera, regardless of the model, always came with one lens that was permanently attached to the camera. This lens has a normal focal length, which was fine for taking snapshots of small groups, but if you wanted to take a landscape photograph you were out of luck. The 600 SE changed all this. It was designed to accept any of three interchangeable lenses in the most popular focal lengths: 75mm f/5.6, 127mm f/4.7, 150mm f/5.6. For the enthusiastic amateur, the 600 SE offers another major advantage: full manual control. It accepts any Polaroid pack films, black-and-white, or color print, and will yield professional-quality photographs seconds after you activate the shutter. Average price: $300 to $500.

COMPACT DISCS

RECORDED music never sounded so pure. That's the consensus opinion on compact discs (CDs), considered the most significant breakthrough in audio since the phonograph. Combining the advanced technology of digital computers with the precision of the laser beam, CDs offer a totally new way of recording and playing back sound.

Sony introduced the first CD player in 1983, and in recent years at least a dozen other major manufacturers have come forward with models of their own. The players are fundamentally the same—low-lying rectangular consoles, similar to a videocassette recorder or stereo amplifier, with a compartment for feeding compact discs (shiny plastic plates only about a third the size of conventional records) into the machine. Inside, a tiny laser beam "reads" the music recorded on the disc, just as the needle on the tone arm of a phonograph senses the grooves on a record, but what the laser is really reading is a set of instructions to a computer, which then interprets the data to make music clear and distortion-free. The CD plays only those sounds that were actually recorded. It is virtually free of the surface noise, distortion, or groove-tracking problems found in even the best of record players. *The sound produced is so clean that first-time CD listeners often swear they are hearing notes and musical phrasing other recording methods must have missed.*

While the CD players now on the market all produce high-quality sound, a few have special features like "audible scan," wireless remote control, and laser videodisc compatibility that make them stand out. *Sony, Technics, and Pioneer are recognized leaders in the new technology.*

The Compact Disc Group, a trade organization of CD hardware and software manufacturers, advises first-time buyers to first determine the price range they can afford and the features they want, then to visit an audio specialty shop and listen to as many different models as possible before making their selection. For those who already have a home stereo system, the CD player can be connected to existing amplifiers and speakers, but it will not play conventional record albums. Approximately 3,000 CD titles of mostly classical and pop music are presently available at $11 to $16 per disc, but as interest in CD expands so will the range of available titles.

The Compact Disc Group operates a toll-free hotline to answer consumer questions. Although the operators replying to calls make no product recommendations, they can answer technical questions and will refer callers to sources of compact discs or hardware. Call (800) 872-5565 or, in New York State, (212) 355-0011.

TELESCOPES

A telescope is little more than a light-gathering tube. It is the quality of the lenses, mirrors, eyepieces, and accessories that determine the scope and power of the instrument. "Fundamentally, you're looking for a telescope that forms a sharp image," says Richard Berry, editor of Astronomy magazine. "I would look for good optical quality and a solid mounting so that the telescope does not vibrate when used at high magnifications."

Size for size, a "refractor" telescope is the best choice for the beginning astronomer. A refractor looks like what most people think of as a telescope: a long thin tube, supported by a tripod, with a lens at one end and an eyepiece at the other. These telescopes tend to have the best optics, or sharpness of image. Among the refractors now on the market, the Celestron C60, available for about $700, would be a good choice. Another reliable, as well as handsome, refractor is the Renaissance, available from TeleVue of Pearl River, New York, for about $1,470. This solid brass four-inch scope, with eyepiece attachments, will magnify Jupiter or another object in view up to 286 times. It is mounted on an ash tripod and comes with its own custom carrying case.

For more power (i.e., magnification), skywatchers must turn to "reflector" telescopes. Using mirrors mounted inside, these telescopes reflect the light of a star or moon through an eyepiece mounted on the side of the tube rather than at its end. Because mirrors can be made in larger sizes than lenses (with support from behind rather than on just the outer edge), reflector telescopes can more than double the magnification power of the strongest refractor. Among reflector telescopes, a reliable model for hobbyists is the brass JSO five and one-half-inch Schmidt-Cassegrain, retailing for $895. "This is a very good telescope," says Berry. "It has nicely done mounting and it is very compact." Berry also recommends the Meade 2080/LX3, an eight-inch Schmidt-Cassegrain reflector with a lifetime warranty. This $875 telescope is mounted on a stand with an electric drive for automatically tracking the star or comet in view as it passes through the night sky.

Beyond the novice class, most authorities recommend reflectors. "Buy the biggest aperture you can afford," is most commonly advised, especially in or near metropolitan areas where city lights can make viewing difficult. The most powerful and most advanced telescope available to amateurs is a two-ton, nine-foot-tall, eighteen-inch-aperture, "catadioptric" observatory-style *Starship,* made in Japan and imported by the Allison Forge Company of Brookline, Massachusetts. This telescope will zoom in on objects in the heavens twice as close as most other amateur telescopes. The basic model costs $98,000. Available accessories include a dome in which to house it, a computer command drive, and a remote TV monitor (you can watch from your living room while the telescope is outside searching the universe). *If the sky's the limit, then this may well be the acme of amateur telescopes.*

PIPES

AS defined in the dictionary a pipe is, "an instrument for smoking, consisting of a tube of wood or clay with a mouthpiece at one end and a small bowl at the other." Within that definition—wood, mouthpiece, bowl—reside the qualities that separate the great pipe from the ordinary. Among pipe shop proprietors, importers, manufacturers, and pipe smokers, there is universal agreement that the world's best pipes come from Dunhill, Charatan, and Comoy in Great Britain; Ivarson, Stanwell, and Nording in Denmark; Savinelli in Italy; and Peterson in Ireland. While some may argue that a pipe is a pipe is a pipe, close examination of the top line of each of the above manufacturers will reveal craftsmanship and quality which a true pipe smoker will quickly recognize.

Dunhill
Generally acknowledged as the number one name in the business, Dunhill has established the hallmark for the pipe. Dunhill pipes start at $180 and range upward. Dunhill, which traces its origins to Alfred Dunhill and the turn of the century, utilizes seventy to eighty different processes in producing a pipe and uses briar from the White Heath species of heather whose shrubs have matured from sixty to 150 years and then, after cutting, are seasoned for another two years. Briar comes from France, Corsica, Italy, and other Mediterranean countries.

Stanley Levy of *Iwan Ries* of Chicago, a tobacco shop that Stanley Marcus in *Quest for the Best* called, "The best pipe store I've ever come across," says, "There is a tremendous amount of handwork involved in any Dunhill pipe. Some of their limited editions have become collector's items and command a good price as collectibles." The Dunhill handwork produces just the right thickness of the wood in both bowl and stem, the accuracy of the boring and the precision with which the mouthpiece is fitted. Then each pipe is shaped for optimum comfort and balance. The toughness and close grain of the briar help to absorb "tars" contained in tobacco smoke and the ideal weight produces pure, cool smoke. It is said that Dunhill rejects ninety-eight percent of all bowls made because of imperfections. The mouthpieces are cut from blocks of compressed vulcanite and shaped to fit snugly and firmly between the teeth. Dunhill's rarefied species are packaged under "straight grains," "special editions," and those embellished with silver or gold.

Charatan

Charatan, a subsidiary of Dunhill, produces pipes of equal quality in its top-bracketed pipes. Established in 1843 and now manufacturing pipes in a wing of Dunhill's London factory, Charatan is renowned not only for its rare Summa Cum Laude, a $10,000 pipe, but for its "Supreme" series, a collection of the tightest, finest-grained (a straight grain is valued for appearance's sake), one-of-a-kind pipes adorned with freehand designs and selling for $350 to $600. As a part of the company slogan reads: " . . . We'll just have to be content with selling the best . . ." Charatan does take its time and never compromises—each year it produces only a dozen of its Coronation style ($1,500) pipes.

Comoy's

Another English manufacturer pipe experts praise is Comoy's, which dates to 1825 and the French village of Saint-Claude. The Blue Riband series is considered one of the top pipes in the world. Made from a flawless piece of briar, it is a lightweight, wonderful pipe. One expert called it "one of the great pipes of all time. Very elegant." Priced at $250, the Blue Riband is hard to find; only forty to fifty are produced a year.

Savinelli

Occupying any best pipe rack would be a selection from Savinelli Pipes of Milan, Italy. Testament to its quality is provided by Neiman-Marcus which sells an exclusive Savinelli pipe designed for the store by Stanley Marcus and called the Chairman's pipe. Savinelli has the most inclusive line in the whole industry. As an example, there is the Autograph series, fifteen pipes of different finishes from smooth to sandblasted and different shades, each bearing the signature of Achille Savinelli on the stem. All are handmade, free form in shape and priced from $150 to $600. Savinelli also has a very limited number of pipes in its Golden Jubilee series, of traditional shape in smooth or sandblasted finish and priced at $200.

Peterson's

The country that made Jameson and Bushmill whisky, Waterford crystal, Belleek china, Donegal tweed, and Irish lace synonymous with the best has made Peterson's Pipes of Dublin among the best pipes in the world. Since 1875, this Irish pipemaker has been producing some of the most elegant and distinctive pipes, particularly its Spigot series which is regarded as one of the most attractive styles produced in bent pipes. They range in price from $110 to $400. If you should ever come across one of the 400 Limited Edition replicas of Mark Twain's 1896 pipe, and can afford to buy, you'll own one of the best collectibles in pipes. Its unnumbered Deluxe version brings about $300.

Ivarson

Denmark was the first country to create free form pipes and its manufacturers are still recognized for their artistic craftsmanship. Iwan Ries' Levy considers Denmark's Ivarson as the top Danish pipemaker. He says, "Ivarson is king. Nobody touches him for his ideas and workmanship." He might also add price. Since no two Ivarson pipes are alike, costs range from $1,000 to $3,000 per pipe. The Danish firm of Stanwell also rates at the top because of its workmanship and innovative design, and another, Nording, was one of the original free-hand manufactures.

• Other fine pipe names to consider: Costello, Micole, Wilmer, Wilke, du Pont, Ascortie, Sasieni, and Radice.

CIGARS

FOR all the cachet of great riches which is traditionally associated with the cigar there is no more easily affordable pleasure in the world than that provided by a tobacco leaf rolled in a fashion not markedly different than it was when Rodrigo de Xeres, who sailed with Columbus to the New World, became the first Westerner to smoke a cigar—according to legend—on October 28, 1492, in what is now the Dominican Republic. Today, you can go to Dunhill's and buy a box of twenty-five Ramon Allones handcrafted cigars for $40. Which means that for $1.60 each, you can enjoy one of the supreme examples of the ancient art of cigar making for less than the price of a Big Mac and a Coke. *Excellent cigars are not only within the economic reach of everyone; they are also readily available.* Iwan Ries, Wally Frank, and Dunhill's are well-known stores for fine cigars. But any tobacconist who wishes to buy stock from a first-class supplier can offer his customers the finest in cigars. Provided, of course, he stores them properly. Unfortunately, very few have the knowledge or the desire to give cigars the attention they deserve. When you go to a cigar store, check to see if it has humidor storage facilities. If it does not, you are almost certain to be in for stale stock. You would be better off buying through the mail from a reputable dealer.

Enormous Variety

The greatest problem facing a cigar buyer is trying to choose from among the enormous variety available. First there is the leaf. There is Cuban leaf and leaf from Honduras, Brazil, Sumatra, Mexico, Jamaica, and the Philippines, just to name a few of the most prominent suppliers of good tobacco leaf. Then there is the cigar shape. The corona and the lonsdale are among the most popular, but there are those who prefer a perfecto, a panatela, a torpedo, or a culebras. And there is the color. Starting with the green double claro, cigars work their way progressively darker to the colorado, the maduro, and finally to the black and bitter oscura. *Strictly speaking, you should order a cigar by its brand, its shape, and its color.* The combinations are almost endless. Zino Davidoff, who has been in business in his shop on Rue de Marche in Geneva for so long he still carries an unpaid bill from Lenin on his books, has calculated there are more than 1,000 possible variations of the Havana cigar alone.

So where do the best cigars come from and who makes them? According to veteran cigar buyers, the following seven brands stand out as truly exceptional and among the world's finest. All are available at better tobacconists around the country.

The Davidoff (Havana, Cuba) is still the reigning king of the Havanas, reminiscent of the pre-embargo glory days. An excellent bouquet with some of the most perfect wrappers ever used on a Havana characterize this cigar. Distributed by Zino Davidoff of Switzerland, it is sold uncellophaned in bundles of fifty, priced from $10 to $20 per cigar, depending on country of purchase.

The J-R Ultimate Line (Honduran) is a well-constructed cigar available in a wide range of sizes and shapes. It comes in a natural wrapper—leaves of tobacco which have all been aged under the sun. Consequently, there are variations in the shades of these cigars because some wrapper leaves were dried in the sun longer than others. *Considered best are the medium brown, silky-looking wrappers.* The top of this superior line is the special Corona series. This is a limited edition cigar, said to number as its devoted followers more men of wealth and status than any other cigar can claim. Distributed exclusively by the J-R Tobacco Company of New York, it is sold uncellophaned to allow the cigar to breathe and is priced from 80¢ to $1.75 per cigar.

The Hoyo de Monterrey-Excalibur (Honduran) is "the closest to the finest Cubans on today's market," says Lew Rothman, president of J-R Tobacco Company, the world's largest cigar wholesaler. An unusually light and smooth wrapper with very little bite is the trademark of this cigar. Distributed by Danby-Palicio of Upper Saddle River, New Jersey, it is sold in beautifully handcrafted wooden boxes for between $1 and $2 per cigar.

The Royal Jamaica and the **Macanudo** (Jamaican) were both said to be favorites of the great cigar connoisseur, British Prime Minister Sir Winston Churchill. The Royal Jamaica is known for an unusual sweet nutty taste. The filler tobaccos used here are superb. Available in natural wrappers only, it is packed in beautiful Spanish cedar chests. Distributed by Lane, Ltd., Tucker, Georgia. Prices range from $1 to more than $4 per cigar.

The Macanudo is made under the consultancy of *Ramon Cifuentes,* a great master cigar blender. The name says it all: macanudo means "a good thing." This is a very light, fragrant, even-burning cigar with a good range of sizes, shapes, and shades. Distributed by Montego Ycia, a company of the Culbro Corporation of New York, this cigar is priced from $1.00 to $3.00

The Punch and the **Hoyo de Monterrey** (Honduran) are both made from the same tobaccos, with some subtle differences. The Punch cigars are stronger tasting with more bite. Hoyo de Monterreys tend to be more aromatic and mellowed. Both have excellent aroma and flavor and represent a real value to the consumer. Distributed by Danby-Palicio of Upper Saddle River, New Jersey, for under a dollar to more than two.

Other distinguished cigars often recommended by discriminating cigar smokers are the **Partagas** of the Dominican Republic, **Te-Amos** of Mexico, **Santa Claras** of Mexico, and the **Rey del Mundos** of Honduras.

Points to Remember

The smoking of a cigar is an endeavor given to much ritual and a great deal of nonsense has been written about the subject. A cigar, after all, is something you light on one end and puff at on the other. But most experts agree there are a few points worth remembering when addressing yourself to a truly fine cigar.

• **Selection.** Pick the style and shape you are most comfortable with, remembering that, in general, the darker the leaf, the heavier and more full-bodied the smoke. You can sniff a cigar if you want to, but that will not tell you much about the condition or the aroma of the smoke to come. A cigar smells like tobacco. One useful test, however, is to roll the cigar lightly between the thumb and forefinger. If it crackles, it is either stale or Dutch or quite possibly both.

• **Preparation.** A cigar has to be opened up at the smoker's end before being lit. It is axiomatic that a cigar with a small hole in the end of it is not a quality cigar. The opening can be made with your teeth, your fingernail, or a cutter. The opening, however, should be clean and a cutter, either a bevel-edged or a guillotine model, is preferred. Do not pierce the cigar in any way. A hole driven into the end creates a tunnel which fills with hot smoke and leaves a bitter taste.

• **Lighting.** A good cigar should not be lit with a live fire. Keep the end slightly away from the flame and let the heat draw in until a small coal of tobacco is formed. This will keep the cigar from getting too hot early on and burning out the flavor.

• **Smoking.** Smoke a good cigar leisurely and let it develop its own cruising speed. Each cigar, depending on how tightly it is wrapped, has a pace of its own and should not be forced. Davidoff estimates that a five-inch corona should yield about fifty puffs and take fifty to sixty minutes to consume.

• **Extinguishing.** When a cigar is ready to go out, let it die a natural death. Don't stub it out on an ash tray. It is the stubbed-out cigar butt that causes most of the smoke odors ladies complain always stay in the curtains.

• **Storing.** All tobacconists sell cigar humidors. However, although humidors may be attractive places in which to store loose cigars, they are not terribly helpful in preserving them for any length of time. Cigars should be stored at no more than sixty-seven degrees temperature and not less than sixty percent humidity. No home humidor box can maintain both of those conditions which are necessary to keep cigars fresh. An old wooden box in a damp cellar would do as well. Some smokers put their cigars in plastic bags and store them in the vegetable crisper in the refrigerator. The fact is, no home storage is really adequate. The best humidor is the cigar store itself. Buy only what you think you might need by the month and let the store keep its cigars fresh in its own facilities.

LUGGAGE: CONTEMPORARY

T ODAY'S traveler, whether in a car, train, plane, or cruise ship, wants luggage that gets him and his belongings to his destination quickly, securely, and in style. To accommodate an increasingly mobile population the industry has evolved *three families of luggage: hard cases, descendants of old-fashioned trunks, which offer the strongest protection; semi-soft luggage, strong but lightweight due to innovative construction; and soft or unconstructed bags,* made, for the most part, to be carried on a plane rather than to withstand the abuses of airline luggage handlers. Dealers, buyers, and spokesmen for the trade make the following choices of the best luggage in each of these three categories. They also provide four general tips on what you should look for when evaluating a piece of luggage.

Semi-Soft Luggage

Any luggage that has some sort of construction that gives it a definite shape, but has a soft top and bottom, is called semi-soft. Semi-soft luggage has taken the place of hard luggage in today's quality market because it is lighter in weight. People buy it, usually in a matched set of several pieces, when they are seriously investing in all-purpose luggage to use over a period of many years. The twenty-four-inch and twenty-nine-inch suitcases (sizes refer to the length of the bag) are the most popular.

• **Hartmann** has introduced the Soft Pullman, a suitcase with sides elastic enough to let you overpack, but constructed with a unique "crushable frame" that springs back into shape after heedless sky-caps have done their worst. Equipped with non-rustable nylon zippers and solid brass padlocks that clearly mean business, the Soft Pullman also has a flexible bottom that prevents the sagging and shifting that wrinkles clothing. The twenty-four-inch Hartmann Soft Pullman lists for $270, and a matching tote bag is $180.

• **French.** The French Company of Covina, California, makes a line of semi-soft luggage that is carried by quality luggage shops everywhere. It is recognized for the high quality of its workmanship. The fabric and the leather for each bag, for example, are cut out individually, rather than in stacks, and the bags are hand-assembled, one at a time. French's unique construction consists of wooden supports that are placed in the four sides of the bag's perimeter to give it a firm shape and to protect its contents. When the bag is not in use, these plywood planks can be removed so that the bag collapses for storage. Priced at around $300 for a twenty-nine-inch bag.

• **Lark.** Another manufacturer of semi-soft luggage respected in the luggage business, Lark bridges the gap between the unstructured and semi-structured categories with its innovative Two-in-One Expandables. Formulated upon the incontrovertible proposition that luggage space requirements tend to increase over the course of a trip, Expandables create extra space with side panels that open and shut by means of exclusive FasTrac zippers. Lark produces Expandable versions of virtually all major pieces including medium and large duffels ($130-$150), medium and long Trippers or "closets away from home" ($185-$215), and packing cases with suit fixtures ($250).

• **Fulton Company.** Another exceptional line of semi-soft luggage is produced by the Fulton Company of New York City. Fulton manufactures two different constructions that are its trademark: a tubular aluminum frame, so strong a person can stand on it, and a spring steel frame that gives under pressure and then bounces back to its original shape. The steel frame weighs slightly less. A twenty-nine-inch bag will cost around $300.

• **Superior** luggage from France addresses the needs of the luxury traveler. Its high-tech shell is molded of soft vinyl, which combines the strength of leather with the weight of a miracle fabric. One turn of an individually numbered key locks the suitcase at four different points and a green Carrera racing stripe encircles the case with a protective rubber bumper. Comes in six colors and two sizes, priced between $225 and $275.

• **T. Anthony.** A New York shop which has met the luggage needs of Park Avenue residents for nearly forty years. Carries its own line of high-quality, semi-soft bags.

Hard Luggage

Hard luggage, although very heavy compared to semi-soft, does have one great advantage. It offers the best protection to its contents. Deflecting rather than rolling with the punches, the hard case itself is more durable under the roughest treatment. Hard luggage has always been favored by people who want to travel with wrinkle-free clothes: it does not have to be packed tightly (the cause of wrinkles) the way softer luggage does and hangers and rods keep everything from falling to the bottom when the bag is lifted.

• **Louis Vuitton.** A name synonymous with luxury luggage since its first Paris showroom opened in 1854. Traditional handcrafted French-made Vuitton luggage consists of solid plywood boards covered with the distinctive Vuitton canvas. Now a new Challenger line has been introduced. Otherwise equal to Vuitton standards, this luggage weighs much less and sports a burgundy-colored fabric, but sans the beloved "LV" monogram. A thirty-one-inch suitcase sells for about $1,250; a twenty-three-inch valise is close to $1,100.

• **Halliburton.** A more modern look in hard luggage is achieved by Halliburton, a line of extremely durable luggage of molded aluminum, made by the Zero Corporation in Burbank, California. Designed in the 1930s in the streamlined Art Deco style, Halliburton is finding new admirers. Fireproof, waterproof (in fact, it floats) and odor-proof, it is a favorite with people who want to insure that their clothes (or costumes) will arrive in perfect condition. Some even use these sturdy bags to carry works of art or other valuables. And in today's world of miniaturized electronics, yet another use has been found: Professionals and business people use it to carry their lap-type personal computers that could easily be damaged in a less durable valise. The luggage does not get dented or scratched, and, at nineteen pounds empty for a twenty-six-inch Pullman bag, it's one of the heaviest lines on the market. A twenty-six-inch silver bag costs from $415 to $495.

• **Samsonite.** The Odyssey line features coordinated pieces of hard and soft luggage. Its hard-side cases have protective bumpers, four recessed wheels, and a leather tether for easy pulling. A twenty-six-inch suiter costs about $175.

Soft Luggage

But a growing number of people reject the traditional style of packing in favor of carry-on luggage—a garment bag and some sort of bag that fits under an airplane seat. Besides being light, carry-on bags alleviate the wait and chaos of the luggage claim and give the owner full control over how his luggage is handled. A wide variety of soft or unconstructed luggage caters to this style of travel. The business person is particularly benefited by this new style in luggage, since he or she often hopscotches across the country making quick stops on a tight schedule.

• **Andiamo.** This California firm manufacturers several lines of indestructible featherweight luggage. Various sizes of unique square duffels, carry-ons, garment bags, Pullmans, and toilet kits in the regular Andiamo line have shells composed of Teflon-coated eleven-ounce Colors nylon, an extremely lightweight, waterproof, and abrasion-resistant fabric. Available in blue, green, and brown for between $30 and $400 per piece, Andiamo luggage has full-grained American cowhide handles and trim plus sturdy, marine-quality nickel/chrome-plated steel hardware.

• **Louis Vuitton.** Offers a hanging bag in vinyl-coated cotton canvas with the familiar "LV" and *fleur-de-lis* pattern that holds six to eight dresses and costs about $500; a men's version is around $450.

• **Trafalgar, Ltd.** Makers of the handsome "Ghurka" collection, which includes a roomy carry-on bag with zippered pouches for tennis rackets on one side, briefcase on the other. Sells for about $300.

• **French.** The extremely well-constructed L'Image garment bag comes in tightly woven brown tweed trimmed with natural and brown suede for about $480.

• **Bill Bayley.** A California company making soft luggage of ballistic nylon. Carry-on and garment bags sell for under $200.

LUGGAGE: LEATHER

U NTIL the advent of the "miracle" materials made possible by
the twentieth-century technological revolution, leather was
considered the only appropriate material for luggage. Now, when
many other materials like poly-canvas, hard plastic, and vinyl can
be used for luggage, leather still remains the first choice of many.
The primary reason for this is its durability. Leather can rebound
from stress that would be catastrophic for other materials. Beyond
its remarkable strength, leather is sensuously beautiful in a way
that no synthetic can be.

The New Book of Bests talked with leather luggage specialists—
buyers, dealers, manufacturers—to determine who makes the top
quality leather luggage and what to look for when investing in these
expensive cases. When choosing a case there are two basic considerations: the type and quality of the leather, and the quality of the
workmanship.

Leather

Because leather is a natural material, its quality can vary
greatly. Everyone we spoke with agreed that high quality leather is
pliable (with the exception of rawhide, about which more later),
smooth and of an even thickness. Leather should be tanned so that
its natural beauty comes through: the small imperfections (veins,
stretch marks) and the grain of the leather should be visible.
Because tanning removes the natural oils that give leather its
smoothness and resiliency, avoid leather that has been tanned very
heavily, recognizable by a thickly polished surface with no
"natural" look to it.

Of the several different kinds of leather used in luggage, by far
the most common is that taken from the cow. There are several
different kinds of cowhide:

• **Belting** is a heavy harness leather that is carefully dressed and
oiled to provide a strong flexible skin that won't stretch. The oil in
the leather makes it water-resistant and encourages the development over time of patina on the leather that masks scuffing and
scratches.

• **Top grain cowhide** (also called full grain cowhide) is the
unsanded top portion of the hide and is usually a first-class piece
reasonably free of scars and blemishes.

• **Grained cowhide** is slightly embossed with a grain and is often
chosen because it conceals dirt and abrasion better than a completely smooth cowhide.

• **Calfskin,** so-called when it is taken from an unweaned calf, has a fine grain and is supple and durable. (Leather made from a somewhat older calf is called veal-skin.)

• **Rawhide** is an extremely durable cowhide that has been processed but not tanned, which gives it a white color and makes it quite stiff. Because it is susceptible to moisture, it must be varnished and can only be used on hard cases.

Other leathers:

• **Ostrich** is a tough, hard-wearing skin but is not widely available because of its expense; for example, a twenty-four-inch ostrich bag sells for $3,000.

• **Water buffalo,** which has a dull matte finish with many markings, has lately become popular due to its strength and scuff-resistance.

• **Alligator and crocodile** are seldom seen in luggage rather than carry-ons simply because they are so expensive.

• **Nappa, sheep, or lamb hide,** is incredibly silky and pliant, and is used almost exclusively on soft luggage. Although it is quite strong, because it is used on soft luggage, it may not protect as well as some other kinds.

The Top Brands

• **Hermès.** The ultimate leather luggage is made by Hermès of Paris. Like many quality leather manufacturers, Hermès started as a saddle and harness maker, then turned to luggage and handbags after the advent of the automobile. Each Hermès case is made completely by hand by a master craftsman who has served years of apprenticeship before he is allowed to make a piece on his own. As a result, every Hermès piece is a work of art. And their prices reflect this superb quality: a twenty-four-inch zippered case with a hard bottom and a soft top—the best of both worlds—in veau graine (a beautiful grained calf) with smooth calf trim sells for about $1,500. One of the most famouse Hermès handbags is the "Kelly" bag, named for the late Princess Grace of Monaco, and they also make a large-size version called the "Travel Kelly," available in two sizes: the "Fjord," in durable and washable cowhide, is $1,500; the "High Handle" at eighteen-inches is somewhat larger and costs $2,300. Famous for its custom work (which is all done in Paris) Hermès has U.S. stores in New York, Chicago, Palm Beach, Bal Harbour, San Francisco, and Beverly Hills.

• **Mädler.** One notch down from Hermès is German-made Mädler luggage, carried in Mädler's stores around the world and in some specialty shops. Their case is a distinctive soft-sided bag with a zipper and straps that starts at $800 for a one-suiter carry-on. Mädler also stocks water buffalo cases starting at $900.

• **Mark Cross.** Another fine manufacturer is the American firm of Mark Cross, which also began as a saddler in Boston in 1845. "All of our leather cases are handmade; nothing is mass-produced," says a Mark Cross spokesman, "Our bags are all crafted for us in Italy by a very select group of craftsmen." Because they are hand-crafted, some of their lines are produced in limited quantities, but can be specially ordered; delivery time is three to six months. Their most popular leather line is Signet, handsome soft-sided cases in luggage-brown calf with dark pigskin trim: twenty-four-inch bag, about $650. Also available in a hard case: $850. One of their new-est lines is an incredibly beautiful wine-colored grained calf bag with a hard case: a twenty-four-inch bag is $780.

• **Karl Seeger.** Karl Seeger is another top German manufacturer available in this country. One of their current offerings is sump-tuous nappa soft luggage in black. These bags, designed to be car-ried on, are lined in elegant gold-and-black striped cotton. A two-suiter is $890; a garment bag, $1,000.

• **Gold-Pheil.** Gold-Pheil, also of Germany, makes quality soft-sided bags of leather that is shrunk before it is fitted on to the frame, so that it is more scratch-resistant. The bags feature a lightweight but extremely strong aluminum frame with the leather stitched to it: a twenty-four-inch case in deep burgundy is about $700.

• **Gucci.** Gucci, famous for its interlocking Gs fabric luggage trimmed in pigskin, also makes high quality leather cases with alu-minum frame and soft sides, zippered and with straps. Made in Italy and available in the fifteen Gucci stores around the U.S., the cases come in several colors and styles, in either leather or suede ($400 for a weekend case; $600 for a twenty-four-inch case; and $650 for the largest size; suede is somewhat higher). One of their best offerings is a set of pigskin cases which look as though they would last practically forever; a weekend case is $675, and a three-suiter, $900. Gucci will add their distinctive red-and-green stripe to any bag at a nominal fee.

• **Bottega Veneta.** Bottega Veneta's trademark is pressed calf etched with a fine diamond pattern. Their luggage, which is hard-sided and square with brass fittings on the corners, is reminiscent of old-fashioned trunks, and comes in deep shades of green, navy, brown, and black: $700 for a twenty-four-inch case; up to $900 for the largest size they stock. (They have discontinued their soft-sided leather luggage, replacing it with a less expensive vinyl version, also with diamond etching.) Bottega Veneta luggage is available in all Neiman-Marcus and I. Magnin stores, as well as in their own New York and Beverly Hills stores.

• **Tanner Krolle.** Tanner Krolle of England makes leather cases that some feel are among the best made anywhere. The hand-stitched, oil-finished cowhide bags have a partial frame with a zip-per and straps, and will expand up to two inches when packed full. A one-suiter is $600; a two-suiter, $650.

• **Other Top Leather Sources.** Many specialty stores carry rawhide luggage from Florence, in creamy white with medium brown trim. The wooden-framed cases also have an old-fashioned look and are often billed as a "lifetime case" since they are so dura-ble. A weekend bag, lined in cotton, is $650; a genuine wardrobe trunk, $1,250. Because of their light color, however, they are best used on private planes rather than entrusted to commercial air-lines. Look also for leather goods by Fendi, Ferragamo, Cartier, Navarro, Nazareno Gabrielli, Roberta di Camerino, and Dooney & Bourke. Many manufacturers of shoes and handbags will, on occasion, produce a suitcase or two. Bally, for example, with seven-teen stores in the U.S., will sometimes carry a suitcase though they don't make a full line of luggage.

Leather in America

High quality bags are produced in America too, but since they are mass-produced, they are not of the same high quality as those imported from Europe. The top brands are Atlas, Hartmann, Fulton, French, and Ghurka.

• **Atlas** bags are made from top quality belting leather with a hard frame and an elegant, tightly fitted, zippered linen interior ($570 for a two-suiter).

• **The Hartmann** bag, also made of belting leather with a partial frame, is a handsome square case that sells for $450 for a one-suiter, $550 for a two-suiter.

• **Fulton** makes soft-sided bags with a spring steel frame, ranging from $310 for a carry-on bag to $610 for a 32-inch three-suiter.

• **French** makes leather and suede versions of its well-crafted soft-sided bag ($380 for a 24-inch suede bag).

• **Ghurka** makes an oiled vealskin version of its well-known twill-and-leather bags: prices range from $25 to $525.

Custom Work

Custom work is a thriving business in leather, since people who can afford leather bags can often afford extra expense to get exactly what they want. And expensive it is—T. Anthony recently produced a custom cosmetic case with interior fittings for almost every kind of jar or bottle. The price tag: $4,000. Most specialty stores will custom-make bags though some like Mädler and Gucci feel that it's sometimes so difficult to get shipments from abroad that custom-made bags are out of the question.

Buying Tips

Always try to buy from a specialty shop whenever possible. Many department stores carry American-made leather bags, and perhaps even some imported cases as well. At a specialty shop, however, the sales people are generally better informed and the selection is usually better too. All specialty shops will repair the luggage they sell, and some, like Dinoffer's, guarantee that they will do repairs for the lifetime of the bag. Quality luggage is available at the following shops, among others.

Atlanta: Mori Luggage and Gifts

Chicago: Deutsch Luggage Shop

Cincinnati: Bankhardt's Luggage Shop

Denver: A.E. Meek Trunk and Bag Co.

Los Angeles: Beckel's Luggage Stores

Miami: Bentley's Luggage

New Orleans: Rapp's Luggage and Gifts

Philadelphia: Robinson Luggage Co.

Phoenix: Leonard's Luggage

Washington, D.C.: Camalier and Buckley

CARS: LUXURY LINES

LUXURY cars, more so than sports cars or mass-produced vehicles of the proles, have always been the showcase for a manufacturer's technical excellence. Unencumbered by weight limitations and price ceilings the grand marques of the past and present have let their imaginations run wild, sometimes too wild, by incorporating every imaginable convenience and luxury item they can think of in their top-of-the-line models.

Some of the daring machines of the past have lived on to become classics. Others died a well-deserved death. Yet, even among the cars of the past which are considered classic milestones you'll find turkeys of the first order. The reason for this was the way cars were made and sold back then. A well-heeled luxury car buyer would stroll into a Duesenberg showroom, pick a chassis he liked and flip through a catalog of finished bodies built by one of the dozens of coachbuilders scattered throughout the country. Arrangements were made to ship the Duesenberg chassis, nothing more than a motor, frame, and wheels at this point, to the coachbuilder of his choice. The customer would then tell the coachbuilder exactly what he wanted. Everything from the number of doors to the color of the border for the upholstery was decided by the customer. For this reason you'll never find two identical cars of the same make. Each was tailor-made.

Coachbuilders with little integrity and lots of greed would execute whatever atrocity a paying customer wanted. Others, like Fleetwood, Brewster, Derham, and Rollston would simply refuse to do the work and send the tasteless *nouveau riche* packing. For the collector, this is an important fact to keep in mind. While a Duesenberg may be a Duesenberg with all the cachet that goes with it, the coachbuilder and his execution of the work are equally important in determining the real value of a luxury car of grand marque.

By the start of World War II most of the coachworks either failed or were swallowed up by corporations such as GM. Post-war luxury cars, therefore, don't vary as much in coachwork, fittings, or execution. They are standardized in that respect and the collector needs to look only at mileage, authenticity of parts, and fittings and general mechanical condition. Here are some of the best.

Pre-War Luxury Cars

• **Duesenberg.** The most desired model and one that makes *the* Herculean Duesenberg statement is the Derham Tourster built on the J Model Duesenberg. It had a dual-overhead camshaft, thirty-two-valve head, in-line eight-cylinder motor that displaced 420 cubic inches. It was one of the smoothest most powerful engines ever fitted to a car, with the exception of the SJ, supercharged version of the same engine. Philip Derham was hired as liaison between the Duesenberg factory and the coachbuilders to make sure the Duesy look and ethic remained intact and not destroyed by fanciful customers. It sold for around $11,000 in 1931 and Gary Cooper, Joe E. Brown, and Johnny Weismuller were among the Hollywood set who owned a Tourster.

• **Cadillac.** The most fabulous of all were the V-16 models which were built in small numbers, comparatively speaking, between 1930 and 1940. There were very few turkeys, except for the later years when GM stylists decided to pursue the AeroDynamic look. One of the best V-16s is the Sports Phaeton of 1930–31.

• **Packard.** Any Packard built by Murphy or LeBaron. The most sought after are the LeBaron-bodied Speedsters, Sport Coupe, and Sport Phaeton. They cleanly made the transition between the traditional straight up radiator and tall tail look and the new aerodynamic look that was becoming the vogue. These models were all V-12s.

Post-War Luxury Cars (Still in production)

• **Bentley.** *The* Bentley to have is the Mulsanne Turbo. Imagine a 4,800 lb. car accelerating 0 to 60 mph in 6.9 seconds and able to maintain a 135 mph speed for hours on end. All this while you're surrounded by leather and wood that's as finely assembled as the lifetime employees can make it. Grace, elegance, and blinding speed isn't easy to combine in a luxury car but for £56,000 Bentley will build one for you. Bentley does not quote horsepower figures. Horsepower for the non-turbo Mulsanne is quoted as "adequate." For the Turbo version "adequate plus 50 percent."

• **Aston-Martin Lagonda.** The first U.S.-legal Lagonda was delivered in February, 1983. They'll be trickling in at a snail's pace and the asking price is $150,000. For that you get a hand-built body, hand-stitched upholstery, and a hand-built four-overhead cam V-8 motor complete with a plaque stating the date of engine manufacture and the name of the man who assembled it. Horsepower rating is undisclosed but the car in U.S. smog trim has been clocked at 140 mph and can sustain that speed all day without even breathing hard. Old World craftsmanship is combined with high-tech electronics to bring a lucky owner a complete digital electronic dash with touch-sensitive controls.

• **Rolls-Royce.** Any of them. Despite socialism, labor strikes, wars, and the incursion of Mercedes into the Rolls market, R-R quality has never wavered. Hand assembly, each bolt brought to the assembly line in its own little plastic baggy, 100-year-old wood for the dash, leather from cattle raised on special diets in farms without barbed wire—all of it part of the Rolls tradition. They've never been leaders in technology, high performance, or heaven knows, *styling,* but every single one of them has been exceedingly well turned out.

CARS: THE PURE SPORTS

THE true and pure sports car, while it may not be dead, is certainly on the endangered species list. It's gotten to the point where most people, including the experts, can't even agree on what makes a sports car. It wasn't always like this. Sports cars were blood red, made an unholy noise, only came up to your belt buckle and, by God, were they fast. Some of them could accelerate to 100 mph and brake back down to zero in the time it takes some contemporary "sporty" cars to barely get up to 55. In short, we're talking *serious* performance here.

Golden Age vs Contemporary

The glory days of the true and pure sports were roughly the two decades between 1945 and 1965. This was the period when the houses of Ferrari, Lamborghini, Maserati, Porsche, Alfa-Romeo, and Lancia came into their own. Their volume was very small, but the proliferation of body styles, engine designs, and displacements were staggering. Along with the great houses were the *carrozerie,* putting some of the most exquisite bodies ever built onto what were essentially road racing cars: People like Bertone, Castagna, Pininfarina, Vignale, Ghia, Zagato, Michelloti, and the master himself, Giugiaro—in constant demand to design a body for this or that street racer. In fact, these cars, even though they had things like headlights, windshield wipers, barely adequate heaters and cooling vents, were nothing more than race cars in thinly disguised street garb. Yes, you could drive them from your apartment's underground garage to your house in the country without too much trouble or overheating, but they were most at home roaring around at full chat on the back roads. Unfortunately, the state of sports cars these days isn't such a pure one. Cars with that kind of uninhibited performance, style, and heritage no longer exist. In their place we have the mass-produced cars like the Datsun 300ZX Turbo, Mazda RX-7, Corvette, and Porsches. *Worthy cars all, but nothing really like the legendary cars of the postwar period.* Certainly they have good sound systems, excellent climate control, velour trim, and all the rest that make a car livable, but they lack that ferocity of purpose, that uncompromising performance that separates the merely sporty from the sports.

Today's U.S. registered sports cars, it must be remembered, are federalized cars: They are built to a rigorous set of parameters from which the car maker dares not deviate. The sports car buyer these days is also a bit more sophisticated that he was in the past. Barely adequate heaters and cooling systems aren't good enough. Suspensions have to be good enough to absorb city potholes and Interstate irregularities without shaking the driver's bones. If viewed in that sense, today's sports cars are actually more *complete* vehicles. Manufacturers of the contemporary sports cars have faced the realities of volume sales and market demand and even though they have deviated from the classical definition (two seats, low slung, convertible, front-engine, or mid-engine with rear-wheel drive), they are sports cars nonetheless. While the purist who may own a Maserati A6GCS can look down his nose at a Celica Supra or a Z Turbo, the fact cannot be denied that these cars still retain some definite performance and handling virtues. *Any comparison of sports cars, therefore, could not possibly include both the cars of the Golden Age and those of the present.* It would be comparing apples to oranges and would thus do an injustice to both sides of the time barrier. When it comes to the best sports cars the line must be drawn between those in production and those which are out of production but still available, more or less.

Best In Production

• **Porsche 928.** Without a doubt one of the finest, best balanced cars ever built. European versions, naturally, make a lot more horsepower than American versions, which are still plenty quick and handle very nicely. Big, all-aluminum V8, Weissach axle, superb interior ergonomics, the whole of it well worth the $50,000 price tag.

• **Porsche 944.** They're lining up around the block for this one. Dealers are getting one a month, two if they're real lucky, and the waiting list gets longer every day. An incredible bargain for the $29,500 suggested retail price. Dealers are asking, and getting, a lot more.

• **DeTomaso Pantera.** The lines are derived from Giugiaro's Mangusta, modified by Ford's styling mavens. They went out of production in '74 costing around $10,000. Eight years later they came back fully legal from the factory at a hefty $60,000. But the Pantera is still the epitome of European styling coupled with a good, old American Ford V8. Stuffed in the back, right behind your ear, it still makes the right noises.

• **Mazda RX-7.** A big price doesn't always designate the best, and this rotary rocket proved the point. At just $12,000 out the door, virtually any clerk can afford one. Sure, they're common as dirt, and you'll see yourself coming and going ten times a day, but the RX-7 is one of the great inexpensive motoring pleasures of all time.

Best Out of Production (But Still Available)

• **Maserati Ghibli.** If there is one car that says it all, it is the Ghibli. Styled by Giorgetto Giugiaro, the Ghibli has style, heart-stopping good looks, and performance, thanks to a 4.9-liter, all-aluminum 330-hp V8. It is so sleek it makes you cry, so fast it can double the national speed limit in third with two more gears to go. It is the car waiting at the end of every sports car lover's rainbow. Only 2,400 were ever built and they're going for around $20,000.

• **Mercedes 300SL.** They call it the Gullwing. They also call it one of the finest road cars ever built, a tubular space frame wrapped around a three-liter slant six, with distinctive gullwing doors. It was good enough for 150 mph, as driven by Stirling Moss to victory in the Mille Miglia and to hundreds of other triumphs by scores of other races, and it is still one of the most desired cars around. Only 1,400 ever built; prices range from $20,000 for a basket case to over $50,000 for a good one.

• **Shelby Cobra 427.** Try to imagine something the size and weight of a VW Rabbit absolutely stuffed to the teeth with a 500-hp Ford 427 CID and you'll have some idea of the performance potential of the Cobra. It is absolutely, without a doubt, one of the most awesome cars ever built. With open exhausts and side-pipes it makes your ears hurt. It took guys like Phil Hill and Ken Miles to make these cars work on a track because the Cobra, like its namesnake, will bite quicker than you think. Only 356 of these brute force animals were manufactured and they run about $50,000. You could have bought one for $6,000 from your local Ford dealership back in 1965.

• **Jaguar XKE.** Front sub-frame, monocoque tub, independent suspensions all-around, and probably the single most beautiful thing the British created since the Spitfire fighter. The best are the 3.8-liter roadsters. They're readily available in poor condition or as completely restored and debugged roadworthies. Prices range from $12,000 up to $30,000.

• **Ford GT-40 MkIII.** Ford built 100 street versions so they could race, and win, at Le Mans. Seventy-five of these 500-hp, mid-engine cars exist and they're the slickest pieces ever to come from a huge corporate investment. They're asking about $90,000 for these. But try and shoehorn one away from its owner. Fat chance.

• **Porsche 930 Turbo.** Like all the really great sports cars, the 930 was built for the public strictly for homologation (race-qualifying) purposes and aimed at the international GT classes. This fat-fendered, whale-tail spoiler contains the turbo inter-cooler; it's fat-tired and diabolically quick. Racing versions have dominated everything they've entered. About $50,000 will put one in your driveway.

• **Ferrari.** Enzo Ferrari and his people have built so many cars with so many displacements and body configurations that they deserve a list of their own. But of all the cars there are three unqualified immortals: The V-12 250 Testa Rossa, 275 GTB/4, and the 365 GTB/4. Each one of them is a platinum-plated investment and each of them with the guts to propel you faster than any man has a right to go. They're worth just about anything the owner asks, but bargain anyway. It might work.

LUXURY MOTORCYCLES

THE *Easy Rider* days of motorcycling—when bikers scorned helmets and wore leather jackets decorated with skull and crossbones—are quickly fading into the horizon. Rebellious young hippies have been replaced by an older, more affluent generation of bikers attracted to the open road. For these riders, who want comfort and convenience as well as the exhilarating sense of freedom that motorcycle touring offers, a technologically advanced type of motorbike called the "luxotourer" has been developed.

Luxotourers are big, powerful motorcycles equipped with stereos, onboard computers, cruise control, and numerous other conveniences you would expect to find in a Cadillac. The seats are sofa-soft, and the air-assisted suspension systems on most of these bikes provide a smooth, jostle-free ride on almost any highway. On the backs of these luxurious machines, bikers cruise cross-country from Alaska to Florida, through parks and prairies, past ocean beaches and redwood forests. "On the back of motorcycle you have more sensory input than you get in a car or plane," says Californian Glenna Stansifer, a veteran of motorcycle touring. "The sense of freedom you feel traveling on two wheels is hard to describe. You have to try it yourself to understand."

In selecting a luxotourer, Jim Kretz of the American Gold Wing Association (of Honda Gold Wing owners) lists the following features as important to long-distance touring: a bike with ample power, a windshield with a clear view, a quality stereo system, and air suspension. Accessories such as trailers or sidecars are convenient, but are not recommended for novice bikers. They alter the handling characteristics of the motorcycle and may cause problems for less experiences drivers.

The top luxotourers which fulfill Kretz's requirements are as follows:

• **Yamaha Venture Royale.** Yamaha's top-of-the-line luxotourer is an $8,300 bike with a huge 1,200cc engine. With its five-gallon gas tank and an average of forty-five miles per gallon, this machine comfortably carries two riders over 200 miles of highway before refueling. Passenger comfort is enhanced by a computerized air suspension system which automatically adjusts the bike's suspension to match the terrain—soft for an ultra-plush ride on smooth roads, firm to maintain stability on unpaved roads. In addition to traditional instruments like a tachometer and speedometer, the Venture Royale is equipped with digital clock, AM/FM cassette stereo, and cruise control.

• **Honda Gold Wing LTD.** Honda has been making its Gold Wing bikes for ten years, and to commemorate the anniversary (in 1985) the company produced a special $10,000 Limited Edition model, its most elaborate luxotourer ever. Even before starting the Gold Wing LTD, it's easy to appreciate the considerations that went into its design. Inside the trunk and saddle bags are a matched trio of soft luggage which, when filled, will carry an impressive amount of clothing and personal items. The seats, for driver and passenger, are the most spacious of all luxotourers, and the body's two-tone gold paint scheme is an attention-grabber. The Gold Wing LTD also sports electronic cruise control, a rider/passenger intercom system, AM/FM stereo receiver and tapedeck, and an on-board trip computer telling time, distance to destination, water temperature, and other details.

• **Harley-Davidson FLT Tour Glide.** An American-made motorcycle with a loyal following. In the touring class, Harley's $9,000 FLT Tour Glide has a completely re-engineered engine that is rubber mounted for a smoother and less shaky ride than on earlier Harleys. It has no on-board electronic gadgetry, but gets an impressive fifty-five miles per gallon on the highway and stops quickly with excellent brakes.

• **Hesketh Vampire.** A leading luxotourer import from Britain, this $12,500 wonderbike sports a wind-tunnel-tested fiberglass design that ensures low wind resistance and smooth handling. Aside from the usual assortment of instruments, it offers a clock, an ambient temperature meter, and an intercom system for conversations between driver and passenger.

BOATS

Sail

UNDER sail, the wind is still free, so with all that money saved on fuel a yachtsman might as well buy a windjammer offering the most speed, comfort, and style. Since the difference in speed between a small sailing yacht and a big one is probably about five miles an hour (eight knots versus twelve knots top speed), a sailboat is seldom the fastest way to travel, and the skipper can pick one that is comfortable to cruise aboard for long stretches of time. Many hours are also spent ashore just admiring the boat at anchor or dockside so, like a pretty car or girl, she should have style that compares well with other craft. Though it's possible to spend years at sea acquiring a knowledge of just what to suggest so that Sparkman & Stephens can design a custom yacht for you, there are already ideal craft ready to sail away.

• **Gulfstar.** Stop in at Gulfstar in St. Petersburg, on Florida's Gulf coast. They'll offer overall lengths in the 36, 39, 44, 50, or Sailmaster 62 models that run from $75,000 up. For about $500,000 get the sloop-rigged 62. That one sleeps eight, parties many more, and can be chosen with ketch rig that allows smaller, easier to handle sails if you'd rather not have a crew do all the work or want to try handling her yourself. Figure at least $25,000 more for outfitting and electronic navigation aids. Gulfstar has been building in fiberglass for thirty years. They know what they're doing.

• **Morgan.** Nearby in Largo, also a suburb of Tampa, is Morgan Yacht, with a six-sailboat line of similar sizes and prices. For all-out racing, the Morgan 45 is available in a stripped-down 45-R option with low silhouette deck, exotic weight-saving fittings and minimum accommodations. For cruising at leisure instead, it comes with niceties like six foot six inch headroom, master staterooms with private bathrooms, teak and mahogany trim, and a cabin table that rides smoothly from cocktail to dining height hydraulically.

• **Cheoy Lee.** Motor sailers are happy hybrids that provide inside steering out of the wind, fulsome accommodations and a chubby design that gives slow and stately speeds under petrol power or sail. Choose a Cheoy Lee 63-footer, and, if you like and have the time, take delivery in Hong Kong where she's built.

• **Hatteras.** Or consider a Hatteras 65. Better known for power craft, Hatteras builds its Sail Yacht in High Point, North Carolina, for a stately $795,000. Budget $1,000,000 for the boat fitted out the way you'll want it for a go-anywhere cruise.

• **Pick Your Engine.** Any sailboat choice today will come with an engine tucked somewhere below decks—for the best of both worlds if the wind goes down or maneuvering quay-side in St. Tropez seems easier under power. Specify your favorite engine: Volvo, Mercedes, BMW, or whatever since most marine power plants are marinized automotive models.

Power

American's hard drinkers have made the world's power boats great. The illegal tipplers of the 1920s were the influence that inspired high-performance on the water. To supply the national thirst, small fast beach boats were needed to bring in the booze from mother ships lying offshore. Little rumrunners, powered with surplus aircraft engines and loaded down with burlap-wrapped bundles of bottles, raced in with the "hooch."

• **Cigarette.** One of the most famous was *Cigarette,* and Miami's Don Aronow picked the name for his boat company, builders of the winningest offshore speed boats. Aronow, a lover of fast cars and fast living, originally had a custom racer built for the 1961 Miami-to-Nassau marathon, and was hooked on boats after finishing fourth in his first race. Since then, he has gone on to win two world offshore championships, and his boats have won many more. He created boat companies named Formula, Donzi, Magnum, and Cigarette. All are still turning out performance craft, the first three now under other owners, but Aronow has kept Cigarette, and his deep-V hull models are built in 35, 36, 38, and 39-foot lengths. His new Cigarette Champion 8 is $100,000 with two 400hp engines and 60 miles-per-hour of speed. Put in bigger mills for added thrill if you want a world title of your own and think you can handle her.

• **Hatteras.** For more sedate cruising, consider a Hatteras from High Point, North Carolina. Start with their newest Sport Fisherman 32 design with a performance hull by offshore champion Jim Wynne. It's $82,000. Move up to the Hatteras 70 Extended Deckhouse Motor Yacht at $986,000, or for seven more feet, there is the 77 Cockpit Motor Yacht. It also sleeps nine, can be furnished with most of the comforts of home, and is delivered for $1,400,000.

• **Rybovich.** Smaller, less well known, but considered the ultimate if you are a sport fisherman, are simple and sleek fishing craft from West Palm Beach, Florida, named Rybovich. There is no name-plate on the outside, you recognize them for their lines, and they run from 30 up to 70 feet. There are many imitations. Some were once turned out in Cuba and known, unofficially, as Cubaviches. Other knock-offs from a prominent American builder were nick-named Chris-a-viches. When you order your Rybovich you don't ask about the price because you may have specified some customiz-ing extras and your favorite brand of turbocharged diesels. You expect it will be launched for under $1,000,000 if you've selected a modest thirty-five or forty-five-footer. But you do know that while you wait a year or so for delivery, you'll be waiting in line with a very select crowd, and once you're out in the Gulf Stream fishing you'll be recognized by the few that know the very best.

ULTIMATE PRIVATE AIRCRAFT

IT'S no news that airplanes come in all shapes and size, not to mention price tags. Just as their large commerical counterparts are designed to fill extremely narrow niches these days—i.e., "ideal for routes of 750 to 1,000 miles in an umpy-ump seat config-uration"—so are so-called "private" aircraft. Since so many of them, in turn, are expensed as company planes, however, the con-cept of what a *private* plane is or really should be has become some-what elusive. But it's not. *A private plane is simply one that can take you, the owner/pilot, anywhere that airplanes can reasonably expect to go—in com-fort, safety, and with at least a modicum of style.*

Now, even it you were prepared to spend a few million dollars, this rules out jets. As some board chairmen are always the last to find out, even the smallest jet aircraft requires more runway than ninety percent of this country's airports have to offer. And, by the way, you *were* planning to have the capability to land, as it were, on water too, right? So you start building the ultimate private plane from the ground up—on a pair of amphibious floats. The best are made by EDO Corp. from aluminum; with extensive compart-menting, some 8,000 rivets and air/oil shocks supporting a landing gear intended to cycle perfectly every time—despite being sub-merged at regular intervals. They will add $50,000 to the cost of the aircraft. (Not including the beefier airframe that must be fac-tory built-in.)

Your choice thus far has dictated a high-wing design. Not because they fly better on floats but because convenient on-water handling, around piers, pilings, and shoreline, demands it. And *because go-anywhere utility was the prime criterion,* you'll want a turbo charged engine. Not only will this pull you out of short fields, including grass and puddle-sized lakes, it will give you a decent cruising speed—over 150 mph—and the ability to climb to 20,000 feet and more (with a supplemental oxygen system) to find tail winds—just like the airlines—on long, cross-country hauls. Pres-sure altitude means nothing to a turbo; our ultimate private plane can go into fields closed off to similar, non-turbo-charged planes not because of runway length but because on a hot day at high altitudes they simply will not be able to get back off the ground.

Note that we're talking single-engine all the way. Twins on amphibious airframes or floats are limited in capability, cumber-some, extremely uneconomical, and they just don't look good at all. Single-engine planes today are quite reliable; in addition, if you do have to make an emergency landing on an unprepared field, the floats (wheels up) are far less likely than conventional landing gear to flip your plane.

The plane should be able to carry four fishing buddies with full gear in total comfort, or three couples if they're just amphibing it to a big game. The social aspect of real private flying—being able to dash off to any tidal and most inland waters in the U.S. (some states have landing restrictions) or forage for low fuel prices and local gumbo recipes at Podunk airports all over the country—this part of it can't be underestimated.

What we have assembled is something like a Cessna Turbo Stationair 6 on EDO 696-3500 floats; it's ready to fly and we've only spent on the order of $150,000. It is not yet the ultimate private plane because we need to put another $60,000-plus into a top-of-the-line, state-of-the-art electronics suite. This is going to include components like a Bendix color radar plus a Ryan Stormscope (which tracks actual lightning flashes), the like of which, in both instances, the captains of most domestic airliners plying U.S. routes *never* see. Add a King radio navigation unit equipped with a microprocessor that lets you go point-to-point rather than slavishly trekking the narrow (and crowded) airways routes like the airliners have to. And, finally, a Century autopilot; you can cut it in 200 feet of the runway and it will literally fly you to within 200 feet of the one you want to land on, 500 miles or more away.

SIX

Shelter

BUYING/RESTORING

Private Islands For Sale

An island away from it all is the ultimate in vacation dreams, but more and more travelers are discovering that their favorite secluded paradise has been invaded by civilization. How can one escape the crush of tourists? For a fee of $20 per year, Donald Ward at Private Islands Unlimited will provide you with a list of several hundred island properties located around the world that are available for purchase, and will send you updates from time to time as he adds new properties to the list. Ward's inventory has included everything from a three-acre wooded island off the coast of Maine to an 8,000-acre property near Honduras, valued at over $10 million. If you don't find what you're looking for on this list, you can describe your particular paradise to Ward and he'll set out to find it.

"My clients include people who want to live on an island year-round, growing crops and fishing, people who want a weekend place, sailors who want a home base. We also hear from investors who want to develop resort condominiums." The client examines maps and photographs of the property before visiting it; Ward does not advise buying sight unseen. "We arrange for a visit to the property, usually with the guidance of the local expert—the real estate broker or the island's current owner," says Ward.

In addition to complete private islands, Ward also lists hundreds of island properties: homes, resort and income properties, established businesses, and land for development, from individual home sites to thousands of acres. For information, CONTACT: *Private Islands Unlimited, Dock 11, Marina Bay, 2176 State Rd. 84, Fort Lauderdale, FL 33312; (305) 584-5343.*

Best Guide to Restoration: Old House Series

An essential for everyone restoring a period home is the Old House Catalog series. Each volume in the series contains a completely different selection of hundreds of items (from reproduction wallpaper to wide-plank flooring to period furniture) suitable for authentic restoration and furnishing, as well as the names of skilled architects and craftsmen who can help with the job. What makes this undertaking unique and enduring is author Lawrence Grow's intelligent text and fierce dedication to good taste and authenticity. Relying on recommendations and evaluations from the experts in the field—curators of historic houses around the country—Grow weeds out the inauthentic, the ill-conceived, and the trite, and lists only those items worthy of quality restoration. *The Fourth Old House Catalog* (1984) is the latest in this excellent series.

CLASSIC WALLPAPERS

GREAT wallpaper can turn an ordinary room into a work of art. It can open up the room with panoramic views, dematerialize walls with trompe l'oeil effects, and add verve with vibrant patterns. **The best wallpapers have always been designed to unite a room's architecture and furnishings,** and bear no relation to the hardware store variety printed with sprays of violets in badly registered colors. Many of the finest papers available today derive from sources of the eighteenth and nineteenth centuries, the era when wallpaper was a legitimate art form. To find out where one gets such wallpapers, we asked Ann Dorfsman, keeper of the wallpaper collection at New York's Cooper-Hewitt Museum, one of the foremost study collections of historic wallpapers, and Catherine Lynn, formerly of Cooper-Hewitt, now a teacher at Yale and author of the field's standard reference work, *Wallpaper in America.*

• **Jean Zuber et Cie.** This historic Alsatian firm still produces—as it has for more than 175 years—what are probably the most awesome displays of the printer's art: the panoramic, hand-blocked, non-repeating wallpapers (called "scenics") that graced the walls of nineteenth-century parlors and dining rooms. These papers, produced at the firm's only factory in tiny Rixheim, depict the exotic locales that were dear to the heart of the Romantic movement. The patterns bear names like *Hindustan, Isola Bella* (Beautiful Islands), and *Arcadie*. They wrap around a room like full-color murals. Jackie Kennedy installed a Zuber scenic, *Views of North America,* during her restoration of the White House.

When you purchase one of Zuber's twelve panoramic designs, you are not buying a reproduction because Zuber's has never stopped making them. They are still made in the same place and by the same process as they were when first introduced during the first decades of the nineteenth century. *As many as 3,000 hand-carved wood blocks are needed to print a single set of the papers.* "Watching this process is like watching a ballet," says Catherine Lynn. (Most other fine papers are also hand printed, but with modern silk screens, rather than wood blocks.) A set of papers to cover an average-sized room runs between $5,000 and $20,000 depending upon the intricacy of the design. The sole American distributor is *S.M. Hexter, 2800 Superior Ave., Cleveland, OH 44114; (216) 696-0146.*

• **Scalamandré.** This New York fabric and wallpaper company founded in 1927 by Franco Scalamandré, has long been known for its beautiful decorative fabrics and authentic reproduction fabrics and wallpapers. In keeping with that tradition, the company recently introduced the Irish-Georgian collection, a series of twenty-two wallpapers and fabrics adapted from the interiors of Ireland's finest castles. The wallpapers in the Irish-Georgian collection range from $45 to $90 per single roll; others cost from $25 to $150 per roll. Scalamandré has showrooms in New York, Boston, Chicago, Los Angeles, Houston, Dallas, Philadelphia, and Washington. Papers must be ordered through a designer or an architect. *950 Third Ave., New York, NY 10022; (212) 361-8500.*

• **Bradbury & Bradbury.** A small craft studio in Benicia, California, which offers exquisite Victorian wallpapers in brilliant colors. In addition to top quality wallpapers, Bradbury & Bradbury offers personal service that larger manufacturers often cannot. Wallpapers are available directly to the consumer, and an extra roll is included with each order—just in case—and if the client is in the area, someone from the company is likely to stop by and help with the hanging. Papers are in the $24 to $100 price range; a brochure is available for two dollars. *P.O. Box 155, Benicia, CA 94510; (707) 746-1900.*

• **Arthur Sanderson & Sons.** A noted British wallpaper company that opened a New York showroom in 1984 with many offerings of top quality. Additional showrooms are scheduled to open in Dallas, Houston, Los Angeles, San Francisco, Atlanta, Miami, and Chicago. Unique to Sanderson is its collection of printed wallpapers designed in the 1880s by arts and crafts master *William Morris;* the company owns and uses the original hand-blocks. The hand-blocked papers run from $97 to $375 per double roll. Screen-printed versions of four of the Morris designs are available from $36 to $52 per roll. A brochure is available. *979 Third Ave., Suite 403, New York, NY 10022; (212)319-7220.*

• **Cole & Son.** Another wallpaper firm that still offers hand-blocked nineteenth-century papers. In the U.S., its papers are available through *Clarence House* in New York, specialists in hand-printed English papers. *40 E. 57th St., New York, NY 10022; (212) 752-2890.*

• **Waterhouse Wallhangings.** Producing authentic historic reproduction wallpaper since 1965, with an extensive selection of eighteenth-century patterns ideal for period homes. Moderately priced, from $15 to $50 per roll. *38 Wareham St., Boston, MA 02118; (617) 423-7688.*

• **Zina Studios.** A relatively small, high-quality house offering 150 designs. Strong in designs ranging from the neoclassical period through moderate, Matisse-like modern. Custom designs ranging from $500 to thousands. *85 Purdy Ave., Port Chester, NY 10573; (914) 937-5661.*

Note: Many of the above firms sell exclusively or primarily through decorators. Consequently, the prices an individual may have to pay could be higher than those quoted here.

TIN CEILINGS, COPPER WALLS, TILE FLOORS

Tin Ceilings
If you've been to Rich's department store in Atlanta, or Maxwell's Plum in San Francisco, you've probably noticed the embos-

sed metal walls that give each place its aura of genteel elegance. Embossed metal ceilings and walls, a turn-of-the-century phenomenon, are making a comeback, and if you want one for your home, you can order from a firm that made them seventy years ago: *W.F. Norman* of Nevada, Missouri. Norman (who did the walls at Rich's and Maxwell's Plum) is a sheet metal firm which had discontinued its wall and ceiling line decades ago. The current surge of interest in older architecture, however, prompted the company to dust off its old molds and go back into business. They're now producing more than 125 of their original designs in copper and brass as well as in the traditional tin-coated steel. The metal panels are still punched out by the same hand-operated rope drop hammers Norman used at the turn of the century.

Among the patterns available are gothic arches, baroque foliate designs, Art Deco geometrics, prim classical motifs, and Oriental fantasies. "All we did was reprint our 1909 catalog," says C. Robert Quitno, who heads the company. A panel, which contains one complete repeat of the pattern, measures two by four feet; costs average $15 to $30 per square foot. *W.F. Norman Corp., Box 232, Nevada, MO 64772; (800) 641-4038. The catalog costs $3.*

Fine Tiles

Hand-painted wall and floor tiles have long been prized decorative items for the home. Today, they are increasingly hard to find. One of, if not the most extensive and beautiful selection of handmade tiles is available through *Country Floors,* importers of designs from Europe and Latin America. Among Country Floors' wide selection of designs are intricate Portuguese tiles in shades of blue and yellow designed to interlock with other tiles in a continuous pattern; a fifty-five-tile seventeenth-century floral panel from France; and subtly-shaded solid tiles in colors ranging from pale mauve to antique green. Prices begin at 55¢ for a four-inch monocottura solid color tile from Italy, and the firm's most expensive tile is a Royal Makkum Chinese-design wall tile from Holland at more than $50, made with meticulous attention by the methods that the family firm has used for the last 300 years. Because it is a highly skilled craft, production of fine tiles is limited. There are waiting lists of up to a year for some of the Portuguese tiles. Country Floors has representatives around the U.S. and fills mail orders. Custom orders are also possible. For a list of Country Floors representatives: *Country Floors, 300 E. 61st St., New York, NY 10021; (212) 758-7414.*

ORIENTAL CARPETS

T HE appeal of fine Oriental carpet making is an ancient one. Surviving specimens of the craft have been dated as far back as the fifth century B.C. We know from the frescoes of Giotto that Oriental rugs were prized by European collectors during the Renaissance. When George Washington posed for his famous Landsdowne portrait, Gilbert Stuart depicted the father of our country standing on an Oushak rug.

Today, appreciation of Oriental carpeting both as home furnishings and fine art is at an historic high. *Although prices for the best quality rugs continue to accelerate, it is still possible to acquire enduring beauty at relatively bargain rates.* A nineteenth-century Mohtasham Kashan carpet, which embodies the highest aspiration of Middle Eastern art, sells for $50,000. When you consider the price of comparable Western art from the same era, it represents an astounding value. On the other hand, the market is as chancy as the political situation in the parts of the world where so many of the best rugs come from and even an expert buyer can be badly stung. A prominent New York dealer recently paid $8,500 at auction for an "antique" Turkish rug which turned out to be a modern Roumanian copy worth not more than $700.

Defining Oriental

Even at the risk of oversimplification, a few definitions are in order. A carpet is a woven fabric usually made of wool or sometimes silk. Oriental refers to just about anywhere between the Dardanelles and the Pacific Ocean but in the rug world is usually limited to Turkey, Iran, Afghanistan, the Soviet Caucasus, Central Asia, and China. Carpeting was originally used for all manner of things including floor coverings, saddle covers, tent adornments, bags for carrying salt, and covers for the pillars in Buddhist temples. *Roughly speaking then, an Oriental rug is a piece of Oriental carpet intended to be put on the floor.* As recently as the early 1970s, Oriental rugs were classed by major auction houses as home furnishings and sold along with silver spoons and lamp shades. Recently, however, the market has broken into two segments; home furnishings and fine art. Again, the definitions are loose. There are some exquisite, flat woven kilim rugs selling for a few thousand that are much too lovely to walk on. But, in general, when the price tag exceeds $10,000 we are starting to talk about "investment quality" art.

A neophyte in Oriental rugs is presented with a bewildering assortment of techniques and styles. There are knotted pile rugs

created by craftsmen who can fashion some 10,000 knots a day and
Persian Mulberry rugs, much sought after by American collectors
during the 1920s, which were bleached coral and then hand colored
to a dark mulberry with an eyedropper. There are light, flexible
kilims where the pattern is created entirely by horizontal threads
(weft) and heavier soumaks where the pattern is achieved by horizontal threads moving across vertical threads fixed on the loom
(warp).

Buying A Carpet

Traditionally, rug merchants have not been eager to share the
secrets of carpetry with prospective buyers and, to a considerable
degree, the old bazaar mentality still prevails. It is up to the customer to know the merchandise. John Edelmann, one of New
York's leading auctioneers of Oriental rugs, suggests a buyer
inspect the rug section by section. "If you won't get down on your
hands and knees to examine a rug, you have no right to buy it," he
says.

Of course, it helps to know what you're looking for. A good
basic introduction is *The Book of Carpets* by Reinhard Hubel. Several museums and galleries offer regular classes in the fine art of
Oriental rugs and one of the best is the monthly seminar offered by
Mr. Edelmann. The quality of the wool is a primary consideration.
It should be springy to the touch and retain its lustre. Be sure to
check for evidence of dry rot and insect damage remembering that
the more a rug has been repaired the less it is worth. Check the back of the
rug as well as the top. If the backing cracks when bent, the rug will
not wear well. Check to see the color dyes have been fixed properly
and are not running. Be sure the fringe is still in place even if it is a
little ratty. As Jimmy Keshishian, a prominent Washington, D.C.,
rug dealer and director of the Association of Specialists in Cleaning
and Restoration (ASCR) points out, "It's better to have a rug with
dirty fringes than with no fringes at all." It is common to find a
large Oriental rug that has been cut down into smaller sizes. This
lessens the value of a rug as a work of art but may be perfectly
acceptable to someone interested only in a floor covering. Any Oriental rug has value, even one in less than mint condition. The
important thing is that you understand the true condition of a rug
before you buy it. When in doubt or when considering an invest-
ment-quality rug, it is best to get an independent appraisal.

Carpets as Investments

The most enjoyable way to familiarize yourself with Oriental
rugs is the auction house. In New York, the two best are at

Edelmann's Gallery and Christie's East where the advice is expert and free. The cardinal auction house rule, however, is never buy anything at your first sale. Try to get a feel for the market before going up against more experienced buyers than yourself.

By common consensus *the most promising investment possibilities among Oriental rugs are to be found in carpeting from China.* Chinese wool textiles have traditionally been overshadowed by the more renowned Chinese silks and ceramics and their prices have been correspondingly lower. Chinese rugs are softer and more loosely woven than their Near Eastern counterparts. A typical Chinese rug will have thirty-five to fifty knots per square inch, while a fine Persian will have several hundred. But the pile is usually much thicker and the quality of the wool is frequently higher. The market for Chinese rugs is still small and collectors have been buying them up for what one auctioneer calls "embarrassingly little money." Small contemporary rugs from the mainland have been going for a few hundred dollars and even fine pieces from the eighteenth century have been selling for well under $10,000.

When considering top investment quality rugs where $30,000 is not uncommon for a large rug, you should look into the show room of such highly regarded dealers as: *Vojtech Blau, 800B Fifth Ave., New York, NY; (212) 249-4525; Beshar Co., 49 E. 53rd St., New York, NY; (212) 758-1400; Joseph M. Fell, Ltd., 3221 N. Clark St., Chicago, IL 60657; (312) 549-6076 and Kaoud Bros. Oriental Rugs, 17 S. Main St., W. Hartford, CT 06107; (203) 233-6211.*

FURNITURE: CONTEMPORARY/REPRODUCTION

THE *laissez passer* of the world of household furnishings is the decorator's card, which admits the bearer to "trade" showrooms that house objects too rarefied (and often too expensive) for furniture or department stores. But there are showrooms and showrooms; only a relative handful carry the finest lines. (A precious few stores carry some of them, too.) **Furniture can be divided into two basic groups: contemporary and historic reproduction.** They have followed opposite paths in recent decades. The best contemporary furniture is now designed and manufactured in Europe, particularly in Italy, Germany, and the Scandinavian countries. The best reproductions, however, are still American-made, even those based on English and French designs.

Contemporary

Although the top American makers remain a strong presence in office furniture, the upper end of the residential business is almost all in the hands of western Europeans. America's residential demise has been hastened by two factors: high skilled labor costs and an increasing shortage of trained craftsmen to produce such special components as hand-sewn leather chair and sofa covers. From the standpoint of design, materials, and workmanship, industry sources consider the following lines the finest in contemporary furniture:

• **Atelier International.** AI, a world leader, imports Italy's renowned Cassina collection, which is high-style and ultra-contemporary (verging into avant-garde). Cassina pieces range across the usual dining room-living room spectrum. It uses outstanding materials—fine wools, precious woods, top-quality leathers—and its very sophisticated wood finishes are distinguished by a handsome high gloss. Like most of the other firms noted here, AI has its principal showroom in Manhattan (*595 Madison Ave.,* in AI's case), with additional showrooms in such other major furniture centers as Chicago's Merchandise Mart and San Francisco's Jackson Square; in secondary centers, the lines are sold by sales representatives.

• **Stendig International.** Stendig imports an estimated seventy percent of its pieces from Scandinavia, Italy, Germany, and Switzerland. They are known for exquisite workmanship, and, although most are highly contemporary, they also include some traditional designs. Among the most notable of the latter: revivals from the Bauhaus period, including such designers as Marcel Breuer and Le Corbusier. Manhattan showroom: *410 E. 62nd St.*

• **B&B America.** A Stendig division, markets a line that vies with Atelier for almost-avant-garde honors. B&B's wares include highly regarded cabinetry: bookcases, bars, stereo cabinets, most of them with the latest innovations in wood finishes, hinges, and the like. B&B's Manhattan showroom, which one importer calls "spectacular," is at *745 Fifth Ave.*

• **Pace Collection.** Pace is a conglomerate of lines, some of them produced in the United States under its own name, most of them imported from makers in Europe. The lines run the gamut in residential furniture, with particularly high marks given the bedroom suites, or "settings." However, to the eye of one knowledgeable observer, all tend to be "a little flashy." Manhattan showroom: *321 E. 62nd St.*

• **International Contract Furnishings.** ICF offers a very diversified collection. It includes revivals of the classic designs of Austrian architect-designer Joseph Hoffmann; pieces by the internationally known Finn, Alvar Aalto, many of them in laminated birch; and a marvelous "Twenty-first Century" kitchen, designed and outfitted in Germany, featuring gadgets and work-saving devices scarcely imagined by the average American cook. Manhattan showroom: *305 E. 63rd St.*

All of these lines include office as well as residential furniture. Just below them in quality are three American makers who also produce both office and residential, though relatively little of the latter. They are **Knoll International** (*655 Madison Ave., Manhattan*); **Herman Miller** (*600 Madison*); and **Brickel Associates** (*515 Madison*). Brickel markets the work of Ward Bennett, one of the most esteemed American furniture and textile designers.

Reproduction

In the reproduction field, several American manufacturers stand out: **Knoll, Miller, Smith & Watson, Wood & Hogan, Baker, Kindall,** and **Kittinger.** Of these, Kittinger has the strongest claim to pre-eminence. The Buffalo, New York, firm has for almost four decades been reproducing designs associated with Colonial Williamsburg—and, in American furniture, you can't get much classier than that. Kittinger is also licensed to reproduce works from such institutions as Historic Newport and Sturbridge Village. Kittinger, however, has no monopoly on impressive connections. Baker takes the designs for its "Stately Homes" collection from English mansions and manor houses, while Kendall has been selected to do the reproductions for Winterthur, the DuPont restoration in Delaware.

Materials form a vital but somewhat subtle measure of quality in reproduction furniture. Ordinary makers do not hew faithfully to the original materials; instead, they substitute—often freely and sometimes incongruously—in the interests of saving money. They also use machines to carve and put the finish on some elements, especially period details.

The best reproductions make very few substitutions for original materials and utilize no machine work. Substitute woods, veneers, or decorative touches are brought in only if the originals are unavailable or prohibitively expensive. Even then, the replacement will be of top quality so as not to lower the overall value of the piece. Whatever mahogany is needed, for example, Kittinger uses the Honduran variety rather than the cheaper, less esteemed kinds from Africa. And, in working the woods, Kittinger and its competitors rely on traditional handcraftsmanship. They often follow more than two dozen separate steps in producing a single table or chest. The result is a piece that not only *looks* good but *is* good—in the sense that it embodies the finest elements of the furniture maker's art and accurately, often painstakingly, represents a classic design.

The best reproductions sometimes look better than mediocre examples of the antiques they emulate. Not that the reproducers try to fool anybody. They are proud to sell their copies as copies, to customers who appreciate the styles and designs, the materials and workmanship, but can't find or can't afford the antiques themselves. It should be noted that some of the top reproductions—lines offered by Smith & Watson and Wood & Hogan, for example—are imported. But the great majority are American made, a comforting fact in an era when quality in so many products (including contemporary furniture) has relocated abroad.

The headquarters of the leading reproduction firms are scattered around the eastern United States. Most of them sell through first-rate department or furniture stores. A few maintain showrooms in New York and elsewhere. For instance, both Kittinger and Wood & Hogan have display space at *305 E. 63rd St. in Manhattan. (That building, incidentally, is a quality-furniture hunter's paradise.* It houses nothing but showrooms of contemporary and reproduction manufacturers, including many of the best lines available.)

Most of Baker's furniture is made in two cities in Michigan—cities where artisans, apprenticing themselves to masters, learned their craft and make their homes. Carving is done in Holland, hand decoration in Grand Rapids. Only a few of the smaller occasional tables come from the south—High Point, North Carolina.

How long a buyer will wait for his furniture depends on the piece—a small torchere may be delivered within three or four months; a more elaborate carved piece in six months.

FURNITURE: LOUNGE CHAIRS

IT'S been said that few architects and designers can resist the urge to design a new chair. The reason is that chairs, more than any other piece of furniture, offer a seemingly limitless variety of technological as well as aesthetic design choices. Nowhere is this variety and range of style, function, size, and texture more evident than in the choice of lounge chairs. The very best ones—whether fashioned out of tubular steel and leather or covered with generous amounts of upholstery—respond to the demands for comfort and art. Often they include the latest in technological advances as well.

The following selection of comfortable chairs ranges from the elegantly stark to the plushly sybaritic, from reproductions of designer classics to high-tech recliners that feature electric massage and wrap-around stereo. These are available through designers, manufacturers, mail-order catalogs, and retail sources:

Le Corbusier Chaise

The Museum of Modern Art (MOMA) in New York City, which has long presented reproductions of graceful, classic furniture in its permanent Design Collection, offers the timeless 1927 Corbusier Chaise. This is the creation of the great Swiss architect known as Le Corbusier. Once available only through designers, the chrome and calfskin chaise lounge which appears to float on its frame, takes its cue from the contours of the human form. Beneath the sleek flat black leather cushion and headrest is a black steel frame welded to twin chrome-plated arcs which slide on a curved track, allowing a variety of position adjustments. The chaise is available through the museum shop for about $3,860. (MOMA members receive a fifteen percent discount.) For information: *The Museum of Modern Art, 11 W. 53rd St., New York, NY 10019; (212) 708-9746.* The Le Corbusier Chaise is manufactured by *Cassina S.p.A.* in Italy for *Atelier International, Ltd.;* for details, contact the company at: *595 Madison Ave., New York, NY 10022; (212) 644-0400.*

Royal Stressless

The Scandinavian leather chair known as the Falcon, with its buttery glove-leather cushions, matching footrest, and splay-footed base has been a perennial favorite. The latest improvement on the theme is the Royal Stressless chair, manufactured by Ekornes in Norway. More massive than the Falcon, the Royal Stressless provides a cushy, nest-like environment. It automatically adjusts to any body position and allows near-total reclining. The chair, which swivels 360 degrees, lists for about $800 in saddle tan, medium or dark brown, or black; for ten percent more, it is available in ten additional shades and colors. For information: *Norsk, 114 E. 57th St., New York, NY 10022; (212) 752-3111* or *Wim & Karen*

Scandinavian Furniture, 319 E. 53rd St., New York, NY 10022; (212) 758-4207.

Massage Lounger

For those who want to be rubbed just the right way, there's the Panasonic Massage Lounger. Hidden beneath the S-curved butterscotch-colored cushions are machines that can perform rolling and kneading motions said to simulate those of specialists in the Japanese massage technique known as *shiatsu.* By means of a hand-held computerized control, the massaging action can be adjusted to perform broad or narrow massage motions or to zero in intensively on specific *tsubos,* or key pressure points. A built-in timer starts as soon as the massage does, to prevent snooze-induced burn-outs. List price for the Massage Lounger is about $990, available from *Markline, P.O. Box C-5, Belmont, MA 02178; (800) 225-8390.* For more information: *Panasonic Appliance Company, Division of Matsushita Electric Corporation of America, One Panasonic Way, Secaucus, NJ 07094; (201) 348-7478.*

Marquise

If Louis XV is your style, you may settle on either an elegant chaise lounge befitting a queen's boudoir, or the Marquise, a king-sized chair commodious enough to fit not only Louis but Henry VIII as well. The chaise has a curved back and optional pillows, and one long cushion with pleated borders, which can be made as plump as one's heart desires. The Marquise, truly a chair-and-a-half, can be turned into a chaise with an optional curved ottoman that fits snugly against it. Both are custom-made in Italy of hand-carved beechwood. Choice of wood finishes and upholstery is up to you, as are the depth and filling for cushions and pillows (duck feather or goose down); prices vary accordingly. List price for the chaise: $4,315. The Marquis: $3,800. For information: *The Devon Shops, 111 E. 27th St., New York, NY 10016; (212) 686-1760.*

Getaway Chair

For the lounger who wants it all, there's the Getaway Chair. Looking somewhat like a streamlined first-class airline seat, the black canvas chair first invites the body to stretch out nearly flat. Then, with the flick of a few switches, any of three independent two-speed massage motors begin vibrating, traveling up and down the spine or focusing on isolated trouble spots in the neck, shoulders, lower back, or hips. All this can be accompanied by music via the stereo AM/FM radio/cassette player installed in the armrest and piped through the headrest through wraparound speakers. A blackout visor and cassette of natural sounds included with the chair make the great escape complete. Price: $1,595. Available from *The Sharper Image, P.O. Box 26823, San Francisco, CA 94126; (800) 344-4444.* For information: *H.W.E., Inc., 11145 Vanowen St., North Hollywood, CA 91605; (818) 760-1801.*

Eve

As for the unabashedly hedonistic, the sleek, frankly sensual Eve chaise from Adesso, Inc., could be the ultimate recliner. Available in buttery soft European pearlized leather or in velvety suede in gray, black, white, or taupe, this American-made chaise combines its arresting, angular design with irresistible comfort. Available for about $3,000. For information: *Adesso, Inc., The Mall at Chestnut Hill, MA 02167; (617) 969-2285.*

FURNITURE: ROCKERS

ONLY one piece of contemporary furniture graces the permanent White House collection in Washington, D.C.—a rocking chair handcrafted by California woodworker Sam Maloof. Purchased at auction for $8,000 in 1982 by a private collector, it was presented as a gift to President Ronald Reagan, who warmly welcomed it into his official residence.

While Maloof has designed more than 400 different pieces of furniture—including cradle hutches, love seats, cabinets, and conference tables—he is most noted for his handsome $5,000 rockers. *Maloof rockers, often carved from Ozark black walnut, are noted for their subtle beauty and genuine comfort.* Museums in Boston, New York, and St. Louis display them for their classic artistry, but private individuals have purchased them for functional use in their homes. Unlike most furniture makers, Maloof does almost all the work on his rockers himself. He personally selects the wood (each rocker has its own distinctive grain pattern), carves the arms and legs and spindles, hollows out the chair seat, and does the joinery. Once the rocker is complete, he rubs it to a fine finish with linseed oil and beeswax. The completed product is a utilitarian piece of classic artistry.

"Working a rough piece of wood into a complete, useful object is the welding together of man and material," says the seventy-year-old Maloof about his craft. He makes only about sixty-five pieces of furniture a year, but each one is a personal statement in wood. Like other works of art, Maloof rockers, desks, or tables are signed, numbered, and dated by their maker. Working in a private studio forty-five miles east of Los Angeles, Maloof never advertises or solicits commissions, but there is always a waiting list for his furniture. To order a Maloof original contact: *Sam Maloof, P. O. Box 51, Alta Loma, CA 91701; (714) 987-2805.*

DOWN QUILTS/PILLOWS

IF you have ever had the good fortune to slowly sink into a bed covered with a down comforter, you may laugh at the controversy and conflicting scientific evidence "proving" that synthetic substitutes for natural down do exist. Down is the underbelly filament of ducks and geese and doesn't contain quills, as do feathers. Holofill, Quallofil, and Fortrel may sound a little like species of waterfowl, but, in point of fact, they can only approximate all of the qualities which down possesses: warmth, softness, resilience, lightness, and durability—all wrapped in one marvelous puff.

Down is admired for its loft, which is both a natural characteristic and one that is aided by the air blown through the filaments during processing. Loft adds height and resiliency. Generally, down from more mature birds is loftier and thus considered to be of higher quality. In the United States birds are often plucked at six weeks of age; in places of higher quality production, such as Poland, birds are often aged six months before being plucked. Weight adds little to the loft or quality of down; *a product claim implying higher quality because of weight is deliberately misleading.* Some states have laws that forbid weight labeling for this reason.

Place of origin is a prime factor in judging the quality of down. The best comes from places where severe climate encourages full development of the insulating down. Almost half of the down that is imported to the United States now comes from China, where the climate varies widely and with it the consistency of its down. Poland is renowned for its superb down, as is the Soviet Union, but market conditions often curtail importation of their products. France, Hungary, and the Labrador coast of Canada also produce fine down.

Iceland and Greenland supply the cream of the crop: eiderdown. Eiderdown comes only from the Eider duck and is increasingly rare and costly. This bird plucks its own down which is then used to line its nest. Thus, to gather down means robbing a nest. There are only 4,000 pounds collected annually, of which perhaps only half is available commercially. Eiderdown's structure has specific interlocking features that trap air. As such it is a top-notch insulator. Eiderdown functions best as a stuffing for comforters or other purely luxury items. Pure eiderdown costs $400 a pound, wholesale. Considering that the average pillow contains twelve ounces, one can easily understand why a top-quality comforter is so costly.

The best way to buy an eiderdown comforter is to ask The Feather and Down Industry Association to buy the eiderdown for you, from wherever they can find it at the time. They will then allow you to examine it before and during its transformation into that epitome of luxury bedding. Contact them at: *4441 Auburn Blvd., Suite O, Sacramento, CA 95841; (916) 481-3812.*

LUXURY LINENS

W HAT better way to pass a luxuriously sleepy night than between cool, smooth linen sheets? A symbol of purity in some cultures, linen is second in strength only to silk among the natural fibers. More absorbent than cotton or cotton blends, linen makes cool sheets for hot summer nights. Linen is derived from flax, which is cultivated in only a few countries. Belgian linen is considered to be of the highest quality. Irish linen, spun wet, is renowned for its fine workmanship, its strength, and its grass-bleached bright white color. French and Italian linens are valued for their design. And sheets made of linen will last. With proper care and use, you can expect to have your sheets for no less than twenty years; some endure for generations. So, if you weren't fortunate enough to inherit your linens, you can choose from the following to start your own collection.

Pratesi Linens

White Italian linen sheets with geometrically embroidered borders come in twin, queen/double, and king sizes and start at about $300. Cases in standard, king, and queen start at $160. With six shops in the U.S., Pratesi sheets are available in Beverly Hills, Bal Harbour, Palm Beach, Chicago, Washington, D.C., and New York. *Pratesi, 829 Madison Ave., New York, NY 10021; (212) 288-2315.*

Leron Incorporated

Leron is a special order house, selling linens available in thirty colors with hemstitched hems, monogrammed or embroidered, made in its own workrooms abroad. Irish, Italian, Swiss, and Belgian sheets are available. For white, Leron recommends the Belgian sheets, which are sold individually and start at about $175. The finest quality colored sheets—in pink, blue, yellow, and green—are Irish and are sold in sets. Special finishes include lace work and hand appliqué in floral and Renaissance designs. Sizes are twin, full, queen, and king. *Leron, Inc., 745 Fifth Ave., New York, NY 10022; (212) 753-6700.*

D. Porthault, Inc.

French linen hemstitched solid color sheets in pastels as well as dark brown, green, and red start at around $290. Porthault's signature sheets in a floral pattern with a scallop border, start at near $500 for the twin size. This family-owned company weaves, dyes, and prints all their fabric in their own factories in Rieux, France. Their products have been available in the U.S. since 1948. They have shops in Toronto, Tokyo, Paris, London, and New York. *D. Porthault, Inc., 57 W. 57th St., New York, NY 10022; (212) 688-1660.*

Maison Henri

Irish and Belgian sheets in white, pink, and blue are available here, but the Irish are recommended as finer. Hemstitched in twin, queen/double, and king. Cases come in standard, king, square, and boudoir sizes. *Maison Henri, 617 Madison Ave., New York, NY 10022; (212) 355-5463.*

E. Braun

Irish linen, hemstitched white sheets are available in twin, queen/double, or king sizes starting at around $165. Open end and French back cases come in standard, king, continental, and boudoir sizes. A mail-order catalog can be had by writing or calling: *E. Braun, 717 Madison Ave., New York, NY 10021; (212) 838-0650.*

R. Jabbour & Sons

White Irish linen sheets in twin, queen/double, and king start at more than $300 per pair. Pink and blue sheets can be ordered but will take six to eight months to arrive. Cases come in standard, king, and square sizes. Monogramming and embroidering are available. *R. Jabbour & Sons, 51 E. 58th St., New York, NY 10022; (212) 355-5126.*

Bergdorf Goodman

This major department store will special order linen sheets—made in Belgium of fabric woven in Ireland, and available in white, pink, blue, and yellow. They can be plain, hemmed or hemstitched, monogrammed or embroidered to taste—as simple as a geometric design or as elaborate as French wallpaper. Sheets are sold in pairs in twin, queen/double, and king sizes; cases come in standard, king, or special order square. Prices vary with each order. *Bergdorf Goodman, 754 Fifth Ave., New York, NY 10019; (212) 753-7300.*

• And the ultimate in luxury linens? A candidate: Pratesi's Royal Set, a line of 100 percent silk sheets which come in two designs: beige silk with silk lace, and a striped silk sateen, with a shiny stripe on a muted silk background of the same color, available in blue or beige. A top sheet for a king size bed runs over $1,000; a pillowcase is $325. Silk sheets feel light and feathery to the touch, just like a fine silk blouse, and while polyester imitations may achieve the same look, they don't "breathe" like the natural fibers.

• Less expensive, but no less luxurious are sheets made of Egyptian cotton. Both Pratesi and Porthault produce 100 percent Egyptian cotton sheets (although Pratesi will add polyester to eliminate the need for ironing). Egyptian cotton's special quality is that it can be woven much finer and closer together. From 280 to 300 threads are woven per inch, as opposed to the 180 to 200 threads per inch in the department store sheets of domestic manufacturers, producing a smoothness and silkiness which must be felt to be believed.

• **The Ultimate in Printed Cottons.** France's highest quality Provencal-design fabrics are made by a manufacturing firm called Souleiado. They are available in the U.S. exclusively through Pierre Deux, Inc., which has nineteen stores. At any one time, Pierre Deux carries more than fifty Souleiado patterns, based on traditional eighteenth-century Provencal designs. What makes these fabrics so special? Most important are the colors: Souleiado fabric comes in extremely unusual shades that make other fabrics look bland and dull. Each season, a few new colors are introduced. Second, the fabric patterns are wonderfully complex; as many as eight different colors may be used in a single design. Finally, the quality of the cotton is superior to other fabrics on the market. Because it is so tightly woven, it repels dirt and is thus suitable for upholstery.

Souleiado fabrics are copied everywhere (genuine ones carry a copyright on the selvage), but, says a Pierre Deux spokesman, imitations are easy to spot: the colors are quite ordinary, and the fabric is limp and loosely woven. Pierre Deux also carries high-quality items made from the fabrics (handbags, pillows, place mats, lampshades, women's clothing), and offers custom decorating and upholstery services. For a store near you: *Pierre Deux National, 350 Bleecker St., New York, NY 10014; (212) 741-7245.*

A BETTER BATH

THOUGH great civilizations have always excelled at the fine art of bathing, mankind's long quest for the perfect bath has always been hampered by a basic flaw in the vessel itself. That bath's waters may be warm and soothing but every bathtub, however large, has been hard and stiff and often cold to the touch—until now.

In the 1970s Scott Bortz of Seattle, Washington, developed a cushioned bathtub, a fiberglass shell lined with inch-thick plastic foam and covered with elastic. The result was the first "soft tub," a supple bathtub which conformed to the human body. Not only did this cushioning make bathing more comfortable for the back and derriere, but the foam actually kept the water warm longer. Soft tubs based on this design are available in the U.S. from two sources: the *Soft Bathtub Company* and *Facetglas.*

The Soft Bathtub Company, of which Bortz is president, offers three models. *The Personal Bathtub,* nicknamed the "reading tub" because its sloped back makes it feel like a plush armchair, is a standard-size, fifty-five-gallon basin with eight whirlpool jets and push-button controls. Deeper and wider is the seventy-five-gallon *Soaking Bathtub.* Both sell for just under $3,000. Top-of-the-line is the *Doublewide Bathtub* (for those who like to share their immersions), available with whirlpool jets for about $3,700.

Soft Bathtub Company also offers such luxury options as underwater illumination systems, solid brass-plated whirlpool jets, and custom finishes. The tubs come in a full range of decorator colors, and a twenty-year warranty is offered. For details, CON-TACT: *The Soft Bathtub Company, P.O. Box 81125, Seattle, WA 98108; (800) 882-7638.*

Facetglas, Inc., manufactures the *Cushiontub,* made of closed-cell foam coated with vinyl. When you step into this tub your toes actually sink into the material. According to the company, laboratory tests on the tub included the ultimate challenge—a fresh egg was dropped from a height of 115 feet onto the foam mat without breaking. Cushiontubs come in three styles: *The Soother,* a standard-size bathtub; *The Serenity,* a more spacious model (a foot longer); *Hearts Content,* a pink heart-shaped tub for two (perfect for Valentine's Day, if you need an excuse). The Cushiontubs are all available with whirlpool units. For prices and information: *Facetglas, Box 10067, Rock Hill, SC 29731; (803) 328-0191.*

CLOCKS

THE world's *most accurate clocks nowadays have atomic measurements.* But they're monopolized by observatories and the like, leaving accuracy-minded consumers to make it with instruments that lose a whole minute in a year's worth of ticking. Even these clocks are not necessarily new-fangled, however: while some utilize the latest thing in the marketable timekeeping, quartz movements, others are mechanically operated, that is, hand-wound. Perhaps the biggest surprise in clockmaking is geographical. The world's best are not turned out by aged Swiss craftsmen in gingerbread houses. Switzerland does make some fine movements, but it makes a lot of schlock as well. In fact, no Swiss clock is listed by our sources among the best. Mentioned instead are: **Elliot** (England), **Seiko** (Japan), **L'Avigne** (France), and two U.S. makers— **Chelsea** and **Herschede.**

Some clock manufacturers specialize in a single type, the grandfather, or "long case." Others make, instead of or in addition to grandfathers, marine, bracket (wall), and mantle or table models as well. Quartz movements can be found in most of these styles. Quartz exceeds mechanical movements in accuracy, but only a very fastidious timekeeper will really relish the difference. As one expert puts it, "People come to me demanding accuracy to thirty seconds a year. I tell them, 'Remember, it took you nine months, give or take a few days, to be born.'" Many first-rate clocks are still made with plain windup mechanical movements, so there's obviously a lot to be said for a key and a bit of muscle.

Clockworks

The ornateness and luster of the case usually sell a clock, but the nature of the case material is a more important indicator of quality. Regardless of exterior appearance, brass is the most valued case material. It should be solid brass casting or, better yet, forging, *not* sheet brass. Inside, it's particularly important that the plates, which contain the bearings and jewels, be of heavy, high-quality brass. "What you're looking for in a movement," says an official of Chelsea, "is something long-lasting and dependable." In grandfather clocks, there is another important interior element— the driving mechanism. Says Robert Tibor, a knowledgeable clock repairman in Manhattan: "Almost all modern grandfathers are chain drive. The real McCoy is *cable*-driven, but it's not easy to find."

Herschede

The Herschede company uses cables in all of its top-line clocks. Herschede (pronounced HER-shuh-dee), a fourth-generation firm originally based in Cincinnati, relocated in Mississippi a quarter century ago, and continues to produce some of America's finest instruments. Although it makes mantel and wall models, *its specialty is grandfathers.* The price of those are the "nine tubular bell" designs, which retail for as much as $8,500. The nine-bellers feature hand-etched dials and hour-marking melodies composed for each namesake style: Canterbury, Westminster, and so on. For clocks costing $5,800 and up, Herschede makes all of its own movements. (Others are imported from Europe, chiefly from West Germany.) For the nine-bellers, it also designs period cabinet styles. Herschede clocks are sold only through dealers, among them: the *Chicago Clock Co.,* Chicago; *Ted's Clock Emporium,* Los Angeles; and *Harris Koch,* New York City.

Chelsea

Despite Herschede's status, Chelsea describes itself as "the last great American clockmaker." The claim, it turns out, pertains to other-than-floor models, *especially to marine clocks; Chelsea's are among the best in the world.* Since the turn of the century, the company has made bulkhead clocks and other types for the U.S. Navy, and its "Boston" line of marine style clocks and barometers has evolved to become the dominant brand used for both pleasure and commercial boating.

The company's "Chelsea" line has recently been expanded to include a variety of contemporary styles. Many of these clocks, including Chelsea's famous Ship's Bell clock, contain the same mechanical striking movement that was designed by Chelsea in 1897. Quartz movement clocks have been added to the line very recently and, like the mechanical movement, it is constructed of gold plated cut brass gears, polished and hardened steel pinions seated on six jeweled bearings. Each is individually made by one of Chelsea's master clockmakers. Prices range from $195 to $1,095.

Chelsea clocks are sold only at better jewelry and specialty stores in the United States. At present, there are just over 300 stores displaying Chelsea clocks. *A catalog is available by calling (outside Massachusetts) (800) 435-2001,* or writing to the company at: *284 Everett Ave., Chelsea, MA 02150.*

F.W. Elliot, Ltd.

F.W. Elliot, Ltd. is an amalgam of two fine old English clock-makers, Elliot itself and the even more distinguished Thwaites and Reed; T and R, established in 1740, built Big Ben and still services it. The combined company also has laurels to rest on: it made the commemorative clock for the Pope's first visit to the United Kingdom. Elliot's products range from "skeletons" (see-throughs) to grandfathers. Those bearing the Elliot name all have wooden cases; of them, the hand-lacquered models—in Chinese red, black, and white—are undoubtedly the best known; they cost between $2,000 and almost $6,000. The Thwaites and Reeds are primarily brass cased and sell for up to $2,000. Elliots are handled by jewelry stores and clock shops and by such department stores as *Marshall Field & Co.* in Chicago, *Galt & Brothers* in Washington, and *Shreeve & Co.* in San Francisco.

L'Arigne/Seiko

Manhattan's Tourneau, a major retailer of clocks and watches, touts two imports: L'Avigne and Seiko. Although not rated by our other sources in the Herchede-Chelsea-Elliot class, they deserve mention. L'Avigne features reproductions of such antique models as English carriage clocks; key wound, with see-through glass cases, they are known for style and elegance. Seiko, famed as a watchmaker, uses metal cases and quartz movements. Its clocks, like its watches, stress sleek and modern design.

PORCELAIN

THE choice among porcelains is difficult. *It is a matter of aesthetics, because the selection among the finest quality porcelains is broad.* Time has given porcelain manufacturers a chance to develop their craft. The basic technique has been known for centuries. The first primitive forms of porcelains were developed under the T'ang dynasty in China, between 618 and 907. Later, under the Yän dynasty (1279–1368), further advances were made in refining the basic clay mixture. In 1575, in a Florentine workshop under the patronage of Francisco I de Medici, the first European porcelain was produced, at Meissen near Dresden, Germany. Designs on these first porcelain pieces imitated Chinese and Japanese pottery. Later, around 1740, European landscapes and flowers began to influence the painting, which was done in polychrome over glaze enamels with frequent touches of gold. The French, who developed their own version of porcelain, using a soft-paste in the mid-seventeenth century, turned to hard paste around 1770, at Limoges and Sevres. Their designs, which were initially inspired by Oriental pottery, then by Meissen, frequently employed fragile but creamy white, deep blue, turquoise, green, yellow, and rose paints.

Today, porcelain is made all over the world with designs to suit any fancy, from classic Oriental to traditional floral to modern geometric. The variety and availability are welcome to anyone keen on setting a special table. But *don't buy porcelain thinking of it as an investment.* Experts at Sotheby's advise it generally does not appreciate in value. So buy it to enjoy, for lovely dinnerware certainly contributes to a wonderful meal. Following is a survey of some of the finest porcelains available today.

Royal Copenhagen

This company's beautiful blue and white signature porcelains—"Blue Fluted" and "Blue Flowers"—bring to mind a large, sun-drenched, flower-filled kitchen, good coffee, and wholesome food. Their patterns date back to 1775 and 1782 respectively; their prices start at $60 for a five-piece place setting. In 1790 a new pattern was introduced based on the wildflowers of Denmark: Flora Danica. The first full set was made for the Empress of Russia. Not completed in time, it remained in Denmark where the King put it on view at Roseborg Castle, where it remains today. It is still being handmade today, featuring pale, muted colors, and extraordinarily delicate painting. It is subtle, understated, splendid. A five-piece dinner service costs $1,850 to $2,000. *Royal Copenhagen, 683 Madison Ave., New York, NY.*

Limoges

All French porcelain is made in the city of Limoges. Hence, the generic name. The finest of these is made by two companies: Haviland and Raynaud Ceralene. Their patterns are similar, spanning the possibilities from subtle geometrics to charming floral, classic Oriental, and innovative Art Deco. Prices for both start at around $150 for a five-piece set, and go up. Both are available at fine stores across the country.

Tiffany Private Stock

In the course of making available to the American public the world's finest porcelains, Tiffany developed design and quality concepts and created their own line of Limoges porcelain hand-painted in France. Patterns derived from Greek and Roman art, from Ming Dynasty and Japanese Kakeimon pottery, from Dresden and Sèvres porcelains decorate these exceptionally beautiful services. Among the finest porcelain available in the world, Tiffany Private Stock starts at $450 for a five-piece setting. Available only at: *Tiffany & Co., Fifth Ave. at 57th St., New York, NY.*

Porcelain Notes

• **Definitions.** A spokesperson for Christie's makes the following technical distinction: you *don't* usually refer to porcelain as china but many people do refer to china as porcelain.

• **Japanese Porcelain.** **Imari** and **Minto** are contemporary Japanese porcelains which are available in Japan and the U.S. and are cheaper when purchased in the U.S. An average vase runs between $1,500 and $2,500. Generally, they are plentiful but not as interesting as two older names dating back to the eighteenth century— **Kakiemon** and **Nabeshima.**

• **Meissen, Sèvres, and Rosenthal.** Meissen, Sèvres, and Rosenthal are still in production and are *very* expensive. While each makes regular dinner service, Sèvres concentrates more on creating individual pieces. Unhappily, both Meissen and Rosenthal have a reputation for being difficult to deal with.

BONE CHINA

DO you love fine dinnerware but are not partial to the stark whiteness of porcelain? Do you prefer the creamy density of bone china white? You are, then, in the company of most savants in England and the United States. **In fact, bone china is the English version of porcelain.** It was created in 1797 when Josiah Spode II added bone ash to a *soft-paste* porcelain mixture and developed what has since become known as standard English bone china. It is harder, more translucent, and requires a lower firing temperature than porcelain. Design motifs have followed much the same path as those of porcelain: Oriental influences, then Meissen and Sèvres landscape and floral patterns. To this day, bone china is made and used primarily in England and the United States.

Spode/Royal Worcester

Founded in the 1760s at Stoke-on-Trent (an English pottery center for centuries), where it resides to this day, this firm pioneered the bone china industry. It was the first company to open a London showroom, one of the first to perfect a transfer printing process, and, as stated above, the virtual creator of bone china. The overall shape of their dishes duplicates that of the silver plates that preceded the development of porcelain and china. The ornamentation is derived from period designs and is still made by hand to a great degree. Their "Lancaster Cobalt" is a dramatically intense pattern that seems to reveal something of the personalities that made it. It sells for $1,500 for a five-piece place setting.

Spode Crested Ware is the name given to custom-designed services, a tradition with Spode that dates back to the time when Josiah Spode completed Chinese import ware services for English customers who had received broken or damaged goods. Today, Spode will custom design and execute a service for twelve within six months time. Also owned by Spode is Royal Worcester, whose most spectacular china pattern is called "Aston" and sells for $650 to $700 the five-piece place setting. Quality of craftsmanship and delicacy of design are hallmarks of both Spode and Royal Worcester. Their dinner services lend dignity and a sense of heritage to any dining table.

Royal Doulton/Minton/Royal Crown Derby

Founded in 1815, Royal Doulton carries on a tradition of excellence in craftsmanship and discretion in design. It is the parent company of such famous china firms as Minton and Royal Crown Derby among others. The combination results in Royal Doulton producing one-third of the world's bone china. Royal Crown Derby's "Old Imari" service calls on the Oriental background of all china to produce a richly vibrantly colored pattern. It sells for $450 to $500 for a five-piece place setting. Minton's "Dynasty" service also evokes the Orient with an unsurpassed intensity and depth. The suggested retail price is $1,100 for a five-piece place setting.

Wedgwood

Founded in 1759 in England, Wedgwood aimed to offer porcelain then china dinnerware to the knowing public at large. Today, about ninety different Wedgwood patterns are available, among them "Ulander Powder Blue," sold at $500 to $600 for a five-piece place setting. It is strikingly beautiful and identifiably Wedgwood. Other world famous creations are Queen's Ware, Black Basalt, and Jasper.

Tiffany Private Stock

As with their private stock porcelain, Tiffany has developed a full line of bone china that is made in England and hand painted in France. With spectacular designs that span the spectrum of taste and prices that start at $450 to $500, Tiffany is a veritable gold mine for dinner services.

Lenox

This top American firm was established in Trenton, New Jersey, in 1889 by Walter Scott Lenox as the Ceramic Art Company. The name was changed to Lenox in 1906. The first American china to be commissioned by the White House, Lenox produced a dinner service for Woodrow Wilson in 1918, another for Franklin D. Roosevelt in 1931, and most recently, a dinner service for Mrs. Ronald Reagan, in 1982. One of their signature patterns is "Autumn." First made in the early 1920s, this service features an elaborate, raised enamel design. It sells today for $150 to $200 for a five-piece place setting. Just as was done for the White House, custom-designed china services can be developed for members of the public.

STERLING SILVER FLATWARE

THE adventure of dining depends on more than delicious food to satisfy the taste. The sense of aesthetics must be fed. Just as the food must be prepared and presented with care, the table must be set with style and elegance. And most crucial to this elegance is the flatware. Design, weight, balance, angle, depth—all are factors determining the real value of silverware.

The eighteenth century saw the arrival of matched sets of flatware for full domestic use and the subsequent disappearance of personal sets. The length of the utensils increased to nine inches, the now customary proportions were developed, forks came to have four prongs, additional serving pieces—like sugar tongs and tea strainers—were created, and handles were curved for easier manipulation. Since that time, changes have followed the dictates of style and fashion: ornate design has given way to a more pared-down look. But the essentials have remained the same. The cost of silver flatware, while never inexpensive, does respond to the pressures of the marketplace. Basically, price is determined by the cost, at the time of purchase of the finished product, of replacing the raw ore added to the cost of the workmanship.

We are all familiar with the standard silver patterns available through such reliable sources as **Reed & Barton, Gorham, Towle,** etc. They offer perfectly serviceable utensils. What follows is a discussion of *sterling silver flatware that goes beyond the merely serviceable, that approaches an art form. Most are handmade: hammered out from the bar of silver into the utensil.* Some are only hand-finished: mold-made, and then refined and polished by hand. All are an unsurpassed pleasure to hold and to use.

Georg Jensen

In business in Denmark since 1904, this is one of the few remaining firms that makes all its silverware completely by hand. They do not believe in compromise. They are very strict about keeping faith with the original concept behind the design; they are very careful about where their products are sold. Since their inception, they have developed forty silverware patterns; today sixteen are regularly produced, but, should you have an heirloom set of a now discontinued pattern and need a replacement or addition, old patterns can be replaced at all times. The best-known and best-selling pattern is "Acorn" at about $750 for a five-piece dinner place setting. "Blossom," the most ornate, sells for $1,800 the place setting. "Koppel," the newest pattern, is very simple, very modern in flavor. And "Cactus," first exhibited in 1924 and produced in 1930, has a timeless weightiness to it. In general, this silverware appeals through its substance, its volume, its integrity. More expensive than most other silverware patterns and not to everyone's taste, it remains singularly independent in look and feel. *Georg Jensen, 683 Madison Ave., New York, NY 10021.*

James Robinson

Unique in the offering of a range of patterns consistent with those of the eighteenth century, Robinson silverware is completely handmade by twenty silversmiths in England. Theirs is the oldest continuing production process in the world, having started in 1550.

Of their eighteen patterns, the oldest currently offered was developed in 1660, the most recent in 1810. Great exponents of the hand-hammering process, Robinson points out that the act of hammering compacts and compresses the silver so that it becomes stronger, tougher, and more durable. The bowls of the spoons are deeper, the prongs of the forks are sharper so more versatile. The patterns are more definitely reproduced and, best of all, special, customized alterations are possible. Robinson silverware is dishwasher-safe and is meant to be used every day. Its patina will only be enhanced by such use. At prices starting around $600 for the five-piece dinner place setting. *James Robinson, 15 E. 57th St., New York, NY 10022; (212) 752-6166.*

Christofle
Since 1830, this firm has prided itself on being silverware suppliers to Napoleon III and the royal courts of Europe. Today, they offer twelve patterns of fine silverplate and five patterns of sterling. Patterns like "Perles," first created in 1872, have an appeal that goes beyond fashion. Neither very ornate or very simple, Christofle silverware, all hand-finished, demonstrates a natural proportion, balance, and feel—all due to a great deal of handwork in the finishing process. Available at fine department stores across the country and through *Pavillon Christofle, 680 Madison Ave., New York, NY 10021.*

Georgian House
Originally an English firm, this company was acquired by Fortunoff. The sterling silverware is still produced in England, as it has been for generations. And it is this sense of history and longevity that provide much of the charm in patterns like "English Onslow," "Queen Anne," and "Coburg." Priced at more than $1,000 per five-piece place setting. Available at fine stores across the country.

Tiffany
The dream of many brides, Tiffany offers seventeen of the most charming patterns in silverware conceivable. Weighty, well-balanced, these patterns carry on the tradition Tiffany established over 100 years ago, a tradition that requires great attention to detail and striving for excellence. Hand-finished to perfection, Tiffany is a time-honored source of fine silverware. *Tiffany & Co., Fifth Ave. at 57th St., New York, NY 10022.*

Sterling Silver: Handmade Is Best. Although sterling silver by law is 925 parts silver to seventy-five parts copper, it can vary widely in quality and in price. We asked Edward Munves, Jr., of New York's distinguished James Robinson, Inc., what the difference is between a $150 sterling silver place setting and the $600 place settings he sells in his shop.

Weight and workmanship account for the tremendous variation in the price of sterling silver flatware. "Handmade silver," says Munves, "is heated, hammered, and compacted. You get more silver per cubic inch. Machine working of silver, on the other hand, tends to stretch it." As a result, handmade silver is stronger than machine-made silver and will last longer. The prongs on a handmade fork, for example, can be pointed because the metal is strong enough to endure repeated use without breaking off; you won't see pointed prongs on machine-made silver. Also, designs on handmade silver will be more sharply defined.

How else can one distinguish handmade flatware? "The terms are confusing," says Munves. "Sometimes 'handmade' means hand-fed into a machine, or hand-finished. The best way to tell is to pick a simple pattern and ask whether minor adjustments can be made. Could the handles be turned up instead of down? Could the fork have four prongs instead of three? If the flatware is handmade, these things can be easily done." (Elaborate handmade patterns are not so easily changed, Munves says, since they are made with molds and even minor changes would require a new mold.)

Silverware Note

Among the best silverware by American makers other than Tiffany, most is machine-made with various degrees of handwork additional, depending on the manufacturer. All of the American makers we talked to quoted prices on a four-piece setting. The average was about $200, with top-of-the-line creations going to $400 to $500. American manufacturers to consider are: Gorham, Towle, Wallace, Reed & Barton, International, and Oneida.

CRYSTAL MADE CLEAR

THE sparkling shimmer of a crystal glass as light refracts off it, as wine is held within it, as it is raised to the lips is incomparable. No other glass is its equal. We have only to thank Englishman George Ravenscroft for this sheer delight. In 1676 he invented the technique of adding lead to glass compounds and created crystal, which was an immediate hit. By the early eighteenth century a standard English style had developed: large, sturdy, stemmed drinking glasses, generally undecorated—the better to see all the optical effects. An industry grew up and prospered such that in 1745 a tax was imposed on the raw materials, causing the English style to change: glasses became smaller, more delicate, and longer stemmed; some even had surface decoration. Because this tax did not extend to Ireland, in the third quarter of the eighteenth century a glassmaking industry grew there. Although English crystal was exported to France, Belgium, Norway, and Sweden throughout the eighteenth century, it wasn't until the nineteenth century that the French began production—Baccarat, of course. And it wasn't until after World War I, in reaction to the heavy English style, that designers with Orrefors, in Sweden, began creating the clear, colorless, free form styles so popular today.

Crystal is a creation which can be (separately or simultaneously) useful, decorative, and aesthetic. Balancing these qualities in your own mind and deciding which is most important is the first step to buying intelligently. *Artistic value is the distinguishing mark which divides the top crystals,* such as Baccarat, from those belonging to the second echelon. The reason: there is a widely recognized artistic element in the top crystals, to the point where they have joined other masterworks in the world's most prestigious museums—including the Louvre in Paris, the Vatican Museums in Rome, the Metropolitan Museum in New York, and the Hermitage in Leningrad. *A second distinguishing note is insistence on perfection.* A top maker of fine crystal, such as Baccarat, will discard as much as forty percent of its finished product at the end of each manufacturing day if it does not measure up to the firm's own high criteria for excellence. Other manufacturers routinely dispose of only ten percent. As one veteran observer of the market says: "At those secondary places, if a piece has made it to the final stages, it's sold no matter what."

What to Look For

• **According to the highest European standards, the best crystal must be made with at least twenty-nine percent lead,** but no more than thirty-one percent. Some objects with as low as twenty-four percent lead content are still considered crystal, but those with less than twenty-four percent (and more than twelve percent) are

only "crystalline." Less than twelve percent lead: merely "glass."
• **When you flick your finger** against the best crystal, it should ring, as top manufacturers will tell you, "like a bell."
• **The crystal must be absolutely colorless,** with no detectable shades of blue, gray, or red. The prism or rainbow effect it gives off, providing it with the diamond-like optical quality it possesses, is an essential part of crystal, but the colors should be the result of light only, not ingredients in the glass. While it's sometimes difficult to detect the slightest shades in a single piece, place pieces next to each other and look for variations in color: poorer products will be easily recognized.
• **It is nearly impossible to make glass articles without** *some* **flaws:** air bubbles called seeds, specks called stones, and slight lines called cords. These can be discovered if the object is held up to the light. The finest, of course, has the fewest flaws.

   The Top Crystal Makers
Austria: Lobmeyr
Belgium: Val St. Lambert
England: Stuart; Webb
France: Baccarat; Daum; Lalique; St. Louis
Ireland: Waterford; Galway
Japan: Hoya; Iwata; Kagami
Sweden: Orrefors; Kosta Boda
U.S.A.: Steuben

• **Steuben.** Steuben makes *the finest American crystal.* Roughly a third of its output is functional: goblets and other drinking vessels, vases, ashtrays, and candlesticks. The remaining two-thirds is termed ornamental or artistic: jewelry objects or sculptures. Prices vary from as low as $125 for a crystal animal figure to $275,000 for more complex, limited edition works. If you are one of those who can never get enough of Steuben's offerings, there is *Steuben Glass: An American Tradition in Crystal* which contains 1,100 photographs of which sixty-one are color, and 1,500 drawings representing the finest Steuben has to offer. It's a must for identifying pieces for collectors and a thing of beauty for glass lovers. The text was written by Mary Jean Madigan, former editor of *Art & Antiques.* Steuben's catalog is available from: *Steuben Glass, Fifth Ave. at 56th St., New York, NY 10022; (212) 752-1441.*

• **Baccarat.** Most experts agree that *Europe's best crystal is made by Baccarat,* with Orrefors coming in a close second. Approximately half of Baccarat's output is tableware; the other half, artistic—or ornamental—objects. Prices vary from $60 for a goblet to $1,000 for a limited edition design. (In his book, *Quest for the Best,* Stanley Marcus singles out Baccarat's ultra-thin goblets as the best in the world.)

• **Orrefors.** With a lead content of 30.6 percent on its art glass and much of its stemware (some stemware is only demi-lead), Orrefors is proud of its broad line of products ranging from practical items like stemware to primarily decorative pieces. Their discard rate, during production, averages at twenty-two percent to twenty-five percent—the more intricate the design, the higher the discard rate. Prices start as low as $20 for stemware and rise to $900 for a bowl, in the practical line. In the art glass line, prices start at $200 and rise to $6,000, again for a bowl.

• **Waterford.** A venerable name in Irish lead crystal, Waterford deserves all the kudos it gets—for consistency, integrity, and adherence to a classic tradition. They have a forty to forty-five percent discard rate in the production of crystal that has one-third percent lead content, which is slightly over the guidelines. Waterford considers all its products to be useful, from glasses right on up to chandeliers, of which they produce twenty-six different models. Prices start at $22 and go as high as $10,000, for a multi-armed chandelier.

• **Val St. Lambert.** As most of this glass is made by hand, this firm claims to have no appreciable overall discard rate on its production line. Their crystal has a twenty-four percent lead content, at the low end of the scale. While they consider their line to be entirely useful, they do allow that the crystal animals, which comprise ten percent of the line, may be thought only decorative. And while they make a very broad range of products, Val St. Lambert is *best known for their candlestick collection.* Suggested retail prices range from $20 to $6,000, for a bowl or a vase.

• **Lalique.** The extremely high level of quality control on the production line results in a very small percentage of discards in this beautiful collection of crystal with a twenty-six percent lead content. Among the primarily useful pieces they produce, about sixty percent of the full line, prices start around $55 for a cache pot and climb to $27,000 for the "Cactus Table." It has a crystal base and eight crystal leg supports topped by a chrome ring and a plate glass surface. This table can be customized, i.e., the diameter of the table can be altered, within limits. Among the purely decorative pieces, a horse's head sells for $8,500. The distinguishing feature of Lalique crystal is a frosted satin finish of the utmost delicacy, often combined on the same piece with a clear finish. Lalique developed this technique and continues, to this day, to be the most accomplished practitioner of the form.

An Investment Caveat

A top glass specialist at Sotheby Parke Bernet warns that there is virtually little or no market for contemporary crystal. "There is far too much of it on the market," she says, "and the best you can expect in resale, even for the top names, is only about 20¢ on the same dollar you paid for it. And that's on a very good day." *The best advice:* if you do buy crystal new and at the retail level and are doing so as an investment, *go with the artistic or ornamental objects.* But buy them through dealers or at auction. The prices are dramatically lower.

HOME SWIMMING POOLS

FOR pointers on what to look for in a top quality pool—and in a quality pool *builder*—we queried John Gedney, president of E.L. Wagner of Darien, Connecticut, America's oldest pool company. Wagner, in business since 1919, operates in the most elite New York suburbs and has built pools for people with names like Rockefeller, Dillon, and Watson. The best pool is *always* made of gunite—concrete sprayed under pressure over steel reinforced rods. "Vinyl- or fiberglass-lined pools can crack, splinter, or peel in a few years," says Gedney. "A normally maintained gunite pool will last virtually forever."

Beyond demanding a gunite pool, says Gedney, it's less important to know technicalities than to know how to find a reputable pool builder. Gedney's pointers:

• **Look for a company that does not subcontract** *any* part of the operation—from digging the hole through servicing the pool after it has been built. High volume, low quality dealers do a lot of sub contracting because they can't afford all their own equipment.

• **Find out if there's a civil engineer on the staff.** If not, the company should at least be able to refer you to one whom they employ as a consultant. "When a professional engineer okays a pool he becomes personally liable," says Gedney. "That's an extra safeguard for you."

• **Visit the company's headquarters and ask to see its inventory.** The number of filters, heaters, pumps, etc., on hand should equal the number of pools the company builds in a year. Says Gedney, "You'd be surprised how many contractors will come up to you when your pool is half-built and say, 'Gee, I'm out of pumps and since it's the height of the season, I can't get one now.'"

• **Make sure that the crew foremen are permanent employees of the firm.** Pool companies are notorious for using large numbers of unskilled college kids during the peak season. The result is that almost no one at the job site has ever built a pool before.

Thirty-seven of the country's high-quality pool builders (including E.L. Wagner) have formed a national company which you can contact to find out if a member firm operates in your area. It's called *Aquatech, 18632 Beach Blvd., Suite 210, Huntington Beach, CA 92648; (714) 964-1334.*

TENNIS COURT ADVANTAGE

IF your tennis passion moves you to invest between $15,000 and $30,000 on your own tennis court, two books are must reading before building. They'll keep you from ending up with the wrong court, or, worse, the wrong contractor. Together they give you the facts you need to choose and deal knowledgeably with a court builder. Total cost $20. The first book is the guide, *Tennis Courts,* revised every two years by the United States Tennis Association facilities committee with the cooperation of the U.S. Tennis Court & Track Builders Association. It is an exhaustive compendium of specifications and guidelines on court surfaces, lighting, fencing, maintenance, depth of sub-bases . . . you name it. If a potential contractor can't quote chapter and verse from this publication, look around for another contractor. Cost $11.

The second book, called simply *The Tennis Court Book,* is written by James Bright and published by the *Andover Publishing Group, 3 Main St., Andover, MA 01810.* ($7.50, plus $1.50 postage and handling). This is a true layman's guide and is a perfect complement to the drier, more technical USTA guide. It's especially good in helping you evaluate which court surface best suits your game, your budget, and your lifestyle. Both books are available from the *USTA Center for Education and Recreational Tennis, 729 Alexander Road, Princeton, NJ 08540; (609) 452-2580.*

If you're thinking about a home court, you should also contact the *U.S. Tennis Court & Track Builders Assn., 223 West Main St., Charlottesville, VA 22901; (804) 971-2860.* This group includes the country's best tennis court contractors and cooperates with the USTA in publishing the annual guide. It can direct you to reputable contractors in your region. It's also a storehouse of information and can answer just about any court-planning questions you may have.

GRACEFUL GARDENS

G REAT garden ornaments confer an aura of elegance on even the most mundane garden or patio. Nothing bespeaks civility more than a well-placed classical urn, a bubbling bronze fountain, or an ornate Victorian garden bench. Only a few firms in this country manufacture garden items with a skill worthy of mention in *The New Book of Bests.* You won't find their products in even the best department or garden furnishing stores. They deal largely with landscape architects and designers, but they will also sell directly to the public.

Robinson Iron

As the name implies, this Alabama firm deals in iron, specifically in recastings of the wonderful cast-iron furniture and ornaments that graced antebellum Southern homes. The firm also does custom historic restoration work. It has, for example, restored the cast-iron Victorian entrance posts that guard Lover's Lane at West Point. You can pay as little as $60 for Robinson's spiral-based flower stand or as much as $5,000 for a life-sized statue of Hebe, Greek goddess of youth. Our favorite: the exuberant fern-patterned chairs at $500 each. CONTACT: *Robinson Iron, Robinson Road, Alexander City, AL 35010; (205) 329-8486.*

Kenneth Lynch & Sons

Kenneth Lynch is one of the country's foremost metal fabricators. Back in the 1920s, the government commissioned him to repair copper work on the Statue of Liberty. Today, his firm makes over 10,000 architectural designs in bronze, lead, cast stone, and wrought iron, including garden urns, statues, weathervanes, and garden chairs. "The cast stone that we use is architectural cast stone such as they use on fine buildings, and we have been making the same product for over 100 years," says Lynch, who is still president of the firm. All work is either of original design, or is an antique reproduction which could not be improved upon. CONTACT: *Kenneth Lynch & Sons, 78 Danbury Road, P.O. Box 488, Wilton, CT 06897; (203) 762-8363.*

Kroin, Inc.

If you like modern patio furniture, you've probably noticed that tubular metal chairs with wire grid seat and back have become extremely popular in outdoor furnishing. We found the firm that introduced the design and still makes the sturdiest version of the chair: Kroin, Inc. Kroin's chairs use approximately forty percent more wire than most versions of the chair. The steel is made in a Bavarian factory which produced steel logging chains 100 years before Kroin approached it to make furniture. Owner Larry Kroin prefers to deal through architects but is willing to accommodate anyone who doesn't have a personal architect or interior designer. The heaviest model chairs cost about $165. CONTACT: *Kroin, Inc., Charles Square, Suite 300, Cambridge, MA 02138; (617) 492-4000.*

GARDEN TOOLS YOU CAN TRUST

THESE days a good workman can, and often should, blame his tools. There is one exception: the tools of **Smith & Hawken,** a California-based company specializing in hand garden tools. Craftmanship is at the heart of Smith & Hawken's tools. Hand-forged steel, seamless or "weldless" heads, and solid stock construction (a process where the tool is forged from one beam of steel and encloses the wooden handle completely), are all requisites for a strong, durable tool. Mass-produced tools just can't equal these qualities. Most of Smith & Hawken's tools are designed and forged by Bulldog Tools, Ltd., in the small mining town of Wiggen, England, where quality virtually excludes automation. Paul Hawken, co-owner and founder of Smith & Hawken, designs some of his tools himself. All of the tools are tried and tested by a board of advisors, active in gardening and farming and sensitive to the frustrations of poor design and careless production.

Smith & Hawken's selection is straightforward. One can't find exotic, highly specialized tools here, although such basics as spades, shovels, saws, and shears come in all shapes and weights. It also carries a line of top-grade axes from Sweden and small-scale tools, useful for children or the urban window-box gardener. Its catalog is full of explanations about how the tools are made, what they do most efficiently, and how the user can help them last the lifetime for which they are designed. As Hawken says, "treat your tools like good friends, and they will be." Finally, a reciprocal friendship. For information and a free catalog: *Smith & Hawken, 68 Homer, Palo Alto, CA 94301; (415) 383-4415.*

SUPER SHADE

THERE is a long shadow on the land and it emanates from Santa Barbara Designs, a fifth-generation home furnishings company. Three brothers, Colin, Doug, and Hugh Hayward, thought they could make a good old thing—an Italian-style market umbrella—into a better new product. The result: **the Santa Barbara Umbrella**—in diameters of eleven and one-half to thirteen and one-half feet. When the Hayward brothers entered their design against recognized leaders in the umbrella field (i.e., Nike, Inc. and Takara Co., Ltd. of Japan) and won an International Achievement Award, they knew they had something.

Each umbrella is constructed by hand, using the best oak and mahogany hardwoods for the frame (easily raised and lowered by a pulley system), solid custom brass fittings, and a choice of rugged Marine Vivatex or color-fast acrylic fabrics. There is a range of color choices and custom linings are also available (to match your outdoor decorating scheme). Delivery time is four to six weeks. Brochure available from: *Santa Barbara Designs, P.O. Box 90610, Santa Barbara, CA 93190; or call collect (805) 965-3071.*

GREAT GRILLS

THE outdoor barbecue is a rite of summer every American enjoys, as a culinary treat and social gathering. Making the most of it means having a first-class grill. Building your own to custom specifications is one option, but, if you're not so inclined, the factory-made grill is the natural alternative. To get the best, consider the following factors and then choose from among the top grill makers.

What to Look For
• **Materials.** The best grills are made of heavy metal—cast aluminum or steel—which keeps them from warping when they get hot.

Handles should be weatherproof and heat resistant. Wheels on heavy units should always be rubber rather than plastic.

• **Covers.** All of the top models are covered grills. Covers protect food and fire from wind and rain, conserve heat, and control the rate of burning.

• **Ventilation.** In a charcoal grill, the charcoal should rest on a grate, not on the bottom of the grill itself. The height of the charcoal-holding grate should be adjustable, in order to regulate cooking speed, as should be the air vents in the body of the grill.

• **Cleaning.** Grilling with charcoal can be a messy business, and the best grills are constructed to minimize your contact with the mess. Most important is a separate tray that effectively collects the ashes from spent charcoal and provides easy removal.

The Best Grills

One of the finest grills on the market today is **W.C. Bradley's Char-Broil Hooded Charcoal Grill,** a heavy-duty, fully covered rectangular "wagon-style" grill made of heavy sheet metal with cast-aluminum sides. The grill body's front door makes it easy to add more charcoal to the first without disturbing the food, and allows adjustment of the grate itself while the fire is on. A removable tray at the bottom of the grill collects ashes. Bradley uses old-fashioned cast-iron cooking grates, which are supposed to be more durable and, with the broader, flat rungs, do a better job of cooking. Model CB-940 is currently the largest and most deluxe grill in a series of four outdoor cookers, featuring a cooking surface of 18¾ by 31¼ inches (586 square inches). Twin shelves on the sides of the grill provide ample work space for the cook. The CB-940 retails for about $300. *W.C. Bradley Enterprises, Inc., P.O. Box 1240, Columbus, GA 31993; (404) 324-2461.*

The most exceptional grill available, though, is the **Cattleman Outdoor Barbecue System,** a 200-pound ensemble which also sports an electric smoker and a propane-fired heating element (with a twelve-quart pot and deep-fry basket). The grill itself is thirty by twenty-two inches—room enough for eight T-bone steaks—and is fronted by an eleven by thirty-three-inch work counter. The grill has its own lid and is vented by a chimney. Made of black-enameled steel, the Cattleman System stands forty-two inches tall, is two feet wide and five feet long. Price: about $1,500. *Hammacher Schlemmer, 147 E. 57th St., New York, NY 10022.*

Gas Grills

Although charcoal still accounts for eighty-five percent of the units sold, gas grills have edged out charcoal in total dollar sales. Obviously gas grills are significantly more expensive, but they are becoming popular because they are so much cleaner than charcoal grills, and the fuel costs are lower: the same meal that's cooked for abou fifty cents using charcoal can be cooked for a couple of cents worth of liquid propane gas. Gas grills give that "cooked outside" flavor to food just as charcoal grills do. Contrary to popular notion, it's not the charcoal itself that flavors the food cooked on a grill. What makes barbecued food taste barbecued is the smoke produced when fat from cooking meat drips onto a heated surface and burns. Any heated surface will do. When buying a gas grill, look for an H-shaped burner, which cooks food more evenly than a single line of flame. Thick cast aluminum is the body material of the best brands. **The big names in gas grills:** *Shepherd* (St. Joseph, Michigan), *Charmglow* (Bristol, Wisconsin), and *W.C. Bradley.*

SEVEN

SPORTS & LEISURE

SPORTS MEDICINE CENTERS

AMERICA'S craze for fitness has at least one of every three citizens over the age of sixteen engaged in some form of vigorous heart-pumping exercise on a regular basis—be it jogging, swimming, bicycling or badminton and volleyball. Correspondingly, the number of injuries suffered by both weekend warriors and determined athletes is dramatically increasing. Recent estimates place injuries close to twenty million, a figure which is costing exercisers and their employers some $40 million in lost work time.

In the wake of this sweat and strain has come a new practitioner of medicine known as the sports physician and a new multidisciplinary treatment center known as the sports medicine clinic. While these clinics have devised amazing ways to repair worn-out arms or shattered knees and developed methods to combat muscular pain and exhaustion, much of the work of a sports medicine clinic is concerned with prevention, fitness, and conditioning as well as body-building and tolerance to injury. One of the pioneers of sports medicine, Dr. James A. Nicholas, founder-director of the Institute of Sports Medicine and Athletic Trauma at New York's Lenox Hill Hospital, defines sports medicine as that which touches on what he calls the "Seven P's": Performer, Performance, Pathology, Prevention, Prescription, Practitioner, and Practice.

Let's say you've decided to join those other millions of Americans and get yourself into some sort of shape. Before you do, it makes good sense to submit yourself to a battery of tests at a top-rated sports clinic to determine just what kind of shape you are in now, what kind of training course to pursue, and how to attain a regimen that will result in a healthier life. Also consider this. You can now be treated by the same doctors that fix up the world's best athletes—the very same ones that lengthened Tommy John's pitching career and kept Joe Namath hopping around on a woefully inadequate knee. These doctors are just as concerned with the average athlete.

The Sports Fitness Evaluation

Just how fit are you and what is your health potential is the focus of sports medicine clinics which, in one form or another, apply the following tests in evaluating your level of fitness:

• **Physical Examination.** A doctor examines you to determine that you are free from heart disease and other conditions which may determine modifications in your exercise.

• **Stress Test.** Conducted on a treadmill or a bicycle ergometer. Your oxygen consumption, heart rate, and blood pressure will be monitored to determine how well oxygen is being delivered to exercising muscles and to detect any heart function abnormalities.

• **Orthopedic Evaluation.** Musculoskeletal strength, joint motion, and nerve functions are evaluated. This is a valuable tool for diagnosing current injuries and abnormalities, as well as preventing future orthopedic problems.

• **Blood tests.** A count of red and white blood cells, hematocrit (percent of blood which is cellular), and hemoglobin (oxygen binding pigment) is usually taken. The tests also look for protein, fats, glucose, electrolytes, iron, and various enzymes in the blood.

• **Body Composition.** An underwater (hydrostatic) weighing mechanism that reveals the body's true proportion of fat to lean muscle tissue and skin fold mesurements.

• **Strength and Flexibility.** A series of tests that evaluate big muscle development and the range of motion of your joints and muscles.

• **Pulmonary Function.** The effects of disease, smoking, pollution, or just plain inactivity will show up in this breathing test.

• **Exercise Prescription.** On the basis of these tests, a comprehensive report will be prepared, including a recommended program for sports activity, specific to your level of physical conditioning and needs.

The Clinics

While sports physicians and sports medicine clinics are sprouting rapidly across the country, *The New Book of Bests,* after extensive talks with athletes, physicians, and administrators of the American Orthopedic Society and the American Academy of Podiatric Sports Medicine, culled the following:

• **Institute of Sports Medicine and Athletic Trauma (ISMAT).** The first hospital-based research facility in America, ISMAT was founded in 1973 by Dr. James A. Nicholas, director of the Department of Orthopedic Surgery at Lenox Hill Hospital in New York City. It soon became widely known for providing care to New York's professional athletes and dancers. Under Dr. Nicholas's continuing direction, ISMAT provides rehabilitation and reconditioning therapy both to professional and recreational athletes who have suffered injuries, while at the same time conducting research into the various biological and physiological responses to exercise and the demands of sport—research which provides the basis on which the staff approaches treatment for each patient. Because of its reputation, the institute has become a testing center for new exercise and rehabilitation equipment, much of which is not available elsewhere. *Lenox Hill Hospital, 130 E. 77th St., New York, NY 10021; (212) 794-4627.*

• **The Sports Medicine Clinic.** Founded in 1983 by Dr. Keith Peterson. Hallmark is its team approach to the prevention, care, and rehabilitation of athletic injury and disease. The Sports Medicine Clinic offers consultation in orthopedics, physical therapy, rehabilitative medicine, nutrition, and family medicine. The clinic sponsors seminars and classes, conducts complete physicals, and provides a speaker's bureau and newsletter. For information: *1551 N.W. 54th St., Suite 200, Seattle, WA 98107; (206) 782-3383.*

• **National Athletic Health Institute.** NAHI was founded in 1973 by Dr. Robert Kerlan and Dr. Frank Jobe, internationally renowned orthopedic surgeons and sports medicine specialists who gained fame by rescuing and repairing athletes from the Los Angeles Rams, Dodgers, Lakers, Kings, and California Angels. NAHI offers medically designed and supervised testing programs—an executive fitness program, health improvement program, and fitness evaluation (costs vary from $200 to $600) that will assist you in achieving your maximum level of cardiovascular health and fitness. In addition, NAHI conducts a sports injury clinic which provides diagnostic care for young athletes of the Southern California area on a regular basis, free of charge. NAHI shares the Inglewood campus of Centinela Hospital Medical Center and concentrates research on the evaluation of sports equipment, artificial turf, helmets, and other protective devices. Centinela's Biomechanics Lab is one of the leading research facilities of prevention and rehabilitation of sports-induced illnesses and injuries. *575 E. Hardy St., Inglewood, CA 90301; (213) 674-1600.*

• **The Cooper Clinic.** The man who some say started America running, Dr. Kenneth Cooper, is the founder and creator of The Aerobics Center with its four components—the Cooper Clinic, the Activity Center, the Institute for Aerobics Research, and the Aerobics Center Guest Lodge. Located on twenty-eight acres in Dallas, the Cooper Clinic, through its best-selling books *Aerobics* and *The Aerobics Program for Total Well-Being,* has long been recognized as a leader in the study of the medical value of exercise. Some 30,000 patients have been given comprehensive evaluations, individual counseling, and specific recommendations at the Cooper Clinic where the theme is simple—an ounce of prevention is worth a pound of cure. The Cooper Clinic has a staff of seven full-time physicians, a nutritionist, a dentist, exercise test technologists, laboratory personnel, and administrative aides. Four different types of exams are given at the Clinic and each includes the physically challenging maximal performance exercise stress test. One result of such testing is a coronary risk profile score which quantifies each patient's risk of having a heart attack based on his or her individual treadmill time, a cholesterol level, blood pressure, family history, and each of the other known coronary risk factors. For information: *Aerobics Center, 12200 Preston Road, Dallas, TX 75230; (800) 527-0362.*

• **The Cleveland Clinic Foundation.** Physicians in this program, founded in 1973 by Dr. John Bergfeld, treat the Cleveland Browns, Cleveland Cavaliers, Cleveland Indians, Cleveland Force, and the Cleveland Ballet. The staff evaluates and treats both acute and chronic sports-related conditions. They also instruct patients in proper rehabilitation and training technique. More than 15,000 patients were seen in 1985. Known for its fully comprehensive approach, the Cleveland Clinic Sports Medicine program also provides nutritional counseling; fitness assessments; and training consultations for beginning, recreational, professional, or elite athletes. Psychologists specializing in the effects of stress on athletes are available for group or individual treatment. Medical exams for high school teams are offered to ensure safe participation in sports. Cleveland Clinic staff conduct an annual seminar for coaches, trainers, physical therapists, physicians, and other health professionals. They also present the courses required for state certification of high school coaches. The staff includes four orthopedic surgeons, a medical orthopedist and a family practitioner as well as four physical therapists, an exercise physiologist, and a certified athletic trainer. Dr. Bergfeld, a strong believer in rehabilitation says, "Most injuries can be treated with rehabilitation and do not require surgery." For information: *9500 Euclid Ave., Cleveland, OH 44106; (216) 444-2620.*

HOME GYMS

THE extraordinary popularity of exercise and fitness in this country during the past decade has been accompanied by an explosion in the manufacture of gym equipment designed specifically for home use. *You can now give yourself the vigorous, thorough workout at home that formerly you could only get at a big gym or a health spa.* In a space as small as seven feet by twelve feet you can set up a home gym that should serve you efficiently in your pursuit of weight control, aerobic fitness, muscle strengthening, and toning.

Unless you know exactly what you need, it might be a good idea to consult a professional before setting up your own gym. A fitness consultant can help you select the right equipment and the right workout program for your needs. You can find one by going to a local gym, health spa, or a university athletics department in your area. Also, most of the better sporting goods stores can recommend consultants, as well as give you advice on equipping your home gymnasium. *The Hardcore Bodybuilding Sourcebook* (Sterling Publishing, $12.95) includes a directory of fitness consultants.

The equipment you will need depends on a number of factors, such as the space available to you, the amount of money you are prepared to spend, and the extent of the exercise program you have planned for yourself. Basically, however, your complete home gym will include: a rower, a stationary exercycle, a multi-station weight and training unit, and free weights. A treadmill, or another aerobic fitness machine, is optional. The criteria for selecting equipment for your personal exercise center should include durability, comfort, compactness, expandability, and appearance.

Finally, you will need a space that is well lit, comfortably ventilated, and carpeted. In order to get the most out of your gym, a pleasant environment is essential. A basement dungeon is not a place in which you'll be anxious to work out on a regular basis. A stereo system will provide a good musical background for your efforts. A television can also be welcome distraction while performing long routines of repetitive exercises.

Rowers

Rowing is a superb exercise for developing overall fitness. It helps improve cardiovascular capacity and works all the main muscle systems of the body. The top of the line in rowing machines is the *Professional Rower* made by MacLevy (approximately $1,250). This big, heavy-duty piece of equipment comes close to duplicating the true feeling of sculling, or rowing across water. If you are seriously devoted to rowing, this would be an excellent machine to choose. Otherwise, a smaller home rower is quite sufficient. These use hydraulic cylinders, or shock absorbers, to provide resistance rather than real oars. The more advanced, like the *Pro Form 935* ($389), are equipped with "ergometers," devices that measure exercise the way the odometer in your car measures miles. Other quality rowing ergometer manufacturers: Precor and Amerec.

The most unique rowing machine is the *Concept II Rowing Ergometer,* which sells for about $600. On this machine the rower pulls on a wooden bar attached to a flywheel. The resistance of the flywheel simulates the pressure of water against an oar.

Cycles

An indoor cycle is another necessity for personal gymnasiums. Among the best models available are those from Monark. Its $2,300 *Monark Electronic Ergometer* has a microcomputer-controlled system that can be used for stress testing or supervised training programs. Electrodes attached to the body constantly monitor heart rate, lung capacity, and other elements of the cardiovascular system. While this machine is used by the professional athlete in training, or the physiotherapist or physician in clinical testing, it is also durable and compact enough for home use as well.

Another high-quality cycle on the market: *Universal Fitness Products' Aerobicycles* ($2,100-$2,500), which automatically adjusts the resistance on the pedals to a target heart rate. If your pulse goes over that rate, pedaling becomes easier; when your pulse is below the target, the cycle makes you work harder. This will help increase heart muscle strength and lung capacity.

Treadmills

You must gauge for yourself the relative benefits of a treadmill versus the real thing, such as road running. If you opt for a treadmill, *Precor* and *Universal* make excellent models ranging in price from $660 to $4,000. The higher priced models have computerized control panels that show speed, running time, distance, and pulse rates on digital displays.

Another option is the *NordicTrack* ($470), the *NordicTrack Pro* ($559), or the *Fitness Master X-C* ($550). These indoor machines simulate cross-country skiing. They're fine for overall conditioning, but you might prefer to get out in the snow.

The most unusual treadmill, however, is the *Swimmer's Treadmill,* designed for those who love to swim laps at home, but who don't have room for an Olympic-sized pool. Following in the wake of the stationary bicycle and the runner's treadmill, this device lets swimmers stroke for miles in a pool just four feet wide by ten feet long. The system consists of a three-and-a-half foot deep pool and a padded belt, or harness, which holds the swimmer in place as he swims. It may sound frustrating, but users report that the system provides a more comfortable and less stressful swimming environment than the typical crowded fitness club pool. Prices range from about $3,200 for a fir-framed unit to about $7,000 for a fully enclosed oak-framed pool. Manufactured and distributed by *Aqua-Motion International (5250 N. Sherman St., Denver, CO 80216; (303) 297-3844).*

Weights

Weight training is important for your total exercise program. It not only increases your strength, but tones your muscles. And, it helps you feel and look better. There are two basic kinds of weight equipment: free weights and weight machines. The advantages of free weights is that they are less expensive and are easier to store. The advantages of weight machines is their convenience and relative safety, i.e., you don't need a "spotter," or someone to catch the weights if your grip should slip.

The best free weight equipment is manufactured by *York*. A set of barbells costs $400 for a 310-pound set, or $600-700 for a 500-pound set. Dumbbell pairs are priced from $50 for three-pound, black-plated weights to $500 for 100-pound weights with a high polish chrome steel finish. Chrome racks for storing dumbbells cost from $250 to $350.

Weight machines can be used as a substitute for free weights, or in conjunction with them. The choice depends on the degree of ambition of your exercise program. *Universal Gym Equipment* developed the first weight training machine in 1957 and their big *Centurion Multi-Station* institutional machine is still top-of-the-line. It has sixteen separate exercise stations, from leg presses to wrist conditioners, with weights from ten to 1,050 pounds. Schools and fitness clubs are the biggest customers for these $13,000 machines. Smaller weight machines, designed specifically for home use, offer many of the same exercises as the Centurion but with fewer stations. The *Power-Pak 400,* also from Universal, enables you to perform up to 100 different exercises at a single exercise station. It comes with a 260-pound stack of chrome weights and costs about $4,300. Other good weight machines for the home are the *Marcy Master Gym* ($1,995), the *Soloflex* ($625), and *Pro Form's Kong* ($545).

Monitors

Another sound idea is to equip your home gym with devices to measure your pulse before, during, and after exercise. This should help prevent dangerous over-exertion. *Universal* makes a series of what are considered very accurate pulse meters that range in price from $100 to $200.

GOLF: EQUIPMENT/SCHOOLS

FOR all golfers a personal best would mean the lowest score he or she has ever posted under good conditions on a great course in front of good friends—or better yet playing a pro-am with Jack Nicklaus. To play our "best golf all the time," in Tommy Armour's words, we need the right clubs, solid instruction, and time to pursue this fascinating pastime.

Equipment
• **Balls:** The best way to choose a ball to fit your game is to know these facts: 1) ODS: The United States Golf Association controls the manufacture of golf balls, in particular with its Overall Distance Standard (ODS) which limits the speed of the ball to 250

yards per second at impact. This means claims by manufacturers that their ball is longest are incorrect. 2) Compression: (low equals eighty; high equals 100) *is* a real factor. The high-handicapper should opt for eighty to ninety compression; only the better player can get the most from a 100 compression ball. 3) Ball Cover: The durable Surlyn cover should be the choice of the average player; thinner, more responsive covers (balata) are for experts and pros. 4) The newer optic balls make for a more colorful game, but have nothing to do with quality.

• **Top Names.** 1) Titleist: Acknowledged as finest overall ball-maker. Surlyn DT and Pinnacle best for majority of players. 2) Spalding. Top-Flite XL ball also one of top two for majority. 3) Hogan. Choice of many of best amateurs and pros. Has same quality that goes into Hogan clubs, which are tops.

• **Clubs**
    A. Standard. 1) AMF Hogan. Still the class act among standard clubs, done with the exacting precision and perfectionist attitude typical of Hogan himself. Radial and Apex PC are top-of-the-line. Look for the Radial 3.5, Hogan's most recent attempt at perfection. 2) PGA Golf. Tommy Armour model is still the best, a contemporary version of one of the great classic clubs. 3) Hillerich and Bradsby Citation Woods. Best persimmon woods; high-quality craftsmanship. 4) Toney Penna Woods by Rawlings. The Penna design plus quality control have kept these in top rank. 5) Two other companies to watch: a) MacGregor. Now owned by Jack Nicklaus, quality on the rise again. Bet on the Golden Bear to produce a super club in the next two to three years. b) Ram. Tom Watson has done a limited edition of Golden Ram Tour Grind model. Look for him to raise Ram standards to the level of one of the very best.
    B. Custom. There are about thirty companies in the U.S. which make custom clubs. Among them we especially recommend:
    1. **Kenneth Smith Golf Club Co.** (P.O. Box 41, Kansas City, MO 64141). Maybe *the* best in the United States. Excellent reputation for care and quality. Takes eight weeks on average.
    2. **Bailey and Izatt, Inc.** (2538 Haverford Road, Ardmore, PA 19003). Four to six weeks.
    3. **Bob Toski Corp.** (160 Essex St., P.O. Box 576, Newark, OH 43055). Former tour pro and leading instructor has translated his experience into clubmaking design.

4. **Hubby Habjan,** (Onwentsia Club, P.O. Box 442, Lake Forest, IL 60045).

5. **The Golfworks,** (Division of Ralph Maltby Enterprises, 4820 Jacksontown Road, P.O. Box 3008, Newark, OH 43055). Equipment editor for *Golf* Magazine; also an expert on repairing and rebuilding clubs.

3. Bags. The contemporary standard dictates a slightly smaller, lighter weight bag made of nylon or cordura. Two companies are still considered the leader in bags: 1) Burton. The traditional leader in fine bags. They make leather models, including steer hide, which can run hundreds of dollars. 2) Pro Group. Their Hotze bag is also a fine example of the craft.

Schools

• **Golf Instruction.** Every golfer wants to lower his or her handicap, but few players do more than take an occasional lesson. However, for anyone seriously interested in improving his game, attending one of the country's premier golf schools is a worthwhile investment. Such establishments offer many hours of intense instruction every day on all aspects of the sport—both physical and mental. In addition, students usually have the opportunity to play a first-rate course, as many of the best golf camps are based at well-known resorts.

Golf schools come in all sizes and shapes. There are schools for men, for women, for men and women, for senior players, and for juniors. They are run by players (Arnold Palmer, John Jacobs, Bert Yancey), by magazines (*Golf Digest*), and by resorts (Disney World). Schools are outdoor and indoor. Some are only one day and take the form of an intensive clinic; others last a week at a plush resort and can cost around $3,000 per person. All involve the golfer in an intensive series of physical and mental drills designed to give him or her enough ideas and techniques to last a long time. The schools provide a discipline and a special golf-minded environment not found in any other teaching situation. Results from golf schools range from minimal improvement to drastic transformation. A list of the top U.S. schools follows:

• **Golf Digest Instructional Schools.** *Golf Digest* magazine manages about fifty schools a year. Its program is one of the most extensive and successful in the country. Most of the sessions are held at first-class resorts; a few are "commuter" schools based at country clubs near large cities. The school's main philosophy is to let students help themselves. Each golfer receives a personal videocassette of his or her lessons; specific drills geared to the individual's exact needs; and a personal notebook to keep a permanent record of all instructions. Itineraries vary for each location, but the basic format for its five-day school remains pretty much the same. Students check in on Sunday night, and check out Saturday morning. The all-inclusive package for a five-day school is about $2,150. A three-day school, with a reduced itinerary, is held several times a year and costs about $1,400. CONTACT: *Golf Digest Instructional Schools, P.O. Box 5350, Norwalk, CT 06856; (203) 847-5811.*

• **John Jacobs Practical Golf Schools.** John Jacobs, a former British touring pro, has long been considered one of the finest teachers in the game. He and his staff pay particular attention to how a student's club strikes the ball. Such factors as clubface alignment, clubhead path, angle of approach, and clubhead speed are all carefully scrutinized. Videotape is used to reinforce lessons, and students are given the opportunity to practice on greens and fairways throughout the week-long school. A typical five-day package includes lodging at a top-quality resort (like Mountain Shadows in Scottsdale, Arizona, or Boyne Highlands Lodge in Harbor Springs, Michigan), most meals, all instruction, green fees, cart rentals, and complete use of the home course and its practice facilities. Prices range from around $650 to $1,000 depending on the resort and the time of the year. CONTACT: *John Jacobs Practical Golf Schools, 5302 E. Cortez Drive, Scottsdale, AZ 85254; (602) 991-8587.*

• **Swing's The Thing.** This school is aptly named, for its instructors—Dick Farley, Rick McCord, and Harry Obitz—are considered masters of swing fundamentals, and have been endorsed by many pros, including Julius Boros, Art Wall, and Ken Venturi. Students get a lot of individual attention, since the student/teacher ratio is a very low 1:4. Based at the twenty-seven-hole Shawnee Inn and Country Club in Pennsylvania's Pocono Mountains. Sessions run June through August. A winter course is held in Orlando, Florida, from February to May. A standard five-day package costs around $990. CONTACT: *Swing's The Thing Golf School, P.O. Box 200, Shawnee-on-Delaware, PA 18356; (717) 421-6666.*

• **Mount Snow Golf School.** Best known as a ski area, Mount Snow also boasts one of the finest golf courses in New England. From May to October, golfers can improve their game in the scenic, lush, rolling foothills of the Green Mountains. A standard five-day program contains twenty-five hours of instruction; some lessons are videotaped. The basic package costs about $700 and includes lodging at the Snow Lake Lodge. CONTACT: *Mount Snow Golf School, Mount Snow, VT 05356; (802) 464-3333.*

• **The Golf Studio.** For those who want to combine a visit to Disney World with golf instruction, this program is ideal. Its chief advantage is flexibility: students take lessons at their convenience. Two-hour studio lessons are given three times each day and cost $35 per person for small groups of three or four. Videotapes are used to analyze each golfer's swing. The Golf Studio is open year-round, unlike all other golf schools. CONTACT: *Disney World Golf Resort, P.O. Box 40, Lake Buena Vista, FL 32830; (305) 824-2250.*

• **Subconscious Golf.** Ed Grant of Phoenix has had significant success with a technique rooted in humanistic psychology. His program of lectures and tapes helps you discover positive powers you may have overlooked. CONTACT: *Ed Grant, Subconscious Golf, Inc., 10601 N. Hayden Road, Suite 100, Scottsdale, AZ 85260.*

• **Ben Sutton Golf Schools.** For players of all ages, from nine to ninety-nine, there is the Ben Sutton Golf School in Sun City, Florida. A coed staff of PGA and LPGA professionals provide personalized instructions on every aspect of the game, from driving to putting, in a relaxed and comfortable atmosphere. Sutton's advice is, "When you come down, don't get over-tired. Pace yourself and do more listening than swinging." One-week sessions from late September through May, about $1,180 per person, double occupancy. CONTACT: *Ben Sutton Golf Schools, Inc., P.O. Box 9199, Canton, OH 44711; (216) 453-4350.*

COURSES: TOP U.S./INTERNATIONAL

THE following course information has two parts. The first is a detailed description of twenty top U.S. courses. The second lists thirty more which receive acclaim and are well worth playing. These lists, in turn, are followed by **fifty courses outside the continental United States.** Those marked with an asterisk are open to the public for a greens fee which averages between $30 and $70. The others are private golf clubs. The best way to get on private courses is to have a member sponsor you as a guest for a round (some clubs require that he or she play with you, but this is not always necessary). Most private club members will do this because they know (if you are a club member) that you will return the favor when they wish to play your course. Either way they are cooperative. Note too that, with the proper introduction, you can get on most all of America's great courses.

Twenty Great American Courses (Listed East to West)

• **Shinnecock Hills Golf Club.** (Southampton, NY) Yardage: 6,697 Par: 70. Located next door to the National Golf Links, Shinnecock is the sixth oldest club in America, founded in 1891, and ranks today as the oldest still on its original property. The striking clubhouse is the work of Stanford White.

• **National Golf Links of America.** (Southampton, NY) Yardage: 6,619 Par: 73. The National Golf Links is the work of one of America's golf pioneers, Charles Blair MacDonald, who spent five years studying all the famous Scottish and English golf holes and then imitated the best to make his eighteen—so well that he bettered the holes he copied.

• **Winged Foot Golf Club.** (Mamaroneck, NY) Yardage 6,881 Par: 72. Built in 1922, Winged Foot was designed by Arthur Tillinghast and derives its name from the Mercury Emblem of the New York Athletic Club. Located in prosperous Westchester County, it includes many celebrity members from the New York area.

• **Oak Hill Country Club. (East Course).** (Rochester, NY) Yardage: 6,902 Par: 71. Oak Hill is another creation of architect Donald Ross and boasts three great finishing holes, which have ruined many title contenders. The course contains some 34,000 trees, which provide both beauty and a challenge to the golfer.

• **Baltusrol Golf Club.** (Springfield, NJ) Yardage: 7,031 Par: 72. In 1895 Arthur Tillinghast designed the two eighteen-hole courses, which remain very much as Tillinghast conceived them. The large stone clubhouse was built in 1909. The challenge of the lower Course, the championship eighteen, is proven by its having been the site of six U.S. Opens, the most recent in 1980.

• **Pine Valley Golf Club.** (Clementon, NJ) Yardage: 6,441-6,765 Par: 70. Probably the most fabled course in America, it often settles the "world's toughest course" argument. Writer Charles Price called it "one big 200-acre, unraked bunker" with some greens and fairways on it. Begun in 1912 by George Crump, who wanted to make it the hardest course in existence, it fulfills his dreams. Crump built much of it himself and others finished it in 1922, four years after his death. Pine Valley is "penalizing architecture," the epitome of target golf, and a mentally terrifying experience for the average golfer who probably won't break 100.

• **Merion Golf Club (East Course).** (Ardmore, PA) Yardage: 6,509 Par: 70. Merion is a course with charm, a place everybody likes. Its Scottish style bunkers, the famous "White Faces of Merion," have provided a challenge for many golfers. It is an inland course with the feel of a seaside links. An accurate and well-placed tee shot is the key to playing Merion well.

• **Congressional Country Club.** (Washington, D.C.) Yardage: 6,900 Par: 72. When you drive off the first tee at the Congressional Country Club, you can count yourself among the "Who's Who" of political, financial, and social titans who since its inaugural in 1924 have played this classic course, located just outside of Washington, D.C. In 1964 it was the scene of the U.S. Open, won by a bone-weary Ken Venturi in one of the Open's most dramatic final rounds.

• **Oakmont Country Club.** (Pittsburgh, PA) Yardage: 7,057 Par: 72. The massive Oakmont punishes the least error severely. Designed by William Fownes, it was begun in 1903 and features huge, fast greens and trademark bunkers with three-foot furrows in them. Once there were 350 traps, but they now number 180, with the famous "church pew" bunkers (fifty yards long with rows of grass in them) the best known.

• **Pinehurst Number Two.** (Pinehurst, NC) Yardage: 7,051 Par: 72. Number Two is the jewel among the seven Pinehurst courses. Designed by Donald Ross in the mid-1930s and revamped slightly in 1948, it displays the lush greenery and pine tree borders characteristic of Pinehurst courses, but adds heavy rough and sand and grass bunkers that make it the championship layout of the golf complex begun by James Tufts in the early 1890s.

• **Augusta National Golf Club.** (Augusta, GA) Yardage: 6,980 Par: 72. Augusta National is storied because it was built by a great golfer, Robert T. Jones, and hosts one of golf's major championships, the Masters. Opened for play in 1932, it was built on a 365-acre floral nursery called Fruitlands, which makes Augusta one of the most beautiful courses in America. It was designed by the master Scottish architect Alister MacKenzie, with Jones overseeing the planning and construction. The course follows Jones's desire to give pleasure to all golfers regardless of ability and to reward the good shot by making the next one simpler.

• **Seminole Golf Club.** (North Palm Beach, FL) Yardage: 6,890 Par: 72. One of the country's most exclusive clubs the majority of its 300 or so members come from the Palm Beach area and read like a "Who's Who" of the Social Register. Ben Hogan is an honorary member. Members and privileged guests come to the elegant club-house to get away from Palm Beach social life and inquiring eyes. The Ormond Bermuda fairways are meticulously manicured and dotted with some 180 bunkers.

• **Pine Tree Golf Club.** (Del Ray Beach, FL) Yardage: 6,900-7,240 Par: 71. Pine Tree is the masterpiece of architect Dick Wilson. Like its neighbor Seminole, Pine Tree caters to a wealthy membership, many of whom have played competitively. Dotted with many bunkers and traps, it is one of America's best kept courses and also one of the toughest to score on.

• **Firestone Country Club.** (Akron, OH) Yardage: 7,165 Par: 70. Firestone is a big hitter's course. Its sixteenth hole, when played from the back tee, measures 625 yards, long enough to make the longest pros take three shots from tee to green. When the tee is up, the drive ends on a downhill lie, making the second shot equally difficult.

• **Medinah Country Club. (Number Three Course).** (Medinah, IL) Yardage: 7,110 Par: 72. Located outside of Chicago, Medinah #3 is part of a meticulously manicured set of fifty-four holes, serving a large, affluent membership. Its lush fairways give short roll and long par fours make it a strength test. Trees line all fairways so that errant shots are heavily penalized.

• **Oakland Hills Country Club.** (Birmingham, MI) Yardage: 6,974 Par: 71. Oakland Hills has the honor of having had Walter Hagen as its first professional. It has also been honored with four U.S. Open competitions. The most famous tournament played at Oakland Hills was the 1951 U.S. Open, when Ben Hogan, shot a closing sixty-seven to win his second Open title in a row.

• **Colonial Country Club.** (Fort Worth, TX) Yardage: 7,132 Par: 70. The room holding Ben Hogan's many trophies marks Colonial as his club, although he now prefers a quieter place across town. It is the site of the Colonial Invitational, called "The Masters of the Southwest."

• **Cherry Hills Country Club.** (Denver, CO) Yardage: 7,042 Par: 71. Built as a men-only club, Cherry Hills favors the big hitter, but the easier front nine is followed by a tough stretch of finishing holes, from twelve through eighteen. Here in 1960, Arnold Palmer made his first great "charge," finishing with a blistering sixty-five for his only Open victory.

• **Pebble Beach Golf Links.** (Monterey, CA) Yardage: 6,747 Par: 72. Annual television coverage of the Bing Crosby National Pro-Am has made the American golfing public familiar with Pebble Beach, in particular its spectacular ocean holes, which make it the best seaside course (technically, a links) in the country. The holes lie along the Monterey Peninsula cliffs and afford tremendous scenic views. They also provide terrifying mental hazards.

• **The Olympic Club (Lake Course).** (San Francisco, CA) Yardage: 6,669 Par: 71. The Lake course is the more challenging of the two Olympic Club layouts, winding diabolically through heavy stands of pine, eucalyptus, and cypress and demanding arrow-straight tee shots and pinpoint iron play to well-trapped greens.

Thirty More Great U.S. Courses

• **Cypress Point Club**
Pebble Beach, CA
Alister Mackenzie
Yardage: 6,464 Par: 72

• **Oakland Hills C.C. (South)**
Birmingham, MI
Donald Ross/Robert Trent Jones
Yardage: 7,088 Par: 72

• **Southern Hills C.C.**
Tulsa, OK
Perry Maxwell
Yardage: 7,037 Par: 71

• **Harbour Town Links***
Hilton Head Island, SC
Peter Dye
Yardage: 6,804 Par: 71

• **Los Angeles C.C. (North)***
Los Angeles, CA
George Thomas
Yardage: 6,813 Par: 71

• **Muirfield Village G.C.**
Dublin, OH
Jack Nicklaus/Desmond Muirhead
Yardage: 7,101 Par: 72

• **Riviera C.C.**
Pacific Palisades, CA
George Thomas/Billy Bell
Yardage: 7,029 Par: 71

• **Jupiter Hills Club**
Jupiter, FL
George and Tom Fazio
Yardage: 7,248 Par: 72

- **Point O'Woods G. & C.C.**
Benton Harbor, MI
Robert Trent Jones
Yardage: 6,906 Par: 71

- **Prairie Dunes C.C.**
Hutchinson, KS
Perry Maxwell/Press Maxwell
Yardage: 6,522 Par: 70

- **Quaker Ridge G.C.**
Scarsdale, NY
A.W. Tillinghast
Yardage: 6,745 Par: 70

- **The Golf Club**
New Albany, OH
Pete Dye
Yardage: 7,237 Par: 72

- **Butler National G.C.**
Oak Brook, IL
George and Tom Fazio
Yardage: 7,083 Par: 72

- **Canterbury G.C.**
Cleveland, OH
Herbert Strong
Yardage: 6,852 Par: 71

- **C.C. of North Carolina***
Pinehurst, NC
Ellis Mapes/Willard Byrd
Yardage: 7,154 Par: 72

- **Inverness Club**
Toledo, OH
Donald Ross
Yardage: 6,982 Par: 71

- **Laurel Valley G.C.**
Ligonier, PA
Dick Wilson
Yardage: 7,045 Par: 71

- **San Francisco G.C.**
San Francisco, CA
A.W. Tillinghast
Yardage: 6,794 Par: 71

- **Saucon Valley C.C. (Grace)**
Bethlehem, PA
David Gordon
Yardage: 7,044 Par: 72

- **Scioto C.C.**
Columbus, OH
Donald Ross/Dick Wilson
Yardage: 6,822 Par: 71

- **Bay Hill Club***
Orlando, FL
Dick Wilson
Yardage: 7,102 Par: 71

- **Bob O'Link G.C.**
Highland Park, IL
Donald Ross/H.S. Colt/
C.H. Alison
Yardage: 6,731 Par: 72

- **Cog Hill G.C. (#4)***
Lemont, IL
Dick Wilson/Joe Lee
Yardage: 7,041 Par: 72

- **Concord G.C.***
Kiamesha Lake, NY
Joe Finger
Yardage: 7,205 Par: 72

- **Doral C.C. (Blue)***
Miami, FL
Dick Wilson
Yardage: 7,065 Par: 72

- **Lancaster C.C.**
Lancaster, PA
William Flynn
Yardage: 6,672 Par: 70

- **Oak Tree G.C.**
Edmond, OK
Pete Dye
Yardage: 7,015 Par: 71

• **Tournament Players Club***   Jack Nicklaus
Jacksonville, FL   Yardage: 7,029 Par: 72
Pete Dye
Yardage: 6,857 Par: 72   • **Spyglass Hill G.C.***
     Pebble Beach, CA
• **Shoal Creek**   Robert Trent Jones
Shoal Creek, AL   Yardage: 6,810 Par: 72

Fifty of the World's Greatest Courses

• **The Old Course, The Royal Ancient Club, St. Andrews,** Scotland (Yardage: 6,960 Par: 72) Cradle of all courses. A must for every player. Open to all.
• **Carnoustie,** Scotland (Yardage: 7,101 Par: 72)
• **Dornoch,** Scotland (Yardage: 6,533 Par: 70) Home of Old Tom Morris, four-time British Open champion and Donald Ross, one of golf's greatest course designers.
• **Old Course, Troon,** Scotland (Yardage: 7,064 Par: 72)
• **Ailsa Course, Turnberry,** Scotland (Yardage: 7,060 Par: 71)
• **Muirfield,** Scotland (Yardage: 6,894 Par: 71) Home of the Honourable Company of Golfers, founded in 1744 and recognized as the oldest club in the world.
• **Royal St. George's,** England (Yardage: 6,136 Par: 70)
• **Birkdale,** England (Yardage: 7,001 Par: 72) Arnold Palmer won his first British Open here in 1961.
• **Royal Lytham & St. Annes,** England (Yardage: 6,673 Par: 71)
• **Royal Cinque Ports G.C.,** Deal, England (Yardage: 6,680 Par: 70)
• **Walton Heath G.C.,** Todworth, England (Yardage: 6,859 Par: 73)
• **Wentworth G.C.,** Surrey, England (Yardage: 6,997 Par: 72)
• **Portmarnock,** Dublin, Ireland (Yardage: 7,103 Par: 72)
• **Royal County Down,** Ireland (Yardage: 6,995 Par: 72)
• **Killarney Golf Club,** County Kerry, Ireland (Yardage: 6,758 Par: 73)
• **Lahinch G.C.,** County Clare, Ireland (Yardage: 6,504 Par: 72)
• **Ballybunion G.C.,** County Kerry, Ireland (Yardage: 6,503 Par: 71)
• **Campo de Golf Cajuiles,** La Romana, Dominican Republic
• **Tobago G.C.,** Mount Irvine Bay, Tobago (Yardage: 6,856 Par: 72)
• **Tryall G. & B.C.,** Jamaica (Yardage: 6,398 Par: 71)
• **East Course, Dorado Beach G. & T.C.,** Puerto Rico (Yardage: 7,005 Par: 72)

- **The Mid-Ocean Club,** Bermuda (Yardage: 6,547 Par: 71)
- **Royal Montreal G.C.,** Montreal, Canada (Yardage: 6,487 Par: 70)
- **St. George's G.C.,** Toronto, Canada (Yardage: 6,797 Par: 71)
- **Banff Springs Hotel,** Alberta, Canada (Yardage: 6,729 Par: 71)
- **Capilano G. & C.C.,** British Columbia, Canada (Yardage: 6,538 Par: 72)
- **Club de Golf,** Mexico City, Mexico (Yardage: 7,250 Par: 72)
- **Lagunita C.C.,** Caracas, Venezuela (Yardage: 6,895 Par: 70)
- **Red Course, Jockey Club,** Buenos Aires, Argentina (Yardage: 6,699 Par: 72)
- **Saint Nom-La-Breteche G.C.,** Versailles, France (Yardage: 6,821 Par: 73)
- **Circolo Golf Olgiata,** Rome, Italy (Yardage: 6,862 Par: 72)
- **Glyfada G.C.,** Greece (Yardage: 6,715 Par: 72)
- **Club de Golf Sotogrande,** Cadiz, Spain (Yardage: 6,910 Par: 72)
- **Golf Nueva Andalucia,** Marbella, Spain (Yardage: 6,815 Par: 72)
- **Penina G.C.,** Algarve, Portugal (Yardage: 7,480 Par: 73)
- **Vilamoura Golf Club,** Algarve, Portugal (Yardage: 6,874 Par: 73)
- **Crans-sur-Sierre G.C.,** Valais, Switzerland (Yardage: 6,813 Par: 73)
- **El Prat,** Marbella, Spain (Yardage: 6,485 Par: 72)
- **Royal Calcutta G.C.,** Calcutta, India (Yardage: 7,331 Par: 73)
- **Durban C.C.,** Natal, South Africa (Yardage: 6,516 Par: 72)
- **Royal Dar-es-Salam,** Rabat, Morocco (Yardage: 7,462 Par: 73) One of the world's real "monster" courses.
- **Pevero G.C.,** Sardinia (Yardage: 6,874 Par: 72)
- **Mauna Kea G.C.,** Kamiela, Hawaii (Yardage: 7,016 Par: 72)
- **Princeville G.C.,** Kauai, Hawaii (Three nines: Ocean: 3,460; Woods: 3,436; Lake: 3,188; all par 36)
- **Royal Hong Kong G.C.,** Fanling, Hong Kong (Yardage: 6,674 Par: 70)
- **Singapore Island C.C.,** Singapore (Yardage: 6,645 Par: 71)
- **Wack Wack G. & C.C.,** Manila, Philippines (Yardage: 7,078 Par: 72)
- **Kasumigaseki C.C.,** Tokyo, Japan (Yardage: 6,934 Par: 72) Japan's oldest club and one of its best.
- **Royal Melbourne G.C.,** Melbourne, Australia (Yardage: 6,946 Par: 71)
- **The Australian G.C.,** Sydney, Australia (Yardage: 7,154 Par: 72)

Golf Tours/Resources

• **Adventures In Golf.** Adventures in Golf is a charter organization which fashions individual trips for pre-arranged groups of four to ninety people who want to go to the British Isles for R&R upon the links. Adventures in Golf comes highly recommended by those who have used it, with costs at approximately $600 to $700 per person for a bed-and-breakfast week, land arrangements only. Luxury weeks cost $1,000 and up. The company will recommend hotels and courses (like those upon which the British Open has been played) and then organize an itinerary and transportation based on the preferences of the travelers. CONTACT: *Adventures in Golf, 29 Valencia Drive, Nashua, NH 03062; (603) 882-8367.*

• **The Old Golf Shop.** The finest source in the U.S. for purchasing books, high-quality golfiana, i.e., clubs, books, paintings, sculptures, etc. Owner James A. Olman has a beautiful catalog and is very willing to help answer questions. *325 W. Fifth St., Cincinnati, OH 45202; (513) 241-7789.*

TENNIS: HIGH-TECH RACKETS

T ENNIS racket design has been undergoing a technological boom the last several seasons, producing a flurry of expensive, exotic frames and a babble of conflicting product claims. In fact, whatever your image may be of what a tennis racket is *supposed* to look like, most of the new breed won't look that way at all. A survey of premium, top-of-the-line rackets by *The New Book of Bests* turned up 200 offerings from twenty-five manufacturers, thirty-five percent of which cost $100 or more, several exceeding the $300 level. Nearly extinct are the handcrafted racket frames where the natural beauty of the wood grain is allowed to show through. In their place are all-black frames designed to look high-tech, with bright and garish cosmetics applied even to many of the all-wood models. Consumers, though, are confused. Is it worth it to spend $100 to $200-plus on a new breed of racket, when $50 to $65 would suffice for a more traditional design? The answer is yes, but with some aesthetic and nostalgic qualifications. Here are some top rackets to consider:

• **Superform XL Stan Smith.** This model is an all-out attack on the vibration problem in a high-tech power rackets. Inside the frame is a graphite/fiberglass torsion box construction (borrowed from ski technology) and outside is an unusual five-sided racket head shape. The racket retails for $149 from *Pacific Sport Inc., 3202 S. Shannon St., Santa Ana, CA 92704; (714) 641-1150.*

• **Durbin Graphite.** There is no claim among tennis equipment manufacturers that arouses more cynicism from players than that of the "largest sweet spot ever." But one racket manufacturer—a relative newcomer to the tennis market—has made some grandiose sweet spot claims and has made them stick. Indeed, the Durbin Graphite racket has been judged as having the largest "sweet zone" in a comparison study released by a leading tennis consumer magazine. The Durbin Graphite offers firmness and the vibration damping qualities desired by strong advanced players. And, most importantly, Durbin's sweet spot claims were vindicated by an independent organization when *World Tennis* magazine released its lab data and play-testing results on top-of-the-line rackets. In lab tests the Durbin Graphite rates a "10"—on a scale of one to ten— for sweet zone, the best score recorded for all rackets. The consensus: the Durbin Graphite is a quality product that lives up to its advertising claims—best in its class. The Durbin Graphite retails for $160 from *Princeton Sports Products, Box 648, Exeter, NH 03833; (603) 778-1997.*

• **Prince Graphite.** When Howard Head introduced the Prince racket in the middle '70s, it revolutionized the racket industry. Head's patented design—the most important feature of which is basic size and shape of the racket head—offered players an enlarged "sweet spot," the ideal contact point for striking the ball, and thus an immediate boost to their games. The suggested retail price for the Prince Graphite is $250. The top-of-the-line Prince Boron, a very lightweight high-performance boron/graphite racket, retails for $450. These rackets do everything the company claims and have one more quality that makes them an excellent buy—durability, another attribute of graphite. *Prince Mfg, Inc., P.O. Box 2031, Princeton, NJ 08543; (609) 896-2500.*

TENNIS: SCHOOLS/RESORTS

ONE of the happiest results of the recent tennis boom has been the rapid growth of camps and resorts dedicated to the sport— to raising your level of play, to pampering your off-court *persona,* and most often, to both. First, however, a cautionary guideline.

These facilities range all the way from intense and neo-Spartan to laid-back and luxurious, so you should place yourself realistically along that spectrum. Evaluate your prospective choices in both on- and off-the court categories. Three general tips: 1) If instruction is your primary interest, you'll receive a more individualized dose if you attend in other-than-peak season. 2) If you prefer a varied social setting, ask which season is best for avoiding large, pre-formed groups. 3) If court surface is important to you, be advised that Western resorts and camps offer "hard" courts (á la The National Tennis Center at Flushing Meadow, New York) almost exclusively, while the East and South tend to have a mixture of hard and soft. Following are locales in four categories from which to pick your best tennis camp experience:

Tough Training Camps

• **Harry Hopman's Tennis.** Hopman developed the seemingly endless string of Australian champions who dominated the international scene from the 1940s through the 1960s. Can he do the same for you? No, but he certainly can improve your game. The Hopman method still dominates every aspect of his camp. His battalion of pros will teach hackers, but they're far more valuable to high intermediates and advanced players—*very* advanced, all the way up to Vitas Gerulaitis, who often works out at Harry's. Hopman's specializes in drills. Done under a Florida sun, several hours a day, they can be exhausting. But they can also quicken footwork and reflexes immensely, and they're combined with as much match play as the student can handle. Set on the grounds of a country club, Hopman's provides decent accommodations and meals. There's little group jollity, however; for after-hours fun, you're pretty much on your own. *Harry Hopman's International Tennis, Largo, FL; (813) 393-5614.*

• **Nick Bollettieri Tennis Academy.** If Hopman's is the tough graduate school of tennis, Bollettieri's is its draconian boot camp. Feisty, promotion-minded Nick has gained a worldwide reputation for turning out promising junior players, and is now ready to apply The System to adults as well. Beginning in 1983, small groups of adults—preferably pals from a single club—were able to submit to the Bollettieri lash for a week or a long weekend. Bollettieri's condos are rather well-appointed, and you won't have to cram into them as the juniors do. *Nick Bollettieri Tennis Academy, Bradenton, FL; (813) 755-1648.*

Tennis-Plus Resorts

• **La Costa Hotel & Spa.** La Costa serves as home base for Pancho Segura, one of the most beloved figures in professional tennis. It is a slick, lavishly appointed resort that contains one of the finest spas in the world: everything from gym classes and saunas to massages and "herbal wraps," wherein the pampered body is swathed in sheets dipped in medicinal herbs. La Costa has twenty-five courts but gives no group lessons or clinics. You can "take" from a cadre of instructors or from the silver-haired Pancho himself. *La Costa Hotel & Spa, Costa Del Mar Road, Carlsbad, CA 92008; (619) 438-9111.*

• **John Gardiner's Tennis Ranches.** If tennis-resort aficionados voted for the best of the lot, one or both of Gardiner's would probably win. His Carmel Valley "ranch" was the sport's first true resort, and it has lost none of its charm. The place has only fourteen guest rooms, and the food and general ambience are so exceptional that people have been known to go for those alone. The Camelback resort, near Scottsdale, Arizona, is much larger but, in its way, equally good. Social life at both places in low-key, plentiful, and pleasant. Like almost all of the best camps and resorts, Gardiner's does not try to remake the student's game. *John Gardiner's Tennis Ranch, Carmel, CA, (408) 659-2207. Camelback, 5700 E. McDonald Drive, Scottsdale, AZ 85253; (602) 948-2100.*

• **Kiawah Island.** Many experts consider Kiawah's program an ideal blend of work and play. Tennis director Roy Barth has a reputation for innovative teaching. Two Barth innovations: hitting at targets on a ball machine-equipped practice court; a videotape projector that can show the student's stroke at any speed or in a single frame—with, if you can stand it, twenty fellow students watching. *Kiawah Island, SC; (800) 845-2471.*

Long-Distance Travel

• **Country Club of Monte Carlo.** This is called the world's most beautiful tennis club, and with good reason. Although not luxurious, the clubhouse exudes Continental charm, and it commands a broad, gorgeous view of the Mediterranean. The two-dozen clay courts, watered after each playing, rank with the finest in Europe. Surprisingly, democracy reigns: anyone can get in, and courts are assigned on a first-come, first-serve basis. The club has no accommodations but does have package arrangements with Monaco's top hotels. *Country Club of Monte Carlo, Monte Carlo, Monaco.*

• **Puente Romano Tennis Club.** This is one of two truly classy resorts on the Costa del Sol, and it's less self-consciously upper crust than the other one. Puente Romano's claim to tennis fame is none other than Bjorn Borg, who jets in from his Monte Carlo home a few times a year to conduct week-long clinics. Maximum clinic enrollment is fifty, and, even at a stiff price, the sessions are heavily booked. What's a quick hit or two with "King Bjorn" (as the club calls him) worth? A good deal in one-upmanship back home, and maybe some real improvement in your game: local pros say Borg works hard and teaches well at his clinics. *Puente Romano Tennis Club, Carretera, Cádiz, Marbella, Spain.*

Closer to Home
• **Palmas del Mar.** Located forty-five miles east of San Juan, Palmas is a large, well-appointed resort that includes a handsome "tennis village." Palm trees and flowers surround the tile-roofed stucco villas, and three and one-half miles of unsullied beach are close at hand. The tennis package offers either two or four hours of instruction (mostly drills) per day. Bob Lutz, a longtime world-class player, is the touring pro, and he teaches a certain number of Palmas sessions. *Palmas del Mar, Humacao, Puerto Rico.*

• **La Terraza.** La Terraza is part of a sprawling resort called Casa de Campo. Even though the resort is better known for golf, tennis patrons rate its courts on a par with the finest. They come complete with ball boys, who also fetch ice water. The courts are enclosed by greenery and flowers, and most of them command a view of the Caribbean. Guests can tailor their packages to include unlimited tennis or nighttime tennis only, as well as a variety of other sports. *La Terraza, La Romana, Dominican Republic.*

• **Cuernavaca Racquet Club.** This club's total of nine courts bespeaks not frugality, but exclusivity. The club is spacious, uncrowded, and exquisite. Hilltop villas open onto a cobbled street that wends its way past arches, sculpture, and fountains. The landscaping around the courts is so lush you may have trouble concentrating on the game. In matters of on-court style, everything is correct: ball boys, obligatory white clothing; if you have orange tennis balls, leave them home. Instruction? Yes, it's available, but not in so coarse a form as drills. *Cuernavaca Racquet Club, Cuernavaca, Mexico.*

TENNIS: BEST WAY TO SEE WIMBLEDON

FOR two weeks each summer the All-England Lawn Tennis and Croquet Club in the south London suburb of Wimbledon hosts the world's premier lawn tennis championships. Tickets for center court, where championship matches are played, and the neighboring No. 1 court, which hosts the world's top tennis professionals, are coveted by sports fans around the world. Most are sold to winners of the annual Wimbledon ticket lottery held in January. Write to the Club Secretary before October to place a ballot in the subsequent year's drawing.

After the drawing a number of tickets will still be available through travel companies as part of tour packages which combine hotel accommodations in London with guaranteed seats. Among these companies are *American Express (800/241-1700), Fourways Travel (800/223-7872)*, and *TravelTix International (212/688-3700)*, all based in New York.

Some of the seats on center and No. 1 courts may also be available on a daily basis through *Abbey Box Office in New York (212/265-7800)*. Prices range from about $100 in the early rounds of the competition up to $500 for the men's single finals. For more information, or to obtain a ballot for the ticket lottery, CONTACT: *The Club Secretary, All-England Tennis and Croquet Club, Church Road, Wimbledon, London SW19 5AE, England.*

SKIING: EQUIPMENT

NOT every ski is best for every purpose of every skier, and the only way to really find out whether a particular model in a particular year fits your needs is to "demo" the skis—actually rent them from the shop at the resort and ski them. (If you buy, you should expect to get the rental charge taken off the purchase price, an almost universal arrangement at the ski shops these days.) However, each season a number of skis stand out, and may be destined to become classic in their time, like the Head Standard in the mid-1950s, the Kneissel White Star of the early 1960s, the Dynamic VR-17 of the late 1960s, and the Atomic Team Bionic and Rossignol Strato of the 1970s. The candidates for the mid-1980s are:

Ready-Made Skis
• **DP Chameleon.** This adjustable flex ski, handcrafted of

fiberglass laminate with a stainless steel adjustable inner camber, can be tuned to match powder, bumps, or ice conditions. Considered the ultimate in technologically advanced ski equipment. (DP Chameleon: $610, 190 to 207 cm in length.)

• **Dynastar Omesoft K.** Special Airflo Tipspoiler System designed to press tip down on snow for stability at high speed. (Dynastar Omesoft K: $320, 170 to 207 cm in length.)

• **Rossignol Carbon K.** Fiberglass torsion box reinforced with carbon and Kevlar fiber. Slalom sidecut, moderate flex. (Rossignol Carbon K: $380, 185 to 207 cm in length.)

• **Heliski.** Designed for superb performance in powder. Research Dynamics is turning this popular handmade ski into a top production model. (Heliski: $598, 173 to 203 cm in length.)

• **Kastle RX National Team Super G.** Metal/fiberglass laminate ski with a wood core. Narrow sidecut for quick turns despite its long length. (Kastle RX National Team Super G: $335, 193 to 213 cm in length.)

Nordic Skis

Eagle River Nordic, the top U.S. distributor of cross-country racing skis uses computer-based technology to ensure a perfect fit. Each year in August, president Bert Kleerup and his staff visit the factories of Europe's leading cross-country ski manufacturers. There they look over the latest crop of new skis and test nearly 2,000 pairs with a unique series of laboratory-type experiments. They test skis for their grip on the snow, their flexibility, and their glide. This information, which is recorded on computer floppy disks, indicates how the ski will perform under specific variables, such as the weight of a skier or specific snow conditions. Later in the year, when customers order a pair of skis, Eagle River asks them for specific information—age, height, weight, number of years skiing, the type of track, and snow likely to be encountered, etc.—and then matches these details, via computer, with the ski data collected by the company.

Like a computerized dating service, Eagle River pairs each of its customers with the most compatible pair of skis available. Eagle River sells its computer-matched cross-country skis at prices ranging from $100 to just over $200 a pair. If a company is not able to fit a particular customer satisfactorily, it will take pre-season special orders and search for the best-fitting pair of skis during the summer European ski-shopping expedition. For a catalog and information: *Eagle River Nordic, P.O. Box 936, Eagle River, WI 54521; (715) 479-7285.*

Handmade Skis
The biggest distributor of hand-built skis is **Lacroix,** which produces 15,000 to 17,000 pairs a season. The flagship of the Lacroix line is the *Le Premier,* which retails for $1,500 (lengths range from 180cm to 207cm). For information call: *Lacroix (303) 371-7205.*

SKIING: CLOTHING

UNTIL not too long ago, looking good on skis was not easy. Many an otherwise impeccable dresser has taken a fashion spill on the slopes. Bulky sweaters, baggy nylon pants, and heavy jackets—while important in keeping the skier warm and dry—have tended to make the wearer look puffy and unkempt rather than svelte and stylish.

Today, things are different. High-tech fabrics introduced in just the last few seasons, combined with the creative talents of a new generation of designers, have substantially improved the appearance of skiers from Aspen to Zermatt. It is now possible to be elegantly protected from the elements without sacrificing comfort or flexibility.

Here are a few of the more recent trends:

Powder Suits
The *dernier cri* in Alpine skiwear, these long-sleeved, one-piece jumpsuits can cut a stylish silhouette on any slope. Alone or layered with parkas or sweaters underneath, they are comfortable, practical, and versatile. Especially popular are loose-fitting suits with exaggerated shoulders and belted waistlines. Broad shoulders, narrower waists, and tapered legs give any skier a great figure.

Willi Bogner's one-piece fashions make bold skiwear statements in designs that range from ultra-sporty to space-age futuristic. The official supplier of the German Men's Ski Team, Bogner's offbeat palette features icy pastels (such as "snow white") and neon brights (rose, mint, lemon, mango, and iris), often used in combination with basic black, white, blue, graphite, and red. Geometric inserts and rubber trim provide splashy accents. Prices

range from \$450 to \$750. *Peter Steinbronn,* another top skiwear
designer, applies a similar use of bright colors to roomy suits fashioned with long zippers, generous pockets, and a matte nylon
finish. Steinbronn's one-piece suits retail at about \$580. Other
quality powder suit designs include Italian-made *Colmar* and *Ellesse*
fashions, *Nils, North Face,* and *Obermeyer.*

Nordic Suits

For the cross-country skier, *Loffler* offers a line of stretchy,
skintight, one-piece racing suits. These allow complete freedom of
movement while streamlining the skier's body. Available for about
\$125.

For maximum ski touring comfort, though, *Loffler's* versatile
knicker suits lead the way. They combine soft and flexible stretch
bib knickers with an overlaying parka. Zip-off sleeves and yoke
convert the parka into a vest on warmer days. Priced around \$160.

Separates

A waterproof "shell"—a parka or jacket—provides essential
protection against wind, sleet, and snow. Shells should be loose-
fitting, with stretch panels at the shoulders for complete freedom of
movement. *Peter Steinbronn's* ski jacket designs blend a stylish T-
shaped silhouette with practical details: zippered pockets for sunglasses and lip balm; powder cuffs to keep out snow; an insulated
collar that turns up to serve as a neck gaiter.

Making use of new synthetic fabrics, *Roffe's* thin, superwarm
Gore-Tex parkas are perfect for high-speed descents down steep
runs. These waterproof and windproof shells come in a variety of
colors, from \$170 to \$260. Other options: *Nino Cerruti's* hunting
plaid high-loft, down-insulated jackets, at around \$275; textured
black leather ski jacket by *Mark Buchanan* with zip-up front and
pockets, for about \$350.

Pants

Successfully reintroduced by Canadian designer Wini Jones
for *Roffe,* stretch ski pants are back in style, utilizing the highly
touted waterproofing laminate, Gore-Tex. These insulated in-the-
boot pants come with knee-high gaiters for protection against infil-
trating snow for about \$195. *Nino Cerruti,* another innovator in
men's ski-pant styles, has texturized nylon bib suits in his skiwear
collection, featuring leather-trimmed suspenders at the shoulders,
for \$175.

Sweaters

Sweaters make up the skier's all-important second layer, beneath ski jacket or jumpsuit. Wool and wool-blend sweaters with ever-popular snowflake and reindeer patterns stitched across the chest have long been favored. But in the place of wool, many skiers are now wearing a new generation of softer and more weatherproof polyester fabrics called *Polarfleece* and *Synchilla*. French skiwear designer Jean-Claude Schmeltz uses Polarfleece in his *Anoralp* pullovers, sweatshirts, and jackets. They can be worn as outerwear in calm, dry weather or beneath a shell in blustery, wet conditions.

Underwear

The best choice in fabrics are polypropylene and silk. Good bets are: *Lifa's* long-sleeved tops and long underwear bottoms in polypropylene ($18 to $22 each) and *Terramar* silk garments. These include long-sleeved tops, T-shirts, long underwear, and silk-insulated quilted vests and pants at $10 to $40 per item.

SKIING: U.S. SCHOOLS

THE best ski schools in the country are those with the most expertise at every level of skiing. However, since not every school has the same amount of practice with skiers at every level and every background, the best bet is for you to go to a school which has successfully taught your friends.

• **In the East,** Camelback, Pennsylvania, and Hunter, New York, are specialists in beginners fresh from the sidewalks, lifelong urbanities. Marilyn Hertz, the director at Camelback, picks her instructors for personality and compassion, and trains them well. Izzy Ture, who runs Hunter's school, is an innovator in moving newcomers right to advanced techniques. The ski school at Stratton, Vermont, gets many of the surburbanite high-performance types who demand and get results. Emo Henrich, the director, is an urbane and experienced Austrian guide and teacher.

• **In the West,** the school at Vail, led by Horst Abraham, the head of the nation's technical instructor organization, has created an innovative and flexible school, expert at teaching anyone and everyone—the school makes a big point of having its instructors learn the theory of teaching as well as skiing. Up in Jackson, Wyoming, at

Snow King, Bill Briggs runs an extraordinary ski school, small but with instructors who have had an immense amount of training in exercises that lead to advances on every level of ability.

The schools at Alta and Snowbird in Utah have the *best powder teaching classes* and the best chance to practice what is learned. Alf Engen, the oldest ski school director in the country, is still one of the best powder skiers anywhere; he runs Alta's school. Junior Bounous at Snowbird has long been an innovator and leader in ski and teaching techniques. *The best expert level teaching,* because of the individual attention that the school is able to give in its small classes, is at Taos, New Mexico, where Jean Mayer teaches. Mayer is rapidly developing a reputation as one of the greatest instructors of his time.

SKIING: EUROPE'S SKI CAPITALS

THE art of building ski resorts originated in the European Alps a century ago, giving that region a head start that has proven all but unbeatable. Although there is skiing outside the United States in such countries as Japan, Yugoslavia, Norway, and Chile, the best alpine resort skiing in the world—with the exception of a handful of American resorts—lies in a rather narrow geographical section of the European continent—in a relatively restricted rectangle, approximately 500 miles long east to west, and 200 north to south; the western edge lies in the French Alps, the northern in German Bavaria, the southern in the Italian Alps, and the eastern cuts through the middle of Austria, leaving most of the Austrian Tyrol within the rectangle's boundaries. Within this heartland of the Alps lie some 500 ski resorts, many of them forming, through their proximity, "resort complexes," interconnected trails, inter-resort lifts, and common services. Some twenty of these European resorts stand above the others. Only one of the selected resorts lie in Germany, and very close to the Austrian border at that.

Austria/Germany

Austria is the smallest and least wealthy of the alpine nations and yet the one most dedicated in spirit and commerce to skiing. Fully half of Austria's population skis regularly, and nearly a fifth of their national income derives from winter tourism. The Austrians quite naturally identify skiing as their national sport and are quietly certain that skiing is to Austria as gastronomy is to France, the standard of knowledge and practice with which all others must bear comparison. We begin with the westernmost of the Austrian resort complexes and work eastward.

• **Arlberg complex.** This is a grouping of five villages lying in the Arlberg Pass not far from the border with Switzerland. St. Anton is the largest and at the same time the lowest in altitude of the villages, being situated on the Tyrol side of the pass, with the greatest number of shops and the only really lively night life, as well as a proud history as the continuous location of the Arlberg Ski School, considered, particularly by Americans, as the "fountainhead" of ski technique and instruction.

The Arlberg represents for many an unbeatable combination of luxurious, hospitable inns, and snow-rich terrain. For a detailed rundown on the Arlberg accommodations and lifts, as well as those of the rest of European alpine skiing, the best source is *Skier's Holiday Guide,* obtainable from *Inter-Ski Services, P.O. Box 3635, Georgetown Station, Washington, DC 20007; (212) 342-0886.*

• **Kitzbuhel** is the most historic of the European ski towns, with shops built into the medieval fortified walls of the city (and it is a city). There are two mountains, one on each side of "Kitz": the Hahnenkamm (where Europe's most fearsome downhill race course is laid), and the Horn. This is historic ski terrain that has been lovingly tended for more than fifty years, giving it lawn-like smoothness on its flatter sections. The rest of Kitz terrain spreads out from the two mountains, encompassing long easy trails to all sides, enabling the skier to ski off trail into farm country ("downhill touring") and come out via local lanes to the roads leading back to Kitz where a "taxibus" will respond quickly to a call and bring the skier back to town.

• **Innsbruck** is the capital of the Austrian Tyrol, its largest "ski city." Within an hour's drive of the town's marvelous hotels and shops lies a choice of skiing to suit any taste from close-by Mutters (easy) to the more challenging slopes farther off. At the very end of the valley beyond Neustift lies the big cable tram up to the Stubaier glacier; its terminal is the marvelous Panorama Restaurant where a 270-degree arc of windows lets you look out at the roof of the Alps.

• **Solden** lies at the center of a web of lifts in the Otztal, or Otz Valley, which runs higher and higher to end up in a wall of peaks that marks the border of Italy, where lie the famous "Gurgls"— otherwise Untergurgl, Obergurgl and Hochgurgl, with terrain at around 10,000 feet, comprising the second highest parish in Europe. These provide some of the best steep, dry-powder runs on the Continent, as well as plenty of easy skiing among chalets decorated with bright traditional peasant motifs.

• **Garmisch-Partenkirchen** is the ultimate winter "spa," with a rather large population whose main business is catering to sport, beauty, fitness and health. "Garmisch" lies just over the Tyrol border in Bavaria which is the German version of Tyrolia. Most prominent buildings are those *kurhaus* (spa) types devoted to slimming, stretching, steam, and sauna, plus swimming in salubrious waters. The main attraction is to take the special mountain train out of the station up through the winding mountain tunnels to the very top of the Zugspitze, Germany's highest mountain. Just about every technological trick that the Europeans have used to open their mountains to skiing is exhibited in Garmisch.

Switzerland

Switzerland is nearly as nationalistic, but not quite, as is Austria about the sport; the Swiss, however, are more inclined to be punctual and unruffled. Nothing goes wrong, you see, because nothing is unforeseen.

• **St. Moritz** is the "Big Apple" not only of Swiss, but of all European skiing, the most sophisticated, oldest established winter resort in the world. It is a regular city of six- and seven-story resort hotels, expensive shops, casinos, and elegant restaurants. The Swiss penchant for polite correctness and scrupulous dealings, as well as their deep appreciation for good food, wine, and natural views, is given full reign in and around St. Moritz. Ski tourism was invented here in the 1870s when a few of the hotels began to stay open in the winter, including the famous St. Moritz Palace, a grand old ark that has survived with some of its Victorian splendor fully intact. For the avid skier who likes to dress for a rather formal dinner and spend his evening thereafter at roulette or baccarat, St. Moritz is *the* place.

• **Davos** stands for a group of related ski regions near the Italian border which includes both the Parsenn and Klosters; taken together the trails of the Davos terrain may add up to the biggest spread of ski runs in Europe. The terrain is largely intermediate, but so fully developed that three-mile runs are not uncommon. Klosters is Davos' neighboring village, one railroad stop up the line; small, cozy and catering to "name skiers" who started coming in the past to rub shoulders with longtime resident Irwin Shaw and such literati and socialites as Shaw inveigled to the village.

• **Zermatt** is the most ski-oriented of the Swiss "Big Three," with the added attraction that no cars are allowed within the village; all skiers arrive by rail or over-the-snow transport. The S-shaped main street is thronged most of the day by skiers shouldering skis and electric baggage carts wobbling along with loads of expensive suitcases and fancy ski bags. Zermatt skiers tend to hit the lifts early and ski late—American style. Many go up and over and down to Cervinia (in Italy) for a day's skiing in a different country. Zermatt has the first "ski subway," an underground track whose cars carry a large number of commuters to the Suneggar Peak, where the skiers can easily reach the other lifts that radiate across the higher ridges. This is terrain that makes skiing Zermatt in Switzerland the equivalent of skiing Baldy at Sun Valley, plus Vail, plus Ajax at Aspen.

• **Gstaad** is *the* glamor town in Switzerland, tending toward social sparkle and celebrity in the warmth of a traditional chalet setting; centrally, the huge, ornate Gstaad Palace towers high over the town which otherwise is in the traditional small-is-beautiful Swiss mountain architecture. This is a marvelous gathering of chalets, each outdoing the next in the intricacy of its woodwork and brightness of outside wall-motifs. The skiing is excellent off the Wisspile, Eggli, and Wassengrat terrains, but Les Diablerets is only sixteen miles away, offering a descent from 10,000 feet on smooth, rolling glacier snow, down through some awesome cirques—a seven-mile run.

• **Verbier** is one of the few resorts to push to the top in the past decade. Begun from scratch on bare mountainside (like Vail), Verbier consists mostly of small apartments and pensions in typical strictly controlled Swiss mountain building modes, but there are more buildings every year, and each year, more lifts. Now eighty lifts connect four valleys, opening up ski terrain that has all the variety of exposure and incline that make excellent skiing for all levels of skiers. Off-trail skiing (with a guide, please) is practically limitless.

• **Crans-Montana** is a second Swiss resort to merit a rank among the best, recently attaining the 20,000 bed capacity that marks the difference between the run of the mill and the extraordinary resorts in Europe. Like Verbier, "Montana" is in the French sector; Gallic custom and outlook prevail. And Montana copies triumphantly the French "new ski towns" concept, being emplaced on a sunny *balcon* (upper mountain shelf) high above the early dark of the deep alpine valleys. The glacier, La Plein Morte, lies at the very top of the lift system. From the restaurant on top of La Plein Morte on a clear day you can see from Mt. Blanc to the Matterhorn.

Italy

• **Cortina,** the site of the 1956 Olympics, is the Italian answer to St. Moritz, Garmisch, and Kitzbuhel, a ski city three blocks long and five blocks wide, with skiing running up both sides of the crenellated, precipitous Dolomites, a mountain range noted for unskiable but spectacular rock towers that form entrancing backdrops. Cortina has links to so many other roundabout trail complexes that it is an ultimate in a way: The skier has access to more than 500 lifts in and around the Dolomites. A three-section cable car, the Sky Arrow (Freca del Cielo), shoots you up to the 10,000-foot peak of the Tofano. Cortina can match terrain with any resort.

• **Cervinia** is a nice informal resort in which to easily enter a skier's "Italian experience" by skiing over for the day from Zermatt. Cervinia's skiing focuses on Monta Rosa, the gently billowing run that drops a dreamlike four and one-half miles from the Swiss border at Zermatt down to one side of Cervinia. It also features a stupendous run from Monta Rosa down to Valtouranche, the first town below Cervinia, a nine-mile descent of over 6,000 vertical feet, one of the longest runs in the world from a lift.

• **Courmeyeur** lies through the Mont Blanc tunnel from Chamonix and is—like many things Italian—cheaper, sunnier, and more relaxed than the proximate French experience. A five-section cable car goes all the way up to Cresta d'Arp and opens an eight-mile run back to Dolonne, for good skiers. The night life is mild but the *après-ski* café life is very good.

France

France has a Big Three that are as different from each other as can be: Val d'Isere, a mecca of hard-bitten skiers and a rather haphazard architecture; Courcheval, sophisticated and luxurious; and Chamonix, a somewhat forbidding village overhung with the most incredible skiing in the country.

• **Chamonix** is France's ancient mountain town, á la Kitzbuhel; what brings skiers to Chamonix is the prospect of some of the world's most varied and extraordinary skiing. Les Grands Montets in its 10,800-foot drop into the valley equals any two American-resort verticals piled one on top of the other. Then, in late season, you can make the ten-mile run down Vallee Blanche—with a guide who knows the way, Vallee Blanche can be the experience of a life-time. Or, you can go the other way and take lifts from the top of the Vallee over the high plateau until you can ski down the Cour-meyeur side, an incredible aesthetic and sports experience, medi-ated by tramways that are strung like skywalker's cables high among the peaks.

• **Courcheval** is the other end of the spectrum, with emphasis on sunny high hotels, a place where the French are at their most oblig-ing, where the systems are concerned with coping successfully for all concerned and where lie the favorite lodgings in France of the American skier. The slopes are, with few notable exceptions, quite easy and groomed constantly. Should you want steeper stuff, go over the top of Meribel, where you have a demanding descent down to a classic alpine village of low-rise mountain inns. From there you can, in the same day, take a lift up the far side of Meribel, and ski into Les Menuires, a stark, modern high-rise resort, on a treeless rolling plain—a bit like skiing on the moon.

• **Val d'Isere** is where the French, and their visitors, ski the hard-est. Home village of the great Jean-Claude Killy, the triple Olym-pic champion, the place is peppered with young Killy-like skiers and their adult imitators, who all ski for skiing's sake. The steep faces overlooking the town are long and satisfying if you are up for them. Above the faces there are various trail combinations facili-tated by a nest of Poma lifts, runs which are somewhat less demanding, with plenty of intermediate terrain. There are, as well, trails going from the two big faces above "Val," the Tête de Solaise and Bellevarde, over to La Daille, another village, and from there to Tigne, a new style condo resort with a glacier on top.

• **Les Arcs** is a French newcomer among the best; built on high, formerly deserted mountain ridges, Les Arcs manages to spread lifts like a spray of tendrils about the Massif de La Vanoise, so that both easy and difficult drops abound in all corners of what was once a land of unrelieved snow and ice: perched high above the old valley village of Bourg St. Maurice, this three-village *balcon* resort allows no cars on its streets and has strictly controlled development; a unified architecture has warm wood and other natural materials predominating. It's a model of what a well-planned and financed ski resort can be, begun from ground zero and built with thought and care.

• **La Plagne** is the second French newcomer, and it, too, erupted from the bald, above-treeline mountaintop. The great French champion and designer, Emile Allais, planned the runs and as the resort has developed in stages, it has been scattered among the ridges quite artfully. It now consists of four quite separate, but connected ski environs: Le Biolly, La Grand Rochette, Roche de Mio, and Les Arpettes, each with its own character and challenges at various ability levels.

SKIING: BEST EXPERT TERRAIN IN THE U.S.

EXPERT terrain means steepness, because it is control of speed on the steeps that qualifies a skier as expert. Among the tens of thousands of slopes at more than 1,200 ski areas in the U.S., there are only forty trails over 3,000 feet long (three-fifths of a mile) that have an average pitch of twenty-two degrees or better, a breathtaking ratio of one foot in drop for every four feet of travel. There are another two dozen trails with drops of seventeen degrees or better over the same distance. To qualify as a true challenge for experts, a resort must offer at least one trail in these two categories and several more trails that are nearly that steep: this is select company indeed.

Best of the West
• **Jackson Hole, Wyoming.** By any measure the steepness king of the country is Jackson Hole, at Teton Village, Wyoming, which has nine runs of over 3,000 feet in length with pitches greater than seventeen-degrees. It has 4,129 feet of vertical drop—greatest by far in the U.S.—but its unique challenge is Corbett's Couloir, a run which requires a death-defying launch into space off the entrance lip and a drop of about twenty-five feet before hitting the sixty-degree slope. Many have tried but few have stood. Jackson Hole also offers the expert marvelous continually steep runs through scattered evergreens. The most challenging of these are the Hobacks, incomparable when the snow is light. *Jackson Hole, Teton*

Village, WY; (307) 733-2291 (area information); (800) 443-6931 (lodging).

• **Sun Valley, Idaho.** Second best in the West is Sun Valley; its trails on Mt. Baldy are steep, with great variety and exposure. The Warm Springs side is the longest continually steep pitch in the country—no let-up at all its whole length. Christmas Bowl is the longest, steepest *lift-served* slope of all, while Exhibition is world-famous, having challenged expert egos since the early 1940s. *Sun Valley, ID; (800) 635-8261.*

• **Vail, Colorado.** Vail's quintet of Northeast Bowl, Prima, Riva Ridge, Rick's Ridge, and Forever will take the bounce out of the legs of *any* top skier who runs these trails in succession. The rest of the terrain at Vail constitutes the greatest ski acreage of any mountain ridge in the U.S., much of it sufficiently challenging to experts. *Vail, CO; (303) 476-5601 (area information); (800) 525-3875.*

• **Ajax at Aspen, Colorado.** This is the steepest and most intricate of Aspen's four mountains. Its runs are a slight cut below Jackson Hole, Sun Valley, and Vail, but Ruthie's is among the longest, steepest runs anywhere. And the runs off the Face, Back and Ridge of Bell Mt. are very demanding—steep through the trees. *Ajax (Aspen Mt.), Aspen, CO; (303) 925-1220 (area information); (303) 925-9000 (lodging).*

• **Arapahoe Basin, Keystone, Colorado.** This veteran ski area, right on the Great Divide, offers the famous Palivaccini, as well as some short steep headwall runs in its top bowl. *Arapahoe Basin, Keystone, CO; (303) 468-2316.*

Steep Running in the East
• **Stowe, Vermont.** Number One in the East is Stowe, whose cluster of Starr, National, Goat, and Liftline trails—side by side—form an unmatched quartet of expert runs: narrow at the top and usually heavily moguled. These four are backed up by another half dozen good trails including the famous Nose Dive, slightly less steep but cut for good, fast skiing. *Stowe, VT; (802) 253-7321 (area information); (802) 253-7321 (lodging).*

• **Sugarbush, Vermont.** With Stein's Run, Castlerock section and Paradise, Sugarbush is a close second to Stowe. Rumble trail in the Castlerock section is the only Eastern match in steepness and difficulty to Stowe's Goat, and Paradise is less steep but has a glade that demands good control of the expert skier. Stein's Run is nearly always full of rather large moguls, due to heavy traffic. *Sugarbush, VT; (802) 583-2381 (area information); (800) 451-5030 (lodging).*

• **Whiteface, New York.** This was the site of the 1980 Winter Olympics, and from the top it's a harsh, demanding mountain. When the trails off the top lift have had machine-made snow laid in—providing the base that nature rarely does—they are as challenging an expert gauntlet as anything east of the Rockies. *Whiteface Mt. Ski Center, Wilmington, NY; (518) 946-2223 (area information); (518) 946-2255 (lodging).*

West Coast Tough
• **Squaw Valley and Heavenly Valley, California.** The two ski areas offering the most extensive steep expert terrain on the Coast face each other across scenic Lake Tahoe. Squaw is the larger of the two ski areas with more lift capacity than any other ski resort in the country. Its KT-22 and steep upper bowl are exhilarating stuff (Squaw put the American skiing boom into gear by hosting the 1960 Olympics).

Heavenly Valley, though, counters Squaw's attraction for experts with some impressive statistics of its own: its Gun Barrel, Upper Face, and Ellie's Run outrank in steepness and length any other trio of trails on the Coast. *Squaw Valley, Olympic Valley, CA; (916) 583-6985; Heavenly Valley, South Lake Tahoe, CA; (916) 541-1330 (area information); (702) 588-4584 (lodging).*

Best Powder Skiing
The world's best powder skiing off lifts lies in the peaks of the Wasatch range which rise right outside Salt Lake City, Utah. The reason for the preeminence of the Wasatch is the amount of snowfall. Some 400 inches fall yearly, almost 100 inches above the average in the Rockies (the *other* powder area in the United States). Of all the Wasatch resorts, **Snowbird** *and* **Alta** *have the longest, most challenging runs,* and therefore, the greatest reputations. The resorts of **Park City** and **Deer Valley,** back to back, run a close third. Alta consists of old-fashioned family style inns; Snowbird has modern condominium hotels; Park City is a real live Western mountain town with streets and saloons. Whereas the atmosphere at Park City is down-home and comfortable, nearby Deer Valley is elite and luxurious.

Best Spring and Summer Skiing

Spring begins officially on March 20, the day when the sun crosses the vernal equinox and day and night become equal. It is also the start of the spring skiing season—the best time of year to enjoy the sport—when "corn snow" conditions prevail. *Corn snow, by contrast, allows all skiers—not just the experts—to taste the sublime.* The best late-season skiing in the United States is at **Mammoth Mt.,** California, where the snowfield lasts into June, and the terrain is smooth and lovely, and the California sunshine is up to its legend. *Mammoth Mt. Ski area: (714) 934-2571.* Conditions are almost as good at **Arapahoe Basin** in Colorado, where the snow stays as long, but the terrain is not as extensive and the temperatures are not quite as mild. *Keystone/Arapahoe Basin: (303) 486-2316.* Our third late-season choice is the Palmer Chairlift at **Timberline on Mt. Hood** in Oregon; you ski on a glacier. Timberline doesn't open the Palmer lift *until* spring and it stays open all summer and well into the first big snow storms of late fall. Mt. Hood is only about sixty miles from Portland. *Timberline ski area: (503) 272-3311.*

For a truly luxury summer ski trip, visit Portillo, Chile, which has the most extensive terrain and lifts of any southern hemisphere resort. Much of the terrain is world-class expert stuff and the Grand Hotel is known for its bar and food. The season runs from June to November—you can get back just in time for the traditional Thanksgiving opening day in Colorado.

SAILING: EQUIPMENT TECHNOLOGY

SCIENCE and engineering *have been moving sailing forward rapidly on four fronts in the past few years.* The first front is *hull construction,* where sandwich hull technology has recently created a new meaning for the phrase, "lightweight hulls." Secondly, in *sailcloth,* where laminated fabric has made possible very light, high-efficiency sails. Third is *computer-driven navigation* and piloting instruments; and fourth, a related phenomenon, *computer-driven performance evaluation,* which report the smartness with which the yacht is being sailed. Progress in these have lifted the sport to a level somewhat comparable to that of modern space hardware and guidance systems.

Yacht Hulls: Up from Fiberglass

Twenty-five years ago, plastic materials began for the first time ever to play a major role in yacht construction. Fiberglass arrived: a wedding of hair-thin glass fibers compressed into mats or woven into cloth embedded in a resin which was applied to the fibers as a liquid and hardened into a resilient skin, taking whatever shape was exhibited by the fiberglass. The use of super-thin fiberglass skins laid outside a core of stiffer lighter material such as balsa or insulation-type foam were tried almost as soon as fiberglass cloth was marketed. The emergence of the core-constructed hull, however, had to await the arrival of stronger fibers (glass and other), stronger glues, and many failures. The strength principle of the "sandwich hull" is that of the steel I-beam; but stresses on the yacht hull tended to tear the disparate layers of the sandwich apart. The bonding problem has only been happily resolved in the past few years.

Today scores of builders are turning out complete balsa hulls, including such names as C and C, Tartan Lancer, and Pearson, along with a bunch of newcomers—Olson, J-Boat, Freedom, Schock, S-2, and Fast 40. Some of these make *ULDBs, ultralight displacement hulls,* which can exceed the standard hull-imposed speed limits off the wind.

The New Laminated Sailcloths

The sails that have been taking over in the racing world are the laminated, multi-material cloths developed around Mylar, nylon, and Dacron in various combinations, along with Kevlar. The new composite sails weigh less, which is of itself an important advantage (less mast wobble and hull bobble). The materials hold shape better in the range of winds designed for, producing more horsepower for the same breeze—like adding a few cylinders to a powerboat engine. Mylar, once the problem material of sail makers (it tore), has been the key. It makes a super smooth laminate into which the sail maker can confidently impress an efficient form and know it will deliver.

The laminates have to be designed and sewn particularly carefully to function within even narrower limits so there is no short cut to quality. The sail makers whose names are household words in racing families—*Hood, North, Ulmer, Shore,* and *Sabstead* come to mind—are the ones whose products are most reliable. Hood makes much of its own sailcloth but cloth making has become so specialized that the remainder buy all theirs at one of the top sailcloth manufacturers, notably *Howe* and *Bainbridge* of Boston, who supply the sail designers with their raw material.

Going Straighter Faster

The advantages of light core-constructed hulls and more powerful sails are quickly dissipated unless a yacht is smartly sailed. The new technology, *the current smart sailors, are on-board micro-processors.* A Grand Prix class racing yacht has more computing power aboard today than did the first-generation orbital satellites. Today there seems to be no limit to the help you can get in navigation and performance by putting down money. The only comfort for less-than-middling-rich yacht owners is that the $5,000 Loran, an acronym for "Long Range Navigation" of ten years ago is outperformed by the $1,000 Loran he buys today.

The top Loran around is Trimble, the choice of nine out of ten Grand Prix class yachts. Trimble Model A goes for $2,500 and lives up to Trimble's peerless reputation for workmanship and reliability. If you can't locate a Trimble dealer near you, call the company direct at: *(415) 962-9893.* A fancier model, used on the biggest yachts around, the "Rolls of Loran," the Navidyne ESZ 5000, has a split screen CRT (television) instead of the usual LED display; one screen contains the raw output figures (longitude, latitude, etc.) and the other screen analyzes the figures for you, and gives you a reliability factor for the particular readings so you can see whether or not it is straining in marginal conditions to get you its readings. Price is $5,000.

Sailing by Satellite

Shooting the stars is romantic, but in these days the high seas navigator tunes in on Transit satellites instead, once his position is outside the range of the land-bound Loran radio towers. Transit is a system of orbiting radio stations whose signals, when properly interpreted by a "satnav" computer, will generate your position within a quarter of a mile, sufficient on the high seas. Transit satellites are so spaced that there may be a three to four hour gap between the eighteen-minute "transit" of one and the arrival of the next. Transit is not something you'd want to use for coastwise navigation except as an occasional check on the Loran. But on the ocean, Transit sure beats standing on a tossing deck trying to center a star in the sextant mirror.

Top satellite navigation computers: Navidyne ESZ 3900 and Furuno FSN 70 at $7,000 each. Any yacht can have a top-of-the-line coastal and high seas navigation system for between $8,000 and $12,000. If he really wants to indulge himself, the owner can buy a Bowditch Navigator, which will interface with the Loran and satnav to plot the ship's position on a nine-inch CRT on which is projected a four-color navigation chart.

A Note: Over the Counter Versus Catalog

Most electronic gear is sold over the counter of your local marine electronics dealer at the yard, in which case you pay the full freight. But *you can order through the mail from discount houses and get a better price.* Your local dealer will undoubtedly be handier if you have any problems: his serviceman—check to see that he has one—will be on hand to fix and, if not, re-ship to the factory without your having to touch a thing. If you buy mail-order and have trouble, you will at the very least have to ship it back yourself to the mail-order house, or factory. The two top houses in the U.S. are:

• **American Marine Electronics,** *1082 Post Road, Darien, CT, 06820; (800) 243-0264.*

• **National Marine Electronics,** *263 Kelly St., Lake City, SC 29650; (800) 845-5927.* The 800 numbers of these two companies comprise a marine electronic hot line.

HELI-SKIING

DEEP powder. Virgin snow. Glaciered peaks. Cozy wilderness lodging. These are the elements that have lured skiers from around the world (including the late King Gustav of Sweden) to a remote mountain range in the Canadian Rockies called "the Bugaboos." Canadian Mountain Holidays, a heli-skiing company based in Banff, Alberta, makes it all possible, guaranteeing 100,000 vertical feet of skiing in a week on mostly untracked snow. In an area the size of Switzerland, its helicopter pilots airlift skiers from one magnificent slope to another. *A day of skiing in the Bugaboos could equal three at any other resort.*

Canadian Mountain Holidays, which operates seven heli-ski resorts in the Rockies, runs the Bugaboo operation out of Bugaboo Lodge, a log structure that houses up to forty-four guests and staff. The lodge is thirty-one air miles from the nearest road and guests stay for a week at a time. The lodge provides living as pampered as any that can be found so deep in the mountains. Copious amounts of hearty European-style food are served up twice daily at cozy common tables, while lunch is flown out to skiers on the slopes.

Accommodation is in doubles or twins. There is also a sauna, ski work bench, a drying room for soggy woolens, and an outdoor ice rink. A lounge with a bar, gargantuan stone fireplace, and picture windows facing the towering Bugaboo Spire is where skiers gather after a full day on the slopes.

Canadian Mountain Holidays is the largest heli-ski operation in the world, and almost seventy-five percent of its guests come back for repeat visits. The season at Bugaboo Lodge runs from mid-December to mid-April; best snow comes in March and April. Skiers should be at the intermediate level or better before trying heli-skiing. The cost for a week of skiing in the Bugaboos can reach $2,400 in high season, but that includes accommodations, meals and transportation from Calgary, Alberta. For information, contact: *Canadian Mountain Holidays, Ltd., Box 1660, 217 Bear St., Banff, Alberta T0L 0C0, Canada; (403) 762-4531.*

SAILING: U.S. SCHOOLS

SAILING is one of the world's oldest experiences. From the moment men confronted the sea they found sailing simultaneously an exploration, an adventure, a sport. In its essence it means mastering the laws of wind and water to get somewhere. Whether you want to learn the rudiments, improve your racing skills, or feel secure enough to charter a boat and cruise the islands of your dreams, there's a sailing school to get you skimming across the water.

Each of the schools listed below receives the consensus recommendation of experienced sailors, graduates, and experts in the boating industry. All guarantee you will know how to race or sail with confidence when you have completed the course they think best for your needs. Most schools teach Beginner, Intermediate, and Advanced courses, and usually Racing and Cruising. All run from two days to three weeks, the ratio is three or four students to a teacher, and each supplies handbooks and a certificate to verify completion of the course.

Annapolis Sailing School

Founded in 1959. Instructor-student ratio is one to four, allowing individual attention as well as plenty of hands-on practice. Fees range from $150 for the "Become a Sailor in One Weekend" course on up to $1,095 for the "Offshore Cruising Course" from Annapolis to St. Croix. Instruction offered at eleven different locations, ranging from Long Island Sound to the Virgin Islands. Hotel arrangements and packages available. *P.O. Box 3334, Annapolis, MD 21403; (800) 638-9192 or (301) 267-7205.*

International Sailing School

Founded in 1981. Elementary and intermediate courses conducted on Lake Champlain each summer using twenty-seven-foot Solings (bigger boats are used for cruising courses). In the fall, the fleet moves to Florida and sets up shop at the Burnt Store Marina in Punta Gorda. Costs run from $215 up to $995 per person. *Lake Shore Drive, Malletts Bay, Colchester, VT 05446; (800) 864-9065 or 1 Matecumbe Key Road, Punta Gorda, FL 33955; (800) 824-5040.*

J World

Stresses racing preparation aboard nimble J 24 sloops in Newport, Rhode Island; San Francisco, California; Key West, Florida, and Kingston, Ontario, Canada. No live-aboard courses, but local accommodations can be arranged. Tuition for Intro Sailing, Sailing, and Racing is around $525 in the U.S. and about $400 (U.S.) at the Canadian school. *P.O. Box 1500, Newport, RI 02840; (401) 849-5492.*

Offshore Sailing School

Founded in 1964 by Steve and Doris Colgate. From its original base on City Island in New York City, the school has branched out to Bar Harbor, Maine; Newport, Rhode Island; Captiva Island, Florida; and Tortola in the British Virgin Islands. One-week courses, abbreviated to three intensive days at City Island, range from "Learn to Sail" through "Advanced Racing" and on to "Coastal Cruising." Basic tuition is about $495 for the beginning course and $525 for all others, with package rates available to cover accommodations. An in-house travel agency can provide assistance with transportation as well. *190 E. Schofield St., City Island, NY 10464; (800) 221-4326.*

Allied Yacht Charters Sailing School

Headquartered in Annapolis and offering a full range of instruction. Allied's pride and joy are the racing courses conducted on weekends by world-class sailor Gary Jobson aboard thirty-foot S2s. For skippers, tuition is $795. For crew, $595. *P.O. Box 4220, Annapolis, MD 21403; (800) 638-5139.*

International School of Sailing
Eight branches spread from Fort Lauderdale, Florida, to San Diego, California. All courses are live-aboard with rates, including meals, running from $325 for a Weekender to $3,500 for an ocean voyage from St. Thomas in the Virgin Islands to Lisbon, Portugal. *1900 S.E. 15th St., Fort Lauderdale, FL 33316; (800) 327-5053.*

Bill Gladstone Sailing Services
Founded 1979. Private sailing lessons on your boat, anywhere in the world. Gladstone and his staff will travel to you. Cost is $300 per day or $1,500 per week, complete. **Specials:** Any number of crew can participate. Courses in sailing, cruising, and racing designed to suit your particular needs and interests. Don't own a boat? Charters available. *Box 122, Addison, IL 60101; (312) 543-2310.*

Cruise Central. Planning a cruise on your own boat or a chartered yacht? If so, you might do well to check with the Cruising Information Center before you sail. Roger Hallowell is executive director of this nonprofit clearinghouse of information on cruising throughout the world. For $25 an hour, he and his stff will search their extensive files for the latest reports on harbor conditions in Barbados, docking facilities in Rio, and even the current political situation in Nicaragua. They will provide you with a complete list of the charts you need, advice on places to visit, and even the name of the best guidebook.

Headquartered in the Peabody Museum in Salem, Massachusetts, the decade-old Cruising Information Center collects firsthand accounts of trips from yachtsmen around the world. This information is compiled with data on cruising gathered from U.S. and foreign publications. An average search, for a transatlantic cruise, for example, will cost $25 to $75. Information for a circumnavigation of the globe would run to $200 or more. For information: *Cruising Information Center, Peabody Museum, East India Square, Salem, MA 01970; (617) 745-1840.*

SPORT DIVING: INTERNATIONAL

TODAY, in the U.S. alone, there are more than two million certified divers—of all ages and sizes. *Hundreds of places offer opportunities for this sport, but only a select few are considered world-class diving resorts. The New Book of Bests* choices were based on interviews with more than thirty expert sport divers, who shared their experience about their favorite diving area.

Eastern Australia

The waters surrounding the Great Barrier Reef off the Queensland coast probably offer the most exceptional diving in the world today. More than 1,000 species of living coral and thousands of species of exotic fish live here.

• **Offshore Islands.** Heron Island is actually part of the Great Barrier Reef. The one resort here is run exclusively for experienced divers. Most diving is done only a few minutes away by boat. The most popular dive site is Big Bommie, which consists of six giant coral heads which rise up to within thirty feet of the surface. From October to March, visitors can see giant sea turtles waddle ashore to lay their eggs.

• **Outer Great Barrier Reef.** Several well-equipped dive boats that usually accommodate from eight to twelve people cruise the waters of the Outer Reef for about a week. The best diving section is Ribbon Reefs, about 160 miles north of Cairns. At the Cod Hole, giant white groupers (called potato cod locally) weighing up to 160 pounds can be hand-fed. Wreck lovers will appreciate the coral-covered *Yongala,* a 350-foot-long ship that sank in 1911.

• **Coral Sea.** Several marvelous reefs are located in the Coral Sea east of the reef. To reach these distant waters, a seven to ten-day excursion aboard a large dive boat is required. At Moore Reef, innumerable crevices that slice through the reef provide shelter to groupers and rays. At Bougainville Reef, divers can explore a large wreck. The waters surrounding Osprey Reef often give divers 250-foot visibility. Marion Reef shelters several kinds of sea snakes.

An Australian company, Dive in Australia, sponsors these trips. Rates for diving packages vary widely, depending on the size of dive boat, location and the season. Generally, prices range from $1,100 up to $3,000. A complete diving package at Heron Island is about $150 a day. *Dive in Australia, 680 Beach St., Suite 498, San Francisco, CA 94109; (415) 928-4480 or (800) 227-5436. Australian Tourist Commission, 630 Fifth Ave., New York, NY 10111. (212) 489-7550.*

Micronesia

The 2,100 islands of Micronesia encompass a huge section of the South Pacific, but three tiny areas—Truk Lagoon, Palau, and Ponape—enchant even experienced divers. The peaceful, calm waters of Truk Lagoon belie a violent past. During World War II, more than 100 Japanese planes, ships, and submarines were sunk here. To find so many shipwrecks so close together, and relatively intact, is unique. These wrecks are now covered with brilliantly colored soft corals, sponges, anemones, and sea fans. Marine Life includes jacks, tuna, and groupers. Ponape is a lush volcanic island. Sharks, manta rays, and brilliant-blue starfish thrive in the shallow coral reefs offshore. Palau is a big coral atoll located in the southwest corner of Micronesia. Perhaps the major highlight for divers is Ngemelis Wall, where there is a drop-off from six inches to 3,000 feet.

The best time to visit Micronesia is from March to June, when winds are the calmest. Diving packages are complicated, and can range from $1,150 to $1,850, plus air fare. *See & Sea, 680 Beach St., Suite 340, Wharfside, San Francisco, CA 94109; (415) 771-0077.*

Bonaire

This island in the Netherland Antilles, some fifty miles off the Venezuelan coast, presents nearly perfect diving conditions: 200-foot visibility with water and air temperatures that are warm and stable year-round. Reefs begin to drop off fifteen to twenty feet from shore, and divers can see such colorful fish as the brilliant purple-and-yellow fairy basslet and the blue-and-yellow queen angelfish. Night diving here is also excellent. Orange tube-coral polyps are particularly luminescent when struck by a beam of light. Bonaire has one big advantage over most other diving areas: easy access. There is a great diving by swimming right off the beach. Another advantage is that it's never crowded. A week of diving costs approximately $600 during the peak winter season. For information write: *Bonaire Tours, P.O. Box 775, Morgan, NJ 08879; (800) 526-2370 or (201) 566-8866* and *Flamingo Beach Hotel, 520 W. State St., Ithaca, NY 14850; (800) 847-7198.*

Tortola

Hundreds of reefs lie just off the British Virgin Islands, located some sixty miles east of Puerto Rico. At Tortola, the Aquatic Centres operation of George and Luana Marler is unsurpassed. Most dive sites here feature narrow reefs, shoals, caves, and pinnacles. But the most famous diving attraction is probably the wreck of the *Rhone*, sunk in 1867. This ship was the site of the movie, *The Deep.* Aquatic Centres sponsors eight-day, seven-night packages, which include lodging and unlimited diving. Meals are extra. *Aquatic Centres, J. W. Pepper, P.O. Box 850, Valley Forge, PA 19482; (800) 345-6296.*

Grand Cayman

Several superior dive resorts are located in the Cayman Islands, but Spanish Cove on Grand Cayman is especially exceptional. The chief attraction for divers is the North Wall—an eight-mile stretch of sheer vertical underwater cliffs. At one point, a wall forming at a depth of sixty feet plunges to 6,000 feet. Other spectacular reefs are located only 150 yards offshore. A typical eight-day, seven-night scuba package costs about $500 per person. *Aquanaut Voyageur, 64 Smull Ave., Caldwell, NJ 07006; (201) 226-4477.*

Red Sea

Despite its location in the troubled Middle East, this calm, clear body of water still offers fine diving. There are two major diving sites: Sharm el Sheikh at the southern tip of the Sinai Peninsula (now controlled by Egypt); and the far northern tip of the Gulf of Aqaba, specifically Elat, Israel, and Aqaba, Jordan. The most thorough way to explore this area is to live aboard a dive boat that cruises the best reefs. These reefs contain lush coral gardens interspersed with countless caves and crevices. A few wrecks can be explored. After ten days of diving, guests visit Jerusalem for two days. This particular excursion costs about $2,750. Trips are run in March, April, August, and September. *See & Sea, 680 Beach St., Suite 340, Wharfside, San Francisco, CA 94109; (415) 771-0077.*

Florida Keys

There are more dive facilities in the Florida Keys than anywhere else in the Caribbean. The center of diving is Key Largo, which has the most extensive coral reefs in the area. John Pennekamp Coral Reef State Park is the only such park of its kind in the United States. It is home to more than forty species of coral and at least 650 varieties of fish. The waters west of Key West are said to contain several wrecks that went down filled with fortunes in gold and silver. This is one of the finest treasure-hunting regions of the world. A week's diving in the Keys usually costs between $300 to $600. An excellent source for information is the Key Largo Chamber of Commerce. It provides a listing of all motels and dive shops

in the area. Write: *Box 274-C, Key Largo, FL 33037; (305) 451-1414.*
In the mid-Keys, one operation with A-1 facilities is: *Hall's Diving Center, 1688 Overseas Highway, Marathon, FL 33050; (305) 743-5929.*
A top-notch dive shop in Key West is: *Reef Raiders, U.S. Highway 1, Stock Island, Key West, FL 33040; (305) 294-0660.*

Cozumel

Located about twenty miles off the coast of Yucatan, Mexico, this island's main attraction is Palancar Reef, a half-mile or so offshore. This six-mile-long structure features steep vertical walls, and towering mounds of coral. Diving in this area can be breathtaking; the corals show magnificent shades of orange and lavender, and, as soon as divers enter the water, fish swim up to divers and eat from their hands. An all-inclusive eight-day, seven-night diving trip, with ten guided dives, is about $500. *Sunseeker Holidays, 1780 Broadway, New York, NY 10019; (800) 422-2020 or (212) 586-3441.*

Multiple-Country Diving Outfitters

Many of the outfitters listed above organize diving packages to several of the resorts mentioned. Below are the names and addresses of these agencies, and the countries they represent:

• **See & Sea,** 680 Beach St., Suite 340, Wharfside, San Francisco, CA 94109; (415) 771-0077. (Australia, Micronesia, Caymans, Roatan, Red Sea.)

• **Sunseeker Holidays,** 1780 Broadway, New York, NY 10019; (212) 586-3441 or (800) 442-2020. (Red Sea, Cozumel, Bonaire, Caymans.)

FISHING: RODS AND REELS

TO give himself every possible chance of landing a trophy game fish, it's imperative that an angler have quality tackle. Fortunately, we are now in a Golden Era of fishing tackle. There are more superior reels and rods available today than ever before. *The New Book of Bests* has examined the finest reels and rods on the market and offers tips on how to identify an outstanding rod and reel; we also highlight specific products that offer particularly innovative features. Since tackle needs vary widely, depending upon the type of fishing you intend to do, *we have divided this tackle section into four separate categories: spinning, bait casting, saltwater (conventional), and fly-fishing.*

Spinning Reels

Several features distinguish an excellent spinning reel: 1) The spool is made of corrosion-proof metal and is strong enough to withstand the pressure of constantly unwinding monofilament line; 2) The drag has a smooth initial pull that prevents a fish from jerking away; 3) The bait clicks or trips very easily; 4) A fast gear ratio is offered, between 4:1 to 5:1. This allows you to retrieve the line very quickly; 5) Handles can be converted to fit either side of the reel.

Spinning reels have relatively simple components. Even the finest models made today only cost about $50. A couple of these reels offer especially attractive characteristics. The Shimano MLX Fast Cast reel allows you to open the bail and cast one-handed in one simple motion. Instead of having to open the bail with your opposite hand, a "bail trigger" on your casting hand does this for you. The Ryobi Dyna-Fight spinner has a no-line-twist feature. On most spinning reels, line becomes twisted when it's stripped off the spool as a fish pulls against the drag. With the Dyna-Fight, the spool remains stationary while the bail rotates. Other top-notch reels include: Pflueger Gold Medalist; Garcia Cardinal 700; Lew Childre S-1 and S-2 Speed Spin; Shakespeare Sigma Supra; and Browning Mitchell 4400.

Spinning Rods

The majority of innovations in fishing tackle during the last ten years have been made with rods. In the 1960s and early 1970s, top-grade rods were made of fiberglass. Then, in the early to mid-1970s, graphite (carbon) rods became the rage. The 1980s trend is toward boron rods, which are even lighter than graphite. A boron/graphite composite rod is lighter and offers more sensitivity (feel), so a fisherman can feel a fish bite easier. A prime graphite or graphite/boron composite rod may cost between $60 to $80.

One of the finest spinning rods is the Fenwick Boron-X, which mixes boron with graphite. Its epicenter is a very thin-walled boron rod. Then the boron is encased in a graphite outer shell, creating an exceptionally strong "rod within a rod." The Shakespeare Ugly Stik mixes graphite, boron, *and* fiberglass. It's so resilient it can nearly be bent into a complete loop. Other high-quality rods include: Eagle Claw Blue Diamond graphite, Lew Childre graphite Speed Stick.

Bait Casting Reels

Bait casting reels are designed to handle large, tough-fighting fish such as big bass, walleyes, pike, etc. They are used to cast bait fish (thus the name) as well as spoons, plugs and other large lures. The best bait casters cost between $75 to $125, and have either a centrifugal or magnetic braking system that automatically slows the spool during casting to prevent backlash—a common problem with this type of reel.

Daiwa's Procaster Magforce reel incorporates a revolutionary magnetic brake. A magnet inside the reel actually prevents the spool from revolving too fast. The Penn Magforce 970 and 980 reels are based upon the same principle. Another innovative anti-backlash device is the V-spool, now found in the Lew Childre BB 1L and BB 1N models, and in the Ryobi AD 4000, AD 5000 and AD 6000 series.

Bait Casting Rods

In most cases, manufacturers' bait casting rods are merely extensions of their spinning-rod lines. (See "Spinning Rod" section above.) However, a bait casting rod must be stronger and able to cast longer distances than a spinning rod. And, as is true with spinning rods, boron/graphite or graphite rods provide the best combination of lightness and strength. Top-of-the-line rods cost between $75 to $100. One noteworthy bait casting rod widely acclaimed by veteran bass fishermen is the Shimano Karate Stik—a graphite casting rod that offers incredible casting power. Another unique rod is the Heddon Magnagraph, which combines graphite with magnesium. Other distinguished rods include Fenwick Boron-X, Eagle Claw Blue Diamond, Shakespeare Ugly Stik, and Pflueger Supreme.

Saltwater (Conventional) Reels

Most saltwater conventional reels are intended for bottom fishing and trolling. Some smaller models are designed primarily for casting. Top-of-the-line conventional reels must have a perfect drag system than can control a 500-pound marlin making a run away from the boat at high speeds.

Two companies dominate the conventional reel market: Tycoon/Fin-Nor and Penn. The overwhelming majority of "serious" big-game fishermen use one of these two companies' reels. Both manufacturers offer several models for both trolling and casting. Fin-Nor's new 12.0 Tri-Gear trolling reel is designed for experts. It features three different gear ratios (3:1, 2:1 or 1:1) that can actually be changed while you're fighting a fish. The Golden Regal models are used for trolling lighter line. The Penn International series is comprised of nine models. It's also one of the great saltwater trolling reels in the world. The prices of these trolling reels range between $230 for small models to $800. The largest Fin-Nor Tri-Gear, however, costs about $1,800.

Saltwater Rods

A superb saltwater rod must obviously be very sturdy. Rods should be made of fiberglass. Graphite and boron rods don't have the power and strength necessary for big-game fishing.

One of the best rods is Fenwick's Big Game Offshore Trolling model. It's composed of Fenglass—a lightweight glass that offers tremendous lifting power. Daiwa's excellent IGFA Tournament models feature a graphite/fiberglass composite. Other high-quality saltwater rods that will last for years include the Eagle Claw Ocean Granger; the St. Croix Buccaneer; the Garcia Big Blue; the Shakespeare Super Stik; and the Pflueger IGFA Custom Trolling model.

Fly Reels

The foremost fly reels are made by a few individual craftsmen who make a limited number of reels a year. These special makers are in such demand that many of them have year-long waiting lists. There's good reason for this—their products are worth it, at least to devoted fly fishermen. The reels are built from scratch. Every part is handmade. And most of these reels are designed to meet the specific fishing needs of each customer. A few, small tackle companies also make top-notch fly reels.

Individual craftsmen, who may spend up to forty hours to make a reel, usually charge between $200 and $350 for a fly reel. Companies such as Hardy or Orvis, which mass-produce reels and therefore don't tailor them for a specific individual, charge between $100 to $200.

The most preeminent fly reel maker today is probably Stan Bogdan, based in New Hampshire. His reel is in such demand that he has a waiting list more than a year long. His clients include such ardent trout fishermen as golfer Jack Nicklaus and the Duke of Wellington.

Another distinguished reel maker is George Gehrke, based in Colorado. His Marryat Centurian reel is considered to have the smoothest, most powerful drag of any reel. Former President Jimmy Carter uses a Centurian.

Other top-of-the-line reels include: Tycoon/Fin-Nor Standard and Anti-Reverse models; the Hardy Perfect, Princess and Lightweight models; and the Orvis CFO models.

Two other superb fly reels, designed for saltwater use, are worth noting. The heavy-duty Billy Pate fly reel is designed specifically for tarpon and billfish angling. Another choice reel for light-line saltwater casting is the Valentine Model 400.

Fly Rods

An outstanding fly rod must allow an angler to do the type of casting required. It must be exquisitely tapered from butt to tip. Guides should be hand-wrapped tightly; ferrules must fit perfectly. The rod should be coated with several layers of high-grade varnish. Above all, an outstanding fly rod must allow an angler to make his cast with pinpoint accuracy, feel the bite of a trout and then withstand the fight.

Though many manufacturers make very good fly rods, truly outstanding ones are produced by a few, select rod manufacturers who make limited numbers of rods each year. These rods are made of either graphite, a boron/graphite composite, or bamboo. *The greatest workmanship goes into bamboo rods.* Such rods are lightweight and easy to cast all day, and will provide superb line and loop control. However, for distance casting or heavy work in rough water, a boron/graphite composite rod generally works best.

A top-notch bamboo rod costs between $600 to $1,200. Some custom-made, special editions may go up to $2,500, though. Boron, boron/graphite composites, or graphite rods are much more inexpensive, usually costing between $200 to $300.

Five rod makers are particularly acclaimed by expert fly-fisherman: Thomas and Thomas, Simroe, Winston, Kusse, Leonard. All offer bamboo, and either graphite or boron/graphite composite flyrods. All of these rods rate a $9^3/_4$ on a scale of one to ten.

FISHING: TOP SPOTS FOR SALTWATER FISHING

A 1,000-pound marlin puts up a four-hour battle; a 150-pound tarpon tail walks along the surface of a jungle lagoon; a streamlined bonefish torpedoes across the flats. Most fishermen can only daydream of such action. But in a few special fishing camps bordering the world's tropical seas, such experiences are common occurrences. *The New Book of Bests* has compiled a list of the world's greatest spots for saltwater fishing, locations that dot the Pacific Ocean and the Caribbean Sea.

Bahamas

Bonefish and permit thrive in the extremely shallow, turquoise waters of the Caribbean Sea. In some areas, anglers can simply wade into the sea and cast; they use both spinning and fly casting tackle. The supply of these fish is particularly plentiful at the east end of Grand Bahama Island, where the Deep Water Cay Club is located. The club is the only first-class accommodation in the Bahamas devoted solely to bonefishing. All of the guides at this resort have had years of experience, and they're particularly skilled at teaching guests the finer points of casting.

An eight-day, seven-night package at the club costs approximately $1,600, including food, lodging, and fishing. For an additional $170, the club provides round trip air service from Palm Beach, Florida. The season begins February 1 and continues through August. *Deep Water Cay Club, P.O. Box 1145, Palm Beach, FL 33480; (305) 684-3958.*

Costa Rica

Few countries on earth are fortunate enough to border one ocean acclaimed for its saltwater fishing. Costa Rica, however, has *two* such coasts, providing the angler with some spectacular challenges. Along the northeastern shore, where the Colorado River empties into the Caribbean, fantastic fishing for tarpon and snook is found in the lagoons and creeks of this river system. Seventy- and eighty-pound tarpon are common; most snook weigh about five pounds. The best season for these fish runs from January to May.

Casa Mar provides excellent accommodations. Nestled in seven acres of tropical gardens, it faces a lagoon where tarpon can often be seen rolling right in front of the dock. A one-week fishing package costs about $1,450; price, based on double occupancy, includes food, lodging, and fishing.

On the Pacific Coast of Costa Rica, *Bahia Pez Vela* offers what is probably the greatest sailfish angling in Central America. Some fishing parties at this camp have raised 500 sailfish in a week. The camp has also witnessed the catch of some of Central America's largest black marlin, blue marlin, and cubera snapper. Sailfishing is best from late May until November; other species can be found year-round. Guests at Bahia Pez Vela stay in modern bungalows overlooking the Pacific. Rates run about $1,500 to $1,700 a week for food, accommodations, and fishing. For Casa Mar, contact: *World Wide Sportsman, P.O. Drawer 787, Islamorada, FL 33036; (800) 327-2880.* For Bahia Pez Vela: *Henry Norton, 150 E. Ontario, Chicago, IL 60611: (800) 621-8091 or (312) 878-3323.*

Yucatan
The water bordering the lush Yucatan jungle is another great spot for finding the Caribbean's rich supply of bonefish and permit. The area has two outstanding fishing camps, Pez Maya and Boca Paila; they are located only three miles from each other. The prime fishing season extends from April to June. An average week of fishing at either lodge runs about $1,350. Guests fly into Cozumel, twelve miles from the camps, on Aero Mexico and Mexicana airlines. For Pez Maya, contact: *World Wide Sportsman, P.O. Drawer 787, Islamorada, FL 33036; (800) 327-2880. For Boca Paila: Pan Angling Travel Service, 180 N. Michigan Ave., Chicago, IL 60601; (312) 263-0328.*

Panama
Near the tropical jungle along Panama's Pacific coast, Tropic Star Lodge and Club Pacifico offer fishermen spectacular action in plush surroundings. More than thirty fishing records have been set by guests at Club Pacifico. Wahoo, cubera snapper, rooster fish, and amberjack, rainbow runners, sailfish, and black marlin are plentiful in the surrounding waters. Guests stay in spacious duplex cottages with an excellent view of the Pacific. A one-week stay costs about $1,900.

Tropic Star Lodge is the envy of all resorts; more than seventy percent of the fishermen who stay there return for another visit. Located on Pinas Bay, on the Pacific side of Panama near the Colombian border, this lodge is the best place in the western hemisphere to catch black marlin, and guests have an excellent chance of landing one: during one week, twenty-three black marlin were pulled in by guests at the lodge. The fish usually weigh between 300 and 600 pounds. Tropic Star is also the most luxurious fishing resort in Central America; guests stay in lovely air-conditioned duplex bungalows and dine on gourmet meals. A week at the lodge will run approximately $2,000 and up, for food, accommodations, and fishing.

January and February are the best months to go after black marlin; striped marlin are usually caught in March and early April. From May to July, Pacific sailfish are plentiful. Heavy-duty offshore tackle is the rule for marlin fishing, but light tackle is used to catch other species. *Club Pacifico, P.O. Box 2866, Hialeah, FL 33012: (800) 327-5662 or (305) 823-8292. Tropic Star Lodge, Suite 200, 693 N. Orange Ave., Orlando, FL 32801; (305) 843-0124.*

Cabo San Lucas

Another good spot for striped marlin is Cabo San Lucas, located at the tip of the Baja Peninsula. Here the great swells of the Pacific Ocean meet the warmer, calmer waters of the Sea of Cortez. Although striped marlin is the number one game fish here, the waters are filled with a diversity of fish species, most of which can be caught year-round. Several line-class records have been set here for rooster fish, dolphin, Pacific blue marlin, striped marlin, black skipjack, and swordfish. Write: *Hotel Palmilla, P.O. Box 1775, La Jolla, CA 92038; (619) 576-1282.*

St. Thomas, Virgin Islands

Long appreciated by vacationers for its white beaches, fine weather, great sailing, and scuba diving, St. Thomas also offers some of the best blue marlin fishing anywhere. A world record for this species—1,282 pounds—was set here. Most blue marlin fishing is done from June through September at the "100-Fathom-Dropoff," where the sea bottom suddenly plummets thousands of feet. Charterboats supply high-quality eighty-pound rigs, which are fished from outriggers. Mullet and balao are used as bait. The boats can be chartered for about $600 a day, and carry up to six passengers.

To book a trip to St. Thomas, contact your travel agent. To charter a boat, contact: *American Yacht Harbor, Red Hook, St. Thomas, U.S. Virgin Islands 00801; (809) 775-6454.*

HUNTING: TOP-OF-THE-LINE SHOTGUNS

PERHAPS no other piece of sporting equipment is as elegant as a high-quality shotgun. Top-of-the-line scatterguns are meticulously made by craftsmen who possess a deft precision equal to that of a master surgeon.

Today, *there are many types of shotguns on the market:* break-action single shots, pumps, autoloaders, or bolt-actions. But for the past century, the preeminent shotguns have been double-barrels: either side-by-sides (where the barrels are horizontal to each other), or over-unders (where one barrel is stacked above another). Doubles are usually lighter and more compact than other shotguns. There-fore, they are easier to grip, hold and point toward the target. In addition, they have traditionally been made out of the finest mate-rials and feature the most fastidious workmanship.

Doubles

The greatest doubles ever made were built between the late nineteenth century and the beginning of World War II. During this period, master craftsmen in England, Continental Europe, and America exhibited a special dedication and were willing to spend the vast amount of time required to build a flawless gun. After the war, many of these artisans retired or died. Therefore—with a few notable exceptions—*most of the foremost shotguns sought by collectors today are those made before 1940.* This is true of both European and American guns. In addition to performing superbly in the field, double shotguns make outstanding investments. In the words of one leading expert on superior-quality firearms, "In many cases, the best double shotguns appreciate in value better than diamonds, antiques, gold, or paintings."

Several qualities mark a great double-barrel shotgun. Its wooden sections should be comprised of European (also commonly called French) walnut. This type of wood is finer grained, with more contrast, than other varieties of walnut, including American black walnut, which is used on lesser guns.

Classic doubles made decades ago all had two triggers—one for each barrel. This is still the type of trigger preferred by purists. Many modern firearms, though, feature a single trigger, which fires the second barrel automatically when the shooter squeezes it.

A shotgun being fired must withstand an incredible amount of stress as the shot leaps out of the barrel. Therefore, the bolting system must be able to withstand thousands of firings without loosening or cracking. All parts must also fit snugly and must allow the gun to open and close effortlessly. The checkering should be sharp and consistent. Every diamond in the pattern should be alike. The engraving, whether it shows a game scene or elaborate scroll, must be excruciatingly precise.

Most of the better doubles use a "sidelock" trigger mecha-nism, which is attached right to the sideplate (the engraved metal strip above the trigger).

Which gun makers do the best job of incorporating the best qualities into their firearms? To find out, *The New Book of Bests* consulted some of the leading gun dealers in the country.

Top Manufacturers

The finest shotguns ever made were manufactured in England between the 1880s and the beginning of World War II. *Three companies—Purdey, Holland and Holland, and Boss—were renowned for their overall excellence then.*

Today, a Purdey shotgun maintains its reputation as the Rolls-Royce of the industry: a firearm fit for a king. In fact, Prince Charles uses one for bird hunting. Less than 100 are made annually, and each part is made completely by hand. These firearms retain the highest market value of any shotgun, whether they are brand new or forty years old. Today, a new side-by-side Purdey may cost $25,000, while a new over-under might cost $35,000, and it may take you three years to get it.

Holland and Holland makes guns of virtually equal caliber, but they just don't have the prestige of Purdey. However, a pre-war Holland, especially an over-under (which the company stopped making in 1960), may also be worth $35,000 today.

While English guns represent the epitome of the art; many experts believe that the quality of these guns has also deteriorated in the past twenty to thirty years. In the small Italian village of Brescia, several firms are making outstanding doubles whose quality, if not their market value, now ranks with the finest Purdeys. Many gun dealers flatly state that today *the Fabbri* is now equal to, if not better, than the Purdey. Only twenty years old, Fabbri makes outstanding shotguns for both hunting and competition. Less than fifty guns are produced a year; most are over-unders. These firearms are especially acclaimed for their "bank note" style of color engraving. A new Fabbri may cost between $16,000 and $20,000. *Famars* offer a wider variety of doubles than Fabbri. Most of them are game guns. The company's 410- and 28-gauge over-unders are especially popular. Top models cost a little less than a prime Fabbri, ranging between $15,000 and $18,000. *Piotti* features trim, compact side-by-sides, similar to English guns. The best-grade Piotti is the King EE-LL, which costs about $14,000.

Trap or skeet shooters may want to consider *two well-known German guns: Krieghoff* and *Merkel.* The best Merkels were built between 1920 and World War II. The top model—the Luxas—was a high-framed over-under. This model is a real collector's item now, and can cost up to $40,000.

Custom Shotguns from Belgium. If you're planning a trip to Belgium, you should know that the country is world-renowned for

its custom shotguns and rifles, made carefully by hand to fit the exact size and shape of their owners. Most of the gunsmiths are located in and around the town of Liège, one of two or three places in the world that maintains the tradition of hand craftsmanship. And Liège guns, while in a class with those made in London, are somewhat lower in price. Liège's best gunsmiths:
• **Dumoulin-Deleye,** *10 Rue Florent Boclinville, Herstal. 32-41-27-39-92.*
• **Dumoulin et fils,** *16 Rue du Tilleul, Milmort. 32-41-78-57-44.*
• **Auguste Francotte & Cie,** *61 Mont St-Martin, Liège. 32-41-23-68-76; telex 41-355.*
• **Pirotte.** *45 Rue St-Laurent, Liège, 32-41-32-34-45.*

American-made double-barrel shotguns are still very much in demand in this country. *Most of the finest American shotguns were made from the 1880s to the late 1930s.* In fact, all of the choice models ever built in the states, only one—the Winchester 21—is still in production. *The Parker,* which was made from 1869 to 1937, is the *crème de la crème* of American-made scatter guns. A side-by-side, as were nearly all of the top American shotguns, the Parker's hand-workmanship rivaled that of the old English guns. It was a superbly engineered, ornate firearm. The A-1 Special was the highest-grade Parker. In fact, a rare 28-gauge, A-1 Special (one of six ever made) sold at auction for $95,000. Other high-quality American doubles include the Fox, Lefever, and L.C. Smith. The Fox FE, the Smith Deluxe, and the Lefever $1,000 Grade are the premier models of those companies. Some of these vintage American doubles are still worth $10,000 or more.

The Winchester 21 was probably the most rugged double ever made in the United States. It was designed so that hunters could use the more powerful ammunition needed to down American game birds. Winchester 21s have been custom made since 1960. As a result, models made today are usually better than those made decades ago. The Grand American is the company's finest shotgun. It's popular among skeet shooters. Some models, with gold inlays, cost as much as $20,000.

Acquiring A Top-Quality Shotgun
Today, smart buyers acquire superior-quality doubles from dealers who specialize in this type of gun. These sellers, many of whom employ professional gunsmiths, can tailor a gun's barrel length, stock, choke, etc., to a buyer's specific needs. Most dealers stock a wide variety of guns from many manufacturers, and

they're usually available in many different gauges. Four of the most prominent dealers in North America are listed below:

- **Bill Jaqua, Jaqua's Sporting Goods,** 315 S. Main St., Findlay, OH 45840; (419) 422-0192.

- **L. Michael Weatherby,** P.O. Box 6451, Laguna Niguel, CA 92677; (714) 831-8512.

- **Bill Ward, Griffin and Howe,** 589 Broadway, New York, NY 10012; (212) 226-5983.

- **Gary Herman, Safari Outfitters,** 71 Ethan Allen Highway, Ridgefield, CT 06877; (203) 544-8010.

HUNTING: BLUE RIBBON TROPHIES

STALKING a lion in the African bush . . . squeezing the trigger on an aggressive polar bear that's closing fast . . . downing a giant sheep on a bleak Mongolian plateau—these are the ultimate hunting experiences: a sportsman's Super Bowl. Fortunately, in a few, select areas of the world, such thrilling hunts are still available—for those dedicated hunters willing to make both physical and financial sacrifices. Many of the hunts described below are necessarily done in some of the wildest, remotest areas on earth. Others are based in plush lodges with all the amenities of a fancy hotel. But all of these hunts offer one thing in common—the hunting experience of a lifetime.

Denmark (Pheasants)

The classic European driven pheasant shoot may be a shotgunner's most rewarding experience. Each November, for one week, this traditional hunt is re-created on sprawling estates in Denmark, as some fifty drivers literally "beat the bushes" to drive out hundreds of birds. On a typical day, 2,000 pheasants might be jumped, with some 500 actually downed by ten or a dozen hunters. Four drives are usually conducted in the morning, and three after lunch. After a day of shooting, spouses and friends join the hunters by the fireplace in the estate's main house for cocktails. Then, guests are transported to nearby country inns. The price for a one-week stay is about $5,300, plus round trip air fare to Copenhagen. Reservations must be made by January. The hunt is usually conducted in November. *Frontiers International, P.O. Box 161, Wexford, PA 15090; (800) 245-1950 or (412) 935-1577.*

Botswana (Lion)

This small country in the southern part of Africa encompasses much of the Kalahari Desert—the last stronghold of the legendary Bushmen. Hunters from around the globe flock here to hunt the black-maned lion, whose rich, dark-colored mane is a much-wanted trophy. Besides the great cat, herds of gemsbok, springbok, cape hartebeest, and greater kudu roam the arid, flat grasslands.

Hunters stay in pleasant tent camps manned by a full staff. The season stretches from April to September. The cost is about $500 a day, fourteen-day minimum. Hunters must fly to Johannesburg, South Africa, then commute up to Gaberone, Botswana. From there, a charter flight takes them to the hunting area. Trophy and license fees are very expensive. For lion, there is a $960 license fee, and an $800 trophy fee. *Safari Travel International, 3505 Hart Ave., Rosemead, CA 91770; (213) 288-2720.*

Spain (Red Stag)

Nestled in the Toledo Mountains of Spain some 130 miles south of Madrid, La Sierra del Castano offers superior red stag hunting. But both the terrain and climate are quite different from Scotland. This section of Spain basks in a sunny, dry Mediterranean climate. The rugged hills are broken by stands of timber and very thick bush that offer a perfect habitat for the deer. The cost of a minimum eight-day hunt is $345 a day, or $2,760. There is also a $2,000 trophy fee for each stag killed. Since nearly every hunter bags at least one animal, expect to spend at least $5,000, plus air fare from Madrid. Transportation and other basic services are included in the fee. *International Big Game Safaris, 977 Butternut Dr., Holland, MI 49423; (616) 399-0501.*

Northern Territory, Australia (Water Buffalo)

In the tropical forests of the Cobourg Peninsula, in Australia's Northern Territory, hunters can seek two of the largest big game trophy animals in the world: the water buffalo and the banteng. Other major game animals include 450-pound Sambar deer, and 250-pound boars. The buffalo are large (up to 2,000 pounds), powerful and dangerous. They have the widest horn spread of any big game animal in the world. Some have measured 90 inches across. The best time to hunt here is between May and November. The banteng hunt costs $8,000; buffalo hunts cost $3,000. Clients must fly from San Francisco to Darwin, Northern Territory, Australia. *Outdoor Adventures International, c/o Sharp's Travel Service, 91 Yonge St., Toronto, Ontario M5C 2R3; (416) 364-0640.*

Mexico (Doves and Ducks)

The Yaqui Valley in western Mexico boasts the largest winter concentration of mourning and white-winged doves in the world, as well as a large wintering concentration of Central Flyway ducks. On a typical day of bird shooting, a hunter arises before dawn and is taken to duck marshes via air boat. Shooting is done over decoys for such species as pintail, gadwall, widgeon, blue-winged teal, green-winged teal, and cinnamon teal. After lunch, sportsmen go dove hunting and are placed among flight lines in corn, wheat, milo and soybean fields. The season runs from November through the end of February. Temperatures are usually in the eighties even in those months. *Frontiers International, P.O. Box 161, Wexford, PA 15090; (800) 245-1950 or (412) 935-1577.*

Montana (Presidential Hunt)

With the exception of Alaska, no other state boasts the abundance of big-game animals as does Montana. The Big Sky state holds virtually every major game animal in North America, including elk, mule deer, black bear, grizzly bear, bighorn sheep, and mountain lion. For most people, getting an opportunity to hunt one of these great game animals is the culmination of their hunting careers. But Jack Atcheson & Sons, a leading outfitter of big game hunts, offers serious hunters the opportunity to take all of these species—in the same thirty-day period. Those participating in the Presidential Hunt start in Montana's eastern prairies and hunt white-tailed deer, antelope, and bison. Then the hunters move to the rugged western portion of the state to seek elk, mule deer, black bear, grizzly bear, and mountain lion.

World's Best Taxidermist. In today's technological society, taxidermy has almost become a lost art. But for seventy-five years, Jonas Brothers—a Denver-based company—has made animal, bird, and fish mounts of exceptional quality. The company regularly handles trophies sent by hunters from around the world. "We probably have made mounts of ninety-nine percent of the big game animals on earth," says Jack Jonas.

Before leaving on a hunt, the client is given detailed instructions on how to field-dress his trophy and how to ship the skin back to Denver so it is properly preserved. Once the skin arrives at Jonas, it is tanned, and then attached to a custom-made plastic mold. A wide variety of mounts is offered, from a simple wall mount of a head to complete life-sized reproduction. Costs vary widely. A head mount of a deer, for instance, costs about $325; a full-size deer mount costs about $1,600. *Jonas Brothers, 1037 Broadway, Denver, CO 80203; (303) 534-7400.*

WALKING TOURS: INTERNATIONAL

MANY potential vacationers fantasize viewing the vast African savannah from the top of Mt. Kilimanjaro, traipsing through flowering alpine meadows in the Swiss Alps, or traversing an emerald-green rain forest in New Zealand. *Today, anyone with an adventurous spirit can join hiking tours to many of the world's most spectacular wildernesses.* Each of these vacations is geared to any man or woman in good physical condition who loves the outdoors.

Swiss Alps
Switzerland may have the finest system of hiking trails anywhere. Several thousand paths slice through this country's beautiful countryside. Most of them are scrupulously maintained; signposts are plentiful and easy to understand. During the day, hikers can follow routes that weave through the moss-blanketed woods and flower-filled meadows surrounded by rows of jagged, white-crested Alps. Each guide-led group will travel six to eight hours daily, and cover six to fifteen miles.

In the summer, several trips are offered that give travelers a choice of visiting two to six villages: Appenzell, Murren, Pontresina, Sils Maria, Saas-Fee, and Zermatt. Saas-Fee and Zermatt are unique because no autos are allowed in them. Zermatt overlooks the world-famous Matterhorn—the symbol of the Alps. CONTACT: *Chappaqua Travel, Inc., 24 S. Greeley Ave., Chappaqua, NY 10514; (914) 238-5151.*

Long Trail (Vermont)
The Appalachian Trail follows the crest of the Appalachian Mountains from Maine to Georgia. But perhaps the most enjoyable stretch of this magnificent 2,000-mile-long path is Vermont's Long Trail, which cuts through the Green Mountains. In fall, when the leaves are in full color, this path may offer the most exhilarating walking experience in North America. Visitors can see an eighty-mile section of the Long Trail as part of an eight-day inn-to-inn hiking package. The season runs from late May to late

October. Total cost for a trip will be about $525. Make reservations early. *Country Inns Along the Trail, Churchill House Inn, R.D. 3, Brandon, VT 05733; (802) 247-3300.*

Milford Track (New Zealand)

People from around the world flock to this jewel-like trail, which runs through the South Island's Fiordland National Park. The Milford has it all: lush rain forests, trout-filled streams, snow-capped peaks, huge waterfalls, and bushy glades overflowing with birds. The thirty-three-mile course begins at Lake Te Anau; hikers travel it in four days. Highlights include 1,904-foot Sutherland Falls, the world's seventh-highest waterfall; lush brilliant-green vegetation; and an absolutely incredible variety of bird life. The excursion ends with a boat ride across Milford Sound, an ice-blue fiord surrounded by snow-capped peaks. Most people take advantage of a sixteen-day tour package, which allows them to make the hike and then visit the major points of interest on both the North and South islands. The sixteen-day trip costs about $1,500 (U.S.), plus air fare. The season runs from November through March. Reservations must be made at least four or five months in advance. *Adventure Center, 5540 College Ave., Oakland, CA 94618; (415) 654-1879.*

Mt. Kilimanjaro (Tanzania)

At 19,340 feet, Mt. Kilimanjaro is the highest mountain in Africa. The isolated, snowcapped peak towers above the great equatorial plain of northern Tanzania. Yet it is one of the few major mountains that can be fully climbed by a person without mountaineering experience or equipment. Hikers start a five-day trek at Kilimanjaro's base outside the city of Marangu. In the early morning blackness of the fourth day, hikers begin the final, arduous 3,000-foot climb to the summit. Several hours later, they will earn one of the great sights on earth—an unforgettable view of the sun rising over the great East African plain. The trek, offered year-round, costs $650, not including airfare to Tanzania. *Overseas Adventure Travel, #6 Bigelow St., Cambridge, MA 02139; (617) 876-0533 or (800) 221-0814.*

Inca Ruins (Peru)

Southeastern Peru was the seat of power of the extraordinary Inca Empire, which dominated the western part of the continent from the thirteenth through the sixteenth centuries. During a two-week tour, travelers can visit some of the 700-year-old ruins from this civilization, as well as savor spectacular mountain and jungle scenery. The trip begins at the former Inca capital of Cuzco (11,204 feet), from which the Incas ruled their vast empire for more than three centuries. Then voyagers take a raft trip down the Urubamba River, gently floating through the sacred Valley of the Incas. Numerous native villages and several sets of rapids are passed along the way. At the small mountain village of Mollepata, the group begins a five-day trek in one of South America's most beautiful mountain ranges: the Cordillera Vilcabamba. After the trek, travelers take a train to Machu Picchu, the "Lost City of the Incas." The cost of this "Highlands of Peru" trek is about $1,200, plus air fare to Lima, Peru. *Wilderness Travel, 1760 Solano Ave., Berkeley, CA 94707; (800) 247-6700 or (415) 524-5111.*

Chilkoot Trail (Alaska)

During the winter of 1897 to '98 thousands of men and women tried to traverse Alaska's Chilkoot Pass on their way to the Klondike gold fields, carrying a year's provisions with them. Many never made it. This grueling thirty-two-mile trek has remained the symbol of the Gold Rush. Today, hikers can travel the same route, enjoying great scenery, wildlife, and many artifacts from this era. This is a backpack trip, so guests must carry their own sleeping bag, change of clothes, and other gear. The guide supplies tents and food. The package tour begins in Juneau. The cost is about $895. Hikes are done in July and August. *Mountain Travel, 1398 Solano Ave., Albany, CA 94706; (800) 227-2384 or (415) 527-8100.*

Grand Canyon (Arizona)

The Grand Canyon is one of the natural wonders of the world. Every year, thousands of people marvel at the resplendent red, orange, and yellow hues of this mile-deep gorge, carved eons ago by the Colorado River. On a guided two-night, three-day hike, outdoor people can stroll slowly down to the canyon's floor, observing rock formations two billion years old. Travelers must carry their own gear and sleeping bag on their back. Trips are run from March to November, but fall is the best season to make this trip. Midsummer temperatures can reach 120 degrees Fahrenheit. Hikers should be in reasonable condition, since everyone must hike back *up* sooner or later. The price of this trip, assuming a typical five-person group, is one of the best recreational bargains in North America—only $22.50 per person, per day, including three meals cooked on the trail. Guided one-day or half-day hikes are also available for those who want a somewhat less strenuous experience and prefer not to have an overnight on the trail. *Grand Canyon Trail Guides, P.O. Box 2997, Flagstaff, AZ 86003; (602) 526-0924.*

WHITEWATER RAFTING: U.S.

R UNNING the rapids of a whitewater river is about as exhilarating a vacation as you're going to find, with lots of time spent holding on for dear life (and getting totally drenched) as your rubber raft rises, crashes, bounces, and twists through frothy chutes. But a raft trip down even the wildest river isn't nonstop whitewater action. There is also the opportunity to explore great wilderness, see native wildlife, swim, dive from rock overhangs, fish, camp out under the stars and perhaps explore a ghost town. *It isn't necessary to have prior rafting experience;* complete beginners can enjoy most trips, be they robust teenagers or senior citizens. *The New Book of Bests* correspondents have investigated the finest riverrunning trips in America and picked the following. All of the trips selected are managed by competent, safety-conscious outfitters with many years experience. These excursions are in high demand, so make your reservations early.

Colorado River, Arizona
This is the ultimate whitewater rafting trip—for seven days, rafters rush down the great river that carved the Grand Canyon. During the 178-mile voyage from Lee's Ferry to Lava Falls, riders enjoy the most awesome scenery on the planet. The thousands of multicolored layers of the Grand Canyon reveal two billion years of earth history. There are twenty major rapids on the Colorado, including two of the wildest rapids in the West—Crystal Creek and Lava Falls. To safely negotiate the treacherous currents, three large rubber rafts are tied together for added stability; they float down the river in tandem. A guide in each of three rafts helps steer. Passengers just have to hold on—and help bail. The season runs from May to August. *Georgie's Royal River Rats, P.O. Box 12057, Las Vegas, NV 89112; (702) 789-0602.*

Rogue River, Oregon
As the Rogue River squeezes through the Coastal Mountains, it picks up velocity and force, offering one of the great rafting experiences along the West Coast. Mule Creek Canyon, for example, offers two straight miles of whitewater thrills and in the Devil's

Staircase, rafters ride huge waves from one ledge to another. The standard three-day, two-night package costs $325 per person, which includes all meals and top-quality equipment and lodging. The season runs from May through September. A special four-day, three-night fall fishing trip is offered from September through late November. The fee is $700 per person, including all gear, food, and lodging. *Rogue Excursions Unlimited, P.O. Box 855, Medford, OR 97501; (503) 773-5983.*

New River, West Virginia

Despite its name, the New River is the second oldest in the world. The New roars through the Appalachians cutting deep gorges; there are twenty-four major rapids along the way, some rated Class IV and Class V. In several sections, rafts must go through—and over—eight-foot waves. For much of the trip, though, passengers can just lie back and enjoy the rolling, heavily forested hillsides. Rafters can swim in quiet pools during rest stops and explore old coal-mining ghost towns. Sixteen-foot rafts are used for this river run and each person is responsible for paddling, following the instructions of a guide. New River rafting trips are offered for one and two days, and cost between $100 and $200. The season runs from April to November, but the best rafting is in May and June. *Mountain River Tours, Inc., Box 88, Sunday Road, Hico, WV 25854; (304) 658-5817 or 658-5266.*

West Branch, Penobscot River, Maine

Henry David Thoreau was enraptured by this great stream and referred to it frequently in his book, *The Maine Wood.* It's easy to see why. Located near Baxter State Park in central Maine, the Penobscot is one of the most scenic rivers in the Northeast and, for rafters, one of the most thrilling. Riders encounter seven major rapids on the thirteen-mile trip; in many places, rafts go thirty m.p.h. and drop as much as twelve feet. In calmer waters, riders can enjoy a spectacular view of Mt. Katahdin, Maine's highest peak (5,268 feet). The season runs from May to early October. The cost for a one-day trip is about $80. *Eastern River Expeditions, Box 1173, Greenville, ME 04441; (207) 695-2411.*

Gauley River, West Virginia

Open only a few weeks a year, mostly in the spring and fall, the wild Gauley River's water flow is controlled by the U.S. Army Corps of Engineers, which operates Summersville Dam above the river. The ferocious current churns up five- to eight-foot waves and many "holes"—sections where the water rushes upstream—that meet the raft head-on. Cost of a one-day trip on the fourteen-mile run is $80 to $100. Only people with plenty of experience in paddling difficult rapids are allowed to participate. *Mountin River Tours, Inc., Box 88, Sunday Road, Hico, WV 25854; (304) 658-5817 or 658-5266.*

Snake River, Wyoming

This is the perfect trip for people who want a lazy, gentle scenic float. The Snake has few rapids between Yellowstone National Park and Jackson Hole, Wyoming, the stretch of the river along the base of the Grand Tetons, some of the most breathtaking scenery in the world. The float begins just south of Yellowstone Park. Cost for the five-day trip is $595 for adults, $495 for children eleven years of age and under. The season extends from May to September. *Parklands Expeditions, Inc., P.O. Box 3055, Jackson Hole, WY 83001; (800) 238-0290 or (307) 773-3379.*

Chattooga River, Georgia/South Carolina

This wild and scenic river in northern Georgia offers the best whitewater excitement in the Southeast, but it's most famous as one of the sites featured in the movie *Deliverance*. Section 4 is a steep, untamed stretch that charges through narrow, thickly-forested gorges and offers the best rafting for a one-day trip. Here, the river drops 275 feet in only six miles and rafters must negotiate tricky seven-foot drops along the way. Rafts hold four people, plus a guide, and everyone is expected to paddle. Trips are run year-round, but most rafting is done from mid-March through October. *Nantahala Outdoor Center, U.S. 19 W., Box 41, Bryson City, NC 28713; (704) 488-2175.*

HIGH CYCLING

LESS than ten years ago there were basically just two kinds of bicycles on the road. About half the world wheeled about on sleek, European-style ten-speeds or English racers. The other half was resigned to heavy, single-speed clunkers, slow but reliable transportation. Then, early in 1981, the "mountain bike" came rolling out of the hills of northern California and the Rockies of central Colorado, bouncing through potholes, tightly gripping wet roadways, and scooting up precipitous trails. These new bikes, equipped with the best features of both the ten-speed (lightweight frame, derailleur gearing, cantilever brakes) and the clunker (sturdy frame, thick balloon tires, upright handlebars), created a revolution in bicycling that has yet to level out.

On the California coast they are called cruisers; in the Virginia Appalachians they are bush bikes. In the South some folks refer to them as "mountain mickies," and among bicycle manufacturers they are officially called all-terrain bikes (ATBs). Whatever their name, one thing is certain: a new era in bicycling has begun. In the U.S., some 200,000 bicyclists were riding ATBs in 1985 and a full ten percent of the bikes sold by forty companies were fat-tired two-wheelers. They are selling so briskly, and the demand for them is growing so fast, that *Bicycling* magazine has predicted that they will soon overtake the dropped-handlebar ten-speed as America's favorite bicycle.

ATBs go places where ten-speeds would fear to tread, like up mountains, down rutted trails, and through both mud and snow. Their wide, knobby tires and sturdy frames carry riders over terrain never before explored by bicyclists. In the high country of Idaho, mountain bikers follow decades-old logging roads deep into the wooded wilderness. Backpackers use off-road bicycles to cross deserts and rocky terrain on their way to more beautiful surroundings. Fishermen use them in their pursuit of brook trout and steelhead salmon.

ATBs also make themselves at home on city streets and flatland roads. Urban riders in New York and Washington, D.C., report smooth rides and carefree commuting on the thick puncture-proof tires and upright handlebars of their "city bikes." On the plains of Kansas and Nebraska they maneuver the gravel backroads and potholed old highways between farms equally well.

While the ATB models now available have a few characteristics in common—fat tires, upright handlebars, saddle seats—they are by no means the same. They are as different in price and design as the terrain they are meant to be ridden over. For example:

City bikes

On city streets eighteen speeds are overkill and the huge, knobby tires of the mountain bike are unnecessary. A "city bike" like the *Metroplex* from the Sterling Cycle Company is excellent for commuting. Its five-speed Sturmey Archer gearing, grooved tires, and leather sprung mattress saddle provide as smooth a ride as you can get on a bicycle. Rather than hunched over curved handlebars, its rider is upright, with a clear vision of the road ahead. The Metroplex is both fast enough to maneuver through traffic and nimble enough to avoid collisions. Its tires will cross curbs, manhole covers, and even broken glass with rarely a flat. It retails for around $575.

Another quality city bike is the *Trek 890*, which weighs just under twenty-nine pounds. The most unique feature of this bike is its radial tires. Similar in design to those on a passenger car, these tires offer lower rolling resistance, longer tread life, and greater shock absorption than most other bicycle tires. Sells for about $500.

Mountain bikes

In mud or gravel, a bicycle rider will want as much traction as he or she can get. That means a mountain bike with tires that look like they belong on a tractor. For off-road racing, or punishing rides through ugly weather, the mountain bikers wants every advantage that science and experience can lend him. Hand-built custom models like the Ritchey Mountain Bikes' *Annapurna* feature the best in bicycle and motorcycle componentry and can cost $2,000 or more. The Annapurna features brazed fillets, chrome-molybdenum alloy tubing, "bullmoose" handlebars, and heavy-duty motorcycle brake cables. With its glossy finish and expert workmanship, it is also a beautiful bicycle in appearance.

Equally dependable but less splashy mountain bikes are the *Diamondback Ridge Runner* distributed by Western States Imports of California, the Mt. Fuji imported by Fuji America, and Specialized Bicycle's *Stumpjumper Sport*. These fifteen-speed and eighteen-speed models retail for about $500, but have proven themselves on the steepest and rockiest of trails.

Newcomers to the sport should, of course, request a test ride before they decide on which model to buy. Although many department stores won't allow this, most independent bike shops will. The small shops will also be able to tell you more about the product they are selling. On even a short ride the differences between the ATB and other bicycle models become apparent. The moment you climb on and begin to pedal, and as soon as you begin to glide across the pavement or dirt, you will start to feel a vast sense of freedom and an inexplicable urge to go out there and conquer new terrain.

For information on ATB models, request catalogs from the following manufacturers: *Fuji America, 118 Bauer Drive, Oakland, NJ 07436; Ritchey Mountain Bikes, Route #2, Box 405, La Honda, CA 94020; Ross Bicycles, 350 Beach 79th St., Rockaway Beach, NY 11693; Specialized Bicycle, 844 Jury Court, San Jose, CA 95112; Sterling Cycle*

Company, 1326 Spruce St., Suite 2702, Philadelphia, PA 19107; Trek Bicycle Corp., 801 W. Madison St., P.O. Box 183, Waterloo, WI 53594; Western States Imports, 1837 DeHavilland, Newbury Park, CA 91320.

HORSE SHOWS: U.S.

THE best horse shows are a breed apart. After a day at a top show, it's easy to understand how people become passionately attached to horseflesh. The following shows garner the highest rating from the American Horse Shows Association (AHSA). They have long and respected traditions attached to them, and several have been held annually for a century or more. (The Upperville show, for example, goes back nearly 130 years and is considered the oldest show in the country.) They feature the best international riders (members of the United States Equestrian Team compete regularly at these shows) and the most respected judges and course designers.

• **Devon Horse Show,** Devon Horse Show Grounds, Devon, PA, held in May.

• **Upperville Colt and Horse Show,** Upperville Show Grounds, Upperville, VA, June.

• **Ox Ridge Charity Horse Show.** Ox Ridge Hunt Club, Darien, CT, June.

• **Santa Barbara National Horse Show,** Santa Barbara, CA, July.

• **Kentucky State Fair World Championship Horse Show,** Louisville, KY, August.

• **Hampton Classic Horse Show,** East Hampton, NY, August, Exact location varies.

• **Arabian and Half Arabian U.S. National Championship Horse Show,** Louisville, KY, October.

• **Pennsylvania National Horse Show,** Farm Show Arena, Harrisburg, PA, October.

• **Washington International Horse Show,** Capitol Centre, Landover, MD, October-November.

• **National Horse Show,** Madison Square Garden, New York, NY, November

For more information on specific shows and exact dates—which vary from year to year—CONTACT: *AHSA, 220 E. 42nd St., New York, NY 10017; (212) 972-AHSA.*

JOINING THE HUNT

YOU no longer have to be a Vanderbilt or a Whitney to get into fox hunting. While riding to hounds is unlikely to displace tennis or golf as a major leisure pursuit, it is certainly attracting a following among prosperous (but not necessarily fabulously wealthy) folks who enjoy the sheer athleticism and sociability traditional to the sport. There are now more than 130 registered fox hunt clubs in thirty-three states and most of them are happy to sign up new members. Even such unlikely places as Arizona and New Mexico—where the landscape hardly resembles the rolling hunt country of the East—support active hunts.

• **What do you need to consider before you take up the sport?** For answers we talked with Benjamin Hardaway, president of the Masters of Foxhounds Association of America and Karen Quanbeck, who writes for *Chronicle of the Horse,* the country's foremost horseman's journal. "The first thing to remember," says Hardaway, "is that you won't be playing pinochle. This is not a pastime for people who are out of shape. You need a horse that won't throw you on your fanny and you need to be physically fit enough to control that horse at all times. The stereotype of the sport as the exclusive preserve of a ruling class is dead. Most of the hunts welcome anybody who's there for the sport and not for the old stuffed up social baloney." In fact, adds Quanbeck, at least seventy-five percent of the hunts (as local clubs are called) are open to new members.

• **How do you find a hunt near you?** Ask at a local stable or feed store; check the annual roster of hunts in the U.S. and Canada which appears each year in a mid-September issue of *Chronicle of the Horse;* call the Masters of Foxhounds Association in Boston. Costs are not excessive—assuming of course that you already have a horse and a way of transporting it if your local hunt is too far from home to reach on horseback. Family memberships often fall into the

$300 to $500 range. Packs of active hunts usually go out at least two or three times a week during the season which, depending upon the club, can run from as early as mid-August through April. "And you'll be decently turned out," says Hardaway, "if you spend $500 or $600 on boots, britches, black coat, and hunt cap."

• **When you are ready to take the plunge,** says Quanbeck "all you have to do is call the master of your local hunt and pay a capping fee—anywhere from $20 to $100—to ride as a visitor. They'll usually ask you to ride as a visitor six times before asking you to join, just to make sure you've got the skills to hunt." (If you want to sharpen those skills, go out early in the season, when the young hounds are being trained. The pace is slower and the dress requirements less stringent.) Once you're in the field, the rules are simple says Quanbeck: "Ride in the back of the group until you're a full-fledged member; never ride up on the horse in front of you; don't talk during a 'check' when the master is listening to the hounds; don't ride ahead of the master; don't kick the hounds."

The best basic introduction to the sport is William Wadsworth's *Riding to Hounds in America* which *The Chronicle of the Horse* publishes and distributes at cost ($1.50). For information: *The Chronicle of the Horse, P.O. Box 46, Middleburg, VA 22117; (703) 687-6341.*

POLO: THE WORLD CUP

POLO is played on a field 300 yards long and 160 yards wide and pits two four-man teams who ride horses (polo ponies) while attempting to drive a willow root ball three inches in diameter through goal posts twenty-four feet apart. A game consists of six chukkers (periods) of play, each seven-and-one-half minutes long. There are about 150 polo clubs in the U.S. and the very finest players achieve a ten-goal rating, i.e., the Argentinian Juan Carlos Harriott, now retired. (The Argentinians have dominated the sport for years.)

High-goal polo at its best can be seen at The Palm Beach Polo and Country Club in Wellington, Florida, the finest polo facility in the world. There are nine polo fields, stables for 226 horses, two private clubhouses, and a polo school where, for a nominal fee, a beginner can learn on a mechanical horse that moves up and down a practice field. From January through March the world's best players compete in a series of matches which climax in the World Cup, the sport's premier tournament.

BEST JIGSAW PUZZLE

FOR anyone tired of tossing off cardboard jigsaw puzzles like boxes of Cracker Jacks, Stave Puzzles of Norwich, Vermont, offers devilish handmade wooden teasers to keep even the most ardent puzzle-solver awake for a month of Sunday nights. Cut from mahogany-backed five-ply laminate and hand-finished, the pieces of a Stave Puzzle interlock in one of three complicated patterns—"Classic," the more difficult "Fantasy," and the hopelessly difficult "Nightmare." Every puzzle includes pieces that are silhouettes of cowboys, ballet dancers, animals, trains, and other creatures and a single clown, signed and dated, that is the trademark in every set. Stave also throws in such tricks to baffle its customers as misleading straight edges on pieces, complicated outside edges on some puzzles, and two-piece silhouettes that surprise you when they come together. They will cut your initials as a large tricky puzzle within a puzzle, include your name in cutout script as a piece, and customize your choice in other ways. You can also have them make a deluxe puzzle out of the photograph or print of your choice.

Stave's top of the line creations are a two-tier "Midsummer Night's Dream" depicting the five acts of the comedy in 650 pieces and "The Doll's House Village," a 2,300-piece, five-part caricature village scene, complete with the story of its citizens' loves and feuds. Both are limited editions, priced at $1,200 and $5,100 respectively. Another unusual Stave effort is a four-part series inspired by the books of James Herriot. Once you've purchased and completed the entire set all four puzzles fit together with the interior edges mirroring each other perfectly. Stave's smallest puzzles start at $85. Custom-made puzzles fashioned from your own photographs or artwork range in price from $145 to $1,200 depending on size and the style of the piece. For Stave's large, whimsical catalog, CONTACT: *Stave Puzzles, Main Street, Norwich, VT 05055; (802) 649-1450.*

HIGH ON KITES

THE ultimate high on a sunny day? The simple art of kite flying. *The New Book of Bests* spoke with kite expert David Klein (of New York's *Go Fly A Kite* store) about the sport that is soaring all over the country. Whether you're building your own kite or buying one, the materials used should be the lightest yet strongest possible. Klein favors Ripstop nylon for all kites except dragon designs. (Dragons require a lighter material because of the drag factor of their long tails.) Synthetics hold up better than natural fibers; cotton has a tendency to shrink and expand near water; silk will rot from overexposure to ultraviolet light.

For a beginner, Klein suggests a Delta design. It is the easiest kite to fly and can handle the widest range of wind conditions. It usually costs under $10. If you are looking for more of a challenge, Klein suggests a two-string acrobatic, or stunt, kite. A six-pack of Rainbow stunt kites will run about $120. The ultimate luxury? Klein recommends the Rokkako, designed by master kite-maker George Peters. This six-sided giant Japanese Fighter kite is made of Ripstop nylon and costs about $550. *Go Fly A Kite, 1201 Lexington Ave., New York, NY 10028; (212) 472-2623.*

DANDY DARTS

FOR the best dart always look for a *tungsten* dart. A recent development in this ancient game, tungsten has only been used in darts for about ten years. Tungsten is heavier than lead and stronger than steel, allowing the dart to have a fine, slender point with sufficient weight behind it to provide needed "umph." It is also half the size of a brass dart of the same weight. Among manufacturers of darts, Accudart was the first to use ninety to ninety-five percent tungsten with an alloy of nickel and iron in their top-of-the-line Pro dart. Because pure tungsten is as brittle as glass, the Pro Line includes just enough nickel and iron alloy to let the lathe work its magic in refining the shape to a pinnacle of accuracy. Larry Rabin, president of the prestigious New York Dart League, gives best marks to Accudart, "You feel positive with the darts, as if they were custom made for *your* hand. The weight is pure, the points are firmly and accurately embedded, the design and craftsmanship are tops."

The same precision design and workmanship go into Accudart's other darts. These include a ninety to ninety-five percent tungsten alloy, and nickel and silver darts and the basic brass dart, the most economical of the lot. But the difference between the $25 brass and the $65 tungsten dart is that between hitting the wall and scoring a bull's eye. Similarly, there is no contest with

Accudart. Accudart's products are available at finer sporting goods stores, or call them at: *(800) 526-0451 or (201) 438-9000.*

PICK OF THE DISCS

O NLY a modest investment lets you join the millions of (in ascending order of devotion) casual players, enthusiasts, and fanatics who while away leisure hours playing Frisbee, or, as it is correctly designated, disc.

While there are approximately fifty companies producing sport discs in the United States, Wham-O, the California-based company that owns the trademark Frisbee has controlled the sport disc market for over twenty years. However, Wham-O does have competition. While many serious disc players prefer the Wham-O World Class 165 for their Ultimate game, most freestylers have developed an attachment to the Sky Styler by Discraft, a small company which also has golf, Ultimate, and all-purpose models. CONTACT: *Discraft Products, Box 275, Westland, MI 48185; (313) 421-4322.*

Not all sport discs are sold in retail stores, either. The Wham-O HDX model, which is made of a special plastic that can withstand cold weather and rough play, is available through *Discovering the World, Box 911, La Mirada, CA 90637; (714) 522-2202.* This specialty shop carries a full line of sport and collector discs. A free catalog is available.

While most discs retail for about $10, collectors will pay much more for prized models. The rare Pluto Platter, Wham-O's first Frisbee, can bring a $100 price tag. *A real treasure would be to acquire an original Frisbee pie tin.* As legend goes, the Frisbee got its name from the Frisbie Pie Tin Company in Bridgeport, Connecticut, when some Yale students passed the time tossing the tins and yelling "frisbie" to warn for the approach.

For more information on discs, CONTACT: *U.S. Disc Sports, c/o Eric Wooten, 462 Main, West Hampton, NY 11978; (516) 288-3371.*

THE BOOMERANG MAN

T HE art of boomerang hurling has become a popular sport in some areas of the country. The best source of ready-made boomerangs is Richard Harrison, who sells them through direct mail. Harrison, known throughout the hobby as "The Boomerang Man," is a longtime thrower, and has competed in the annual boomerang-hurling tournament held at the Smithsonian each spring. His catalog includes handcrafted boomerangs from all over the world, and he will personally recommend the boomerang he thinks is right for you, if you send him your specifications.

He sells boomerangs for all sizes of thrower and special boomerangs for left-handed throwers. Harrison suggests the light but durable "Stick Around" boomerang for novices and children; a more ambitious adult beginner might prefer the "Bakwood," made of steam-bent ashwood, which has a longer throwing range. Experienced throwers will be interested in the "Gerhard Hook," made and flight-tested by Al Gerhard, who holds the world record for the distance throw. Unlike the boomerangs available in many sporting goods stores, all Harrison's boomerangs have been tested and are guaranteed to fly. Prices range from $5 to $75 depending on size, shape, and materials. For a catalog, write: *The Boomerang Man, 1806-B N. 3rd, Monroe, LA 71201.*

BEST BILLIARD TABLES

THE finest billiard tables made today are the ornately carved models turned out by furniture maker Charles Porter and Company at *Renaissance Billiards* in Santa Ana, California. Porter uses the hardest Honduras mahogany, rosewood, oak, and teak to build tables that are fancy (some say gaudy) pieces of furniture as well as excellent playing surfaces. Using only inch-thick Italian slate bolted securely between the rail and the table frame, Porter assures his customers of the truest and steadiest surface for play. The heavy wool-and-nylon cloth he uses is a durable covering comparable to the sort used on casino tables. Elaborate carving techniques requiring hours of handwork complete these masterpieces. Top-of-the-line models start at about $15,000 to $20,000. *Renaissance Billiards and Accessories, 3304 W. Second St., Santa Ana, CA 92703; (714) 835-8265.*

Two other companies—Golden West and World of Leisure— make tables with comparable playing surfaces, but without the carving and handwork that distinguish the Renaissance tables (and make them so expensive). The Trafalgar table ($5,000) made by World of Leisure is used by CBS and ABC television for broadcast tournament play; their top models also include the Versailles

($7,000) and the Paulmier ($3,500 to $4,000). *World of Leisure, P.O. Box 347, Covina, CA 91723; (818) 331-2911.* The top of the line at Golden West is the Victorian ($7,000). *Golden West Billiards, 21260 Deering Ct., Canoga Park, CA 91304; (800) 423-5702.* Accessories also affect the play of a table: choose the English-made Super Crystalite billiard balls, about $170 a set.

FABULOUS FIREWORKS

IT'S a booming, colorful business which serves satisfied customers such as the Olympics, Yves St. Laurent, Walt Disney World, and Macy's. It's the fireworks game and competitors George Zambelli *(Zambelli Internationale Fireworks)* and Felix Grucci *(Fireworks by Gucci)* play it better than anyone else.

Started in Italy over eighty years ago, Zambelli Internationale is the largest fireworks company in the United States and is still completely controlled by the family from the creation of the designs to the manufacture of the shells, right up to the grand finale in the sky. Every Zambelli program is customized for individual clients, which include the cities of Indianapolis, Miami, and Philadelphia as well as the Orange Bowl and Hershey Park in Pennsylvania. Certainly one of the grandest and largest displays that Zambelli creates is the Macy's Fourth of July celebration in New York City. It is a fantastic piece of choreography which combines fireworks, fountains, and music—all erupting over the Hudson River and the Statue of Liberty. These grand shows cost an average of $1,600 per minute. However, the company will gladly organize smaller shows for private parties, weddings, and companies. A complete show would cost a minimum of $2,000.

Fireworks by Grucci, run by Felix Grucci and his family, boasts six generations of fireworks experience. As with Zambelli Internationale, the Grucci family prepares a completely customized display for a client, from design to firing, such as the fireworks productions for the Brooklyn Bridge Centennial in 1983, and the 1981 and 1985 Presidential Inaugurations in Washington, D.C. The minimum cost for a show on the scale of private parties for business or family celebrations would be in the $1,700 to $2,000 range. Every year George Plimpton, the Official Fireworks Commissioner of New York City, hires Grucci to put together a show at his Long Island home for his friends.

For information about hosting your own fireworks display anywhere in the world, CONTACT: *Zambelli Internationale Fireworks,*

P.O. Box 1463, New Castle, PA 16103; (800) 245-0397 or (412) 658-6611. Fireworks by Grucci, Association Road, Bellport, NY 11713; (516) 286-0088.

EIGHT

Travel

A GALAXY OF GREAT HOTELS

CHOOSING a hotel is like choosing a lover. The right choice brings immediate delight and fond memories long after. The cost? Who would put a price on bliss? But consider the wrong choice: it's not soon forgotten. Recriminations abound. Why weren't you more discerning? Why didn't you sense, from the very first, that such and such would never be to your liking? As for expense, suffice it to say that every dollar spent becomes a dollar begrudged. Your retrospective considerations are fraught with regret and laden with rue. Of course, even with the best of planning, a wrong choice in love or in lodging occasionally is unavoidable. We firmly believe, however, that expert advance briefing in both categories can allay disaster.

What follows, therefore, is a list of hotels which have consistently pleased, satisfied—even delighted—the connoisseur, the discriminating world traveler, and, yes, the hard-to-please. Each hotel, in our considered opinion, has a unique mixture of those attributes that distinguish the best—locale, architecture, design, cuisine, and service. Our choices are ours and ours alone. Other experts may take issue with an inclusion, with an omission. Let them. We know there are more great hotels. For now we stand four-square behind our picks. If you, the reader, trusting our judgment, choose your hotel from our listing, and in so doing, discover a truly special place to which you will surely return, then know that we will count our efforts well expended. Our choices follow:

Hotel Imperial
16 Kärtner Ring, Vienna, Austria
65-1765
Conceived and constructed as a pleasure palace for the Duke of Wurttemberg in 1869 this hotel does opulent justice to its ducal origins. It presides over the city's Ringstrasse and on a snowy winter night, its floodlit majestic façade evokes all the romance and grandeur of imperial living. Within, all is well-bred, not a fork misplaced or a guest's title mispronounced. One of the last of the old great bests.

Hotel Amigo
Rue de l'Amigo, Brussels, Belgium
(02) 511-59-10
Just a step or two in from the magnificence of the Grande Place this delightfully intimate hotel makes certain that every guest is served with care and courtesy, easy enough to say, too seldom seen. In a city where the commercial, the scientific, the military, and the scholarly are forever arriving and departing, the Amigo manages to provide a much needed preserve of gracious civility.

Royal Crescent Hotel
Bath, Avon, England
(0225) 319090
Dramatically situated in the city's Royal Crescent, a one-of-a-kind architectural wonder, this hotel is listed in Royal Archives as "Grade I Building," meaning of peerless historical value. Its flawless restoration and refurbishing in its original Georgian style does ample justice to its setting. Impeccable service in charmingly sumptuous surroundings.

Claridge's
Brook Street, W1 London, England
(01) 629-8860
All the elegance of a fine private town house, all the concerned coddling of a superior hotel. No bar per se but instead a charming lounge with a letter-perfect staff in attendance. Bedrooms and baths of exceptionally generous dimensions.

Connaught
Carlos Place, W1 London, England
(01) 499-7070
Small, unfussy, traditional with emphasis on unobtrusive, personalized service. From the white portico and window boxes outside to
the splendid, sweeping staircase and utterly comfortable bedrooms
inside, this hotel in a quiet residential section gets unanimous
approval from us. Some people's choice for *the* hotel in London—
and the world.

Ritz Hotel
Piccadilly, W1 London, England
(01) 493-8181
Once down on its uppers and coasting on its gilded origins, this
centrally located, palatial establishment, now under new
ownership has been magnificently restored to former glory.
Though the Rivoli Bar is gone, the Palm Court is still very much
there and still the poshest place in Londontown at teatime.

Hotel de Crillon
10 Place de la Concorde, Paris, 8e. France
296-1081
Louis XV obviously didn't know what he was missing when he
passed up the chance to reside in this magnificent structure,
designed and built originally for his needs alone. Fortunately, the
rest of us can enjoy what the king overlooked: a stately, luxurious
hotel where excellence permeates everything from the view to the
tea sandwiches, from hemstitched linen sheets to the marble baths
and the wine list, surely the most comprehensive in all of Paris.

Hotel Plaza Athénée
25 Avenue Montaigne, 75008 Paris, France
(1) 723-78-33
Red awnings and masses of geraniums against beige stone façades
. . . silk-covered couches, Porthault sheets, marble fireplaces, not
with gas jets but with crackling logs, a just-right courtyard garden
and roses on your bedside door. It suits us perfectly just as it suits
Fellini, Dior, both Hepburns, and half the royalty of Europe. Other
hotels are larger, more streamlined but none, repeat *none,* is more
elegant.

Hotel Vier Jahreszeiten Kempinski
17 Maximilianstrasse, Munich, Germany
(089) 22-88-21

Bastion of the finest tradition of German hoteliers. Intelligently brought up-to-date insofar as amenities are concerned, yet always with respectful attention to the safeguarding of paneling, tapestries and furnishings that have, for well over a century made this Germany's most distinguished hotel.

The Athens Hilton
46 Vissilissis Sofias Ave., Athens, Greece
720-201
Of all of the Hiltons, this we say, is the finest. Its setting is without equal in the Mediterranean: on one side, the lofty ridge of the Hymettus, on the other the noble wreckage of the Acropolis. Out of deference to its Hellenic surroundings, the architects have made lavish, and altogether appropriate, use of marble, acres of marble. The food served in the Taverna Ta Nissia and in the rooftop Supper Club may well be the best to be found from Gibraltar to Beirut.

Budapest Hilton
1014 Budapest, Hess Andras Ter 1-3, Budapest, Hungary
853-500
Hilton et al., could so easily have taken the simple route: building their brand new hotel (opened 1977) right from scratch. Instead, to their great credit, they chose to construct this quite beautiful building in and around the remains of a great house, built in the days of Ottoman splendor. The very latest in modern comfort has artfully been wedded to the concepts of a long past era of elegance. Hotels with this degree of opulence *plus* efficiency are very few and far between in this sector of Europe.

Berkeley Court
Lansdowne Road, Ballsbridge, Dublin, Ireland
601711
From the moment you drive into the tastefully planted courtyard with its palm trees and other subtropical surprises, you know you're in for a treat. The cheery courtesy of the doorman is prototypical of what you'll find throughout your stay at this comfortable, spit-and-polish hotel, blessedly set apart from the downtown traffic chaos. Everyone from the manager down to the busboy takes an interest in your well-being.

Le Grand Hotel
3 via Vittorio, Emanuele Orlando, Rome, Italy
(06) 4709

Enough marble, gold leaf, crystal, and damask to please the great
Lorenzo himself. Opulence neatly, efficiently paired with expert
service. It's a combination that earns this CIGA hotel a rating
among the very best.

Hassler Villa Medici
Trinita dei Monti 6, Rome, Italy
67-82-651
Long a favorite of discerning Americans who value privacy as well
as elegance. As for its location, well who could ask for more than the
Spanish Steps almost at the threshold? Apart from the view atop St.
Peter's, the Roof Garden at the Hassler provides the finest views
that one can have of the Eternal City.

Hotel Excelsior
125 via Vittorio Veneto, Rome, Italy
48-90-31
Conveniently close to the American Embassy this Roman hotel
caters with aplomb and courtesy to the needs of film stars, heads of
state, and royalty. The electricity of life along the via Veneto infects
the hotel's atmosphere, making it undeniably the place in which to
see and be seen.

Hotel Gritti Palace
Campo S. Maria del Giglio 2467, Venice, Italy
(041) 26-044
In the fifteenth century, when the silk and spice trade routes from
the Orient passed through Venice, making it the world's most fascinating city, then it was that the Doge Andrea Gritti built his palace. All the comfort, charm and opulence that he demanded then is
just as evident today. Just a few steps from St. Mark's Square, com-
manding a splendid view of the Grand Canal, the Gritti Palace is
indeed one-of-a-kind in the world of great hotels.

Hotel De Paris
Place du Casino, Monaco
(93) 50-80-80
Here everything is outsize: the guests are the most famous, most
notorious, the richest, the handsomest, and, of course, the most
demanding. Drawing up before its massive portals is a constant
stream of Jaguars, Porsches, Mercedes, Rolls-Royces, and
Bentleys. You'll likely find yourself next to a rajah, a movie star, or
a prime minister, and rest assured that such a clientele stays here

because the ambience, cuisine, and room appointments are, hands down, as superb as can be had in all of Europe.

Hotel Ritz
Plaza de la Lealtad No. 5, Madrid, Spain
22128-57
Built just after the turn of the century by that luxury-loving monarch, Alfonzo XIII, the Ritz happily exemplifies all the splendid and baroque grandeur of Europe before the Great War. During the "bad years" under Franco, hard times came and stayed at the Ritz. Not that you would know it today. Recent renovations have left intact all the best, whilst handsomely updating baths, kitchens, telephones, and lifts. A truly grand hotel on a truly grand scale. Classifies as one not to be missed.

Villa Magna
Paseo de la Castellana 22, Madrid, Spain
261-4900
A stay in this small, distinctive hostelry should be on the list of special requisites for anyone who aspires to enter the field of hotels, as a manager, architect, or owner. Despite its convenient location in the center of the Spanish capital, this hotel maintains beautifully manicured gardens which perfectly complement the building and its interiors. The rooms are a joy to live in . . . comfortable, opulent, and in pluperfect taste. One presumes that all employees are sent through language school prior to signing on, since English, Italian, French, German, even Arabic, all seem to come trippingly off the tongue.

Grand Hotel
S-103 27 Stockholm, Sweden
(08) 221720
There it sits, right on the edge of the harbor, looking exactly the way a grand old European, super-deluxe hotel should look. When monarchs or heads of state are in residence, which is often enough, the proper national flag flies from the rooftop poles. Yachts from all nations tie up just in front of the spacious verandah where, in summertime, you have your coffee and pastries with the likes of Bergman, Ullman, and Sweden's leading rock group, Abba. On the Cafe Verandah the smorgasbord buffets are, in and of themselves, well worth the round trip ticket to Sweden.

Hotel Beau Rivage
13 Quai du Mont-Blanc, 1201 Geneva, Switzerland
(022) 31-02-21

Superbly located at the very end of Lake Geneva, this small—120 rooms—hotel has been pleasing the great names of Europe for well over a century. When one tires of strolling its tasteful public rooms, of dining in elegance in its charming restaurant, or of residing in bedrooms as comfortable as the ones at home, then there still remains the terrace, overlooking the lake with the Alps providing the backdrop. A lovely spot, graced by a hotel that has magnificently withstood the tests of time.

Cataract Hotel
Abtal El Tahir Street, Aswan, Egypt
2233
Here in Upper Egypt on the east bank of the Nile stands what must surely be one of the world's very last, truly *dernier siècle* hotels. By that we mean the rooms are huge, the tubs are long, the corridors broad, the service is painstaking. The great wide covered terrace overlooks the Nile where it splits to flow around Elephantine Island. All day long the fellucas ply the river, their odd-shaped sails dazzling in the undiluted sunshine. To sit, drink in hand, either on one's own balcony or on that same terrace, at day's end and watch the western sky turn fiery is one of life's most thoroughly satisfying experiences.

King David Hotel
26 King David Ave., Jerusalem, Israel
221111
Of no other Israeli hotel can it so truthfully be said that the history of the country is written on its walls. When, during the struggle for independence, patriots blew up one entire wing of this venerable establishment, few people believed that the doors of the hotel would ever reopen. But like the country itself, the management and staff of the King David have proven themselves to be both resilient and diligent. Consequently, a guest will find not just concerned and courteous service but also an almost tangible pride in the hotel's firmly established reputation for excellence.

Red Sea Palace
P.O. Box 824, Jeddah, Saudi Arabia
(02) 6428555
Just as its name suggests, this recently opened hotel, under eagle-eyed Swiss management, reflects all the grandeur and incredibility of this desert kingdom. From its balconies one peers down on the

rooftops of the fascinating old town of Jeddah. Look the other way and there's the Red Sea, right at your doorstep. To live in the Red Sea Palace while sightseeing in and around Jeddah is, in the truest sense of the phrase, to experience the best of two worlds, that of historical wonder plus that of bone-deep luxury. It's a contrast that very much appeals to us.

Hotel De La Mamounia
Avenue Bab Idid, Marrakesh, Morocco
(04) 32381
In the very center of the city of Marrakesh, walled off from the clamor of the teeming streets, this fabulous hotel overlooks its seventeen acres of landscaped serenity. The snowcapped Atlas Mountains on the horizon accentuate the exotic charm that is Morocco. It was Churchill's favorite retreat and one visit will confirm that great man's discernment insofar as lodgings are concerned. Bedrooms are large, airy, usually with a balcony. Furnishings are typically Moroccan with a preponderance of gleaming brass, beautiful leather, and, of course, the handwoven rugs for which the country is justly famous. One of our favorites among the nonurban choices.

Lanzerac Hotel
Jonkershock Road, Stellenbosch, South Africa
5020
This is one of the very few hotels we've chosen to list that is not strictly urban. One hundred and fifty years ago this hotel was a Cape Dutch homestead, one of the handsomest in all of the lovely Jonkershock Valley. Its conversion from a stately private home to a small but perfect hotel has been handled with exquisite taste. The results are worth the less than one hour's drive from the center of Capetown. The gardens are extraordinary, the rooms are as individual in their furnishings as those in your own house. The food is beautifully prepared and presented with all the *éclat* it deserves. Burnished brass, polished wood, huge bowls of proteus, the national flower, make this a very special find.

The Regent
199 George St., Sydney N.S.W. 2000, Australia
238-0000
Of all the hotels we've covered in the book, this is the youngest. We firmly believe that time is the ultimate test of every hotel, so naturally we qualify our judgment here with the reservation that the future must substantiate the present. But the present, as we see it at

the Regent, Sydney's very newest deluxe hotel, is glowing indeed. No detail has been overlooked: telephones are handily placed in every room at three locations, bedside, desk top, and bathroom; stocked refrigerator, completely appointed office-size writing desk, and AM/FM radios and color TV are all standard equipment. For business people the hotel provides a "business center" which includes a library devoted to Australian business information. Its location, on "The Rocks," overlooking Sydney's dramatic harbor is among the most impressive we've seen.

Four Seasons Hotel
1050 Sherbrooke St., West, Montreal, Canada
(514) 284-1110
We've discovered the Four Seasons and so have a great many others, or so it would seem given the lead time required to secure a room reservation. Never mind, the wait is worth it. To stay at the Four Seasons is to indulge oneself in every sense. The food is just plain superb. The public areas are as comfortable as they are striking. The eye of management is evidently everywhere since one rarely sees a half-filled ashtray or a diner in the throes of trying to attract a waiter. Good taste, concern for the needs of guests, and a refreshingly courteous staff and there you have the Four Seasons in this Anglo/French city.

The Royal York
100 Front St., West, Toronto, Canada
(416) 368-2511
Far, far too big was our first impression of this 1,600-room hotel, at least for those whose tastes run to the smaller, more intimate hotel where we can count on being recognized, welcomed, and made to feel at home. No exercise of imagination could transpose this into anything we could ever call "cozy." Yet we include it here because, indisputably, its suites are among the most comfortable we've found anywhere in the world. As for the rooms, particularly the larger ones, we found them more than adequate by half. In part this is due to the fact that the service is absolutely top-notch. Off-hour requests are fulfilled without a murmur, iced champagne and smoked salmon arriving just as promptly at midnight as if requested at noon.

Windsor Arms
22 St. Thomas St., Toronto, Canada
(416) 979-2341

If you're not careful, you'll be very apt to pass right by its front door, never dreaming that this could be anything other than a very well kept private residence. Which is exactly why it's very much a favorite of ours. Once inside, the impression persists. Logs crackle in huge stone fireplaces, and light streams in through well-polished leaded windows. Every square inch of mahogany and brass gleams, and the food served in all four of its delightful restaurants is right up there with the best to be found in Toronto. Katharine Hepburn makes it home whenever she's in the city, proof positive that she likes to live as well as she acts.

Beverly Wilshire Hotel
9500 Wilshire Blvd., Beverly Hills, CA
(213) 275-4282
How exactly right that in the world of the super-extravaganza, this hotel exists: a living, breathing monument to the ultimate. Its suites are all balconied and/or duplexes. Christian Dior's namesake suite does magnificent justice to his unerring taste and his penchant for the perfect detail. Nothing understated here but, on the other hand, the garish or excessive have miraculously been held at bay. Comfort on a grand scale in a semitropical atmosphere that gloriously complements the hotel's ambience.

Ritz-Carlton Hotel
15 Arlington St., Boston, MA
(617) 536-5700
Here the most venerable name in the world of hotels is definitely in good hands. Looking out over Boston's Public Gardens, the Ritz continues to provide skilled service, scrupulously appointed rooms, and a vastly comforting permanence insofar as its elegant ambience is concerned. Unbeatable in Beantown.

The Drake Hotel
140 E. Walton Place, Chicago, IL
(312) 787-2200
Where else (except Rio) can you stay in the center of a great metropolis with a beach right at your doorstep? The Drake, within easy walking distance of Chicago's best galleries and concerts, has, if you please, its very own beach on the shore of Lake Michigan. The Drake's restaurant, Avenue One, boasts some of the city's most interesting cuisine, including the famed Cape Cod Room, carefully prepared and served by an intelligent staff familiar with the needs of an appreciative clientele.

The Tremont
100 E. Chestnut St., Chicago, IL
(312) 751-1900; (800) 621-8133
Whenever Henry Fonda visited the Windy City, he stayed at the Tremont, which only proves that Mr. Fonda was as astute offstage as he was effective on. It's small (140 rooms), personal, and as close as you can come to staying in a private home circa 1920. Chicago has several absolutely first-class hotels but, as of this writing, we're casting our first ballot with this pleasantly diminutive oasis of comfort.

Brown Palace Hotel
17th and Tremont Place, Denver, CO
(303) 825-3111
In 1896 when it first opened its doors, it was a source of wonder and remains so today. For a century now, architects from all over the world have visited Denver to marvel at its nine-story central atrium, encircled by balconies. Periodic refurbishings have kept this memento of the Old West right up to date insofar as comforts and amenities go. The staff is knowledgeable about the hotel's place in the history of the Mile High City and they share that knowledge with refreshing pride.

Four Seasons Hotel
1300 Lamar St., Houston, TX
(713) 650-1300
If this is Texas, where's the chrome, the cowboy mural, the gilded six-shooters over the bar? Instead we find understated elegance and sophistication. The reception area is suffused with a muted color scheme of terra cotta and beige. Space, light, and ingenious use of tropical plantings make this relatively new hotel a visual delight. Service is impeccable, rendered by a staff of cheerful, competent professionals. Quite possibly the finest hotel cuisine in the U.S.

The Carlyle
36 E. 76th St., New York, NY
(212) 744-1600
Chinese Chippendale mirrors, Gobelin tapestries, and Savonnerie rugs set just the right tone for the food, wine, and service which makes this delightful hotel an "uptown favorite."

Mayfair Regent
610 Park Ave., New York, NY
(212) 288-0800; (800) 545-4000
A longtime favorite of visitors who will make no compromise with quality, either in service or accommodations. Its restaurant, Le Cirque, rates as the finest hotel dining in the city.

The Pierre
61st and Fifth Ave., New York, NY
(212) 838-8000; (800) 228-3000
For more than half a century the Pierre has been quietly sheltering, feeding, and entertaining the discriminating and the chic.

U.N. Plaza Hotel
1 U.N. Plaza, New York, NY
(212) 355-3400
Second to none in its dramatic location, overlooking both the United Nations and the East River, this quietly sumptuous hotel combines the very best of modern design with concepts of Old World elegance and service. Full of light, charm, and chic with delicious unexpected extras and touches. If you can find a more delightful swimming pool than that which perches on the twenty-seventh floor, by all means, buy it.

The Stanford Court
Nob Hill, San Francisco, CA
(415) 989-3500
As much a city landmark as the cable cars, this splendid hotel stands where Governor Leland Stanford first constructed his famous family mansion. The earthquake of 1906 destroyed the mansion but the hotel's construction incorporated many features salvaged from the ruins. Authentic Carrara marble, original nine-teenth-century French antiques, Baccarat chandeliers all artfully combined to produce an atmosphere that is gracious without being austere. From Fournou's Bar, to the left as you enter, can be had one of the best views of the Bay area, more dramatic than any mural, any decorating scheme.

Ouro Verde Hotel
1456 Avenida Atlantica, 22021 Rio de Janeiro, Brazil
257-1800
In a city whose shoreline is studded with one faceless high-rise after another, this fifty-six room hotel comes as something of a sur-prise—an exceedingly pleasant one. Built shortly after World War

II, the Ouro Verde has managed to capture the nicest touches of European hotels plus the ambience of a well-to-do Latin home. You may well also cross paths with longtime Rio residents who periodically come here to dine, knowing it to be the finest food in the entire city.

Ritz-Carlton Hotel
2100 Massachusetts Ave., N.W., Washington DC
(202) 293-2100
Formerly the much respected Fairfax, the Ritz continues to gladden the hearts of Washingtonians and their visitors. Here you can count on the very finest of cuisine, service, accommodations, and appointments. A decided credit to our nation's capital city.

Hotel Avila
Av. Jorge Washington, San Bernardino, Caracas, Venezuela
515155
How delightful in a city that has been overwhelmed with the hustle and bustle of the petroleum-paced tycoons to find this one small oasis of quiet, calm, leafy, altogether civilized living. The terraces are sun-swept, the service is courteous and swift, the ambience reflects the elegance that was old Venezuela at its best.

The Mandarin
5 Connaught Road Central, Hong Kong
(5) 220111
Often said to be the finest hotel in Asia, the Mandarin is to hotels what the Concorde is to air travel, what Everest is to mountains. Here Eastern serenity and Oriental opulence meet and merge with Western efficiency. Say not that you have dined on Chinese food unless you've sampled the fare that is served in the Chinese Man Wah Room.

The Regent
Salisbury Road, Kowloon, Hong Kong
(3) 7211211
We said it couldn't be done: a brand new hotel that aspired to eclipse in style, service, and opulence the time-tested, much respected, world-famous hostelries of which Hong Kong is so justifiably proud. But Regent International Hotels has managed, in our opinion, to do just that. Its octagonal swimming pool of truly emperor-ish dimensions is a wonder in itself, as is the quality of the cuisine, the grandeur of the harbor views, and the all-glass lobby.

The Taj Mahal Inter-Continental Hotel
Apollo Bunder, Bombay, India
243366
In all of Asia, few places so magnificently capture the grandeurs of the East. Comfort? Elegance? Unequalled luxury? All safely sequestered in this truly splendid hotel. Consisting of two parts, the old, original structure which dates back to 1906 and the last-word-in-modern-design tower block. Each has its own very special charm. The service throughout the hotel is as close as any hotel can ever come to round-the-clock perfection. The cuisine is excellent, said by many connoisseurs to be the finest served in India outside of a few private palaces.

Hotel Okura
10-4 Toranomon, 2-Chrome, Minato-ku, Tokyo 107
(03) 582-0111
In this incredible citadel of international cuisines and eclectic decors it's possible to sup on *coq au vin,* preceded by a very American, extra-dry martini with a twist, and then retire to your room which is exquisitely decorated in the very essence of Italianate. On the other hand, it's also possible to sample the very best of Japanese cuisine, to be served tea in the most meticulously observed tradition, and to be accommodated in rooms that could easily pass for the master bedrooms of a wealthy Japanese family. Despite its size (980 rooms), the staff manages to convey a genuine concern and interest in the comfort and well-being of every guest.

Shangri-La Hotel
22 Orange Grove Road, Singapore
737-3644
Situated close to the pandemonium of the shopping along Orchard Road this is a haven of tropical landscaping, trickling fountains, swift, soft-footed service, and a view from your bedroom of sampans and sailing yachts. The excitement of Singapore, the luxury of the Shangri-La—in our view an unbeatable combination.

To augment our list of best hotels we polled the editors and correspondents of *The New Book of Bests,* asking each of them to list his or her favorite hotel anywhere in the world. The list that follows is the result of that poll.

The Oriental (Bangkok)
The 1976 addition to this century-old bastion of empire grandeur has, miraculously, left unimpaired the delight of staying in this time-honored favorite.

Peninsula (Hong Kong)
Its distinctly Colonial ambience plus its marvelous view of the Kowloon waterfront makes it distinctive in the midst of world-class hotels.

Dolder Grand (Zurich)
Only a quarter of an hour from the downtown clamor and well worth every second of the journey.

The Ritz (Paris)
If Cleopatra came to Paris, where would she stay but right here, overlooking her very own obelisk in the Place Vendôme.

L'Ermitage (Los Angeles)
A one-of-a-kind place to stay where no two rooms look alike and the privacy of guests is still a high priority.

Habitation Leclerc (Haiti)
Of all the gifts bestowed by Napoleon, quite possibly the land on which this exotic hotel stands, is one of the very best. Gratefully received by the Emperor's sister, Pauline, and today a tropical refuge for sybarites.

Anatole (Dallas)
Not to everyone's taste but heaven for the inveterate shopper since everything from le petit boutique to the grand slam retail outlet is right on the doorstep.

The Mansion (Dallas)
Depending on your tastes, this is either a hodgepodge or a cornucopia of wildly varying styles, from Ye Old England and Venice under the Medicis to Lone Star Kitsch. But its devotees are near-fanatics.

Nova-Park Elysées (Paris)
So what if it was conceived and constructed primarily for the petro biggies of the Middle East? One of our staffers swears by it as do many of the world's movers and shakers.

The Inn On the Park (Houston)
Where else can you count on center-city outdoor swimming and tennis just beyond your bedroom door? All this plus a chef who obviously was sent straight from heaven.

The Westwood Marquis (Los Angeles)
Says one of our editors, "I'm pro-home, anti-hotel which probably explains why this is my favorite West Coast crash pad."

11 Cadogan Gardens (London)
Four Victorian town houses, delightfully merged into a small and just-about-perfect hostelry where personal checks are Yes but credit cards are No.

The Plaza (New York)
At seventy-five years plus, still one of America's *grande dame* hotels and a name synonymous with New York. Centrally located, elegant, it combines the leisurely charm of Palm Court tea with the sophistication of its Oak Bar. Everyone should stay here once.

Hyatt On The Park (Chicago)
The Windy City's most recent arrival and already high in the ratings.

A SAMPLER OF LUXURY SUITES

T HE sumptuous, elegant, shamefully luxurious suite is truly the pampered world within the pampered world. Step from the clamor of the thoroughfare into the hushed serentiy of a United Nations Plaza or a Dorchester, and at once the senses are soothed. If you wish to escalate your level of self-indulgence to an even higher level, move then from the public reception areas to the private suite. Here's a world designed and maintained with no other objective than to serve and please you—laundry, valeting, letter mailing, or the turning away of unwanted callers, all handled on your behalf, discreetly, even invisibly. Like an aria superbly rendered, your stay in any of the following suites should linger in your memory for a long time.

Imperial Suite (Okura, Tokyo)
Bizarre as it may seem, the Imperial Suite in Tokyo's Okura Hotel is a glowing tribute to classic English decor. Recently renovated, the suite's large living room has a floor-to-ceiling window overlooking the city. In addition to the dining room, two bedrooms, dressing room, and two baths, there is a spectacular, spacious master bath with all marble and gold fixtures. Guests will also appreciate the suite's library, stocked with the classics—in

English of course. *Hotel Okura, 10-4 Toranomon 2-chrome, Minato-ku, Tokyo 105, Japan; (03) 582-0111.*

Marco Polo Suite (Peninsula, Hong Kong)

The Marco Polo Suite on the penthouse floor of Hong Kong's Peninsula Hotel consists of large, lavishly decorated rooms filled with Chinese art, T'ang bronzes, figurines, porcelain, and large bathtubs made of Carrara marble. The semicircular, sunken dining room features a Ching dynasty screen (on loan from a private collection). The living room with its built-in stereo is a cheery blend of formality and comfort. A private valet is assigned to occupants of the suite for the duration of their stay. And, to sweeten the visit, a supply of fruits, chocolates, and liquor, is constantly replenished. *The Peninsula Hotel, Salisbury Road, Kowloon; 3-666251.*

Presidential Suite (Beverly Wilshire, Los Angeles)

During the Bicentennial, most of the visiting royalty and heads of state, made appropriate excuses in order to visit Los Angeles, primarily just to stay in the Beverly Wilshire Hotel's Presidential Suite. Prince Charles, King Hussein of Jordan, and the Kings of Norway and Sweden are but a few who've passed that way. What makes this suite so special? Surely not just authentic reproductions of Louis XV and Louis XVI furniture, or the huge terrace overlooking the city of the stars; nor the spaciousness of the living room, dining room, two bedrooms, and four bathrooms. In this gilt-edged corner of the world, the Presidential Suite, despite its title reflects the most imperial of tastes. Need we even mention that, of course, a butler is on twenty-four-hour call? *Beverly Wilshire Hotel, Wilshire Boulevard and Rodeo Drive, Beverly Hills, CA; (213) 275-4282.*

Ralph Bunche Suite (U.N. Plaza, New York)

New York has plenty of luxury hotels, most of them overflowing with Old World ambience which is why we find the Ralph Bunche duplex suite, at the United Nations Plaza so refreshing. With its emphasis on airiness, light, and space, it stands as a fine example of contemporary design. It also enjoys one of the most extraordinary views in New York, looking over both the East River and the gardens of the United Nations. Throughout, the suite's mirrors and windows create a delightful sense of openness. Exceptionally comfortable sofas and chairs, a piano, an intriguing circular staircase which joins living and sleeping space, and an excellent stereo system make these accommodations particularly appealing. *United Nations Plaza Hotel, 1 United Nations Plaza, New York, NY; (212) 355-3400.*

Presidential Suite (Hyatt Regency, Maui, Hawaii)

The most spectacular suite to be found in the Hawaiian Islands is the Presidential Suite of the Hyatt Regency on Maui. Over 2,200 square feet, it boasts a travertine marble entryway, a Steinway baby grand piano, a sauna, and a Jacuzzi. The decor is an artful blending of fine Italian marble with original American art and Oriental accents. The library, with its ash-grain paneling and light-teak parquet flooring, stocks a selection of current bestsellers. From the living room guests look out over a panoramic view of the Pacific and the Maui mountains. *Hyatt Regency Maui, 200 Nohea Kai Drive, Lahaina, Maui, Hawaii, (808) 667-7474.*

Suite #224, 225, 226 (Hotel de Paris, Monte Carlo)

In the Hotel de Paris, the finest suite, #224, 225, 226, is invariably reserved by the international jet set and government VIPs. Each of the two bathrooms has a large marble bath, while the bedrooms are done in soothing rust, beige, and blue. The sitting room furniture is modern, lacquered, while the walls are graced with paintings of Japanese gardens. All three rooms open over the casino, and, of course, the Mediterranean. *Hotel de Paris, Place du Casino, Monte Carlo, Monaco; (93) 50-80-80.*

Winston Churchill Suite (La Mamounia, Marrakesh)

When at La Mamounia, his favorite Moroccan hotel, Winston Churchill always insisted on staying in his favorite "regular" suite. Named—what else? The Churchill Suite. Two bedrooms and a living-room where Eastern wall hangings and European furnishings are nicely-blended. The living room opens on to a furnished balcony with a spectacular view of the hotel gardens and the Atlas Mountains. Exactly where Churchill sat to paint those glorious mountain sunsets. *La Mamounia, Avenue Bab Jdid, Marrakesh, Morocco; 323-81.*

The Royal Suite (Nova-Park Elysées, Paris)

The Royal Suite of the Nova-Park Elysées, likely the most expensive hotel in the world, was designed exclusively for kings and heads of state. Five bedrooms, seven bathrooms, sitting rooms, conference rooms, and three different terraces with outstanding views of the city; security includes bulletproof windows and an automatic alarm system. For government leaders who simply cannot be out of touch with new developments, a special business room is equipped with telex and wire services. *Hotel Nova-Park Elysées, 51 rue Francois-ler, Paris; 562-63-64.*

Suite 11-300 (The Biltmore, Los Angeles)

The Biltmore believes that anyone who pays for a home away from home deserves exactly that. Suite 11-300 with its three-bedroom, three-bathroom duplex suite comes complete with a large fully-equipped kitchen, plus dinette. For guests in search of a quiet hour, there's a well-stocked library. Mies van der Rohe furniture and Barcelona chairs dominate the living room. In the dining room an Italian marble table with Marcel Breuer chairs seats eight. *The Biltmore Hotel, Los Angeles, CA; (213) 624-1011.*

The Royal Suite (The Waldorf Towers, New York)

Suite 42-R, as it's called, may be the grandest of all American suites. You can hold a reception for 100 in its living room and serve dinner for twenty-four in the dining room. Two bedrooms and a kitchen complete the suite. The decor is a mixture of French Regency furniture and a variety of antiques, wall coverings, and a Persian rug. You have a private entrance, a personal file of your special needs, and one of New York's finest views.

RESORTS AND RETREATS

IN our view, the criteria for a great resort are simple and clear: A great resort must be aesthetically pleasing. Whether it commands a view of the Alps or the Andes, a sweep of perfect Caribbean beach, or perhaps a vast expanse of East African forestland, it must be situated in a place that delights the eye.
• A resort must be comfortable. Spartan accommodations are fine in a duck blind or below deck on an ocean-racing sailboat. But at a resort, ordinary needs must be met with comfort.
• A resort must provide opportunities to indulge one's fancy in sports and games. Be it skiing, trapshooting, bowling on the green, or a rubber of bridge, a resort must make it not just possible but also easy for you to find your own brand of fun.
• Finally, a resort must be peopled with other congenial fellow-vacationers with whom you're at ease, people whose companionship you enjoy.

Each of the resorts listed here, meets these criteria and meets them with style and consistency. We list them *alphabetically.*

Antumalal (Pucon, Chile)

Queen Elizabeth and Prince Philip stayed here. So did Senator Barry Goldwater, but then the management of this 3,000-foot high hotel is quite unfazed by the arrival of international VIPs. As perhaps South America's poshest resort, Antumalal prides itself on guarding the privacy of its guests while they revel in the spectacular scenery of Andes vistas and the snowfed clarity of Villarrica Lake. Only twenty rooms with a handsome stone reception house. We are hard put to find any resort on any continent where the views are more dramatic, or indeed, the hospitality more warm-hearted and unaffected. Splendid fishing and mountain hiking and for those who thrive on near-Arctic temperatures, marvelous swimming as well.

Armacao (Brazil)

Only a few years back this was a sleepy fishing village about seventy-five miles closer to the equator than Rio. Only the tax collector and the priest ever ventured down its tiny streets with shoes on their feet. Today private jets streak into its newly-built runways and its waterfront is lined with yachts that fly the pennants of the greatest yacht clubs in the world. The beach is less than great. The surf can be downright dangerous, but the bikini-clad sun worshippers have obviously decided that Armacao is the right place for solar communion. If you prefer not to sleep aboard your yacht, then the Auberge de l'Hermitage provides the closest thing to a sumptuous hotel that you'll find this side of the French Riviera.

Baden-Baden (Germany)

A century ago the merchant princes and lesser nobility of Europe took for granted their midsummer fortnight stay at Brenner's Park, Germany's beloved spa. Today things have changed very little. The violins are heard at teatime, the coach-and-four still clatters down the pebbled drive, and only the chauffeur-parked rows of Daimlers, Mercedes, and Porsches, remind one that this is the 1980s. Guests at Brenner's Park, many of whom reserve their rooms a year in advance, can (and do) count not just on some of Europe's most superb cuisine but also a chance to try their luck in one of Europe's handsomest casinos.

The Burgenstock (Switzerland)

The Burgenstock, situated in the heart of Switzerland 1,500 feet above Lake Lucerne, is a mountaintop eyrie and private kingdom belonging to Fritz Frey. It is Switzerland's best private estate hotel complex, a sanctuary that includes over fifty buildings, miles of private roads and a privately maintained fire brigade and water and power supply. There are three hotels from which to choose: The Grand, The Palace, and the slightly less luxurious Park. The Grand, built in 1873, was the first hotel on the site and to this day maintains an art collection that rivals a museum. Every guest room at the Burgenstock has a view—one the Frey family has maintained free of any commercial intrusion. Although the regular (and anonymous) clientele includes heads of state, celebrities, and VIPs from around the world, Frey cautions, "We consider everyone an honored guest at the Burgenstock." Those looking for night life and city lights here will be disappointed. The routine is leisurely with an emphasis on nature activities—hiking, boating, etc. Elegant serenity is the Burgenstock's best offering.

Capri

For our taste we'll take Capri out of season, if you please. In May when the roses are big as pie plates and the lanes are abuzz with nothing more sophisticated than the honey bees . . . or in mid and late September, after the multilingual hordes have departed and once again the waterfront is populated not with double-breasted, gold-buttoned navy blue blazers but with fishermen's caps and scuffed-up rubber working boots. But in season or out, there's little that can match the splendor of the view of the Faraglioni, the island's rocky ramparts, or the clarity of the awesomely deep waters that surround this fabled isle. Adopted by royalty, adored by the titled, and the wealthy, immortalized in verse and song since Homer's time, Capri yet retains a certain unspoiled charm that even a casual visitor would find hard to resist.

Casa De Campo (Dominican Republic)

Picture 7,000 lush tropical acres devoted entirely and exclusively to pleasure and you have a pretty good idea of this Gulf + Western-owned playland. Breaking it down into its playful components: La Terraza, as the tennis complex is dubbed, ranks as one of the best facilities in the Caribbean. There is a polo field and beautifully run stables whose tenants are very definitely not for beginners. Two golf courses by master designer, Pete Dye, give the place a special allure for golfers. A carefully manicured beach and a generous choice of pools . . . plus dining in any one of a variety of restaurants. Decor is by native Oscar de la Renta and accommodations range from large, tile-floored, balconied rooms to suites and villas.

Fisher's Island (New York)

Quite the most laid back, understated island spot in Long Island Sound but no point in flying out there unless your Uncle Algie or your Cousin Eustacia has room for you. "Commercial" on Fisher's is limited to the grocery-liquor store, the gas station, and the island hardware store. Rambling Victorian houses with wraparound porches nestle in dunes and any suggestion of "landscaping" is decidedly no-no because out here we're tastefully, wealthily back-to-nature. Dress-up means clean L.L. Bean khakis and very dress-up means your monogram worked in needlepoint on your patent leather pumps. A good reputation as an offshore sailor and/or a wicked net game is all you need to get you in with the very best of Fisher's . . . provided you've also been veddy, veddy careful about your ancestry.

Hobe Sound (Florida)

The post office is on the mainland but the Hobe Sound Club is out on Jupiter Island, accessible at the south end by a draw-bridge, at the north end by a pleasant little, easily-patrolled bridge. In other words, in the best of resort traditions, access into Hobe Sound, in more ways than one, is completely controllable. Along Hobe's (the in-terminology) only two roads, Ocean and Gomez, the houses are discreetly screened from view by well-behaved pines and hedges. The golf course is definitely not great . . . (who cares, everyone who plays the game belongs to Seminole anyway) but the tennis courts, all ten of them, are perfect—shielded from unruly breezes by Australian pine windbreaks and supervised by the courtly Jim Pressley whose staff does a splendid job of building a two-handed backhand for the next generation of Hobe Club members.

Hotel du Cap (France)

Every bit as luxurious (and luxuriant) today as when Scotty and Zelda were in residence. Let every other villa, hotel, and resort that aspires to indulge its guests, take heed of the *modus operandi* that prevails here. As the French say, it "gives on the sea" (i.e., overlooks the Mediterranean) and within its generous walls, this hotel offers the very best that can be had in the way of oversized rooms, salon-sized baths, easy access to your yacht mooring, some of France's finest tennis courts, and chefs who value their reputation far too much to ever send forth a platter that is less than superb.

Gibson Island (Maryland)

It's not true at all that unless you're a Symington with ump-teen generations' worth of Baltimore-dwelling ancestry behind you and a couple of legs on the Maryland Hunt Cup that you can't get into the Gibson Island Club. But it is almost true. But if, with the right credentials, you make it past the gate of this Chesapeake Bay Island kingdom, just off the shores of Annapolis, you'll find your-self in Bay boating heaven. Not every resident regularly rides to hounds, has a seat on the stock exchange, or graduated from Gilman's but you can bet your bottom farthing that every one of them has a tidy little fiberglass number with furling sails, rainbow-hued spinnakers, and a sweet touch on the tiller.

The Greenbrier (West Virginia)

As they say, for the "complete resort experience," nothing can touch the Greenbrier. Three superb golf courses, twenty tennis courts, bowling alleys, swimming pools, thoroughbred horses, skeet and trapshooting, and a chef whose reputation was made in heaven. The property covers a modest 6,500 acres, bordered by the Blue Ridge Mountains. Sneer if you like at the outdated customs of the quote unquote Old World but still we challenge you to come up with anything more pleasant than afternoon tea at the Greenbrier, served to the discreet strains of Viennese waltzes. In our eye, big is usually synonymous with bad, but this time around we have to make a gold-star exception.

Los Portales (Costa Rica)

Only an even dozen rooms comprise this Central American deliciously deluxe retreat, known not to many but cherished by those who've been fortunate enough to be steered its way. An hour's drive from San Jose, up into the mountains, will bring you to this small and quite perfect property. Each room is a delight in size, appointments, and vista. The cuisine is French but with some imaginative and altogether successful inclusion of regional recipes. The gardens are, in themselves, quite worth the trip. Tennis and trout fishing about complete the "in-house" entertainments although excellent golf can be had within just a few minutes' drive.

Lyford Cay (Bahamas)

Some people might think it a shame to fly all the way to the Bahamas only to ignore the beach in favor of the pool, but that's the way life goes out at Canadian millionaire E.P. Taylor's ultra-club creation. Tennis is something of a stepchild while golf, on a beautifully maintained course, is very much the favorite. The rooms are nice though certainly not spectacular and if you want a dockside mooring for your yacht, you'd be well advised to notify the harbor master well in advance. The cuisine, just like the rooms, is also not spectacular, which probably explains why so many guests prefer to eat aboard their boat where at least the chef can be counted on to know his quenelles from his quiches.

Mackinac Island (Michigan)
If you make it rhyme with Cadillac you prove at once you don't belong on this woodsy bit of heaven that sits prim as a tea rose in the Straits that separate the Upper Peninsula from the rest of Michigan. Even the pigtailed moppets know that it's Mack-in-Aw, as in My-Rich-Paw, without whom they wouldn't even be here. In the state where Henry Ford gave birth to the automobile, this fresh water island enforces a strict ban against same. If you object to walking, or maybe biking, you're welcome to avail yourself of one of the island's many handsome horse-drawn carriages. If you're without your own summer house, then of course you can stay at the Grand Hotel which is, indeed, exactly that. Chosen as the settings for goodness knows how many movies, it continues to dispense, between Memorial Day and Labor Day, an antiquated, quite delightful brand of hospitality.

Mount Kenya Safari Club (Kenya)
"But of course, it's not really *Africa.*" Its detractors sniff and profess a preference for long, dusty treks with bearers out through the bush, following the spoor and pug marks of the wounded whatever. But the fact remains that this handsome lodge-hotel is very hard to fault. It sits squarely on the equator but at an altitude that guarantees crystal-clear days and blanket-cool evenings. Its walls are hung with fascinating old photographs of the Grand Old Days of empire. Yes, that's Prince Philip and, yes, that's Lord Randolph Churchill, squinting into the camera, flanked by grinning guides and stalwart "white hunters." The view from the Lodge, towards Mt. Kenya is extraordinary. And the food? Well, you'll not find its equal from Capetown to Cairo.

Northeast Harbor (Maine)
Except of course it's never known as anything but "Northeast." Here's a seaside resort where no one ever swims in the sea. Too cold by half. Never mind, there's "the pool" around the edges

of which you'll have ample chance to chat about last Winter's Assembly and this fall's Yale-Princeton game. It may be August but bring your woolies. The fogs of June have been known to settle in and still be much in evidence come Labor Day but then isn't that all part of the fun of being down East? Otherwise, why should all the *sangs-bleus* from Philadelphia, Baltimore, and Pittsburgh pack their retrievers, tennis racquets, and tooth-banded children into their station wagons for the annual trek to "open up the house"?

Palm Beach (Florida)

You buy, not a house, but a villa in Palm just to have the children attend dancing class at the B & T which is not a sandwich but the, no, *the* Palm Beach Club, otherwise known as the Bath and Tennis. If you can't find what you want along Worth Avenue, then you don't want it. It's as simple as that. Servants of course are a problem. But there are brand new ways of achieving status such as installing the most sophisticated alarm system, hooking up your own Dow Jones ticker tape machine out on the pool patio, and bringing the kids down from St. Paul's and Foxcroft via your private plane for spring vacation.

Palm Springs (California)

As the man says, "You asked for a resort . . . I give you a resort," and that's Palm Springs, the mostest, biggest, wealthiest, plushest. Within less than twenty square miles there are forty eighteen-hole golf courses, 500 tennis courts, 5,000 swimming pools, all divided up between fewer than 25,000 residents. This is the desert playland to which ex-presidents, CEOs, Hollywood stars and starlets, and heirs of every size and description funnel in from all over the U.S. If your "ranch house" is not yet completed, you can book into non-Spartan accommodations at the Spa or the Tennis Club, but one's own place is preferable . . . provided it was designed by Philip Johnson or the equivalent and has one swimming pool that's sheltered for the windy days.

Pinehurst Hotel & Country Club (North Carolina)

Of its golf we all know: seven superior courses featuring the Number Two course, and each one kept in mint condition. But what about the tennis? It is only fair to mention the twenty-four courts, four of them under lights for night play. Plus the staff of tennis pros who can provide individual instruction, group lessons, or fill in as the fourth in your doubles game? We're also obliged to mention the gun facilities which include both trap and skeet plus live bird. There's also a 200-acre lake with excellent bass and bream fishing. And the stables keep a fine assortment of riding horses with which to cover some of the 200 miles of wooded bridle trails. The gracious four-story hotel with its green awnings, cheerful lounges, excellent food, and letter-perfect service is as pleasant a resort hotel as the South has to offer.

Windermere Island Club (Bahamas)

Don't be surprised if you don't find it listed in your all-Bahamas guide. The people who own and run this little tropical microcosm, and the people who annually retreat within it for a soul-restoring fortnight, seek publicity about as avidly as a bear seeks bees. Palm-shaded privacy is what vacationers at this small oasis want, and get. Time was when Lord Mountbatten fished its tarpon-laden waters. Today his two married daughters both manage to find time in busy schedules every spring to fly to Windermere for their out-of-England holidays. Here it was that Charles brought his bride, confident that the royal pair's hunger for peace, quiet, and no questions please would be honored with good grace, as indeed it was. A faultless beach, a tasteful club, a few villas that can be leased in their owners' absence, some good tennis and sailing plus an invisible but absolute barrier between yourself and the intrusive outer world.

BEAUTIFUL BEACHES

A good beach is hard to find. And one person's idea of the perfect seaside strand doesn't necessarily coincide with the next person's. In the face of such hazards we will nevertheless share part of our own list of *America's great beaches*. (We've excluded Hawaii, since good beaches there are too numerous to mention.)

Looking over our list, we can't find any particular criteria that unite our choices. Some are near long-established resort areas; others are so isolated that you'd better bring a tent if you plan to stay over. Most tend to be relatively free of dune buggies, surfers, hot dog stands, and oil slicks, but beyond that their only real link is that *we think you'll find them delightful*. Here they are, in approximate geographical progression from east to west.

• **Cape Cod's Atlantic shore from Monomoy Point on the south to the northern tip.** Wonderful dunes around Province Lands and Truro; great birdwatching on Monomoy Island.

• **Mohegan Bluffs on Block Island.** This beach looks like it should be on the West Coast rather than the East. Tall headlands face out to sea; brushy arroyos drop down precipitously to secluded coves.

• **Long Island's entire south shore from the New York City line to Montauk Point.** Good sand; nice surf; water that's neither too warm nor too cool. Within these 130 miles of beaches you can find any social milieu that suits you—from the democratic precincts of Jones Beach to the chic enclaves of the Hamptons.

• **Assateague Island off the Delmarva Peninsula.** A constantly shifting barrier island of great beauty (and of relative isolation considering how close it is to East Coast population centers). Very little undertow for an Atlantic beach. Home of the famous Chincoteague wild ponies.

• **Cape Lookout, North Carolina.** Not as genteel as the sea islands further south; not as honky-tonk as the shore to the north (from Cape Hatteras to Virginia Beach). Just three nice, long, primitive barrier islands.

• **Gulf islands of northeast Florida and Mississippi.** Despite lots of development, there are still spots that show what this area must have been like before it was discovered. Especially nice: Ship, Horn, and Petit Bois islands off Mississippi. St. George Island across from Apalachacola in Florida is nice too.

• **Indiana Dunes on Lake Michigan.** An eerie moonscape in the midst of America's most industrial area. (450-foot high *Sleeping Bear* in northern Michigan is an equally fascinating dunescape.)

• **Point Sal, California.** This beach, about thirty-five miles south of Morro Bay, is relatively undiscovered by California standards. A rough, nine-mile entry road helps maintain its privacy.

• **The Three Capes area of Oregon from Cloverdale north to Tillamook.** Crowded in spots, but still one of the most beautiful areas of the Northwest Coast.

• **The Washington coast from Cape Alava to about fifty miles south.** Picking your way along the Olympic National Park coastline, you won't find many congenial swimming holes, but you'll experience a grand, brute wilderness by the sea.

ISLAND PARADISE

P RIVACY, sun, and vacation are three heartwarming words for anyone ankle-deep in winter blues. A single-resort private island in the Caribbean brings all three words vividly to life. It assures you a soul-satisfying place in the sun, plenty of elbow room, and, frequently, luxury comforts beyond fantasy. Guest capacity can be as few as thirty people and rarely more than 100. You can even rent the entire island if you'd like.

The Island

Perhaps the ultimate and most exclusive of the island resorts in the Caribbean is The Island, an imposingly lavish, ten-bedroom villa resting atop the highest point of a seventy-four-acre island called Necker in the British Virgin Islands. The owner, British entrepreneur Richard Branson, has spared nothing in delivering a Balinese style villa furnished with plush, oversized sofas and chairs clothed in fabrics from Bali. A fleet of boats awaits the pleasure of the villa's guests, along with tennis courts, a Nautilus gym, swimming pools, and fine dining. Local staff, under British management, run the house, which will accommodate up to twenty persons. Available, totally inclusive, for $5,500 daily. CONTACT: *Resorts Management, The Carriage House, 201½ E. 29th St., New York, NY 10016; (212) 696-4566 or (800) 225-4255.*

Guana

Another intimate one-resort island is Guana, named for an iguana-shaped rock formation and located near Tortola in the British Virgin Islands. The 850-acre Guana has room for only thirty guests, giving visitors the impression of being on their own island. Guests of the Guana Island Club live in seven white-washed cottages which sit atop a ridge with stunning views of the Atlantic Ocean and Caribbean Sea. The island boasts seven beaches; one of them is a half-mile stretch of white powder sand. Double room rates are $295 per day; the rate for the entire island is negotiable. CONTACT: *Guana Island Club, Timber Trail, Rye, NY 10580; (914) 967-6050.*

Mustique

Mustique Island is in the northern Grenadines, eighteen miles south of St. Vincent in the West Indies. Spaced thoughtfully over its 1,400 acres are fifty-two extraordinary and uncommonly exclusive villas. For example, there is the Marienlyst, a two-bedroom house designed by the late stage designer and architect Oliver Messel, situated high in the Endeavour Hills overlooking the entire northern end of the island; the Mulberry, a split-level rustic wood plantation house with veranda, patio, and lovely garden with swimming pool; the Sea Star, a three-bedroom beach cottage complex with a pavilion for entertaining; Windsong, a tropical chalet in Vincentian white and yellow wood furnishings accented by thick gardens of rare flowers. Weekly rates for the villas, which have as many as six bedrooms and accommodate up to twelve guests, range from $1,200 to $10,000 CONTACT: *Resorts Management, The Carriage House, 201½ E. 29th St., New York, NY 10016; (212) 696-4566.*

Petit St. Vincent

Petit St. Vincent is the southernmost of the Grenadines and offers perhaps the utmost in beauty and privacy. The island is a maze of forests and bluffs, with twenty-two wood and fieldstone cottages dotting the landscape. Each cottage has a patio with an exquisite sea view and is separated from neighboring cottages by a huge hedge-lined lawn. One could spend an entire vacation here without any outside contact: meals can be taken via room service, requests are conveyed to resort personnel via a mailbox behind each cottage (checked daily by a moped-riding employee), and neighboring guests are always at least a lawn away. Double room rates range from $240 to $450 per day. CONTACT: *Petit St. Vincent, P.O. Box 12506, Cincinnati, OH 45212; (513) 242-1333.*

Long Bay

Located on Antigua's trade-wind-cooled northeast coast, the Long Bay Hotel is a lush, landscaped estate nestled on a point of land between the sea and a lagoon. Just five villas and twenty rooms with private balconies keep the number of guests small and the mood intimate and informal. Double room rates are from $165 to $210. CONTACT: *Resorts Management, Inc., The Carriage House, 201½ E. 29th St., New York, NY 10016; (800) 225-4255 or (212) 696-4566.*

Jumby Bay

A "Jumbie," in Antiguan folklore, is a playful spirit, and this privately owned vacation retreat lives up to its name. Situated a mile north of Antigua, the only other inhabitants on this 300-acre island, besides the guests and staff, are exotic birds and a flock of wild sheep that freely roam white cedar and loblolly forests. There are thirty-four guest accommodations, each with a private terrace overlooking the sea. Daily rates, based on double occupancy, are from $300 to $475. CONTACT: *Jumby Bay, P.O. Box 243, Long Island, Antigua, West Indies; (809) 463-2176.*

The Meridian Club

The Turks and Caicos Islands, situated southeast of the Bahamas, are a British Crown Colony. Pine Cay, the site of The Meridian Club, is one of several major islands and several dozen small cays that comprise the Colony. On this 800-acre private island, The Meridian maintains twelve spacious accommodations, each fronting a virtually deserted, two-mile beach. Double room daily rates range from $200 to $350. CONTACT: *The Meridian Club, P.O. Box 350367, Fort Lauderdale, FL 33335; (800) 327-3139 or (305) 942-5563.*

Caneel Bay

Located on St. John in the U.S. Virgin Islands, the Caneel Bay resort occupies a 170-acre peninsula adjoining the Virgin Islands National Park. There are 170 guest rooms set around the peninsula, close to seven white sand beaches, three dining areas and seven tennis courts. Daily rates for double rooms are $180 to $305 per day, with special packages available. CONTACT: *Rockresorts, 30 Rockefeller Plaza, Room 5400, New York, NY 10112; (800) 223-7637 or (212) 442-8198.*

Peter Island

Of all the attractions found on Peter Island, the scuba sites are perhaps the most alluring. There are some thirty-six around the 1,050-acre island, from coral forests to a nineteenth-century wreck. There are three white sandy beaches, Land Rover tours of the island, horseback riding, tennis, and a host of water sports. Rooms in the eight harbor houses and five beach houses are complete with verandas overlooking the sea. Double room rates are from $315 to $1,500 per day. CONTACT: *Resorts Management, Inc., The Carriage House, 201½ E. 29th St., New York, NY 10016; (212) 696-4566 or (800) 225-4255.*

Little Dix Bay

Little Dix curves around a crescent bay in the British Virgin Islands. Green hills cradle its white-gold beach; a coral reef shelters its translucent waters. There are eighty-two rooms at the Little Dix Bay Hotel, sprinkled along the beach, available for about $380 per day. For those who prefer a house, the St. Thomas Bay Cottage and Handsome Bay Cottage overlook Virgin Gorda Yacht Harbour and the scenic Sir Francis Drake Channel. CONTACT: *Little Dix Bay Hotel, Box 70, Virgin Gorda, British Virgin Islands; (809) 495-5555 or (800) 223-7637.*

Young Island

Two hundred yards off St. Vincent Island in the Grenadines is Young Island, a twenty-five-acre haven with thirty rustic cottages set on the beaches and hillsides. Double room rates are $330 to $370 per day. CONTACT: *Ralph Locke Islands, Inc., 315 E. 72nd St., New York, NY 10021; (212) 628-8149 or (800) 223-1108.*

Palm Island

Named for the graceful coconut palms lining its beaches, Palm Island in the Grenadines is the 100-acre hideaway of John and Mary Caldwell. Guests stay in twenty beachfront stone cottages and spend the day swimming, snorkeling, scuba diving, water-skiing, sailing, and windsurfing along beaches hailed as some of the finest in the Caribbean. Double room rates are $185 to $195 per day. CONTACT: *John Caldwell, Palm Island, St. Vincent, West Indies; (809) 458-4804.*

COUNTRY INNS: U.S.

SAMUEL Johnson, who was always saying something important and to the point, once declared, "There is nothing which gives so much pleasure as an inn or tavern." The Great Lexicographer was referring to those havens of refuge within a busy London where people could gather for a convivial cup and good conversation. Indeed, one of the most celebrated, "The Club," was founded by David Garrick just so friends would have a place to hear Johnson talk.

The inn of today usually takes on a more rustic tone. Mention an inn to most Americans and they think of a spot in the country set away from the turnpike where they can collapse in quietude and repose; a place such as The Ark in Deer Isle, Maine, where the principal activity is, according to its owners, "to do nothing, pleasantly." The Ark is a classic small New England inn. There are only nine rooms and guests shift for themselves, often sharing the house with the owners' spaniels. Evenings are family get-togethers with snacking in the common room and dinner served in an old barn.

But there are those among us to whom the most favored pastoral experience is being driven in a limousine with the windows open. When we go to a country inn, we want to be spared the telephone and the Seven O'Clock News. But apart from that we want to be pampered, stuffed with good food, and slathered in luxury. Fortunately, America is as amply stocked with grande luxe country inns as any land on earth. *The New Book of Bests* found the even dozen establishments listed below are all true to the comfortable traditions of the country inn, but each has its own sumptuousness that places it on a par with the finest city hotel. They are followed by ten offering the traditional rusticity prized in the best inns.

The Inn At Sawmill Farm (West Dover, Vermont)

Architect-owner Rodney Williams and his decorator wife, Ione, have devised a stunning country inn. Unlike many New England inns where the rooms tend to be like cubbyholes, the Inn at Sawmill Farm is spacious and free flowing. The accommodations range from singles to two-bedroom suites with fireplaces and are all first class. Each room is individually decorated; sometimes Victorian, sometimes colonial. The old hayloft has been converted into a fine library. The food is the best in the area. All the produce is locally grown but the meat and fish are trucked in from Boston and the crab is flown in from Maryland. Figure on two hours for dinner. Not waiting. Just enjoying splendid cuisine in a relaxed atmosphere.

Jared Coffin House (Nantucket Island, Massachusetts)

The Jared Coffin House was and still is the finest mansion on Nantucket. Built by a prosperous ship owner in 1845, it is virtually a museum within one of the most famous guest houses in New England. Rich with the fruits of the old China trade, the house displays magnificent Oriental rugs along with Chippendale and Sheraton antiques. Although there are excellent rooms in the Eben Allen wing and the nearby Daniel Webster House, the best accommodations are the ten rooms in the main house, two with marble fireplaces. The food is not up to the architectural standards of the house; but the area is full of excellent restaurants. The best time to visit is Christmas when the place is bedecked with laurel and holly. There is a giant Christmas tree downstairs and a present for each guest.

Blantyre Castle (Lenox, Massachusetts)

It may not be the Taj Mahal but Blantyre Castle was a love token just as sincerely felt. Built in 1902 this replica of a Scottish castle was an anniversary present from William Patterson to his wife. The accommodations would please the most demanding laird. There are good modern rooms in a separate house on the grounds, but try to stay in one of the master bedrooms on the second floor. Enormous affairs, they overlook the sweeping grounds and take you back to the time when a person didn't need a tax shelter to be rich.

Wheatleigh (Lenox, Massachusetts)

Even the best country inns are not usually long on service. There is rarely a sufficient staff to do more than give a hand with the luggage. But Wheatleigh is not a usual country inn. It is a thirty-room pleasure dome built by a wealthy industrialist at the turn of the century who wanted a Florentine palazzo set in the Berkshires. So when Leonard Bernstein came to stay in the Aviary suite, it was no trouble for the management to move in the maestro's grand piano as well. The original owner spent well over one million late-nineteenth-century dollars to create this edifice and the work of some 150 Italian craftsmen who came to carve the ceilings and the mantels can still be seen. The rooms at Wheatleigh come in regular and deluxe. The latter are sun-struck rooms with canopied beds and huge fireplaces. The best time to come is when the Boston Symphony is playing at Tanglewood, a ten-minute walk from Wheatleigh.

The Inn At Castle Hill (Newport, Rhode Island)

The Inn at Castle Hill is a perfect movie setting for an elegant house party weekend at the ocean or, if the weather is a bit overcast, an English murder mystery. A great shingle ramble of a place, the inn is a center of social activity for Newport. There always seems to be a new America's Cup victor or tennis tournament champion to celebrate. Overlooking the Atlantic, the inn gives a sense of traveling first class on an ocean liner. The best room in the house is the pentagonal room in the turret where author Thornton Wilder worked on his last novel, *Theophilus North*. Stay there and share Theophilus's view where he could see, "the beacons of six light houses and hear the booming and chiming of as many sea bouys."

L'Hostellerie Bressane (Hillsdale, New York)

The rooms at L'Hostellerie Bressane are perfectly all right—country Spartan but comfortable. However, they are hardly the reason why people journey to this charming French inn located in rural Cumberland County. The restaurant ruled by the owner, chef Jean Morel, is the three-star attraction. A native of Brest and schooled in Paris, Morel came to his country inn by way of New York City's Chateaubriand and Lafayette restaurants. The result is the most elegantly prepared French cuisine of any country inn in America. Nothing ordinary comes out of the kitchen. Every French restaurant offers onion soup; at L'Hostellerie it is served with eggs, Madeira, and Cognac. And so it goes. Classic food with a personal touch. In your rush to the table, however, don't forget to stop by the bar. It is a little bandbox that merges French elegance with American hospitality.

Chalet Suzanne (Lake Wales, Florida)

Don't try to make sense out of the Chalet Suzanne. It follows its own perverse logic. It is one of those places where nothing fits but everything works. The Round Dining Room is heptagonal and the Swiss Dining Room is fitted with Oriental tiles. No spoon matches any other on the table and in a single room there are eight different lighting fixtures from a Venetian glass lamp to a Singapore ship's lantern. But the important thing is that there are some thirty enchanting rooms spread out in a series of small buildings overlooking a private lake and a restaurant that is world-class. For a special evening pretend you are newlyweds and ask for the Honeymoon Table. It is a table for two overlooking the main dining room that is so private not even a waiter intrudes. You hoist your own food up in a glass enclosed dumbwaiter.

Maison de Ville (New Orleans, Louisiana)

How about staying where Tennessee Williams wrote *A Streetcar Named Desire,* where John James Audubon created many of his most famous wildlife drawings, and where the Sazerac cocktail was invented? Then come to the finest small hostelry in the South. The rooms in the main house are without peer in the city for sumptuous furnishings and the nearby cottages offer country relaxation in an urban setting. Only a continental breakfast is available at Maison de Ville but the concierge will book you a table at any restaurant in New Orleans.

Rancho Encantado (Tesuque, New Mexico)

Situated in the high chaparral country only eight miles outside of Santa Fe, the Rancho Encantado looks as if it has been there since Coronado arrived in the sixteenth century searching for "gold, glory and God." Actually, it was built during the 1920s and only brought to its present luster fifteen years ago. The Rancho is a smoothly run modern resort facility that retains the traditional sense of Western comfort. The restaurant is excellent and, surprisingly, famous for its seafood which is flown in daily from the Pacific.

Tanque Verde Ranch (Tucson, Arizona)

Tanque Verde takes the idea of the dude ranch and pushes it as far as it can go. The emphasis is on trail riding but there are tennis courts, indoor and outdoor swimming pools, whirlpool baths, air-conditioned rooms, and a kitchen which serves up such non chuck wagon fare as mocha marzipan tortes. Founded on a Spanish land grant in 1862, Tanque Verde is one of the oldest working ranches in America. Traces of its early history are evident from the small windows on the valley side of the main house which were once used as gun ports. But today nothing goes wrong at Tanque Verde that cannot be fixed by a snooze on the hammock.

San Ysidro Ranch (Montecito, California)

This mountainside inn has been receiving guests one way or another for more than a century. First it was a way staion maintained by Franciscan monks and in the first part of the twentieth century it was a resort hotel. For more than thirty years it was the country retreat of film star Ronald Colman. Now it is run by James Lavenson, formerly president of the Plaza Hotel in New York. Spread out over 540 acres, the ranch has some forty guest accommodations in individual cottages around the property. There are also stabling facilities for guests who bring their own horses. Of all the cottages, the best is Forest Cottage complete with a modern kitchen and private outdoor whirlpool bath screened from view by a cedar fence. Many guests never leave the privacy of their cottages but those who do find a superb continental restaurant in what was the mission's fruit-packing house.

Heritage House (Little River, California)

In the days when it was a rumrunners' haven, Baby Face Nelson used the barn as a hideout but now it is for people who want to look out over the ocean not their shoulders. The accommodations are in separate cottages, and each has a separate identity. There is a duplex called the Water Tower and Maison 2 with its outsized beds and first-class city hotel that just happens to have a view of the Pacific. Breakfast in the sunny dining room balcony is the best way to start a California morning. Have the silver-dollar hot cakes; made from a special house recipe, they are so delicate they dissolve on your tongue before you can even start to chew them.

And here are some more of America's finest country inns:

The Old Tavern (Grafton, Vermont)
Restoration on a grand scale. Not only the tavern but the entire community has been restored to its 1830 mint condition when it was a favored spot for such Boston literati as Nathaniel Hawthorne and Ralph Waldo Emerson.

The Homestead (Sugar Hill, New Hampshire)
In the same family since 1780, the Homestead is the kind of comfortable old home people envision when they dream about that "little place in the country." Breakfast at the Homestead is famous throughout the state and Thanksgiving Dinner brings old customers flying in from California.

Lyme Inn (Lyme, New Hampshire)
Joe College meets the Country Inn in this neatly restored hostelry that has been a social center of the town since 1809. Dartmouth is only ten miles down the road and win or lose every Saturday night is Homecoming Week for faculty and alumni. Set within an hour's drive of five major skiing areas, the Lyme Inn has its own skating pond for guests who don't want to get out of eyeshot of the taproom.

Griswold Inn (Essex, Connecticut)
A seafaring inn that has just about everything you could ask for: one of the handsomest bars in America, a library of more than 1,000 volumes, a world famous maritime art collection, a firearm display that goes back to the fifteenth century, and a superb kitchen that has been serving magnificent English hunt breakfasts ever since the British occupation during the War of 1812. There are 20 slightly quirky rooms upstairs where you will never hear a phone ring.

Old Drovers Inn (Dover Plains, New York)
A country inn since 1750 and a one-time favorite of the Marquis de Lafayette, this charming stopover combines rustic charm with urban sophistication. The rooms are tiny delights and the food is excellent with New York City standards. But watch out for the martinis. They're the biggest in the state.

The Inn at Phillips Mill (New Hope, Pennsylvania)

As close to perfection as a small inn can be. There are only five rooms but each one is a bandbox delight. Overnight guests have their own dining room upstairs in front of a fireplace and breakfast is brought to the bedroom. This is the kind of place that was made for people who want to forget the twentieth century ever happened.

Red Fox Tavern (Middleburg, Virginia)

If you are a history buff, this is the spot. George Washington surveyed the land, and Thomas Jefferson always stopped here when traveling between Monticello and the White House. Set in the heart of the Virginia hunt country, the Red Fox is now a popular spot for the sporting set and it helps to know something about horses if you want to get into a conversation in the taproom, once a headquarters for the Confederate Army.

Nu-Wray Inn (Burnsville, North Carolina)

There's nothing fancy about the Nu-Wray but if your appetite runs to sweet cured hams, platters of fried chicken with cornbread stuffing, and thick milk gravy and homemade biscuits they serve it all family style at the Nu-Wray and everybody helps themselves. When people talk about Southern hospitality and home cooking, they are talking about an inn like the Nu-Wray.

St. Orres (Gualala, California)

As much a triumph of the spirit as it is of design, St. Orres seems to be straight out of a Pushkin novel. But its nineteenth-century Muscovite domes are actually the creation of a pair of young American carpenters who put the place together piece by piece only six years ago. And when customers drive up from San Francisco just for dinner, you know they must be doing something right in the kitchen as well.

Union Hotel (Los Alamos, California)

The Union Hotel is a cheery evocation of a California Gold Rush hotel that is furnished with everything from ancient Egyptian funeral urns to a pair of swinging doors taken from one of New Orleans's most elegant bordellos. Guests choose their own rooms on a first come first served basis and in the morning there is a traditional miners' breakfast that includes gingerbread cake and, for the strong in heart, a bottle of brandy.

For More Information:

- **The Inn At Sawmill Farm**
  West Dover, VT
  (802) 464-8131

- **Jared Coffin House**
  Nantucket Island, MA
  (617) 228-2400

- **Blantyre Castle**
  Lenox, MA
  (413) 637-3556

- **Wheatleigh**
  Lenox, MA
  (413) 637-0610

- **Rancho Encantado**
  Tesuque, NM
  (505) 982-3537

- **Tanque Verde Ranch**
  Tucson, AZ
  (602) 296-6275

- **L'Hostellerie Bressane**
  Hillsdale, NY
  (518) 325-3412

- **Chalet Suzanne**
  Lake Wales, FL
  (813) 676-6011

- **Maison De Ville**
  New Orleans, LA
  (504) 561-5858

- **San Ysidro Ranch**
  Montecito, CA
  (805) 969-5046

- **Heritage House**
  Little River, CA
  (707) 937-5885

COUNTRY INNS: GREAT BRITAIN

Gravetye Manor (West Sussex, England)

This delightful, ivy-covered manor house, built in 1598, was once an illicit storage house for contraband along England's famed "Smuggler's Lane." But it reached its greatest fame in the nineteenth century as the home of William Robinson who pioneered in the development of the English "natural garden." The grounds immediately surrounding the house are still maintained as the great gardener ordained.

The Lygon Arms (Worcestershire, England)

The Lygon Arms has been a celebrated English inn since the reign of Henry VIII and with a fine historical evenhandedness, still maintains a pair of suites in honor of two of its most famous visitors, Charles I and Oliver Cromwell. Over the centuries, the Lygon Arms has amassed a museum-quality collection of fine English antiques which are lovingly maintained. This impressive stone mansion is particularly well situated for day tripping in the surrounding area. Stratford-upon-Avon is only fifteen miles away and within an easy drive guests can visit Blenheim Palace, the seat of the Dukes of Marlborough and the birthplace of Winston Churchill.

Maison Talbooth (Essex, England)

Small by English standards, Maison Talbooth has just ten suites in a charming, cream-colored Victorian house set in three acres of gardens overlooking the Vale of Dedham, everyone's idea of what a traditional English countryside should look like. About half a mile down the road is Le Talbooth, a superb restaurant in a fifteenth-century Tudor country house on the banks of the River Stour. The house is prominent in (John) Constable's famous painting of Dedham Vale, which now hangs in the National Gallery of Scotland.

The Priory Hotel (Bath, England)

Something of a newcomer among the ranks of great English inns, the Priory was converted to a hotel in 1969. The original house, built in 1835, is a prime example of Georgian-Gothic architecture. The community of Bath, long the favored resort of British regents, is in the heart of some of England's most historic countryside. Some of the finest Roman remains are nearby and Stonehenge is just south near the historic cathedral town of Salisbury. The picturesque Thomas "Hardy" country of Dorset lies southwest and to the west are the famous caves of Cheddar Gorge.

Ardsheal House (Argyll, Scotland)

Ardsheal House is an engorgement of the senses. Motor down the private driveway and you are amid some of the most beautiful woodland in Scotland; enormous rhododendrons, oaklike holly trees, and ancient sycamores growing up amid a blanket of heather. The house itself sits on top of a peninsula overlooking Loch Linnhe, and its view of the Morven hills beyond is the sort of scene the minstrels sang about. If, on your first visit, the place seems familiar, it may be because Robert Louis Stevenson used it as a setting for his novel, *Kidnapped*.

Isle of Eriska (Argyll, Scotland)

If you really want to get away from it all, how about your own island? Pass over the vehicle bridge and you are in a private natural wildlife sanctuary where Roe Deer, heron, and, on occasion, the famous but all too rare Scottish Golden Eagle can be seen. The main house is a handsome example of Scot-Baronial architecture in soft gray granite. A model of the ideal Highland estate, Eriska seems like a self-contained principality within a half day's scenic drive to Edinburgh and Glasgow.

Inverlochy Castle (Fort William, Inverness-Shire, Scotland)

Queen Victoria was not given to handing out extravagant praise lightly but when she stayed at Inverlochy in 1873, she confided in her diary, "I never saw a lovelier or more romantic spot." More than a century later the setting is still much the same. Built in 1863, Inverlochy with its frescoed ceilings and period decorations exemplifies Victorian architecture at its finest; solid and proper but without fussiness. You might not want to drink the water elsewhere but be sure to do so here. The pure sparkling water drawn from nearby mountain slopes is so good it is used by the local distillery to make "Dew of Ben Nevis," one of the Highland's most fabled whiskies.

Dromoland Castle
(Newmarket-on-Fergus, County Clare, Ireland)

The ancestral home of the ancient kings of Ireland, who traced their heritage back in an unbroken line to 1014, Dromoland Castle, like the nearby Cliffs of Dover, is one of the most sung about spots in the republic. Truly palatial, Dromoland is the most sumptuous hotel in Ireland. Ireland is a land made for leisurely sightseeing and Dromoland Castle is uniquely situated to take advantage of the opportunities. Bunratty and Knappogue Castles, which still serve authentic medieval banquets, are only ten miles away and Limerick, the oldest city in Ireland, is but sixteen. Even Dublin's itself is only a day's drive away.

HOT SPRINGS: JAPAN

THE traveler to Japan who wishes to experience one of the country's most pleasurable diversions, should plan a visit to an *onsen*—a thermal springs resort. Onsen range from large, multifaceted hotels offering many types of thermal pools in single-sex communal bathing halls to small *ryokan* (Japanese inns) where private indoor facilities or *rotenburo* (outdoor thermal springs) accommodate couples, family groups, and individuals on an hourly rental basis. Participants sit and soak in the tiled, shallow baths, which are filled with bubbling thermal waters. Embodying a particularly Japanese esthetic, the pools are often surrounded by charming indoor gardens and waterfalls or face out onto magnificent vistas.

For those new to the centuries-old custom of onsen bathing, note than certain rules of etiquette apply:

• Before entering the bath, remove your clothes and take a seat on one of the small benches near the pool. Wash yourself with soap and hot water; then rinse off thoroughly.

• Take the small towel you will have been given into the pool with you to preserve your modesty. Then soak in the bath for a few minutes. Emerge and repeat the washing and rinsing process. Then return to the bath and soak for a longer period—up to about thirty minutes.

• The Japanese bath is extremely hot, but temperatures can be adjusted through the addition of cold water.

• Try bathing in the evening as most Japanese do; then climb into a fresh yukata robe (cotton kimono) and enjoy a satisfying dinner on the spa's premises.

Japanese onsen are open year-round, but the autumn and spring months (when maple foliage and cherry blossoms are at their respective peaks) are the ideal times to visit the country. Here is our selection of noteworthy Japanese onsen:

Hakone-Yumoto

Just ninety minutes from Tokyo's Shinjuku station via the Odakyu Railway's plush Romance Car, the popular resort area of Hakone-Yumoto is situated between Mt. Fuji and the Izu Peninsula, and is famous for its rugged volcanic topography and countless thermal springs. The exclusive 100-year-old-plus **Fujiya** is probably the best hotel in town. It offers 150 Western-style rooms, hot springs bathing, indoor and outdoor swimming, golf, and enchanting hillside gardens.

Kinugawa Spa

Also conveniently close to Tokyo—a two-hour train trip via the comfortable Tobu Railway—is the Kinugawa Spa, located in Nikko National Park. When not luxuriating in the steaming hot springs, be sure to visit Nikko's dazzling seventeenth-century

Toshugu Shrine. Its spectacular presence rivals Bangkok's Grand Palace with its ornate architecture and towering ancient cedar trees. The best hotel at the Kinugawa Spa is the **Asaya,** which offers a cordial atmosphere and a variety of thermal bathing facilities.

Beppu
On Kyushu, Japan's southernmost island, is Beppu, one of the country's most famous spa resorts. Here, naturally occurring bubbling pools of different colors (called "hells" by the Japanese) dot the region's mountains and valleys. These *jogoku* ("hells") are extolled for their therapeutic treatment for ailments ranging from skin diseases to the common hangover. The **Suginoi Hotel** features glass-enclosed bathhouses as large as aircraft hangers. Dozens of hot baths in every size and temperature are ornamented by giant ferns, palm trees, and topiary flamingos. Guests have their choice of Western or Japanese-style (with futons) accommodations, some overlooking Beppu Bay.

Noboribetsu Spa
Located in Hokkaido, in the extreme north of the country, is Japan's largest and most renowned onsen. Stay at either the **Noboribetsu Grand,** featuring seven different hot springs facilities, or the **Dai-ichi Takimotokan,** which has nineteen different bathing facilities. The Dai-ichi Takimotokan is one of the few remaining spas left in Japan that features mixed nude public bathing in large communal halls.

DUDE RANCHES

THE laconic, self-sufficient cowboy. Immortalized in Louis L'Amour novels and John Ford westerns, he remains one of the most popular figures in American folklore. Every year people who can afford the poshest resorts eschew them for the opportunity to share, for a time, a hardier, simpler life on dude ranches. While many modern Western resorts style themselves as "guest ranches," the true working ranch accepting guests is a vanishing breed. Our selection of the best dude ranches is based on criteria favoring those operations which provide guests with a genuine ranching experience:

• **Longevity.** We chose only those ranches that had weathered sufficient seasons to know their business—inside and out.

• **Location.** Size isn't everything. Each ranch we mention is large enough to provide a variety of landscapes—forests, streams, open range, and mountainside.

• **Facilities.** Each ranch must have the necessary variety and number of facilities and mounts to meet the needs of a varied clientele.

• **Function.** We looked for places where the actual ranching was an ongoing, vital operation. We avoided full-blown resorts offering Western activities on the side.

Eaton's Ranch

The most venerable dude ranch in the United States may well be Eaton's Ranch located on the eastern slopes of Wyoming's Big Horn Mountains. Established in 1879 by three Eaton brothers in North Dakota, the ranch was subsequently moved to Wolf Creek, near Sheridan, in 1904 to provide a more suitable and varied riding country for its guests. Its management is now being handled by third and fourth generations of the founding family. Accommodating up to 125 guests, the 7,000-acre ranch also owns some 200 to 230 Western-bred horses which are allowed to run free from sundown to sunrise, then corralled and saddled again if needed in the morning. Guests enjoy unlimited riding except on Sunday afternoons. Overnight pack trips into the mountains are also available. Lodging is provided in simply furnished cabins suitable for singles, couples, or families. For additional relaxation, Eaton's also boasts a well-stocked trout stream, heated pool, informal rodeos, and dances in its Howard Hall. Rates: $475 to $500 per week, depending upon date of visit and age of guest. CONTACT: *Eaton's Ranch, Wolf, WY 82844; (307) 655-9285.*

H F Bar Ranch

Established in 1902, the H F Bar Ranch has retained its authenticity as a working ranch, raising horses and cattle. Situated in the timbered hills of the Big Horn Mountains, H F raises beef cattle year-round and accepts guests from June 15 to September 15, and from October 15 to November 15 (approximate) for the deer and elk hunting season. Good hunting is so close that sportsmen can operate right out of the ranch, though pack trips can be arranged up in the mountains. H F can handle about ninety guests at one time in its twenty-six cabins; suitable mounts are available for riders of every skill level in the 145-horse stable. Weekly barn dances, hayrides, and a heated pool add to the activities. Rates:

About $75 per day, all inclusive; fifteen percent discount for children under twelve. CONTACT: *H F Bar Ranch, Saddlestring, WY 82840; (307) 684-2487.*

The Sixty Three Ranch

For those guests who want to assist cowboys with their daily chores, the Sixty Three Ranch offers an opportunity to assist them in branding, roundups, and animal care. Accommodations are available in electrically heated cabins set at the foot of a canyon and by Mission Creek which flows through it. Guests have an infinite variety of activities available to them: an excursion to nearby Yellowstone Park, a climb up Shell Mountain to explore the fossils of an ancient sea bottom, or a day's trout fishing. Founded in 1929 by the Christensen family, the ranch has operated continuously since then, and now owns about 2,000 acres and a stable of sixty horses. Sixty Three prides itself on its high percentage of repeat guests. If you want to pay a winter visit, the ranch offers a cross-country ski season in December and January. In addition, with advance notice, three-day or longer pack trips can be planned. Rates: $390 to $450 a week, depending on age and accommodations; $15 deduction per week for children under twelve. CONTACT: *Sixty Three Ranch, Livingston, MT 59047; (406) 222-0570.*

Trail Creek Ranch

Owned by Elizabeth Woolsey since 1943, Trail Creek Ranch has developed a loyal clientele, including parents who were brought to the ranch as children returning with families of their own. On 320 acres of deeded land bordering wilderness-designated National Forest, Trail Creek can accommodate thirty guests during the summer season running from June 15 to September 15. Children can be housed in bunkhouses, adults in comfortable doubles and singles with private baths. There are also family cabins. A working ranch, with about sixty-five head of horses and mules, Trail Creek offers daily riding and also pack trips of up to ten days in length. These are separately priced, starting as low as $90 a day depending on the size of the party and the destination. Canoeing, white water rafting, and trout fishing are also available. During the winter, Trail Creek offers cross-country skiing on its own track and downhill skiing at the nearby Teton Pass ski area during February, March, and early April. Rates: $60 to $100 per day. CONTACT: *Trail Creek Ranch, Box 10, Wilson, WY 83014; (307) 733-2610.*

Diamond D Ranch

Located in central Idaho, the Diamond D Ranch is a small working outfit with thirty-two horses and some pack mules. Purchased in 1948 by John Demorest, the ranch is surrounded by a wilderness area that becomes completely impassable in winter. Diamond D accepts guests from mid-June to mid-September, and hunting parties from mid-September through November. The ranch, which has its own private lake and several streams, can accommodate up to forty people. So attractive has this healthy scheme appeared to vacationing businessmen that the ranch has also been used as the site of some dead-serious business meetings. Can time spent riding the trails be as conducive to a fruitful exchange of ideas as a three-martini lunch? You decide. Diamond D provides a wide variety of hunting and fishing experiences, having exclusive rights to more than 600 square miles of National Forest. Weekly rates per person are $425 to $475 for adults, less for children. Week-long guided fishing trips are planned from June through early September and are priced slightly higher. CONTACT: *Jack Demorest, Diamond D Ranch, 2836 N. Beachwood Dr., Los Angeles, CA 90068; (213) 205-7614.*

VACATION HOME EXCHANGES

IF a house swap fits into your vacation plans, then now is the time to look into the Vacation Exchange Club. David Ostroff founded this international club for travelers trading and renting homes and condominiums. A classified directory of homes, villas and apartments available for exchange is published every February; an update is issued in April. To receive either publication, you must pay a $15 membership fee (without listing your home), or $22.70 with a listing to the Vacation Exchange Club. A black-and-white photograph of your home will be published with your listing for an additional $8.65. Newcomers to house-trading often join without listing their own home to preserve anonymity, but this makes recruiting a swap a one-sided burden.

Past listings have included a country club condominium in Palm Springs, a Spanish villa by the Mediterranean, and an apartment in the sixteenth arrondissement of Paris. Members write to each other to make their own exchange or rental arrangements. The Vacation Exchange Club has listings from New Zealand, Germany, Austria, Holland, and expanded lists of homes in France.

The club is linked with Home Interchange, Ltd., of London, Holiday Home Exchange in Australia, Aloha Exchange in Hawaii, and Intervac, a federation of nineteen European home exchange operations. For information, CONTACT: *Vacation Exchange Club, 12006 111th Ave., Suite 12, Youngstown, AZ 85363; (602) 972-2186.*

LUXURY TOURS

WHETHER you're traveling by cruise ship through the sun-baked Caribbean, by railroad through the Orient, or on foot through the busy streets of London, there are a select but varied number of tours and tour operators who cater to those who want small groups, personal service, and an experience removed from the ordinary holiday. Top tour companies now pride themselves on having the flexibility to meet their clients' most unique whims, frequently tailoring tours to meet individual interests. Following is a listing of some of the best tours available. These and others are limited only by the imagination.

• **Pakistan and India.** How about a tour of a venerable monastery at Shey, a shopping spree in the ancient bazaars of Rawalpindi, and, if they're home, a visit with the Royal Family of Hunza? Lindblad Travel can't promise Shangri-la, but they do offer a journey through Pakistan and India that includes a Jeep ride across a 600-foot suspension bridge in Gilgit. The accommodations, like the itinerary, run the gamut: one night in a rustic inn at Gilgit, another at a tent camp in Ladakh; two nights at a newly remodeled hotel in Swat; and three on a luxurious houseboat on Srinagar's Dal Lake. The excursion concludes with three nights at Delhi at the posh Oberair InterContinental Hotel. Price: $2,700 per person double occupancy. Air fare to and from New York and India is about an additional $1,650. *Lindblad Travel, One Sylvan Road North, Westport, CT 06881; (800) 243-5657 or (203) 226-8531.*

• **Opera Tours.** The leading American tour agency for opera buffs is Dailey-Thorp Travel of New York. The agency operates dozens of opera tours each year throughout the world, including trips to major summer festivals such as the Aix-en-Provence Festival, the Salzburg Festival, the Bayreuth Festival, and the Edinburgh Festival. Food and accommodations are as good as the music. *Dailey-Thorp Travel, Park Towers South, 315 W. 57th St., New York, NY 10019; (212) 307-1555.*

• **Arrangements Abroad.** This New York agency plans deluxe, one-of-a-kind tours, usually at the request of alumni, museum, and professional groups that want an in-depth look at a particular subject. The trips are highlighted by lectures, gallery tours, and visits to places not generally open to the public. Cruises with expert lectures are also offered to destinations such as Scandinavia, Russia, Australia, New Zealand, and Alaska. Arrangements Abroad executives describe their clients as "educated leisure travelers," not scholars, and add that "people who normally will not travel with groups will go with us because of the personalized attention they receive." Though the trips are commissioned by specific groups and limited to between twenty-five and thirty-five people, there is often room for other interested applicants. Costs vary, but the average two-week land tour runs about $3,000. Arrangements Abroad also handles meetings and conventions for associations and corporate clients. *Arrangements Abroad, Inc., 50 Broadway, New York, NY 10004; (212) 344-0830 or (800) 221-1944 outside of New York.*

• **The QE2.** For luxury cruises, there still is nothing like a voyage on that monarch of the Seven Seas, the QE2, which crosses the Atlantic on a regular basis, cruises the Caribbean, Bermuda, and Iberia, and circles the entire globe each year. Travelers may also, if they wish, combine a round-trip transatlantic crossing with a QE2 seven- or eight-day Iberian cruise in April, May, or August. In all, QE2 makes twenty-two transatlantic crossings between April and October. On board, travelers will find the Golden Door Spa at Sea, a computer center, and the first and only floating Harrod's of London. *Cunard Line, 555 Fifth Ave., New York, NY 10017; (212) 661-7777 or (800) 223-0764.*

• **Nature Tours: Birdwatching.** Victor Emanuel Nature Tours (VENT) of Austin, Texas, is offering some of the best bird tours in the world. Each of the leaders at VENT is an expert on the birds of a particular area. Roger Tory Peterson, author of the famous *Peterson Field Guides to the Birds* and one of the foremost naturalists in the world, and Peter Matthiessen, a leading nature writer and novelist, are among VENT's more celebrated tour leaders. Sample tours: a Grand Texas Tour, where participants can expect to see over 350 different species of birds; a trip to Cambridge Bay, the richest area for birds in the High Arctic; and, a three-week tour to Peru. Groups limited to fourteen people outside the U.S., sixteen within, and costs vary depending on the length and location of the tour.

VENT will also custom-design tours for groups. *Victor Emanuel Nature Tours, P.O. Box 33008, Austin, TX 87864; (512) 477-1727.*

• **Ballooning.** Balloon adventures offer the seasoned traveler a taste of the exotic, if the spirit is willing. There are a variety of them to choose from: one can drift over the wildlife terrain of Kenya or settle into a "balloon ranch" in Colorado for instructions on the fine art of hot-air travel. Consult your travel agent for details on these and other available packages. An outstanding figure in the field of commercial ballooning is Buddy Bombard, who offers weekly balloon trips over the Burgundy region of France from mid-April to early November. Trips cost from $1,990 and up. *The Bombard Society, 6727 Curran St., McLean, VA 22101; (703) 448-9407 or (800) 862-8537.*

• **Photographic Safari.** The Nairobi-based outfitter, Ker & Downey, has been leading safaris since before the days when the sun set on the British Empire. Today, the forty-year-old company outfits custom photographic safaris rather than expeditions by great white hunters in search of bull elephants or lion trophies. The hunting background doesn't hurt, however, as K&D's veteran British and Kenyan guides are said to be masters at stalking wild game. K&D is known in particular for its tented Kenyan expeditions. Tents furnished with real beds and mattresses are made up daily with freshly ironed sheets and fluffed-up blankets. The staff— headed my major domo and chef—transports the camping gear by truck as the travelers move out with safari guides in four-wheel-drive vehicles for a day of game viewing. Iced drinks and hot showers await the photographers at each new campsite. The K&D custom-camping safaris cost $570 a day per person, based on double occupancy. As the safari group increases in size, the rates go down. *The East African Safari Company, 250 W. 57th St., New York, NY 10107; (800) 7-SAFARI or (212) 757-0722.*

• **Rajasthan.** Literally "land of the Raja," Rajasthan is the India of palaces and splendor. A twenty-one-day tour of this north-western province includes accommodations in several former palaces that have been converted into hotels; visits to the 500-year-old temples of Ranakpur; drives through the dramatic Aravalli Mountain Valley Range; shopping in the labyrinthine streets of Jaisalmer; and transportation on the Maharaj Gajsingh's private train. Cost is about $3,240 per person, based on double occupancy. Air fare additional. *Special Expeditions, 133 E. 55th St., New York, NY 10022; (800) 762-0003 or (212) 765-7740.*

• **Around the World by Luxury Jet.** This may be the tour to end all tours. Your jet, a Boeing 727 originally configured for 140 passengers, will accommodate just you and another twenty-three fortunate individuals who will spend thirty-one days globe-trotting—sometimes in the world's best hotels, but more often in private chateaux, villas, and castles. Included on the itinerary: in Florence, accommodations in a thousand-year-old, sixty-bedroom castle, hosted by its owners, Baron and Baroness Ricasoli; two days of touring in Cairo, with a cocktail party on a houseboat on the Nile; camel races in Saudi Arabia; a visit to the monkey temple in the hills of Kathmandu. Cost: $29,450 per person. No baggage limits. *Society Expeditions, 723 Broadway East, Seattle, WA 98102; (800) 426-7794.*

• **Fishing in China.** If you haven't been lured by the opportunity to see the Great Wall of the Forbidden City, perhaps the chance to fish for spotted maigre, Crucian carp, or the Oriental yellowtail (tuna) on China's lakes and shoreline will catch your interest. Klineburger Worldwide Travel of Seattle, one of the top international big game outfitters, has organized the first fishing tours of China with seventeen-day trips scheduled monthly from May through October. The all-inclusive price for these angling adventures is $2,950 for West Coast departures (add $280 for New York departures). *Klineburger Worldwide Travel, 3627 First Ave. South, Seattle, WA 98134; (206) 343-9699.*

• **Wine Country Bicycle Tours.** France's wine country is the setting for deluxe bicycle tours offered several times a year by Progressive Travels, Ltd. of Colorado Springs, Colorado. On each trip, cyclists pedal along scenic wine country roads on European-style ten-speed bicycles (provided by the tour organizers), pausing along the way for wine tastings at some of the country's premier cellars and chateaux. They stay in first-class country inns and hotels, dine in Michelin-starred restaurants, and, because a support van is available to transport luggage from inn to inn, they travel without baggage on itineraries flexible enough to suit all riders, from novice to expert. The most popular tour is a Burgundy & Beaujolais trip exploring the two adjacent and world-famous wine-producing regions. *Progressive Travels, Ltd., 30 E. Kiowa, Suite 104, Colorado Springs, CO 80903; (800) 245-2229.*

SPECIAL TOURS FOR THE HANDICAPPED

EVEN the most enthusiastic globe-trotter knows that traveling can at times be physically draining and mentally stresssful. For the handicapped person, the demands posed by travel may discourage the idea altogether. But that need not be the case. There are organizations that cater specifically to handicapped persons interested in traveling both in this country and abroad. The Society for the Advancement of Travel for the Handicapped recommends the tours of two travel organizations as particularly interesting and responsibly planned:

• **Evergreen Travel.** In business for over twenty years, was the first travel company to offer luxury tours overseas for the handicapped. The tours are led by Betty Hoffman and her son Jack, president of Evergreen and son of its founder, and his aides. The cruise ships, hotels, and ground transportation used on Evergreen tours are designed to meet the specific needs of the handicapped, with ground level accessibility to all rooms and facilities. The Evergreen touring staff does not include medical personnel, so customers with special needs should arrange for medical aides to accompany them. Friends and family members are also welcome to join the tours. Sample tours include: Spain, Portugal, and the Canary Islands; a Nile River cruise; a tour of China. *Evergreen Travel, 19505L 44th Ave. West, Lynnwood, WA 98036; (206) 776-1184.*

• **Mobility Tours.** Offers custom tours, catering exclusively to the needs of the disabled traveler. Since its beginning in 1976, Mobility Tours has done extensive work with institutions, as well as public and private organizations that provide services for the disabled population. Its staff has a background in both travel and human services, experienced in providing the kinds of highly specialized services that the disabled require. All tours are custom designed to suit the needs of the particular group traveling. Groups range in size from five to 100, with support staff generally provided by the sponsoring agency or organization. However, Mobility Tours can provide staff if required. *Mobility Tours, 26 Court St., Brooklyn, NY 11242; (718) 858-6021 or 625-4744.*

TRAINING UNLIMITED

THOSE who long for the bygone era of leisurely and luxurious transportation, or perhaps aren't in much of a hurry, will find an increasing number of superior train adventures to choose from.

Venice-Simplon Orient Express

The original Orient Express was the high-style conveyance of diplomats, aristocrats, tycoons, and spies traveling between Paris and Istanbul between 1883 and 1897. Those who wish to indulge in opulent nostalgia have the choice of three private incarnations of the Orient Express (plus one down-scaled version that runs between Paris and the Romanian city of Bucharest). Since 1982 the Venice-Simplon Orient Express has run London-to-Venice excursions in sumptuously restored 1920s Pullman cars that ride high and smooth on oversized white wheels.

Continental breakfasts on the privately owned train are delivered to cabins; buffet brunch is served in the restaurant car; dinner is an elegant Continental affair for which many passengers choose to dress formal. Operating year-round, and three times a week between March and November, the entire London-to-Florence trip takes about thirty-three hours and costs around $730 to $770 per person double occupancy, or $910 to $960 single occupancy. Shorter duration trips are also available. *The Venice-Simplon Orient Express, One World Trade Center, New York, NY 10048; (800) 223-1588; (212) 661-4540.*

The Bullet Trains

Combining the aesthetics of the Orient with the speed and practicality of the West, Japan's Shinkansen or bullet trains, are among the world's fastest trains. The Tokaido/Sanyo Shinkansen covers the 1,069 kilometers (680 miles) between Tokyo and Hakata in under seven hours. Two additional Shinkansen—the Joetsu and the Tohoku—were added in 1982, providing service to Northeastern Japan and the Niigata-Gumma region. Six additional Shinkansen lines are planned. Not only an efficient way to travel from city to city in Japan, these trains also provide an eyeful, passing through national parks and farmlands and affording views of Mt. Fuji (12,397 feet). Japan Rail Passes are available to foreign tourists visiting Japan from abroad and are valid for unlimited travel on Japan National Railways rail, bus, and ferry lines. They must be purchased before arriving in Japan, however. *Japan National Railways, 45 Rockefeller Plaza, New York, NY 10111; (212) 757 9070.*

Around the World in Forty-five Days

E.M. Frimbo would jump for joy at the train tours offered by Bayliss International Journeys. Best of all: An exotic forty-five-day London-to-Hong Kong trip tracing the overland route that, until the 1930s, was the main link between these two cities. The tour goes around the world, passing through some of the most fabled cities in Europe and Asia. About $6,600 covers everything: first-class accommodations in hotels and on the train, meals, flights to and from the U.S., English-speaking guides, medical insurance, even baggage insurance.

Several other international train tours are available through Bayliss. For a catalog, contact Bob Bayliss. *Bayliss International Journeys, 2392 Telegraph Ave., Berkeley, CA 94704; (800) 435-4334 or 641-3366.*

The World's Fastest Train

Attention all siderophiles: you can book the fabled TGV (*train a grand vitesse,* or "very great speed train") from Paris to Lyon (averaging thirty departures daily). At 168 m.p.h., it takes two hours. In 1981, the prototype TGV broke its own earlier world record with a test run at 238 m.p.h.—a demonstration of safety and capability establishing it as the fastest train in the world. TGV service was then extended to regular lines (where the trains are limited to 125 m.p.h.) to Burgundy, Provence, Languedoc, and through Savoy to the Swiss Alps, essentially streamlining southern France. While en route, in eight air-conditioned cars (an electric motive unit at each end), you can buy hot meals and service from 111 first-class seats, or cold meals at the 275 second-class seats. Reservations are required and are available until five minutes before departure. Eurailpasses accepted; fares no higher than conventional trains. *French National Railroads, 610 Fifth Ave., New York, NY 10020; (212) 582-2816.*

The Canadian

VIA Rail operates the best transcontinental train in North America. Departing from Montreal and Toronto, The Canadian travels close to Lake Superior through Thunder Bay, then heads across the vast prairies via Winnipeg, Regina, and Calgary. The train, complete with dining cars and lounges, affords passengers an opportunity to view the majestic panorama of the Canadian Rockies from its two dome cars. The cross-country trip takes three days and three nights, with departures daily. The basic fare is $250 each way. Supplemental fares for accommodations range from $100 for a lower berth to $175 per person for a bedroom. *VIA Rail, 2 Place Ville Marie, Suite 400, P.O. Box 8116, Montreal, Quebec, H3B 2G6, Canada.*

Private Railroad Cars

Compared to private planes, what do private railroad cars have to offer? Aside from speed, almost everything. Traveling in a "private varnish," as the splendidly polished wooden railroad cars of the past were often called, is like taking your home and/or office along with you, no matter where you go. You can have every luxury and conveience at hand as you travel by rail: plush seating, private baths, gourmet dining, wet bar, stereo music of your choice, and many other accoutrements of gracious living. Fully staffed with chef and porters, and sometimes even office personnel, the private car can become a world unto itself. Then, of course, there is the spectacular natural theater of shifting panoramas—from cityscape to craggy mountains to verdant forests—to be viewed and savored.

The American Association of Private Railroad Car Owners (AAPRCO) maintains a referral list of over sixty private railroad cars nationwide that are available for private charter. Dave Schumacher is chairman of the Charter Referral Committee for the association and will provide details to interested persons. He will give advice on charters or send a free brochure listing the cars available. *American Association of Private Railroad Car Owners, Inc., 3751 E. Dartmouth Ave., Denver, CO 80210; (303) 740-0761.*

BEST CITY MAPS

WHEN was the last time you wished you *didn't* have a map? Most of the maps on the market often hinder rather than help the traveler. For example, a cumbersome map costs sightseeing time and increases your vulnerability as a target for potential muggers and con artists on the watch for errant tourists. The moral of this familiar situation is that maps should be perfect. A really good map offers: 1) correct information, 2) practicality of scale, detail, and size, 3) readability, and 4) convenience in handling. Every cartographer and map producer consulted by *The New Book of Bests* listed these criteria for a good map. But not every map provides all of them and more often than not, one map was rated excellent for a specific purpose and another for a different one. The few that consistently met the demands of their versatile functions are as follows:

Falk

Falk, a West German company, produces pocket-sized maps of the United States and Europe that fold like an envelope, on all four sides toward the center. When all of the flaps are unfolded the map reveals the entire country. Sections of subsequent folds reveal smaller and more detailed areas of one state or one country. The scale is small and Falk's maps are thus best used as road maps, but the design is impeccable and the size, even at its largest, is well within the scope of your steering wheel. About $10 with laminated cover. Available at better bookstores.

Michelin

Michelin maps also rank consistently high among experts. Their scope and variety are enormous, although they are best known for European maps. They are particularly strong in France, their home base, producing the most detailed travel map of Paris available, plus many single maps of small out-of-the-way areas. These are particularly useful for the seasoned traveler who sidesteps the big sights that maps concentrate on.

Michelin scales run the gamut from $\frac{1}{1},000,000$ (1" = 16 mi.) to $\frac{1}{10},000$ (their "plan de Paris" where 1" = approximately 800'). Their maps are reliable, updated annually, and designed to coordinate with their annotated green and red guidebooks. They are currently working to coordinate their guidebooks even further, so that one comprehensive map, instead of the current four or five, can cover the areas in their guides. *Michelin Guides and Maps, P.O. Box 3305, Spartanburg, SC 29304, (803) 599-0850.*

London "A-Z"

The London Map called "A-Z," endorsed by the British Tourist Authority, is the most comprehensive street map of London available. It is a pocket-sized atlas containing detailed maps of specific areas. The index in the back lists every street and the corresponding page and coordinates on which to find it. The front contains an excellent map of the London Underground, the entire system on a one-pager the size of a small notebook. This map is not particularly beautiful; its black and white pages and newsprint index bespeak practicality above all else. Available at finer bookstores in the United States and on every street corner in Great Britain. *Note: Don't buy the condensed version* which is very similar in appearance.

Paris "A-Z"

The Parisian counterpart to London "A-Z" is the "Paris par Arrondissements" published by Taride. It is in pocket atlas form, so it is not ideal for a total picture of Paris (try the Michelin for that), but is an excellent street guide complete with an index listing every major street. It also gives addresses of major monuments, museums, and all of those larger tourist attractions that are a must-see even for Parisians. As the name implies, it is one of the few maps that makes sense of the "arrondissements," or districts, of Paris. Not readily available in the U.S. but can be ordered from *Alliance Française Bookstore, 27 E. 60th St., New York, NY 10022; (212) 355-6100.*

Access Press

For the United States, Michelin has served an obvious inspiration for a budding company named Access Press. Access specializes in combined map/guidebooks that are designed to give the traveler complete access to a city in one slick bundle. Los Angeles, San Francisco, Hawaii, London, Washington, D.C., Rome, Tokyo, Las Vegas, Paris, and New York are in the Access plan. Specialty, stylized maps of the entire area are found in the front of each 140- to 200-page book, showing such things as the public transportation system or freeways. Detailed maps are reserved for the guide-notes section which divides the city into small areas listing restaurants, sights, hotels, and architecture. All of the information is color-coded, numbered, and extremely well organized. It even includes such small but useful details as the seating arrangements of the Hollywood Bowl, and descriptions of those strange pastries that whiz by on dim sum carts in San Francisco's Chinatown. About $10 to $12. *Access Press, 59 Wooster St., New York, NY 10012; (800) ACCESS-4 or (212) 219-8993.*

INDEX

Wilson International Center for Scholars, Woodrow, 81
Wilson School of Public & International Affairs, Woodrow, 89
Wimbledon (tennis), 321
Winchester 21 (shotguns), 355
Windermere Island Club, 402
Windows on the World (restaurant), 104
Windsor Arms (hotel), 385–86
Wine, 142–62
Wine auctions, 161–62
Wine cellars, 102–4
Wine Country Bicycle Tours, 425
Wine events, 161–62
Wine resources, U.S., 160
Wine Spectator, The (newspaper), 102
Winged Foot Golf Club, 309
Winston (rods), 349
Winston, Harry (jeweler), 175, 201
Winter Antiques Show, The, 50
Winterthur Museum and Gallery, 3
Wisdom & Warter (sherry), 150
Wise Distinctive Shirt Makers, Nat, 190
Withington, Richard (auction house), 47
Wittamer (bakery), 139, 177
Wittamer (chocolates), 139
Wolfers Freres, Henrion (jewelers), 177
Wood & Hogan (furniture), 266
Woods Hole (oceanography), 88
Woolf Bros. (shirtmakers), 190
Worcester Art Museum, 3

Worcester County Horticultural Society, 131
World Class 165 (Frisbees), 372
World of Cheese, The (book), 114
World of Leisure (billiard tables), 373
Worth Avenue (Palm Beach), 176
Worthington Gallery, 66
Wurlitzer (clarinets), 26

Y

Yacht hulls, 335–36
Yachts, 250–51
Yaddo (art fellowship), 78
Yale University, 83, 84, 89, 90, 91, 92
Yale University Art Gallery, 3
Yamaha (instruments), 28, 29, 33
Yankee Silversmith Inn, 104
Yemen Mocha (coffee), 168
York (gym equipment), 304

Z

Zabar's (gourmet food), 175
Zabriskie Gallery, 62
Zambelli International Fireworks, 374
Zermatt (ski resort), 328
Zeiss (lens), 224
Zeiss (binoculars), 222, 223
Zeiss (sunglasses), 221
Zina Studios (wallpaper), 260
Zuber et Cie, Jean (wallpaper), 259